# INDIA
## EMERGING POWER

# INDIA
## EMERGING POWER

## STEPHEN PHILIP COHEN

BROOKINGS INSTITUTION PRESS
*Washington, D.C.*

*Library of Congress Cataloging-in-Publication data*

Cohen, Stephen P., 1936–
  India : emerging power / Stephen P. Cohen.
    p.     cm.
Includes bibliographical references and index.
  ISBN 0-8157-0006-7 (cloth : alk. paper)
  1. India—Politics and government—1972– 2. India—Economic
conditions—1947– 3. India—Foreign relations—1984– I. Title.
  DS480.852 .C634  2001                                    2001000219
  954.05′2—dc21                                                   CIP


9 8 7 6 5 4 3 2 1


The paper used in this publication meets minimum requirements of the
American National Standard for Information Sciences—Permanence of Paper
for Printed Library Materials: ANSI Z39.48-1992.


Typeset in Sabon

Composition by
Betsy Kulamer
Washington, D.C.

Printed by
R. R. Donnelley and Sons
Harrisonburg, Virginia

# ฿ THE BROOKINGS INSTITUTION

The Brookings Institution is an independent organization devoted to nonpartisan research, education, and publication in economics, government, foreign policy, and the social sciences generally. Its principal purposes are to aid in the development of sound public policies and to promote public understanding of issues of national importance. The Institution was founded on December 8, 1927, to merge the activities of the Institute for Government Research, founded in 1916, the Institute of Economics, founded in 1922, and the Robert Brookings Graduate School of Economics and Government, founded in 1924. The Institution maintains a position of neutrality on issues of public policy to safeguard the intellectual freedom of the staff.

*To my wife, Roberta*

# Foreword

Forty years ago ties between the United States and India were very close. India, the world's largest democracy, was viewed as a front-line state in the cold war, a natural balance to communist China, and a critical battleground in the ideological struggle with the Soviet Union. A near alliance was in place, with Washington providing significant economic assistance to New Delhi. After the 1962 India-China war, the United States provided military aid to India and there was close cooperation between the two countries on intelligence issues. By 1968 most of those links were gone. As far as most Americans were concerned, India was relegated to the status of a second-rank power. It was seen as an economically stagnant state, a proliferation "problem," the leader of the nonaligned movement, and for several years, even a strategic partner of the Soviet Union.

The past few years have seen a revival of American interest in India. The prospects seem excellent for closer political and strategic ties. Stephen Philip Cohen argues, however, that while such a development is long overdue and should be welcomed, both states will have to proceed cautiously to avoid the inflated expectations (or deep disappointments) that have characterized relations in the past. The two states have very different strategic styles, they embody different civilizational traditions, they have different strategic interests, and they have not worked together closely for many years.

While India is now emerging as a major pan-Asian power, this evolution will be conditioned and shaped by a series of dramatic internal social and political developments that are transforming much of India. These developments will occupy the attention of Indian politicians for years. As a strategic power, the country is likely to continue its cautious policies toward China. On the basis of the evidence presented in this book, it would be unwise to expect that even a more self-confident India would be willing to challenge China directly. India's relations with Pakistan present another area of vulnerability. New Delhi seems unable to develop a strategy that would resolve the Kashmir crisis.

Nevertheless, although strategic and political ties between the United States and India may be developing slowly, other areas are very promising. The new social and economic ties—epitomized by the million-plus Indian-American community, with its growing political clout, and India's highly publicized successes in software and high technology—are giving some real content to the relationship between the world's oldest democracy and the world's largest democracy.

Cohen wishes to acknowledge the many individuals who provided assistance in the research and writing of this book. He is especially grateful to Dennis Kux and Ashley Tellis for detailed suggestions on an early draft and also to Marshall Bouton, James Clad, Howard Schaffer, Teresita Schaffer, and several anonymous readers for their comments. Three of Cohen's former students made significant contributions to the project: Kanti P. Bajpai, a visiting scholar at Brookings in 2000–01, and Dinshaw Mistry and Sunil Gupta, who provided important research assistance at Brookings. Margaret Cederoth, Yusuf Khan, Ravi Purohit, Shomikho Raha, Mona Sehgal, Bharat Srinivasan, and Sowmya Swaminathan served as interns. The author also acknowledges the contributions of the many South Asian journalists, scholars, and public officials who have shared with him their insight and wisdom over the years.

Cohen wishes to thank Richard Haass, former director of the Brookings Foreign Policy Studies program, who conceived of an India–South Asia project and chose him to direct it. This book is the first major product of that project, and Haass made a substantial contribution to both its shape and its substance.

At the Brookings Institution Press, Vicky MacIntyre ably edited the manuscript, Carlotta Ribar proofread the pages, Julia Petrakis provided the index, and Todd DeLelle verified the manuscript.

Brookings is grateful to the W. Alton-Jones Foundation, the John M. Olin Foundation, the Smith Richardson Foundation, the Starr Foundation, the United States Institute of Peace, and other donors for their financial support to the India–South Asia project.

The views expressed here are solely those of the author and should not be attributed to any person or organization acknowledged above or to the trustees, officers, or other staff members of the Brookings Institution.

MICHAEL H. ARMACOST
*President, Brookings Institution*

*Washington, D.C.*
*May 2001*

# Contents

# INDIA

## EMERGING POWER

# Introduction

THIS BOOK EXAMINES the proposition that India is becoming a major power and that such a development has important implications for the United States. I first addressed this subject twenty years ago with the late Richard L. Park. We concluded that if one took a twenty-five year perspective, then India would loom large as a crucial factor in America's policies toward all of Asia, and beyond.[1] Sufficient evidence is now available to demonstrate that we were essentially correct.

To its smaller neighbors, India has always been a great power. It has had a strong impact on their cultures, their economies, and even their identities. This power has been of great concern to Pakistan, the only state in the region to have challenged India. To China, most Western states, Japan, and the economic and political arrivistes of Southeast Asia, however, India has not counted among the most important states in the world.

In American calculations, India has assumed at best a secondary place, although it did seem very important during stretches of the cold war such as the years before, during, and immediately after the 1962 India-China war. Some Americans saw this rivalry as one of the armatures around which the cold war revolved and expected India to become a showcase of noncommunist development. That interest faded by 1965. Toward the end of the cold war, India's quasi alliance with the Soviet Union created anxiety in Washington, resulting in yet another "opening" to New Delhi. This interest also waned, and U.S.-Indian relations again reverted to the pattern of mutual attraction and disillusionment that has characterized the relationship from the time India achieved its independence in 1947.[2]

One is therefore tempted to ask whether India is destined always to be "emerging" but never actually arriving. Will it remain lodged in the second rank of international politics? Some believe it could drop from even this position into extreme chaos and disintegration, beset by population pressure, the demands of India's 20 language groups, 50,000 castes, and 500,000 villages. This would in addition seem to ensure that for several decades India is likely to contain over half of the world's poorest people. No wonder some are asking not whether India will emerge but when it will collapse, bringing down much of South Asia with it. Presumably, the United States would want to avoid ties with a faltering state.

Others would counter that India has actually overcome many of the obvious obstacles to its growth and expanding influence, although some critical issues (social and political cohesion, the success of economic reforms, and the flexibility and imagination of its leadership) remain to be addressed. In this view, India is now one of the three most important Asian states, and American policy must accommodate itself to this new reality. Like China and Japan, India is acquiring the capability to influence developments throughout much of Asia and other regions of the world. It is not yet a dominant military or economic power, although its capabilities in these spheres are rising. Rather, it is a state with great cultural and civilizational influence and an increasingly skilled political and strategic leadership that is learning to exploit India's strengths. It also has a diaspora that constitutes a potential asset for the Indian state, as well as a new link with the United States.

In the 1990s the United States paid a price for failing to understand India's broad capabilities and qualities. An India that did not seem to count for very much (in Washington, at least) was embroiled in two major regional disputes and detonated several nuclear devices (provoking Pakistan to follow suit) and stymied America's global nonproliferation strategy. India also took on an important role in an area of great importance to the United States: software and information technology. Furthermore, a new community of Americans of Indian origin came to maturity, forming a new domestic political force.

These developments did lead to heightened American engagement in South Asia, including the first presidential visit to South Asia in twenty years in March 2000, and six months later a reciprocal visit by India's prime minister, Atal Behari Vajpayee. Clear thinking, a long-range perspective, and closer attention to the way in which the United States addresses India are long overdue. India will become increasingly important to the United States because it will be a major player in at least two critical areas, the high-technology revolution and the nuclear revolution. An India that does well in these areas could be an important partner. Conversely, an India that is hostile to American interests but whose influence is expanding could block important American goals. In particular, the prospect of a nuclear conflict between India and Pakistan (or between India and China) makes the stakes very high in South Asia. India's domestic developments are also important to key American values. Independent India has been the world's largest democracy for most of its brief history. Although imperfect and punctuated by an authoritarian "Emergency," its democracy has survived and is thriving under conditions of enormous social, economic, and geographical diversity. Indians clearly have a talent for political accommodation and management that is sorely lacking in many other parts of the world, such as the Balkans and much of Africa and the Middle East.

While Indians themselves will by and large determine when and how India plays a role as an Asian or even a world power, there are critical areas in which American efforts might make a significant difference. The American policy community needs to understand what is beyond its grasp in influencing this megastate, as well as what is achievable.

At the time we published *India: Emergent Power?* studies about India fell into two categories. Those in the first group were written by advocates of India who thought that it already was (or had been) a "great" power, that this reality would soon be acknowledged by the rest of the world, and that its "emergence" was a matter of time.[3] The failure of the United States to recognize this greatness (often defined in civilizational terms) was variously attributed to American obsession with the cold war, ignorance, and cultural parochialism, or to the inability of the Indian government to project a suitable image or to fully explain India's self-evident greatness. Americans therefore needed to be better educated: about the futility of the cold war, and about the arts, culture, and history of India. For their part, Indian officials needed to work harder, and perhaps hire lobbying firms (or support American scholars), to better convey the message of India's greatness.

A second stream of analysis led to very different predictions about India.[4] There is both an indigenous and a "foreign" tradition of pointing to India's crippling or disfiguring social and political ills. One of the earliest and most influential American writers of this persuasion, Katherine Mayo, wrote a scathing book, *Mother India,* that negatively influenced successive generations of Americans.[5] With relish, they highlighted the plight of Indian women (Mayo was an early feminist), India's vast untouchable population, and its generally low standard of hygiene (Mahatma Gandhi called Mayo's book a "drain-inspector's report"). Many concluded that Indians were incapable of self-government or, in the postindependence years, incapable of good government. The implications for U.S. policy were clear: India was barely a country; it was mired in caste conflict, social malignancies, and poverty. The Indian state had to look to its survival, not its greatness. Americans could, and should, help India climb out of this pit, but India was an object for American charity, not strategy. These two approaches, one optimistic about India's prospects, the other deeply pessimistic, have, when combined, created a bifurcated high-low American perception of India.[6]

More recently, there have been a number of attempts to come to a balanced assessment of India and to highlight policy implications for the United States. These include the work of several American task forces, stimulated in part by the almost simultaneous end of the cold war, the de facto nuclearization of India (and Pakistan), and the near collapse of the Indian economy in 1991.

Among these are two 1994–95 studies by the Asia Society, one optimistically expecting closer economic relations between the United States and all of the states of South Asia, particularly India, the other arguing for a regional as well as a nonproliferation approach to the nuclear issue.[7] The latter was greeted with a distinct lack of enthusiasm by the Clinton administration, but most of its analysis and policy conclusions were subsequently confirmed by George Perkovich's history of the Indian nuclear program.[8] Sandy Gordon's assessment of India as a major power, written for an Asian and Australian audience, provides considerable information on India's domestic political and economic infrastructure.[9] (Generally, experts working on Indian foreign policy have ignored domestic social and economic factors, while the scholars who work on Indian domestic politics tend to be unconcerned with strategic issues.)[10] And a Council on Foreign Relations Task Force recently called on the United States to devote greater attention to its relations with India and Pakistan, though its members were not unanimous in their views on nuclear proliferation and U.S. relations with Pakistan.[11] In effect, the task force's report accurately reflected the fissures within the American academic and strategic policy communities.

Beyond this, there is a large literature on specific issues, most notably the proliferation problem. The 1998 nuclear tests, followed by the government's declaration that India was a nuclear weapons state, yielded a further crop of nuclear studies. India's new economic policies have drawn widespread attention, too, as has its turbulent domestic political scene. A number of case studies of South Asian conflict detail the way in which India has asserted its regional influence while managing its relationships with major outside powers, especially the United States and China. In addition, the onset of the fiftieth anniversary of the independence of India was the occasion for several introspective reviews of past failures and successes.[12] These indicate that Indians have edged toward a new realism in reconciling the possible with the desirable and have begun to acknowledge the significant changes in the international order as well as America's unique role in that order.

In one way or another, these studies offer a perspective on one of the central puzzles of contemporary India: the large disparity between India's own view of its "greatness"—past, present, and future—and the skepticism in this regard voiced by many others. The contrast between the visions of past Indian greatness and the acute reality of a still-poor people is one major reason why it is difficult for Americans to come to a balanced assessment of this complex country, let alone formulate consistent policies toward it. American policymakers tend to see India in terms of a blur of favorable and unfavorable stereotypes generated by the images of the saintly Mahatma Gandhi and Mother Teresa, or of the villainous Krishna Menon or the "dragon lady," Indira Gandhi, or of ugly scenes of saffron-clad mobs tearing down the Babri Masjid, or of India's "untouchables" mired in human filth.

This book attempts to move beyond these stereotypes to arrive at a "net assessment" of the major factors critical to India's emergence as a great power. It opens with a survey of old and new measures of power, influence, geography, and culture in an era of economic interdependence, political deregulation, and technological innovation. Chapter 2 turns to the dominant strands of thinking of the Indian strategic community and the growing regional elites. What is their vision for Indian power, their conception of a just and equitable world order, and India's role in it? Chapter 3 is about India's unique and highly developed approach to formulating and implementing strategic policies. Chapter 4 provides an overview of important domestic factors that are helping to shape India's foreign and security policies and to build the material and organizational capabilities that would underpin India's position in the international system. Chapter 5 summarizes India's fifty years of experience as the region's dominant—if not always successful—power. Although there is a widespread (if unexamined) assumption of its regional superiority, does India have the ability to project power beyond the region? Can it develop the technological, logistic, and military capacity to be more than a South Asian power in years to come? Chapter 6 describes a new element in Indian and regional calculations: the move, in May 1998, to become a nuclear weapons state, perhaps the most important recent attempt to break out of the mold of a second-tier power. Chapter 7 examines India's recent and past relations with its key neighbor and foe, Pakistan. Chapter 8 traces India's relations with its other Asian neighbors and its giant twin, China, while chapter 9 looks at relations with the United States (especially the growing economic links, increasing numbers of Americans of Indian origin, and the entry of India into the nuclear club). Chapter 10 sums up the prospects for India as a major strategic power and sets forth a range of policy options for the United States as it copes with India's emergence as a great power.

# ONE    *Situating India*

THE INTERACTION BETWEEN economic and military strength of the "great powers" has been the subject of much recent debate.[1] Whether one argues that military power is the means to acquire economic power or that a strong economic base is a prerequisite to becoming a great military power, both kinds of power can be measured, at least crudely. One obvious indicator of a great power is the outcome of war; another is the ability of a state to recover from a military or political setback. Leaders and leadership are also important in that they enable a state to make its way in the world efficiently, and to move up (or down) the hierarchy of states.

Much of the literature on this subject focuses on the rise (and fall) of great states over the past several hundred years. These are usually the major European states and the United States, which have much in common culturally and socially, and Japan, which emerged as a great power in the first half of the twentieth century by carefully emulating the armies, bureaucracies, and economies of the West.

From a broader view, however, important states and empires flourished and declined throughout the world long before the rise of the West.[2] Most of the earlier ones were flattened by the expansion of Europe, some (such as India, Indonesia, and most of those in Africa and Latin America) became colonies, and some (such as China and large parts of Central Asia) fell under Western control. That a "world system" existed before the rise of the West remains uncertain, as does its possible structure, whether a single system composed of major civiliza-

7

tional-imperial entities or several successive world systems of changing form, each with its own set of hegemons.[3] Whatever the case, India was clearly one of the major civilizational entities of the world, retaining cultural and often political consistency through the millennia.

India most closely resembles China in its current reemergence as a major state, although it trails far behind in many respects. China's importance in recent decades can be traced not only to its military potential and economic strength gained by making others dependent on its cheap labor and efficient manufacturing processes.[4] Also important is its role as a counterbalance to Moscow and as a growing player in the Persian Gulf and Africa (through its arms exports and aid programs) and throughout Southeast Asia (through overseas Chinese communities). As a result, some analysts now see China as a new "superpower" and rival to the United States.[5]

Although India lags behind, it is on an economic path similar to the one that Beijing took twenty-five years ago. India also took advantage of global bipolarity, although unlike Beijing, New Delhi was leaning toward the losing side when the cold war ended. With the disappearance of bipolarity and the era of overseas conquest, new factors have come into play. Nuclear weapons, for example, now make large-scale war between the major powers improbable, although not impossible, and changes in the international economy provide new opportunities for states with a broad economic base such as India. If India were able to harness the managerial and scientific talent of its large population, it could achieve a comparative advantage in a number of sectors beyond high technology.

Some of the pre-Westphalian factors that contribute to the rise (or fall) of a major power are newly important. India, like China, has a distinct civilizational identity, composed of a number of cultural patterns, social structures, and a special view of history. These factors enable it to mobilize its own people around a unique set of values, images, and ideas. These include the idea that India is a source of profound ideas and values, that India (and Indians) has something to teach the rest of the world, and that of the major civilizations India is uniquely unassertive toward others. India also has a distinctive way of organizing society, which inevitably influences its outlook on the rest of the world and the way others see it. Some of these qualities appeal to other states, near and far, and enable India to balance, contain, and synthesize outside influences, whether from the West, the Islamic world, or other directions.[6]

As this chapter shows, a number of factors need to be considered when placing India in the modern hierarchy of states. The complex civilizational traditions that derive from Hindu/Buddhist, Islamic, and British influences are but one of these. Another is geostrategic context, how this has changed over the past hundred years, and thus how India's place in the international system has altered, even though its physical location remains the same. Conventional measures of economic and military power need to be taken into account as well.

## The Historical Legacy

Over a span of two thousand years or more, South Asia has experienced many political orders, but it is only one of two modern states—China being the other—that embody distinct civilizations. During most of its known history, the area that is present-day India was home to several regional political systems, a few of which eventually expanded to encompass most of the Subcontinent. Of the nine powers that achieved pan-Indian status (covering at least four of India's five major regions), seven were centered in the North Indian Plain.[7] Of sixty-three pan- and supraregional powers (defined as powers that covered at least two regions), twenty-eight had their base in the North Indian Plain, and pan-Indian rule was based there for all but five or six decades. The rise of the Mughals in 1526 A.D. led to a major change in the political integration of India after 600 years of numerous regional states and dynasties in the manner of medieval Europe. The previous pan-Indian dynasty, the Guptas, had been in power from 319 to 950 A.D.. Because India's recent dominant political systems were centered in the north, its strategists have historically looked north and west for their threats, and Indians have paid little attention to the sea, the Indian Ocean region, and naval power. The dominant tradition of statecraft also rests in the north.

The formative period of Indian civilization spanned the writing of the Hindu scriptures, the Upanishads, and the development of the Mauryan Empire (321–181 B.C.) under Emperor Asoka. During these years the foundations of Indian social and philosophical thought were laid down and codified, as epitomized by the Indian manual on statecraft and political organization, the *Arthashastra*. This text, written about the same time (fourth century B.C.) as Thucydides' *The Peloponnesian Wars* and Sun Tzu's *Art of War*, is one of the most remarkable applications of rational thought to the problems of social organization. It remains influential today as an entirely indigenous political text, analogous to the writings of Aristotle and Plato but with an admixture of a police manual. Written in the service of a northern empire, it refers to parts of Central Asia, Afghanistan, China, South India, and Para Samudra (contemporary Sri Lanka).[8]

The Indian imperial vision defined during this period was to dominate succeeding centuries of Indian political life, even though by 180 B.C. this first experiment in imperial government had ended.[9] Other empires in later centuries never enjoyed quite the same conditions, particularly the same degree of central control or revenue to support a vast army or subsidize imperial enterprises.[10] The desire for empire remained but lacked the intensity of the Mauryas. The same can be said of free India's first fifty years: there has been ambition aplenty, but marked underachievement.

The Mauryas achieved Subcontinental reach about the same time that the Greeks and Chinese began to implement their own visions of imperial and civilizational order. India established contacts with the Greeks, the Persians, and the Chinese, but it was not a conquering system in the military sense of the term, although the Mauryas conquered through the attraction of their culture. The Mauryas were Buddhists, and under their reign, all of India's neighbors fell under Buddhist influence. Buddhism spread eastward through Central Asia and Ceylon, and long after the Mauryan Empire had collapsed into a series of rival Buddhist and Hindu kingdoms, their cultural influence, carried largely through the wide-ranging South Indian Chola dynasty, penetrated the societies of China, Japan, and especially Southeast Asia.[11]

## The Hindu Tradition of Indian Statecraft

Contemporary Indian analysts argue that the central strategic problem facing India goes back at least two thousand years: how to achieve the strategic unity of the Subcontinent and protect it from the incursions of outside powers. For the most part, the early Indian tradition had an answer to the problem of maintaining stability and security in a closed political system but not to the problem of extraregional incursions. The basic system of foreign policy, the *mandala,* or circle of states, was rooted in the geopolitics of the North Indian Plain. Since this was a relatively open and underpopulated area, extended military movement was possible, and aggressive kings were the norm rather than the exception.

Kautilya's *Arthashastra,* which codified Mauryan doctrine and practice, describes an elaborate range of foreign policy options based on the
*mandala.*[12] It assumes the existence of many states; from the perspective
of any one of them, there is a circle, or ring, of neighbors. One's immediate neighbors are likely to be the enemy; beyond that ring are a number of potential allies (who are the enemy's enemy), and so forth. For
any given ruler, the *mandala* will consist of twelve neighbors: some
allies, some enemies, and some neutrals.

For Kautilya, this circular arrangement of states suggested six types
of foreign policies: agreement with pledges (peace), offensive operations
(war), threats to the enemy, indifference (neutrality), subordination
within an alliance, and "duplicity," or the "dual" policy (allying with
one power while making war against another). Those portions of the
*Arthashastra* that deal with statecraft assume cultural and military
homogeneity and offer a set of rules for the conduct of statecraft and
war. These rules are utterly realistic and rest upon a shared culture and
military technology. Thus the *Arthashastra* is more a guide to Subcontinental than international (or intercultural) politics. Indeed, when later
dynasties applied Hindu norms and doctrines to invading Greeks, Huns,
Scythians, and Muslims, they were devastated. Although each of these
conquerors viewed the Subcontinent as an extension of their exogenous
power base, they later came to see the world through Indo-centric eyes.
The absorptive power of Indian society has always been impressive.[13]

Although Indian treatises refer to the legitimacy of political and military expansion, they cite few examples of Hindu rulers seeking to
expand beyond South Asia. The 1,500 years of Hindu colonialism,
mostly in Burma and Southeast Asia, were largely economic, cultural,
and religious in nature, comparable to the Sinicization of parts of East
and Southeast Asia. In the ninth century Indians sailed great distances
and established Hindu kingdoms throughout Southeast Asia. The physical remnants can be seen at Angkor Wat and elsewhere in Cambodia
and Indonesia, while the cultural remnants permeate these societies.
However, these kingdoms were not extensions of an India-based power.
It may be that Indian society was so well adapted to overseas colonialism that little or no force was needed.[14]

Muslims came to India's Sind in the early eighth century via the Arabian Sea and later to the Malabar coast in the south. By 870 A.D. Islam
had conquered Kabul, bringing with it the notion of an expanding
world of the faithful. It also brought new military technologies, theolo-

gies, and political ideas, but it did not destroy Indian civilization as it had destroyed pre-Islamic Persian culture. Eventually, under the Mughals, much of India was again unified within an imperial system. With this new order even Islam was powerfully influenced by Hindu culture, just as Islam shocked and transformed Hinduism.

The theory of an Indian empire was so popular and strong that the British East India Company developed the idea that it was ruling on behalf of the Mughals. Following the Mutiny of 1857 (termed by Indian nationalists the First War of Independence), this fiction was discarded, and India came under direct British rule. Because India had been apprenticed to the idea of unity earlier, they built on bureaucratic and symbolic foundations already in place. Large numbers of Indians accepted the empire under the British (the "Raj") as legitimate, although some ambivalence existed in the hundreds of Indian princely states that were never formally incorporated into the Raj. Some of these, such as Hyderabad in the south and Kashmir in the north, were themselves vast enterprises, with their own traditions of regional dominance and statecraft. The manner of British rule (especially its racism) rubbed the wrong way; most of India's important nationalist leaders were the victims at one time or another of racial discrimination, although few rejected the imperial system that exercised power in the Subcontinent.

### The Bureaucratic State

Much of India has long been familiar with the idea of the bureaucratic state. The Mauryans replaced traditional military-tribal patterns of governance with a system based upon rules and regulations. This survived for hundreds of years, but eventually collapsed because of excessive decentralization. The Mughals, under Akbar, and then the British, reintroduced bureaucracies (based upon Persian and Chinese models). These bureaucracies accommodated ambitious and powerful local leaders who might otherwise have broken away from central authority or banded together to depose that authority. This was the typical pattern for most of India's history; even when there were no pan-Indian empires, there were long spells of orderly, organized governance at the regional level lasting for hundreds of years.

A distinctive feature of both early and later Indian dynasties was the modest role of the military. As in ancient Greece and China, the civilizing impetus led to the curtailment of the authority and power of the soldier. In Indian terms, this is reflected in the status accorded various castes: the Brahmin (priestly) caste ranked higher than the Kshatriya, or warrior, castes. The *Arthashastra* was written (or compiled) by a Brahmin adviser, and Brahmins were influential in all of the great Hindu dynasties. In similar fashion, the later Muslim rulers did not accord divine authority to the ruler-soldier. Though India produced many great Muslim soldiers and warriors (and the Mughals solidified their rule by an alliance with the most martial of the Hindu warrior castes, the Rajputs), the Mughal Empire was based on consolidation, not conquest, and weakened only when Emperor Aurangzeb overreached himself in attempting to conquer the far south.[15] And although the military played an important role in establishing Britain as an Indian power, in its last fifty years the Raj was run by civilians exercising tight control over the armed forces. India's first prime minister, Jawaharlal Nehru (1889–1964) and his Congress party extended this practice. As discussed in chapter 3, the armed forces play a smaller role in decisionmaking in India than in any other major state in the world.

The Subcontinent has a weak record of protecting itself from foreign invaders. The ancient Hindu armies conducted extensive military operations within India, but their strategies were based on the war elephant in the context of plains warfare. While elephants were formidable weapons platforms when facing foot soldiers or other elephants, the invention of the stirrup in Central Asia and the rise of mobile armies transformed warfare in the Subcontinent. Successive invaders swept into South Asia on horseback at will, bringing down a thousand years of Hindu rule.[16] The successor Muslim dynasties, including the great Mughals, were not in the forefront of technological or organizational innovation and in any case had no naval force capable of keeping the Westerners at bay.

However, it was not so much superior military technology that enabled the British to defeat Muslim and Hindu armies as it was superior organizational skills. By recruiting and training Indian soldiers in large numbers, they went on to create a reliable army that not only defeated the French forces in India but subsequently conquered the rest of India, Nepal, and parts of Afghan territory. Later, because of British imperial politics, the Indian military was kept at a very low level of technology and Indian industry was prohibited from developing and manufacturing modern arms. Virtually every Indian nationalist politician and strategist noted this chronic technological lag under British rule, and correcting the problem became a high national priority. Autonomy, self-reliance, and freedom from outside restraints are still important themes in Indian strategic thinking. Thus economic development, the pursuit of advanced technology, and strategic autonomy are inextricably linked in the Indian mind, even though the achievement of these goals has been inadequate and incomplete.

## State and Ruler

The great imperial systems of India shared a common veneration of the emperor-ruler. In ancient Hindu tradition, the ruler was said to be made of the same cosmic material as the gods. As the king reintegrated and reordered his kingdom, he was also renewing the macrocosmic level of the universe.[17] Yet the Hindu ruler was still subject to the constraints of caste and an overriding duty to preserve the Hindu social system.

Although India's Muslim rulers did not invoke divine sanction, some moved in this direction in an effort to hold together their diverse Muslim-Hindu population. The most comprehensive effort in this regard was that of Emperor Akbar, who founded a cult of the monarchy in addition to creating a bureaucracy and an imperial civil service that lasted well into the nineteenth century. To restore the concept of imperial sanctity established by earlier Hindu rulers, Akbar drew upon powerful symbols such as the nimbus, or halo, which was added to the imperial head in Mughal paintings. He also established a syncretic religion, "the Divine Faith," which portrayed him as a superhuman or semidivine person. In Indian estimation, the Mughals rose above the general run of kings and princes; they had acquired a level of divinity.[18]

After a modest beginning, the British eventually surrounded the viceroy with both Hindu and Muslim imperial trappings. Through ceremony, doctrine, and architecture, the British tried to awe their Indian subjects with the majesty and near divinity of the viceroy and of the British king-emperor back in the motherland. Most of this imperial panoply has been retained in free India, not only in New Delhi but also in states such as Andhra Pradesh and Tamil Nadu, where film stars famous for playing the role of various gods have turned to politics and it has been hard to tell where the worship of the god ended and that of the politician began. Even though India has always been a political system enmeshed in law and regulation, it has also been one where authority is embodied in a great political figure.

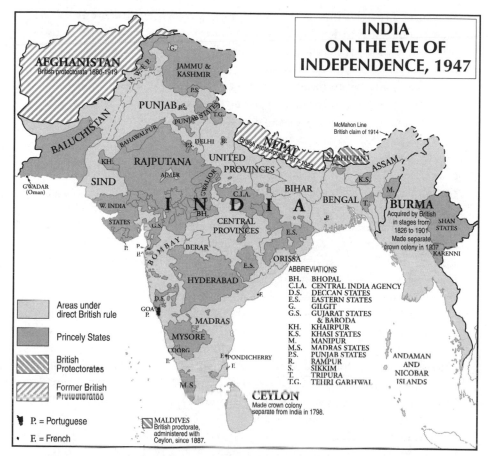

*Figure 1-1. India on the Eve of Independence, 1947*

## The Raj

The British-Indian Empire—eventually known as the "Raj" (Hindi and Sanskrit for "rule," or "government")—went through several strategic phases. The initial conquest was organized and led by professional soldiers such as Lord Cornwallis, who had lost the war in the American colonies. They were in the service of the East India Company, a private company chartered by the British Crown that developed a civil and military administrative structure throughout most of the Subcontinent well before 1857, when India formally became a colony. By the end of the nineteenth century, a debate was under way between those (such as Lord

Curzon) who saw India as the "jewel in the crown" of the empire and those (such as Lord Kitchener) who saw it merely as another imperial possession, and perhaps less important than some of the resource-rich colonies. The latter view won out early in the twentieth century, and from that point on India became an imperial base camp. Its shipyards and ports were vital to Britain's Far Eastern naval strategy, although the tiny Indian navy was controlled from Britain's Far Eastern naval headquarters in Singapore. The army had deeper Indian roots, and after it was used to conquer the remaining parts of India itself, it became central to Britain's regional and Asian strategy. It was sent into Afghanistan several times, and there were expeditions to Burma and Tibet. Whereas Hindu rulers had not ventured out of the region militarily, the British linked the Subcontinent to their global strategy. Indian Army units were commanded both by British and by Indian officers and fought in Africa, Europe, and Southeast Asia in World War II, and served as occupation forces in Indochina and Japan after the war. Earlier, they served as a near-permanent police force in parts of the Persian Gulf.

A crucial element of the Raj was the Royal Navy, whose dominance at sea ensured access to India (and other possessions) while preventing invasions of the kind Britain, France, and Portugal had undertaken. This, also, was a sphere that the British kept to themselves. Though a tiny Royal Indian Navy (RIN) existed, it performed only minor naval tasks while Indian shipyards were restricted in the number and displacement of ships that they could build.

Within South Asia, the British tailored their ambitions to fit their resources. They signed controlling treaties with Nepal and all of India's princely states; British India also had special rights in Tibet and contested Russian and German power in Afghanistan. However, the history of Britain's Afghan policy reveals a steady diminution of effort and ambition. On the eve of World War II, the Indian Army was prepared to let a foreign power come right up to the Durand Line, the modern-day division between Pakistan and Afghanistan. Indian manpower was needed elsewhere in the empire, and Indian industries could not produce the weapons needed to launch a preemptive invasion through the Khyber Pass.[19]

The British Empire bequeathed a number of important geopolitical norms. These included buffers to the north, sea protection in and around the Indian peninsula, and "the existence of a core and periphery in the Subcontinent, the core being postindependence India and the periphery being the smaller states ringed around it."[20] As discussed in chapter 5, the new Indian state did not have the Raj's resources, and its strategic environment was greatly weakened by the creation of a hostile Pakistan. India has struggled for half a century to close the gap between the strategy inherited from the British and its resource base, the latter considerably diminished because of the demands of social and economic development.

The British were divided over the idea of India becoming a nation. Some found it idealistic and unrealistic, arguing that India was at best a congeries of peoples or nations and needed a firm hand to keep these different elements from tearing one another apart. The Mughals and the British had provided such a hand, and many British officials and politicians were wary of handing control of the Raj to a disputatious collection of politicians. Some were also reluctant to see the princes, those Indians loyal to the Raj, and the Muslim population left to the mercy of Indian nationalists.[21]

Other British officials recognized early in the century that their place in India would be supplanted by a class of Indian administrators, politicians, and military officers. Although the pace of this development was not fast enough for the nationalists, by the time India achieved independence it had a strong core of bureaucrats and even some military officers. In fact, Indians had been engaged in electoral politics and legislative activities from the late nineteenth century in the provinces, and arguably from 1935 onward in New Delhi.[22]

## The Nationalist Response: An Imperiled State

Early generations of Indians saw the British as just another power contesting for dominance in South Asia. By the time Britain departed from the Subcontinent, that generation of Indians who assumed leadership had come to their own understanding of India's 2,000-year-old history. This was shaped both by Indian traditions and the example and tutelage of the British.

With the exception of some princes and a few politicians who lacked a strong political base, Indians were eager for independence from Britain and believed that they could manage the security of the Subcontinent as well as, if not better than, the British. While they differed in their estimate of the threats to the new Indian state, they were in agreement on a number of points.

One was that the state had to be enlarged rather than shrunk, and it had to play an active role in Indian economic development and social reform. Colloquially known as *Maa Baap* (Mother and Father) even in British India, the state was thought to play a benevolent and essential role. And despite its imperiousness, it fulfilled vital regulatory, economic, and developmental functions at the local and national levels.

Indians also believed that London needed to return full control over the state to India and place strategic planning in Indian hands, though some disagreed over the appropriate degree of postindependence cooperation with the British. Sovereignty was to be extended to all parts of "India," that is, to all territory under the Raj's control and influence, including the princely states. For some nationalists, the idea of territorial India became fused with the idea of holy India; as successive generations of Indian leaders were to discover, there was little support for territorial concessions to neighbors.

Indian nationalists and the British alike believed that this new ship of state would be difficult to govern and needed a firm hand on the tiller. Jawaharlal Nehru, India's first prime minister and the dominant figure in Indian politics for twenty-five years, saw only two factors standing in the way of India's greatness: international pressures and a lack of domestic unity. In his view, "fissiparous tendencies," the standard euphemism for domestic disorder, posed the graver danger. Many Indians blamed these tendencies on quarreling rulers who let outsiders enter and conquer the Subcontinent. A short story by the Urdu writer Prem Chand ("The Chess Players") recapitulated the experience for modern Indians: it portrays two idle Muslim princes wasting their time playing chess while the British gain a foothold in their territories. The lesson cannot be lost on anyone who has read the story (or seen the film by Satyajit Ray): Indians had only themselves to blame if they succumbed to rapacious outsiders.

The differences between the Indian leadership and the British were also marked. Several important Indian leaders, such as Jawaharlal Nehru, shied away from the use of force, and for the most part the Congress party was committed to peaceful protest. The most famous advocate of nonviolence, of course, was Mohandas K. Gandhi (1869–1948).

Indian strategic tradition emphasized defense, rather than imperial expansion. As a result, many of the so-called extremists in the independence movement such as Aurobindo Ghose (1872–1950), though tough nationalists, did not favor the use of force across India's borders. Believing that their culture, embodied in Hinduism, had universal appeal, they saw no need to force it upon other societies or peoples.[23] Other leaders, however, were even more eager than the British to turn to the gun, as seen in the activities of India's militants and militarists. Both traditions continue to this day (see chapter 3).

Nehru differed from the British and from Gandhi and the leading Muslim separatist politician, Mohammed Ali Jinnah (1875–1948) in another important respect. He believed that the national state (such as the Soviet Union) was giving way to the multinational state (such as the United States) and large federations.[24] He accepted the partition of British India, believing that it would only be a matter of time before a basic feeling of unity would reunite India and Pakistan. For him, the idea of Pakistan was a "fantasy," and "the loss of certain parts of India a temporary phenomenon which would soon right itself."[25] Like many Indian leaders, he argued that India had to remain whole and united to fulfill its great historical mission; because of its multinational, multi-ethnic nature, threats to Indian unity were as likely to come from within as from without. Furthermore, it would be easier for a united India to meet these challenges than a divided India.

Note, too, that few Indian leaders could match the British in their experience with the application of force and its relationship to statecraft and diplomacy. The Indian nationalist movement achieved independence largely through peaceful means, and the real Indian experts on defense and military matters were politically marginalized after independence or went to Pakistan.

## The Societal Legacy

Indian leaders were also the product of a unique and distinctive society composed of a complex blend of the very new and the very old. Such features as the caste system and India's linguistic and cultural diversity may have altered somewhat over the centuries, but descriptions of ancient India by early Greek and Chinese travelers clearly refer to the country now called India.[26] How well does Indian society support the requirements of a modern state, especially one with ambitions beyond South Asia? Are the classical scriptures, the theoretical political hand-books, and the practical advice of earlier Hindu, Muslim, and British rulers still relevant to contemporary Indian leaders? Does this past provide an insight into future Indian ambitions and objectives?

### Caste: "The Great Wall of India"

India is a modern state but an ancient civilization. In this respect it is
one of the few contemporary states that are largely coterminous with a
single "great" tradition. African, Arab, Latin, and European civilizations are divided among many states, but India, like China, is the heart-
land of a civilization of great antiquity. While several aspects of this
society are relevant to its possible emergence as more than a regional
power, the caste system (termed "The Great Wall of India" by the theo-
rist Charles Drekmeier) is the most characteristic of all Indian institutions.[27] Though a dominant feature of Hinduism, this system has influenced other religions, even egalitarian Islam, Judaism, and Christianity,
not to mention Sikhism, which is indigenous to South Asia.

Caste is a social construct rooted in endogamy: it refers to the largest
group in which a couple will seek a marriage partner for their child.
There are tens of thousands of castes. The word itself derives from the
Portuguese *castas,* meaning tribes, clans, or families.[28] The Sanskrit
term for caste is *jati.* Some *jati* are found throughout India; others are
small local entities. Many castes in different regions of India are similar
but because of linguistic differences are considered separate entities.

The origin of the extraordinarily hierarchical caste system is still a
matter of dispute among scholars.[29] Castes may have evolved from a
functional or occupational specialization, acquiring their present form
from the four major *varna* recorded in the early Hindu scriptures (ca. 500
B.C.): Brahmins, the teachers and priests of society; Kshatriyas, the war-
rior-rulers; Vaishyas, merchants and businessmen; and, at the bottom,
Shudra, or farmers.[30] The *varna* hierarchy is somewhat similar to the
social model of Plato's *Republic.* Outside the system were the non-Hindus, or those so low in the hierarchy that they were ritually despised.[31]

Although the "great *varna* tradition" has clearly influenced the status
of individual castes, the divisions are not always clear-cut. There are
Brahmin farmers, merchants, and soldiers (the British Indian Army even
had a regiment of "martial Brahmins"), and other castes carry on a wide
variety of occupations. Even in ancient India, the Brahmin often served
as the minister or adviser to the warrior-ruler, and a Brahmin compiled
the *Arthashastra.* Recently, Brahmins have tried their hand at business
and make up a large percentage of the booming computer industry. This
could lead to attitudinal changes in India concerning business and
moneymaking.

The salient features of the caste system are its adaptability and its complexity. Castes are not static or unchanging. They rise and fall, and they split and create new castes. They also use power and money to enhance their ritual status. Often a newly prosperous lower caste will have a Brahmin priest create a new caste legend, helping a farmer caste or even an untouchable caste edge into the ranks of the warrior or Kshatriya castes. Castes (or individuals within a caste) can change their status in other ways as well. Over the centuries the system has been successively (but not always successfully) challenged by Buddhism, Islam, Sikhism, Christianity, and many reformist Hindu movements. Some caste identities are not easily shed, and caste-based differences are still to be found among Indian Sikhs, Muslims, Christians, and Jews.

Although the caste system has always adapted to changing circumstances, the rate of change has accelerated in the past hundred years, reaching a revolutionary pace in the past decade. Some of these changes have been fostered by the state itself. Others are due to the logic of India's newly established democratic framework.

One of the best examples of how the state has adapted itself to and altered the caste system is seen in India's military system developed 200 years ago, where the British both drew upon traditional "martial" castes and shaped the identity of those castes. Infantry recruits for the Indian Army are still chosen on the basis of religious, regional, or caste quotas.[32] The British called these different recruitment groups "classes" (essentially ethnic groups) and the term is still in use. Various army regiments—Sikhs, Rajputs, Garhwalis, Mahars, Gurkhas, Dogras, and so forth—correspond to some of these classes. Each class has an elaborate tradition anchored in the "martial" history of the particular caste or ethnic group, and the different classes engage in friendly competition. The raw material of the army, the *jawan,* or ordinary soldier, is still drawn from the villages of India. Here he is inculcated with traditional notions of obedience, but he remains tied to the village authority structure; his behavior in the army reflects upon his village, and caste elders ensure that any runaway is returned to the army for discipline.

These diverse castes and classes were held together by a British officer corps, subsequently replaced in India (and in Pakistan) by indigenous officers within a few years of partition. They are still English-speaking officers, recruited nationally and competitively, and drawn largely from India's vast middle class. They received a modern military education and viewed the army as a long-term professional commitment. Thus today's armed forces, especially the army (the air force and the navy more closely resemble their Western counterparts), represent the melding of ancient practices, recently invented "traditions," and modern professional norms. Even though they lacked advanced technology, Indian forces proved very effective when used as an extension of British imperial power in Europe, the Middle East, and East Asia. The blend of old and new now provides a defense force competent to deal with basic regional security demands or various peacekeeping operations in Africa, the Middle East, and Asia. In India's most recent conflict with Pakistan in the Kargil district of Kashmir, the Indian infantry demonstrated that it had not lost the capacity for bravery and self-sacrifice.

### Caste and the Indian World View

India's social and cultural systems influence its approach to the world in many ways. First, the very complexity of Indian society can be frustrating to the political and strategic community, let alone baffling to outsiders. Despite the growth of an all-India culture and outlook (especially among the middle and upper classes and castes), India is still a country of staggering social, cultural, and political diversity. With its mixture of ancient Hindu, Muslim, British, and now even American components, it is more like a marble cake than a layer cake (or to use a regional metaphor, it is more like an Indian *kicheri*, which is a mixed dish of rice, lentils, and vegetables). Indian leaders have proclaimed this complexity and diversity to be a source of India's greatness. "Unity in diversity" is practically a national motto. However, these same leaders worry about this diversity exploding into chaos if the various castes and regions should get out of hand. One of the main objectives of Indian national policy has been to manage that diversity while insulating the Subcontinent from foreign influence.

Second, the caste system is a way of measuring others, and of being measured according to one's status in a hierarchy. This may help explain why Indian leaders, still drawn largely from the upper castes, are extraordinarily sensitive to the tiniest perceived slight to themselves, or their country, by foreigners.

Third, growing up in an enormously complex society with crosscutting themes of caste, language, ethnicity, and religion, as well as social class, constitutes an advanced course in practical politics. Indians are especially skilled at detecting nuances, searching out complexities, and calculating advantages and disadvantages within the social setting. All of these skills are put to good use in the realm of foreign policy. Indeed, Indian officials and strategists tend to overanalyze, to read too much into events. This tendency is reinforced in many cases by an enormous talent for historical detail. The Indian educational system, which still bears the imprint of the traditional ritual education reserved for Brahmins and other high castes, emphasizes the mastery of facts and the memorization of enormous amounts of detail. Indian officials find it easy to comprehend the minutiae of a negotiating record (they are aided by an exhaustive information system). They take pride in demonstrating this mastery during negotiations and often assume that superior knowledge about a particular issue signifies a superior position.

## Geography and Destiny

In ancient and medieval times, India was known to peoples to the East (Chinese, Southeast Asians, and even Japanese) and to the West (Persians, Arabs, and Greeks). It was renowned for its philosophy, its spices, and its social diversity. From the Mughals onward, there has been a belief, shared by the Indian nationalist movement, that South Asia formed a single cultural/geopolitical region. Even Muhamed Ali Jinnah and the Pakistan movement agreed: while arguing that Indian Muslims were a separate "nation" and could not live in a Hindu-majority state, they were still Indians.

Even though South Asia is a distinct region, its international significance, including that of India as the region's dominant power, has undergone dramatic changes over the past century. The location of a country and its natural and human resources would seem to be the immutable building blocks of a foreign policy. Yet such policy is powerfully influenced by the changing international environment.

During the British Raj, for example, India had three successive identities. In the eighteenth and early nineteenth centuries, it was an object of plunder and the basis for many British fortunes. By the late nineteenth century, India had become Britain's most important overseas possession, the "jewel" in the crown. Finally, at the beginning of World War II, it came to be seen as merely one component of a larger imperial strategy. When the anti-imperialist Labour party won power after the war, Britain beat a hasty retreat from its Indian possessions and granted India independence.

The cold war once again transformed India's strategic position. It was relegated to the backwaters of U.S.-Soviet competition. This isolation was abetted by the decision of the ruling Indian Nationalist Congress party to pursue a neutralist or "nonaligned" foreign policy. This policy also stressed anticolonialism, and by coincidence, ran counter to the interests of many of the European powers and the United States. After the United States and the Soviet Union achieved a stand-off in Europe and Northeast Asia, the cold war was fought in the former colonies and in the newly independent states of Asia and Africa. Even so, South Asia and India remained peripheral, except for brief periods when the region appeared to be threatened by China or the Soviet Union. Ironically, India's relatively stable political order caused Western interest to decline. New Delhi was considered more important for its ability to contain communism internally than for its role as a "frontline" state such as Turkey, Taiwan, South Vietnam, or South Korea.

India's strategic marginality was reinforced by the widespread view of Asia as a series of subregions, some more important than others. Seen merely as a state in "South Asia," India jostled for attention in the foreign ministries of the world with other cold war battlegrounds such as Southeast and East Asia and the Middle East. These constructed subregions displaced the older, expanded notion of "Asia."[33]

Indian strategists, such as Nehru and Ambassador K. M. Panikkar, objected to having India placed in this cold war framework at the margin of the new global strategic order and separated from regions with which it had a long cultural and strategic association. The cold war was seen—correctly—as an extension of a European-dominated system that might yet prove to be transient. Panikkar, an academic-diplomat who once served as India's ambassador to China, argued for an expanded notion of an "Indian Ocean region" that included the territory stretching from East Africa to Southeast Asia.[34] Like many other Indian historians, he was aware that the global system had changed after Europe expanded its power in the wake of Vasco da Gama's journey to India, but he prophetically argued that this could change again. Nehru, the dominant figure in Indian foreign policy for two decades, urged his fellow Indians (and the rest of the world) to recognize India's importance in the Middle East, Southeast Asia, or the Far East, pointing out that "while the Middle East may not be directly connected with Southeast Asia, both are connected with India."[35]

Nehru saw China as India's natural Asian partner, and he hoped that together they would shape the destiny of Asia by challenging, and defeating, the Eurocentric world that had made India a colony and China a weak, semi-occupied state.[36] Nehru's sustained policy of anti-colonialism began well before India achieved independence. This policy was motivated in part by his powerful desire to restore a world in which India was truly one of the major powers.

Though not incorrect, Nehru's concept of India as something more than a South Asian power fell on deaf ears in the 1950s. It was dismissed by China, rejected by its one strong regional neighbor, Pakistan, and ignored by the superpowers. But Nehru was right in predicting an end to the cold war and a transformed international order, although he was wrong in his expectation that India and China might form the core of an "Asian" alliance. In part, this was because he assumed that China, like India, would emerge as one of the security managers of a post-Vasco era, keeping European influence at bay in an alliance of the region's two megastates. Nehru died at the peak of the cold war (1964), but more than a decade after its termination India's hitherto marginal position is as geopolitically salient as it was for much of the eighteenth and nineteenth centuries.

### Ranking India

There are at least three ways to determine India's position in the hierarchy of states. One is to examine the present judgments of other states, as well as of Indians, in order to assess India's *reputation* as a great power. A second is to look at India's material strengths and weaknesses. Third, one can attempt a "class" analysis, to determine its rank among other states.

#### Reputational Power

For the past several decades, India has had a weak or at least highly variable reputation, as judged by the ability to influence without attempting to exercise influence. Such influence flows naturally and silently; it is what Joseph Nye Jr. has termed "soft power."[37] For the United States, China, Japan, and most of Europe, India has long been considered a state with a vast poor population and slow economic growth. India was easily written off as a "regional" power and even as a nuisance or impediment to some larger strategic objective. It was clearly not "on the radar screen" of the United States or of Asia's two other major states, China and Japan. Of the major powers, only the Soviet Union developed a broad appreciation of India as a power. While Moscow was primarily motivated by strategic and economic calculations, Indian culture penetrated somewhat into Russia and many of the Asian Republics.

Much to the chagrin of the Indian strategic elite, India has stirred the Western imagination more because of its exotic and esoteric qualities than because of its power and influence as a state. It became the "Other" that the West used to understand itself: "Whether Westerners praised India for its spirituality and its high creative achievements, sought it for its wealth, or denigrated it for what seemed barbarous and inhuman customs, its value was in relation to the West."[38] Ironically, this notion of an exotic India defined in opposition to the West made its way back to India itself through the introduction of Western histories and curricula in Indian schools, colleges, and universities, and in the education that tens of thousands of Indians received in Britain and Europe. Many of these elites experienced racial or other forms of discrimination and proceeded to invert the Europe-Indian relationship, defining India (and the rest of Asia, or subsequently the "third world") as morally and spiritually superior. Upon being asked, "What do you think of Western civilization?" Gandhi once wryly commented, "I am in favor of it." This summarizes the Indian nationalist response, which constructed (often in collaboration with Western scholars) a distinctive view of India's past that helped shape their vision of India's future.

The major powers may not have paid much attention to India, but its reputational power in the capitals of its neighbors is enormous. They regard it as a state that can do them great damage, and New Delhi need not say or do much to command their full attention. The foreign policies of Nepal, Sri Lanka, Bangladesh, Bhutan, and even Pakistan are oriented primarily around the fact that India is the dominant power in the region. But this is inadequate fare for much of the Indian strategic elite, which is both angered and embarrassed by comparisons with mere Pakistan, let alone smaller states like Bangladesh, or Nepal or Sri Lanka. This is not the high table.

In recent years India's reputation as a major power has grown steadily. The nuclear tests of 1998, the rise of the bold and decisive

Bharatiya Janata party (BJP), its ability to maintain a stable political coalition at the center, a "victory" in the Kargil war, and Bill Clinton's accommodating visit to India in March 2000 (followed by an equally obeisant visit by Russia's president Vladimir Putin), all point to a more respected India. Furthermore, its leaders have demonstrated an ability to persuade the United States and other major powers to take a more positive attitude toward India. This newly elevated view of India could be reversed quickly, but the net trend seems to be upward.

## Economic and Military Power

Demographic, economic, and military indicators place India in a very high rank in some respects. (Of course, this does not necessarily mean that India can do much more than maintain the status quo or that it has "discretionary" military or economic capabilities of diplomatic or strategic use.)

—India has the world's second largest population, having just passed the billion mark, and could surpass China in the next few decades, moving far ahead of the United States (270 million). Russia and five other states (Indonesia, Japan, Pakistan, Brazil, and Nigeria) all fall between 100 million and 250 million.

—According to the World Bank's *World Development Report 1999/2000*, India's economy is gigantic in terms of overall gross national product (GNP). It ranks eleventh in the world, with a total figure of $421 billion, compared with China's $929 billion, and Japan's whopping $4,090 billion, the world's second largest economy.

—India ranks low in terms of GNP per capita, with a figure of only $430. China has nearly double that at $750. The two states rank 165th and 149th, respectively. Again, this does not begin to compare with Japan's $32,380 GNP per capita.[39]

—When measured by purchasing power parity (PPP), India scores somewhat higher at $1,661 billion, the fourth largest in the world (PPP adjusts national accounting figures for price and exchange rate differences), behind China ($3,984 billion), and not far behind Japan ($2,928 billion). However, PPP per capita is much lower, India ranking 163d in the world, with a PPP per capita of $1,700 (the figure for China is 129 and for Pakistan 169).[40]

On social indicators, India does very poorly at the gross aggregate level and is not even found among the first hundred states on several measures.[41] The human development index of the United Nations Development Program (UNDP) (a summary measure of a number of social indicators) is a feeble 128 (China is higher at 98, and Japan ranks ninth in the world).[42] When judged by the UNDP's gender-related development index, India ranks 108th, barely ahead of Pakistan (115th) and Bangladesh (121st), and somewhat behind China (79th).[43] India's illiteracy rate is still high, but has fallen significantly: in 1947, 88 percent of Indians were illiterate. Today the adult literacy rate is 56 percent, far behind that of China (83 percent), but well ahead of that of Pakistan (44 percent).[44] Finally, life expectancy at birth in India is now sixty-three years, a dramatic increase from the colonial years (when average Indian life expectancy at birth was about thirty-two years), but marginally behind the levels in Pakistan (sixty-four years), Russia (sixty-seven years), and China (seventy years).[45]

India thus presents a somewhat contradictory picture. Its economy is huge, but so is its population; while standards of living are rising, India, like China, remains a poor country at the aggregate level. The quality-of-life indicators are all moving upward, but very slowly. India is home to more than half of the world's poorest populations, and though many are gradually improving their lot in life, this is still a large, overcrowded, largely peasant, half-literate society with pockets of terrible poverty and deprivation. There are areas of spectacular wealth and high technology as well, and these have benefited greatly from recent reforms. It is also an intensely politicized society, with an incomparably dense web of political parties, associations, and local governments, all of which make India the world's largest "producer" of politicians, elections, and democratic political activities. It produces more in this regard than the rest of the world combined.[46]

India is usually in the top dozen states in terms of overall military expenditures, ranking twelfth in 1999–2000 with spending at about $14 billion.[47] This is a paltry sum compared with China's $40 billion or Japan's $37 billion, which is about the amount spent by most major European powers. Russia, the rump superpower, still spends $54 billion, but of course all of these numbers are overshadowed by the United States, which spends well over $250 billion in military equipment and personnel each year.

India's relative defense burden is low, and the state spends only 3 percent of its gross domestic product (GDP) on defense, amounting in 1998 to only $14 per person. By comparison, Pakistan spends over 6.5 percent of national income on the armed forces, about $28 per person, while China spends 5.3 percent and $30 per person.[48]

What does India get for its money? Here, the low wages and generally high quality of Indian armed forces magnify the effect of India's mere $14 billion in defense spending. India has the largest volunteer military establishment in the world, with well over 1 million regular soldiers, sailors, and airmen, and nearly the same number of paramilitary forces. India has fewer military personnel than the People's Republic of China (2.8 million) or the United States (1.4 million), and its total manpower is about equal to Russia's. If one were to add the burgeoning Indian paramilitary forces (estimated at nearly a million men), they would put India just behind China, although Beijing is rapidly expanding its own paramilitary forces.

India's armed forces have not only large numbers of personnel but also a great deal of equipment of all kinds. India maintains a significant number of armored vehicles: 4,000 tanks (some are in storage), and about 500 armored personnel carriers organized into 60 tank regiments, and 300–400 infantry battalions. India also has almost 200 artillery regiments, including a few equipped with short-range "Prithvi" missiles manufactured in India. These forces are organized into two strike corps and six to seven independent armored brigades, plus many independent infantry brigades and battalions scattered about the country, many of which are tied down in internal security duties. India's ground forces are somewhat bigger than Pakistan's all across the board, and the ratio of armor has been approximately 2.5:1 for many years. Indian air dominance over Pakistan is somewhat greater, with almost double the aircraft (India has 774 combat aircraft, mostly multipurpose fighters; Pakistan has only 389). China, by contrast, has a vast armored force, with more than 8,000 tanks and more than 3,000 combat aircraft. All three countries have few modern aircraft, most of which are old Soviet models (in China's case, they are copies of Soviet aircraft, many of which have been sold to Pakistan). However, each of the three possesses a small core of advanced fighters, capable of challenging another regional power for air superiority or serving as delivery vehicles for nuclear weapons. India and China now possess the nuclear-capable Sukhoi 30; India and Pakistan each possess a variant of the Mirage 2000, although Pakistan is the only air force in this triad that flies the advanced but rapidly aging American F-16.

The Indian armed forces, critics say, are suffering from gross waste and corruption and are sadly underequipped compared with even Pakistan.[49]

A recent 17 percent increase in defense spending will still have a limited impact on India's power-projection capabilities since there is no indication that India could prevail in a short conflict, or that others might not assist Islamabad in a long one.[50] Furthermore, the impact of the "revolution in military affairs" on this large establishment remains uncertain. Much of it still resembles a colonial military establishment, and doctrine and theory have not kept up with advances elsewhere in the world.

Now that India and Pakistan have declared that they hold nuclear weapons, these devices must also be figured into the regional military balance. China is thought to have a relatively modest force of nearly 300 deployed nuclear weapons, India to have enough plutonium to fabricate between 25 and 100 warheads, and Pakistan (whose weapons are based on uranium) to have enough fissile material to produce between 10 and 15 devices, although recent reports suggest that Pakistan holds the larger inventory.[51] Whether India and Pakistan have made all of the weapons that their fissile inventories would permit, and whether these have been mated to delivery systems, are difficult questions to answer. It is widely assumed that each has fielded at least a few devices and could produce many more on fairly short notice.

The delivery vehicles for these weapons are likely to be aircraft, but Pakistan is moving toward a missile-based capability (partly because it is so short of modern aircraft). With Chinese and North Korean assistance, Pakistan has accumulated about twenty medium-range nuclear-capable missiles. India lags in this category, with only a few short-range missiles (the Prithvi) in its inventory, and a medium-range missile (the Agni) still under development. China has nearly seventy medium-range missiles, a few long-range intercontinental ballistic missiles (ICBMs), and a dozen sea-launched medium-range missiles (India has neither an ICBM nor a sea-launch capability, although programs for both are under way). Most of these Chinese systems could theoretically target major Indian cities or Indian nuclear weapons based in northern and eastern India.

In terms of naval power, India's fleet is smaller than China's, but anecdotal evidence suggests that it is better trained and more experienced. Indian ships range throughout the Indian Ocean, paying regular calls on ports in East Africa and Southeast Asia. Its aging submarine fleet, almost entirely Soviet/Russian in origin, is shrinking.

Like China, India has been unable to produce high-quality weapons without external assistance. At present, it is in the midst of a major arms-buying spree. A recent purchase from Russia for more than $4 billion worth of equipment will augment India's tank force and air fleet considerably and permit the acquisition of several important ships, including a second aircraft carrier.[52]

It is more difficult to measure the relative quality of Indian forces, since much depends on leadership, both civilian and military (see chapter 5). However, the Indian military, when adequately led and given a clear and reasonable political objective, can obviously perform extremely well, albeit at a low to intermediate level of technological sophistication. The Indian armed forces certainly compare favorably with those of Pakistan and China, although they would have a hard time coping with naval or air units from a truly advanced military power.

### Rising and Emerging Powers

The notion of an emerging power implies movement upward in a hierarchical or class system. To make such a move, a state must acquire the capabilities (be they economic, military, strategic, or some other criteria by which nations are graded) to change its rank. Such movement is also relative: if neighbors, rivals, or a superpower lose their capabilities, a state may rise by virtue of the decline of others. With the fall of the Soviet Union, a number of countries found themselves with the opportunity to "rise" through the international order and assume some, if not all, of the Soviet Union's special international status. In the present unipolar international order, or even the earlier bipolar system, great states would appear to be one notch below the top. Most often, these are states that are regionally dominant but are unable to project power into another region.

Being a "great" power also implies certain attitudes and policies in keeping with a particular position in an international order. "Great" states have both a class identity and an ambition. They are, it seems, in the habit of claiming superior rights and accepting special responsibilities and often cast themselves as the managers of the international system. At the end of a major war, for example, they attempt to arrange peace settlements and to restore an international system that would ensure their own influence in peacetime politics.[53]

Middle powers have no such ambitions and no such class identity. Great powers do: they need to defend their collective authority against challenges from below and to maintain their superior position against would-be great powers. This can be a strong incentive to restrain their rivalries and to sometimes coordinate their policies.[54]

As for weaker states, their chief preoccupation is survival. Great powers have broader interests: to organize their region, to promote an ideology or a concept of political order. In this sense, small states need not be weak states, and powerful states are not necessarily big ones.

Some states may also be monothematic, in that they are economically powerful but have not attempted to convert this to military power or strategic influence; or they may project their cultural or ideological influence on adjacent or distant regions yet lack a global or multiregional reach. Relations downward are as important as relations upward. Almost all Indian writers have focused on India's relations with the "great" or superpowers, but few have paid much attention to relations with the smaller states. From the perspective of its small regional neighbors India is already a superpower. It constrains them in every possible way; its cultural and economic power is projected on them far more strongly than American, Chinese, or European power is projected on India.

The most significant exception to this is Pakistan, the only South Asian state that has tried to resist Indian predominance through military and ideological means. Pakistan is strongly opposed to India's "emergence" from a regional power to a state that has resources available for extraregional influence. Since Pakistan has become a nuclear weapons state, has powerful allies, and a strong military establishment, India-Pakistan relations are important to India's place in the international order, and the Pakistan-China alliance places a critical restraint upon India, seemingly confining it indefinitely to the status of a "regional" power. It has been said that "India has yet to succeed in translating its regional preeminence, which can be measured by objective criteria, into regional predominance, which is dependent on the other regional states' acceptance of such a role as legitimate."[55]

India's emergence as a great power also depends on the kind of international system that prevails at any given time. From the Indian perspective, the ideal world would consist of many great powers, each dominant in its own region, and pledged to avoid interference across regions. For five decades, Indian diplomacy has worked to bring about such a world, but it seems as distant now as it did in 1947. When the world assumed a bipolar shape, India's response was to seek systemic leverage by forming, and for many years, leading, the nonaligned movement. This did not prevent India from having a close association with each of the superpowers in order to strengthen its regional position and, it was thought, ultimately make possible its accession to a higher rank.

With the end of the cold war, the prospect of an emerging India arose again. Indian strategists held their breath, as great strategic change took place. While the Soviet Union, then India's most important external ally, collapsed, there was still the possibility that the other superpower, the United States, would also go into decline or reject a global role.

The Gulf War and the revival of the U.S. economy in the 1990s belied these expectations. The United States has continued to act as a power with global reach, although one with fewer interests in South Asia itself after the Soviet pullout from Afghanistan. A new world consisting of several major powers (including India) was not at hand. Indeed, Indians became alarmed, because by the mid-1990s it seemed that one of its rivals, China, was emerging as a major Asian state. This prospect was especially worrisome to New Delhi because of the close U.S.-China ties that had developed over the years.

India's rise to "great power" status was thus confounded in part by the form of the international system. As a classic middle power, India waited expectantly for either a call from one of the superpowers or their decline. The call never came, and the decay of one superpower was not followed by the other, but instead by the growing capabilities of a some-times regional rival, China. India's reputation and its interest in assuming a greater international role were also clouded by domestic political crises from the late 1980s onward, with Rajiv Gandhi's assassination, a series of weak coalition governments, and a failing economy.

India's ambivalent status as a major or great power can also be seen in its frustrating relationship with the leading international organization, the United Nations. India emerged from World War II as the world's fourth largest industrial power and second most populous state. A permanent seat on the UN Security Council (with veto power) would have been the ultimate certification of India's status as a major power, but because of a peculiar conjunction of dates, the United Nations came into being at almost the same moment British India was moving toward partition. Focused on gaining independence in 1945, Indian leaders let pass the opportunity to stake a claim as a permanent member of the council. Sir Girja Shankar Bajpai, a senior Indian civil servant who represented the Raj in Washington during and immediately after World War II, apparently did not have the question of UN membership on his agenda, nor were the British eager to have India on the council. Britain, which was still regarded, in William Fox's terminology, as one of the three "superpowers" of the day, was expected to protect Indian interests.[56]

India's inability to secure a seat on the Security Council is ironic, because Jawaharlal Nehru was a staunch supporter of the United Nations, and cooperation with international organizations is mandated in the Constitution of India. While Indians have found a prominent place in the UN system itself, serving in important political, economic, and even military roles, a permanent seat, with a veto, eludes their country.

In recent years India has revived its campaign to secure a seat on the Security Council. India's views toward the United Nations have shifted somewhat. Instead of seeing it as an important global organization in its own right, India seems primarily concerned with status and security. As for status, the government's strategy is to move the UN debate away from selection by region (which is how current non-veto council members are chosen) and toward a set of principles (size, income, past contribution to UN activities), which would lead to the conclusion that India is an appropriate candidate for a permanent seat.

Implicit in this argument is the view that some of the existing council members have less right to be there than India. Should Communist China be on the council when democratic India is denied a seat? What about the smaller council members, France and Britain, which not only have small populations but are no longer world powers? As for security considerations, India wants a UN seat because it may at some time have to veto a UN resolution dealing with Kashmir or South Asia. For New Delhi, the UN's military involvement in Kosovo and the Persian Gulf were worrisome precedents for a renewed involvement in Kashmir, and it can no longer count on the Russians for such a veto.

## India as a Different Great Power

India has a 3,000-year history of growth, decay, and renewal; of invasion, absorption, and survival; of imperial conquest and imperial subordination. This has left its imprint on Indian society and its political elite. While this past does not dictate contemporary policy, it does influence it. India's foreign policy rests on an expansive vision of the country's destiny; yet to date India has lacked the resources that could turn vision into reality. *India has long been counted among the have-nots. This situ-*

*ation is rapidly changing, which is what will make India such an interesting "great" power for the next dozen years.*

Although India's ability to extend its military power or play a balancing role elsewhere remains relatively modest, this power is increasing, as is the skill with which that power is now wielded. In the economic arena, Indian influence is mixed: while it does have significant capabilities in advanced and high technology, it was slow to develop an export capability of any consequence. This, also, is changing. On balance, India has long been regarded as a state that has failed to live up to expectations. Indians, of course, argue that there are reasons for this lack of performance, the primary one being that New Delhi remains enmeshed in a needless conflict with Pakistan that prevents it from becoming a major power. But even the propensity to blame others for India's ills is changing, and a new sense of confidence has become apparent in the past several years.

Though India may be the weakest of the great states and still unable to do some important things, it is capable of surprises. It cannot be ignored, but neither will it act like a great power at all times. Like China, which periodically pleads that it is still a "third world" state, India will have one foot in the "developing" world and one in the world of advanced economic and military powers for the indefinite future.

TWO  *The World View of India's Strategic Elite*

As India moves toward major power status, what course will its leaders follow? Their intentions may be difficult to decipher. India is a parliamentary democracy, but it is an Asian, not a Western state. It has a federal structure, but one in which central authority plays a disproportionately large role in national security affairs. India's armed forces are powerful, but they play a smaller role in security policymaking than their counterparts in almost all other countries. As in the United States, the most sensitive security issues are freely and abundantly discussed. If holding a rich variety of complex theories about peace and war is a mark of a great state, then India more than amply meets this criterion. However, this garrulousness sometimes complicates the task of determining intentions in what can be a remarkably opaque state. Although Indians acknowledge that they keep a secret by telling it to one person at a time, the system is capable of deception and stealth, as in the case of the 1998 nuclear tests.

One more qualification is in order. As in any other great country, India has experienced important changes in perception over time. Elsewhere I have described how different generations have responded to major formative events in the history of the Pakistan Army.[1] Similarly, India has now had two generations of Indian strategists and foreign policy experts coping with varied experiences and creating multiple angles of vision on the same problem. My approach in this discussion may flatten out these differences, but important new trends have appeared since the Bharatiya Janata party and its allies have moved from the opposition to form one of the stablest governments that India has seen for years.

## The Major Components of Indian Strategic Thought

Until recently, it was possible to speak of "the" Indian strategic perspective. Centered in New Delhi, it was dominated by Jawaharlal Nehru's view of India and the world. The Nehruvian consensus has long since broken down. Many profess to subscribe to Nehru's *principles* but assert that circumstances have changed, and so must Indian policy. Several emerging ideological and regional perspectives now provide alternatives to the Delhi-centric strategic community and Nehru's vision of India in the world. Finally (sooner rather than later), a new generation of Indians is coming to power, and their experiences, memories, and possibly their policies could differ markedly from those of their predecessors.

### The Nehruvian Tradition

Jawaharlal Nehru was not only India's chief foreign policy theoretician, he was its dominant, almost sole, practitioner for nearly twenty years. Nearly forty years after his death, his ideas and policies remain influential, partly because the environment of Indian foreign policy did not change much for twenty years. The international system of bipolarity remained intact, India's struggle with Pakistan has been a constant, and the conflict with China—which crushed Nehru personally—was already well under way before his death in 1964. Furthermore, Nehru's views persisted because he was succeeded in power by individuals who were either unskilled in foreign policy (Lal Bahadur Shastri, prime minister from 1964 to 1966), or who were committed to Nehruvian principles. Among the latter were his daughter, Indira Gandhi, who served as prime minister in 1966–77 and 1980–84, and Nehru's grandson, Rajiv, who succeeded her from 1984 to 1989. Both Indira and Rajiv made many changes in Indian foreign policy, but they and the Congress party establishment insisted that a national consensus on foreign policy based on Nehruvian principles was in place, even as they departed from them. This long inning of Congress party rule created two generations of Indian politicians and bureaucrats committed to Nehruvianism. Indians whose political and strategic views were formed in the early 1970s now hold positions of responsibility in the bureaucracy, although the changes are coming somewhat faster in the political parties and the business sector, where recruitment is more fluid and open.

Strongly influenced by interwar British socialist perspectives, Nehru adhered to a combination of liberal internationalism and the idea of a strong state, including its domination of the "commanding heights" of the economy. His views, also shared by the pre–World War II British Left, included a skeptical view of the United States, on cultural as well as ideological grounds. Nehru also held a sympathetic, even romantic image of the economic and social accomplishments of the Soviet Union—although he rejected Soviet totalitarianism—and he admired the way that Moscow stood up to Western pressure. Many of Nehru's generation saw this as a model for a weak, recently independent India. Above all, India's first prime minister was sympathetic to the anticolonial movements then stirring around the world, and he made this a central theme of free India's diplomacy.

Both Nehru and his successors believed that India was a great state and would produce leaders who would act wisely. They also had something to teach the rest of the world. In part, this may have been a consequence of the dominance of Brahmins and other high-caste Hindus in the policy process, including Nehru himself. Whatever the explanation, the role of global teacher, as well as leader, is highly valued in India. A lesser state can be led astray by a corrupt or unrepresentative regime, but a truly great state will, in the Indian view, produce leaders who combine nobility and strategic skill. The *chakravarti*—the classical Hindu leader who protects and orders society and brings order to the world, or guards the state against the chaos and anarchy of the outside world—is an honored role in the Indian tradition.

Nehru resisted playing the role of *chakravarti* even as he filled it. His ambiguity about his special place in Indian history and his charismatic appeal are amply reflected in his speeches and statements. A bit of self-criticism, first published under a pseudonym, then reprinted as part of his autobiography, is revealing:

> *Jawaharlal ki jai*! (Hail Jawaharlal!) The Rashtrapati [state leader] looked up as he passed swiftly through the waiting crowds; his hands went up, and his pale, hard face was lit up with a smile. . . . The smile passed away and the face became stern and sad. . . . Men like Jawaharlal, with all their great capacity for great and good work, are unsafe in a democracy. From the Far North to Cape

Comorin he has gone like some triumphant Caesar. . . . He calls himself a democrat and a socialist. . . . but a little twist and he might turn into a dictator. . . . It is not through Caesarism that India will attain freedom, and though she might prosper a little under a benevolent and efficient despotism, she will remain stunted and the day of the emancipation of her people will be delayed.[2]

Nehru also held that India's interests are relatively permanent and unchanging (since the state is an enduring entity with extensive territory and civilizational roots). He claimed only to have given "voice" to Indian policy:

I have not originated it. It is a policy inherent in the circumstances of India, inherent in the past thinking of India, inherent in the whole mental outlook of India, inherent in the condition of the Indian mind during the freedom struggle and inherent in the circumstances of the world today. I come in by the mere accidental fact that during these few years I have represented that policy as foreign minister. I am quite convinced that whoever might have been in charge of the foreign affairs of India and whatever party might have been in power in India, they could not have deviated very much from this policy.[3]

Thus, under Nehru's guidance, India's foreign policy was seen to be inevitable because it was grounded in the geostrategic realities of India. Nehru's supporters argued that to the degree that he failed, it was because, being only human, he may have misread these realities or was led astray by flawed advisers, such as his right-hand man, Krishna Menon, or was tricked by India's foes, especially the Chinese.[4]

Nehruvian internationalism is "realist" in its assumption that the world is not necessarily friendly to a weak and vulnerable state such as India, and that national interests must shape the foreign policy of any state. But Nehru was also a liberal and thought that states can rise above "the rigors of anarchy and fashion at least seasons and locales of peace and cooperation. They must do so because power politics is flawed and will end in catastrophe."[5] Nehru himself wavered continually between idealism and national egoism, or realism, arguing that idealism was, for India, a pragmatic and realistic policy. Under this reductionist realism, virtuous and wise leaders (such as Nehru) would be led to pursue realistic policies that advanced the national interest; these policies included a measure of idealism, or liberal internationalism. In brief, India would do well by doing good, and when it could not do good, the essentially just and moral India could, when necessary, use force to protect its vital interests. As in other great states, this national egoism permeates Indian foreign policy.

Jawaharlal Nehru profoundly influenced the first generations of Indian strategists. While fast disappearing, they include K. R. Narayanan, the current president of India, and Inder K. Gujral, who served as India's ambassador to the Soviet Union, foreign minister (twice), and then as prime minister in the United Front Government (1997–98). Gujral and his contemporaries could be called the "classic" Nehruvians. They remain suspicious of the "sole" superpower ("Today, the global system has to reckon with unimpeded power and authority centered around one superpower of which there is no equal in terms of pure military might") and concerned with the global spread of other states' nuclear weapons.[6] Like Gujral, they regret the passing of the Soviet Union on pragmatic grounds—it was an ally of India and a balancer of the United States and China—but also on grounds of principle: the Soviet Union was a noble, albeit flawed, attempt to build a modern state that practiced social justice and featured a state-centric economy.

The Nehruvians accommodated themselves to the new global realities and retreated from state-directed economic policies. As Gujral wrote, "It is no longer possible for nations or national markets to operate as self-sufficient units. Although a latecomer to liberalization . . . [there is a] growing integration of India's economy with the rest of the world." Globalization has also led, according to Gujral, to the "spectacular emergence of regional cooperation and integration," providing an opportunity for India to revive the spirit and substance of regional cooperation in South Asia, something that interested Nehru, but not his daughter. Gujral's major accomplishment as foreign minister and prime minister was his success in alleviating some of the fears of India's smaller neighbors. This was tagged the Gujral Doctrine and represented an attempt to return to Nehru's more accommodating relationship with India's neighbors.

## Gandhi's Influence

The Nehruvian core was also influenced by Mahatma Gandhi, directly through the Gandhi-Nehru relationship and indirectly through the influence of the Mahatma on Indian thinking at large. Although there are still vestiges of this legacy even fifty years after Gandhi's death, no significant element of the foreign policy community in India would claim to be "Gandhian" without some important qualification. With the exception of a few nongovernmental organizations (NGOs) and some environmentalists, authentic Gandhians are rare in the foreign policy arena.

However, Gandhi was a consummate Indian nationalist and patriot. This aspect of his political philosophy finds acceptance across the political spectrum and has been appropriated by the Hindu Right, much of the liberal Left, and even the communists. The great theoretician and practitioner of nonviolence, Gandhi has even been interpreted as favoring India's wars and the development and deployment of nuclear weapons.[7] This grossly distorts his central concern with how individuals, communities, and states could overcome violence. Throughout his life he argued that the major obligation of all individuals, including politicians, was to resist evil. The major instrument for such resistance had to be nonviolence. He frequently chose jail or resorted to fasts to combat some evil practice. For Gandhi, the worst course was to accept evil; he only reluctantly conceded the possibility of resisting evil with violence. Violence was doubly dangerous. First, it corrupted the person committing violence, since it was immoral to use a bad means to achieve a good end; second, there was always the possibility that one's position was incorrect. In this case violence was not only self-corrupting, but it hurt the innocent. These distinctions are glossed over in contemporary India, where politicians have deployed the nationalist and patriotic Gandhi, while the creator of principled nonviolent resistance to evil has been largely forgotten.

### The Militant Nehruvians

The Nehruvian world did not survive the trauma of the 1962 loss to China. It was supplanted by a tougher attitude concerning the use of force and the threats facing India. The dominant Indian perspective for the next twenty-five years could be characterized as "militant Nehruvian" and was best exemplified by Mrs. Indira Gandhi, Nehru's daughter. This approach shared many of Nehru's assumptions about the greatness of India and the unbalanced international system but differed from Nehru in the use of force. The militant Nehruvians were more likely to cite the model of the *mandala*—Kautilya's ultrarealist model of geopolitics—than the precepts of the Buddha, and they rejected Nehru's "softness" toward Pakistan and China.

To this group, the world was composed of threats, not opportunities. Where Nehru tried to carve out a role for India in the wider world, assuming that this would enhance India's prestige and thus lend weight to its diplomacy, Indira Gandhi dismissed this as "idealistic." The threats to India were found at all points of India's horizon. First, the smallest neighbors (Bangladesh, Nepal, Sri Lanka) were all too willing to serve as cat's-paws for the major powers, or their political incoherence created problems for Delhi. Second, Pakistan, an outright hostile state structurally destined to oppose India because of its reluctance to give up the two-nation theory, argued that the Subcontinent held two separate and incompatible nations, one Hindu, one Muslim. Third, China had humiliated India in 1962 and was bent on keeping it from emerging as an Asian equal. Fourth, after 1970, the United States entered the picture. Nehru was ambivalent about America, but his successors found strategic reasons for institutionalizing his distrust of Washington. America had armed Pakistan in the 1950s and 1960s; it had opposed India's just support for the Bangladesh movement in 1971, and had allied with China in the 1970s and 1980s and brought down India's friend, the Soviet Union, in the 1980s.

In addition, the strategic community came to a near-paranoid understanding of the domestic threats to Indian security. Taking their cue from Indira Gandhi, many concluded that these threats were largely, if not entirely, due to the machinations of foreign powers ranging from Sri Lanka to the United States. Such powers meddled in Indian affairs for the same reason they countered India internationally: they feared the rise or the coherence of India. The smaller regional states were led by misguided leaders; the larger, more distant ones wanted to prevent the rise of an alternative power center based in India.

If the militant Nehruvians disagreed among themselves, it was only over the direction and magnitude of the threat. For about twenty years (1972–92), no major strategic community in the world could match India's in terms of the number and variety of perceived threats. The eleventh-century Islamic historian, Alberuni, once wrote mockingly of Indian claims to greatness (there being no civilization like India's, no science like India's, no culture like India's, and so forth).[8] For many years Indians seemed to believe that no state was as threatened as India, and Delhi could point to actions by the Pakistanis, the Chinese, the Americans, or even the smaller regional states as "anti-Indian" in intent. All of these outsiders, together or separately, were trying to dilute India's natural and proper regional dominance.

## The Rise of Alternative Perspectives

The Nehruvian mainstream has been credibly challenged by an alliance of two different perspectives on security and foreign policy. The first is a renascent conservative-realist perspective, the second a more ideologically driven "Hindutva" (or revitalist Hindu) viewpoint.[9] Both groups have found a home in the BJP.

## Realists and Revitalists

In the mid-1960s, the Swatantra party attempted to offer a classical conservative perspective on domestic and foreign policy issues. It was led by the veteran Congress politician (and Lord Mountbatten's successor as governor-general), C. Rajagopalachari. Swatantra's supporters were drawn from three major groups: former government bureaucrats, members of princely families, and the business community. What united these disparate factions was a distaste for Nehru's Fabian economics and nonalignment; they were more sympathetic to the market and to private enterprise and were strong anticommunists. The Swatantra party never did well at the polls. It had no mass base, and Indira Gandhi attacked it as a tool of the neocolonialist West. However, several Swatantra party members continued their political careers in other channels, and one, Jaswant Singh, finance minister in one BJP coalition government and foreign minister in the second and third, has emerged as the leading spokesman for a realist foreign policy.

The realists differ from the Nehruvians in that they believe the world has fundamentally changed.[10] While Nehruvian self-reliance and third world solidarity might have sufficed during the cold war, the new world order is led by economics. Power, including military power, flows from economic strength. They do not see the United States as the enemy, but as a potential friend; China is just another state that has managed to play the new world order game very well, but there is nothing to inhibit India from going down the same road, in its own way, and at its own (accelerated) pace. China is not India's chief rival or enemy, nor is it a natural ally, as the Nehruvians might suggest; in any case, India must develop its own economy and then its own power in order to be able to settle the border conflict with China. China is a model for India in how to operate in the new world order and deal with the United States.

While sharing Nehru's belief in India as a great civilization, and the militant Nehruvians' willingness to use force, a new generation of politician/strategists, such as Jaswant Singh, are realists. Although tough on past leaders, especially Nehru, for their mistakes, Singh has been sympathetic, as a politician himself, to their plight.[11] Strategic matters rarely offer a choice between good and bad decisions, yet those who make these decisions must be held accountable, especially in a democracy. Indeed, Singh argues, most internal security problems in the Subcontinent are directly traceable to bad policies by governments (whether those of Pakistan, in the case of East Pakistan, or those of India, in the case of the Northeast, Punjab, and Kashmir) that ignored the legitimate demands of ordinary citizens. While foreign governments may have meddled in India, disturbance in these cases were also caused by flawed Indian domestic decisions. Singh is also keenly aware that in a democracy foreign and defense policies cannot be based on narrow *realpolitik,* since all major decisions will eventually have to face the test of the polls. On the other hand, he does not think that a policy based on idealism alone will work. All policies are necessarily a balance between idealism and self-interest. Finding that balance is the most difficult but important task of the statesman.

Nowhere is this more apparent than in nuclear matters. According to Singh, India now faces the same dilemma confronted earlier by the United States and other nuclear weapons states. Nuclear weapons cannot be used for any legitimate military purpose, yet they have become the symbol of national power. Although nuclear weapons cannot be seen as a solution to India's myriad external and internal security problems, he notes, as a country of unique status and civilizational influence, India cannot do without them.[12]

Jaswant Singh has argued for the restoration of a strategic perspective that reaches beyond India's immediate borders. This does not imply expansionism but recognition that India's strategic frontier may not be coterminous with its political borders. Quoting both Nehru's cousin, the distinguished retired diplomat, B. K. Nehru, and Jagat Mehta, a foreign secretary in the late 1970s who had worked closely with Nehru, he concludes that Nehru—and by extension, his successors—did not get their priorities right. Instead of accommodating the weaker Pakistan and recognizing the stronger China, Nehru pursued an excessively firm line toward Islamabad and too soft a line toward the Chinese. Furthermore, by adopting a socialist economic policy, the Nehruvians failed to provide India with the economic base upon which great power status could be erected. Finally, Singh is critical of the anti-American stance of Indian foreign policy: it makes no sense, he says, for India to gratuitously alienate a state that will remain economically important and strategically central to India for the foreseeable future.[13]

This center-right realist perspective has other prominent exponents. K. C. Pant, the son of one of Nehru's closest associates and a member of the Congress party until he joined the BJP in 1998, has long advocated similar policies. Pant's maiden public speech, delivered to the annual meeting of the Congress party in 1965, favored the development of an Indian nuclear weapon (to the shock both of several Gandhians and of Krishna Menon, who were in attendance). The first Indian test was conducted while Pant was minister of defense in 1974.

Both Jaswant Singh and K. C. Pant have staked out a center-right position on the political spectrum, constituting an important and influential new voice on foreign policy.[14] Yet both are members of the BJP, which is also more ideologically driven.

One of the major supporters of the BJP is the revitalist Hindu organization, the Rashtriya Swayamsevak Sangh (RSS, or "national service society"), founded in 1925.[15] Today it is one of India's largest and most important social service organizations.[16] The revitalists subscribe to a culture-driven view of the world in which India represents one of humankind's supreme civilizational accomplishments. Unlike the Nehruvians, they stress the active nature of the conflict between civilizations and believe that India's Hindu-dominant culture is still under attack from other, hostile civilizations. This is all the more unfair, because the RSS, like many other Indian groups, thinks that Indian culture is nonaggressive, and that this has given a false sense of Indian weakness and submissiveness.[17] During World War II, the RSS remained neutral in the struggle between the Allies and the Axis powers, although it did encourage their cadres to join the Indian Army and receive military training, looking ahead to the day when these skills might prove useful in a struggle against separatist Muslims and other forces antithetical to the RSS notion of Hindutva ("Hindu-ness").

While Nehru emphasized India's contribution to the Western and even global scene, especially the contribution of Gandhi and organizations such as the nonaligned movement (which India cofounded), the revitalists see India's primary influence largely confined to South Asia and areas where Indians have emigrated. In the mid-1960s the then "leader" of the RSS, M. S. Golwalker, drew a picture of the "motherland" "dipping its arms in the two seas, at Aryan (Iran) in the West and at Sringapur (Singapore) in the East, with Lanka (Ceylon) as a lotus petal offered at her sacred feet by the Southern Ocean."[18]

In the RSS view, the root cause of conflict in South Asia is the artificial division between the people of the region. South Asia is equated with India. It cannot be divided along territorial lines, since it has a common people and a common culture. Pakistan is an aberration, and most Pakistanis are, in fact, converts from Hinduism. Liberal Hindus, especially the Nehruvians, are faulted for battling what they misrepresent as a Hindu communalist movement (the RSS) while making concessions to a threatening Indian "Islamic communalism" and to Pakistan. Nehru and his followers failed to realize that many Indian Muslims are a "Pakistani fifth column entrenched in strategic points all over the country" (that is, many happen to live in cities), conspiring with Pakistan to bring about the further vivisection of India. Pakistan itself has distributed "various types of lethal weapons among the Muslims in the border areas. Probably, they feel that this is a golden opportunity for them to revolt, to bring our leaders to their knees and force them to part with another chunk of land as before."[19] This language, dating from the early 1960s, had entered the Indian mainstream description of Pakistan's intentions by the 1990s.

The RSS would like to organize all of South Asia along religious lines. India's Hindu culture, it argues, is the dominant strand that ties the region together, and as long as this powerful social force is artificially suppressed in India and it is arbitrarily separated from other Hindu-based societies, the region will never achieve full economic and strategic importance. To achieve this, the militant Hindu organizations argue, India must be militarily strong.

Among the political parties that have received RSS backing are the Hindu Mahasabha, the Jana Sangh, and most recently, the BJP. The Jana Sangh was the first Indian political party to advocate the acquisition of nuclear weapons. Hindu conservatives in the Congress party shared some of the Jana Sangh's outlook, but even Nehru's great adversary (and Gandhi's close supporter) Sardar Patel was willing to recognize Pakistan as an Islamic state and the reorganization of South Asia along religious lines. Nehru, on the other hand, had contempt for the militant Hindus who rejected secularism, even if he shared their distaste for religious-based Pakistan.

Much of the inspiration behind the strategic vision of the revitalists stems from their preoccupation with domestic matters, formerly known as "Indianization," a term coined by the BJP's forerunner, the Jana Sangh, and adopted by that party in 1952.[20] It refers to this purification of India through Hinduization, which consisted in part of eliminating foreign holidays and improper concessions to "foreign minorities" who came to India from abroad. Though such minorities include Jews, Parsis, Christians, and Muslims, only the latter two are regarded as potentially hostile to Hindutva, because they allegedly came to India with the intention of conquering and converting, and also retain ties to powerful foreign (and anti-Indian) forces.[21]

If one individual represents the successful synthesis of Indian realist perceptions and the more ideologically driven views of the RSS and its sister organizations, he is Atal Behari Vajpayee (1924–), who served as foreign minister in the Janata government of 1979 and has been prime minister from 1998 onward. Vajpayee was once a member of the RSS and still attends RSS functions, where he is widely revered. But he is also a political and strategic realist, able to forge workable alliances at home with disparate partners and improve relations with a wide variety of states hitherto regarded as anathema, among them the United States.[22] Vajpayee shares realist views about the importance of force and has written (in language reminiscent of Western realist thought) that "peace and strength are not incompatible," and that lasting security in the "real world" must be based upon security for all.[23] Of the states in the world, India's security is "central to Asia's security and stability," and American and other observers have to acknowledge both India's peaceful intentions and its right to possess weapons of mass destruction, which would be used responsibly by India.[24] While unpersuasive to many foreign observers, this position neatly fuses a number of Indian positions, and coupled with Vajpayee's transparent sincerity and avuncular style, has made him one of India's most popular (and effective) prime ministers.

## The Growth of Regional Indian Perspectives

For the most part the Indian security and foreign policy community is concentrated in New Delhi and has a Delhi-centric perspective of the world. Many of its leading thinkers are dispossessed high-caste elites from various states (especially the south) who have gravitated to Delhi, where they provide a disproportionate component of the strategic elite. However, the main regions of India have a latent potential to articulate different perspectives. For many decades, this was kept in check by the dominance of a single party (Congress) and a centralized economic policy. Now, however, there are a number of signs of a growing articulation of differing western, southern, northern, and eastern perspectives about Indian foreign policy interests in years to come.

This is especially the case in the booming regions of India's south and west. These states see new opportunities abroad. Some are closely linked to the international development of high technology, especially in information technology. While Karnataka's capital, Bangalore, has been much discussed as India's Silicon Valley, Hyderabad and Chennai (Madras) are not far behind. Some of these states relish their growing independence from New Delhi: a recent "anticolonialism, anti-imperialism" celebration in Hyderabad, the capital of Andhra Pradesh, was not a rally against America or the West, but marked the formation of the state forty years earlier, the unification of Telugu-speaking people, and their "liberation" from Delhi's dominance.

Some states now actually have the means to influence India's foreign policy. The gradual dispersion of political power in India with the Congress party's decline has given rise to a number of powerful regional political parties. Often these do not control many votes outside their own state, but in some cases they have elected enough members of Parliament to decisively influence the fate of a coalition government in New Delhi and now exercise this power. In recent years the defection of state-based parties in Tamil Nadu and West Bengal threatened to bring down the BJP-led coalition government in Delhi. Border states such as West Bengal, with a strong interest in normalizing relations with its cross-border neighbor (in this instance, Bangladesh), can now encourage the center to pursue conciliatory strategies. Tamil Nadu parties similarly influence India's policy toward Sri Lanka. A number of other states boast strong overseas communities, and those with large overseas Indian communities (Andhra Pradesh, Tamil Nadu, Kerala, and Gujarat) have a special interest in developments in the Middle East, East Africa, Fiji, and Malaysia, where persons of Indian origin (PIOs) are numerous.

Some Indian states also have a strong interest in expanding relations with potential investors. Chief ministers from economically dynamic states such as Andhra Pradesh, Karnataka, and Maharashtra regularly troop to Washington, New York, and Los Angeles to woo potential American investors, and they eagerly receive American officials and investors in their state capitals. While Prime Minister Atal Behari Vajpayee was visiting the United States in September 2000, several states were more interested in the visits to India of Microsoft's Bill Gates and General Electric's Jack Welch. These trends run counter to the residual autarchic tendencies of many in the Delhi strategic community, who do not want to see India become overdependent on outside powers for technology and investment, least of all the United States.

## A New Generation?

The reductionist realists may argue that a nation's interests are eternal and unchanging, but any policy community is profoundly shaped by its historical experiences. After 1962, when the moderate Nehruvian perspective was discredited, more militant attitudes took its place. This traumatic event "taught" a whole generation of Indians that the role of force in international politics had been underestimated by Nehru, even though they clung to his view that India had to remain outside of the major international alliances. Fortunately, India was able to move closer to both of the major cold war rivals in order to acquire the resources to balance China and rearm. From that date onward, India has been a psychologically militarized state, although paradoxically the already insignificant political power of the armed forces declined further.

While most older members of the Indian foreign policy community remain Nehruvian in all essentials, a new generation of Indian strategists has emerged. They have different perceptions of the international order, the use of force, the desirability of the international status quo, and India's major national strategic objectives. This successor generation (now assuming leadership in all of the major bureaucratic, policy, press, and academic institutions) will shape Indian thinking on strategic issues for many years. This generation has no firm memory of the 1962 defeat, or the victory of 1971. It has little direct knowledge of Pakistan, except through televised images, and these range from cricket and Pakistani soap operas (very popular), to the 1999 conflict in Kargil, India's first televised war, when Pakistan was depicted to the Indian nation as a traitorous, duplicitous adversary.

The overwhelming interests of this generation are domestic issues: caste reservations, job opportunities, and, to some extent environmental and gender problems. The "generation X" of India is patriotic, nationalistic, but (like its counterparts elsewhere in the world) less engaged with the outside world. Its understanding of China is no more sophisticated than that of its predecessors, except that China is seen as a country that has "made it" economically, whereas India has not. Their understanding of the United States is strongly colored by the fact that many of India's urban elite have relatives in America, and many of this generation aspire to higher education there. To them, their parents' (and their grandparents') anglophilia seems quaint and their anti-Americanism misguided.

In summing up his somewhat different categorization of Indian strategic thinking, the Indian scholar Kanti Bajpai noted that "there are few pure Nehruvians, Gandhians or Hindutva civilizationists. Indian elite views are a complex mix of all three tendencies. . . . [T]he Nehruvian vision has thus far predominated. Gandhianism resides increasingly in the shadows. Hindutva is declaring itself publicly and winning supporters, but full-blown Hindutva is still a minority view."[25] If one adds the growing regionalist perspective and the emergence of a new generation of Indian thinkers (of which Bajpai himself would be one), there is no shortage of Indian strategic perspectives. Indian humor understands this: as was once said about Bengalis, "One Bengali is a poet, two Bengalis are a debating club, three Bengalis comprise a literary magazine (editor, publisher, reader), four Bengalis a political party, and five Bengalis are Section 144" (the section of the Indian Penal Code that banned gatherings of five or more individuals in the Raj). Outsiders can be overwhelmed by an overabundance of articulate, well-thought-out views on a wide range of issues, yet a strong if evolving common core exists.

## The Common Core and Its Variations

Since so many of these different strands of Indian strategic thought overlap, it is possible to think of a "core" Indian perspective, as long as one is careful to note exceptions and new trends. How does this Delhi-centric core strategic community view India's strategic legacy and its role in the present international system? What is its vision of a desirable international order?

## The Impact of History

India baffles many foreigners because of the great contrast between its obvious poverty and apparent political turmoil on the one hand, and the self-confidence and pride of its leaders, on the other. The description of Alberuni, the eleventh-century Muslim scholar-traveler still fits: "The Indians believe that there is no country but theirs, no nation like theirs, no king like theirs, no religion like theirs, no science like theirs."[26] One reason for this discrepancy is rooted in the view held by Indians of their own civilization.

Despite foreign policy failures and much debate over tactics, the Indian elite holds fast to a vision of national greatness, as I discuss in subsequent chapters. Although this vision was revived during the years of struggle against the British, it has its roots in imperial and civilizational traditions that go back several thousand years.

The fact that India's history was punctuated by long spells of foreign domination made the past more, not less, relevant to the leaders of the Indian nationalist movement. Jawaharlal Nehru took advantage of extended imprisonment to write several interpretative volumes of Indian history, one of them in the form of a series of letters to his then teen-age daughter, Indira.[27] His views have been challenged by political rivals and professional historians, but not his notion that an exploration of the past is vital to an understanding of the present.[28]

When they examine the historical record, and compare it with that of other great civilizations, Indians come to two conclusions. First, the accomplishments of the great Indian Hindu rulers of the past—and even some of the deeds of the Muslims and the British—are second to none. They point to the richness of ancient Indian philosophical and political thought, the profundity of its religions (India is the home of four religions: Hinduism, Buddhism, Jainism, and Sikhism, and made a major contribution to Islam), the mastery of mathematics and science, and the development of a complex social and political order at a time when Europeans, for example, were organized into primitive tribes.[29]

Of the great world civilizations, only India and China embody a civilization in a single great nation-state. Like the Chinese, Indians understand how they came to be distinct and great and have a set of fundamental premises and assumptions, and a particular way of ordering both their own societies and guiding relations with the outside world. Moreover, like China, Persia, and Greece, India produced a language (Sanskrit) and a vocabulary that covered the entire range of human experience and knowledge. Sanskrit has a particularly rich political vocabulary. The root *raj*, roughly equivalent to the Greek *pol*, was borrowed by the British to describe their rule in India and is found throughout the modern Indian political vocabulary: Rajya Sabha (the Indian upper house of parliament), Raj Bhavan (governor's house), Raja (princely ruler), Rajasthan (place of rulers, the western Indian state), Rajpath (the ceremonial avenue in front of the President's house), and so forth.

Second, the historical memory of a great Indian civilization has practical consequences. Indian officials believe they are representing not just a state but a civilization. Few state-civilizations are India's equal. Believing that India should be accorded deference and respect because of its intrinsic civilizational qualities, many Indian diplomats and strategists are wary of having to depend upon states that do not appreciate India's special and unique characteristics.

Furthermore, Indians believe that India-as-civilization has something to offer the rest of the world. Contemporary Indian leaders also see India as playing a global, albeit benign, role. These beliefs explain Nehru's tendency to moralize, and the Indian propensity to lecture other powers, great and small. They are embedded in India's constitution: it decrees that as a matter of state policy India shall "endeavor to promote international peace and security; maintain just and honorable relations between nations; foster respect for international law and treaty obligations in the dealings of organized peoples."[30] Therefore, while India primarily seeks regional dominance, it takes its global mission seriously.[31] As just mentioned, New Delhi sees that mission as essentially benign: Indian politicians and scholars point to the largely pacific tradition of cultural and social expansion. Whether via ideology (Buddhism) or cultural colonialism (in much of Southeast Asia), or its influence on Greek and European thought, Indian philosophies and social patterns have traveled well and for the most part have been nonviolent. Only under the British did India become a base for extensive foreign military operations, and only under British tutelage was a global strategic tradition based on the Subcontinent established. Furthermore, India can wait until the rest of the world comes around to its way of seeing things, or at least acknowledges India's right to do things "its way."

India need only wait until others understand and accommodate to the Indian position. Nehru expounded this view for forty years, and his successors continue to do so. K. C. Pant, a former minister of defense and now a member of the Bharatiya Janata party, expressed the consensus on the long-term influence of culture and civilization: "We in India are aware that these attitudinal changes are not likely to come about overnight. However, we are optimistic that [they] are bound to take place. . . . I belong to a civilization which holds *Ekan Sat Viprah Bahudha Vadanti* [Truth is one, the learned expound it in many ways]."[32]

As for India's special social and cultural heritage, most Indian leaders still see their multiethnic, multicultural state as very well suited to the modern world. India's size, also, is considered an asset, not a liability. India has a depth of human and material resources matched by few other states. In this regard, Indian elites believe their country falls into the same class as Russia, China, and the United States. India embodies a great civilization, perhaps the greatest of all, because it is composed of so many other cultures, and (unlike China) has been tolerant of extreme diversity. What others insultingly refer to as "polyglot" is, to the Indian elite, a rich and diverse land of unlimited potential.[33] In its diversity India was a match for Europe or America, but in the eyes of the Indian nationalists, it is far superior in its spiritual heritage.

However, India's very diversity and complexity have been a mixed blessing. They have allowed foreign invaders to play off one group against another. Indian history is filled with examples of rapacious barbarians (or jealous neighbors) practicing "divide-and-rule" strategies against India. In the view of Indian leaders, Britain's cynical use of such a policy to rule India by catering to the Muslim League resulted in the partition, rather than the complete unification, of India. The fear of a "foreign hand" exploiting internal politics is endemic to Indian social structure. Outside powers (such as the United States and China), it is said, are intent on weakening India internally and support India's weaker neighbors militarily to "keep India down."

Finally, history has bequeathed to Indians a political and strategic tradition remarkable for its sophistication and complexity. India was not only the land of the realist Kautilya but also the home of the Buddha. Indian emperors felt no compunction in shifting from ruthless conquest to philosophical nonviolence. Pragmatism, realism, and idealism exist side by side; Jawaharlal Nehru displayed all of these traits—sometimes simultaneously—which is one reason why he remains such an interesting figure today. Contemporary Indians thrive on the legacy of complexity: their ideal is to combine the diverse strands in a truly Indian outlook, an Indian approach to the world. That is why few in government would accept the notion that India is a mere "pivotal" state, one of a cluster of eight or nine powers that are, for one reason or another, important to America as it pursues its objectives in the "developing world."[34] India is clearly no mere third world "pivot," but whether it will be regarded as belonging to the same class as China will depend in part on thinking in the Indian strategic community itself, which at present has no doubt about India being a world power, though it is deeply divided over the kind of role that India should play as such a power.

This view of culture and history helps explain the Indian understanding of the relationship between poverty and national greatness. For most Americans and Westerners (and the Japanese and even the Chinese), India has been *defined* by its poverty. But for Indians, poverty is an accepted cultural fact, not an inherently evil condition, and not a sign of failure or a civilizational flaw. Indian leaders are sincere in their attempts to reduce poverty through economic development, but they also believe that a poor state (more precisely, a state that contains many poor people) should not aspire to lesser goals. India's past anticipates a great historical destiny; dependence on others must not interfere with a national policy designed to fulfill that destiny. Many in the Indian strategic elite would rather see their country fail on its own than succeed with the help of others. This attitude is sometimes perplexing to foreigners, who are puzzled by the juxtaposition of poverty and high ambitions, although Indian accomplishments in high technology and a few other areas are rapidly changing images of India.

### The Present International System

A generation ago India placed its chips on the Soviet Union, economic autarky, and military might. It lost all three bets. The past decade has seen a wrenching reappraisal of Indian grand strategy in a changing international environment.

While Indians envision a more perfect and just international system in which New Delhi would play an important role, India remains a deeply status quo state, one that needs international stability to develop at home. The cold war in some ways provided an ideally stable environment: it allowed India to play (in its own eyes) an exaggerated role on the international stage for many years, where it could moralize about the inequities of bipolarity and the "cold war mentality" while still benefiting materially and politically from its ties to both the Soviet Union and the United States and its skill at playing one against the other.

For most members of India's strategic community, the end of global bipolarity forced India to operate in an unbalanced world. Most of the world's power, resources, technology, and status accrue to the former imperial powers and their clients. Even the United States (or perhaps particularly the United States, which by all logic should share the Indian distrust of empire) seemed to have turned its back on much of the "third world" (a term that Nehru himself would not use). Washington cared about this world only in areas where its resources and investments drew it in, or where peripheral states became pawns in a larger strategic struggle.

Although the current distribution of power is unipolar, this is seen as a temporary state of affairs; the larger struggle ahead will be between those major states that benefit from and manipulate the present status quo and those (such as India) that strive to join the first rank of major powers and will be able to influence the policies of the still-dominant America. Thus the issue of emerging or rising powers is important. During the cold war India was a flanking power that could afford to wait before entering a conflict or siding with one bloc or another. It rationalized its nonengagement in moral terms, although the underlying realist calculation was similar to that set forth in George Washington's Farewell Address of September 17, 1796. Similarly, India could also argue that it was so large, important, and democratic, that it need not join an alliance to serve the interests of the West: just maintaining itself as a democratic, status quo power was an adequate justification for putting a claim on the resources of others. To the Indian strategic community, India is not merely a "pivotal"—second-tier—state.[35] Moreover, in a more perfect world, its importance would be self-evident. Such a world would be one in which each major power acted responsibly to keep order and promote justice in its part of the globe. International politics would be governed by a group of such mature and responsible states that would be careful not to meddle in the affairs of other regions. But little thought has been given to how the policies of such states could be coordinated or how deviance from the system could be sanctioned.

The Nehruvians assumed that the United States would eventually retreat to its own hemisphere and cease its interference elsewhere around the world. Failing that, in the short term, the United States (and to a lesser extent its allies and dependencies, such as Japan) could possibly be "educated" into the proper norms of international behavior.

At one time, the same was said of China. Nehru believed that an India-China détente could stabilize Asia and keep the superpowers at bay. The 1962 war put an end to such hopes, and it is unlikely that the subsequent characterization of China as a strategic rival will soon fade. Beijing has supported separatist and autonomist groups within India, while remaining an authoritarian state. Indians understand that China is scornful of its "soft" democracy and has acquired a substantial lead over New Delhi in economic capacity and weaponry. As its own requirements for Middle Eastern oil draw it into the Indian Ocean, China could also emerge as a naval rival to India. The realists in Delhi see China continuing its strategy of encircling and counterbalancing India, preventing it from achieving its rightful dominance of the Subcontinent.

This next decade is seen as a transition period, when India must gingerly cope with expanding Chinese power, achieve a working relationship with the Americans, and cautiously use each to balance the other's military, economic, and strategic influence. India's new balancing act combines appeasement of China (on such issues as Tibet and Taiwan) with the pursuit of improved ties with China's other potential balancers, especially Vietnam and Russia. There are also conversations with China on how to prevent the abuses of unipolarity, but as reinsurance, India is eager to maintain a "strategic dialogue" with the United States, one subject on the table likely to be the problems that both face in containing Beijing.

Still another dilemma for the strategic community emanates from India's slow economic development. For several decades, Indian strategists were content with India's modest growth rate and dependence on outside sources for assistance and military technology, despite their claims of autarky in the area of defense. In the 1960s they derided Taiwan, Malaysia, and South Korea as flunkies of the West and stated that their own economic lead over China was decisive. With the end of the cold war (1989) in tandem with a major economic crisis in India (1991), it became clear that the state-centric economic policy (which was very hesitantly challenged from 1983 onward) had failed to transform India into a modern country. The lesson was all the more shocking because the economic crisis was partly brought on by a decade of military adventurism and high levels of military expenditure that produced no tangible strategic gains. Most of the Indian strategic community has abandoned Nehruvian socialist economics and come to favor at least the first wave of economic reform, which involved opening up the Indian economy to greater foreign investment, reducing the role of the state in economic policy, and eliminating or selling some state-run enterprises. Some have argued that this will generate the resources to afford a major military capability. Although India's earlier emphasis on military power has not changed, the economic facts of life imposed constraints on the acquisition of military power for some time. Today, a large strategic community views the country as having slipped back in the past fifteen years, in the region as well as the country. The conflict with Pakistan has been debilitating; the failure to move early on to economic reforms has weakened India's capacity to project power; and the new international structure, consisting of one dominant power and a number of major (and aspiring) regional powers, may not include a place for New Delhi.

## Global and Regional Security Regimes

India is also reexamining its approach to international and regional organizations. Nehru was an early supporter of the United Nations (he took the Kashmir conflict to the General Assembly) and peacekeeping and mediation initiatives. In fact, the Constitution of India mandates cooperation with international bodies, including the United Nations.[36] Also a staunch advocate of Asian regional cooperation, it was Nehru who organized the Asian Relations Conference even before India achieved independence.

Today, few in India share Nehru's faith that international organizations will emerge as a force for global peace. The UN system is widely recognized as another arena of realpolitik where India can advance its interests and where Indians have played a significant role in both political and military capacities. The United Nations is also seen as a dangerous place, where India runs the risk of having its Kashmir policies come under critical scrutiny, and perhaps fresh UN resolutions, and even sanctions. For this reason, India worked closely with the former Soviet Union, which protected it with a veto, and New Delhi now seeks a seat on the Security Council.

At the regional level, assessments of the prospects for cooperation are more realistic. Almost all Indians, especially the realist-hawks, are wary of the South Asian Association for Regional Cooperation (SAARC), preferring to deal with neighbors on a bilateral basis. According to most realist strategists, regional cooperation will only work when one of two conditions exists. The first is the presence of a benevolent, dominant regional power that can regulate regional behavior (as the United States does in the Western Hemisphere). The other is the existence of satisfied and roughly equally capable regional states (as found in Europe or Southeast Asia) that can balance each other yet still keep outside powers at bay. Neither arrangement yet obtains in South Asia. However, as discussed in chapter 8, there are new opportunities open to India via various Asian and Asian-Pacific organizations, especially those with an economic orientation, or that might someday serve as a framework to balance expanding Chinese influence. India is welcomed in such groups as the Asian Regional Forum and recent Indian governments have begun to develop various economic groupings that tie India and Southeast Asia together but that exclude Pakistan.

Views toward international intervention, even humanitarian intervention, are framed by India's own experience, especially with outside interference in Kashmir. While Nehru originally agreed to such international mediatory-diplomatic involvement in Kashmir, all successive Indian governments have moved away from the idea of an international role there, and New Delhi's support for such international intervention elsewhere is strongly conditioned by its concern with setting the wrong example.[37] This is an area where Indian policy is likely to remain ambivalent: giving lukewarm support to intervention elsewhere, but firmly opposed to it at home.

## Solutions and Stratagems

Given that India sees itself as a civilizationally blessed, responsible, and peaceful state, how can it influence its neighbors and outsiders in a way that strengthens the India-centered regional security system and enables India to play a greater international role? Indians have three answers to this question: a more forceful policy, a more conciliatory policy, and a policy that attempts to change perceptions of friend and foe alike.

### Firm India

From the late 1970s to 1990 the idea that India should project itself as a firm, powerful state and be able to use force freely was the dominant strategic theme in Indian policy. Partly inspired by Indira Gandhi's reliance on military symbolism and the successful use of force in creating Bangladesh, this approach was also a reaction to the perceived weakness and vacillation of Nehru in the face of Chinese, Pakistani, and American pressure.

In his authoritative 1982 survey of Indian strategic thinking, former Indian diplomat U. S. Bajpai concluded:

> When our image weakened as a result of the 1962 military setback it emboldened Ayub Khan to test whether one Pakistani was not equal to ten Indians. Our weak image was responsible for the Chinese decision to arm the [rebellious northeast tribal groups such as the] Nagas and Mizos and to extend support to a Maoist revolutionary group in West Bengal, the Naxalites. Finally, our weak image tempted Yahya Khan to force ten million refugees into our territory.[38]

The solution is not to accommodate the desires of India's neighbors, but to address "the gap—the credibility gap—between the actual (or real) and expected (i.e., aspired or potential) power capabilities of India in playing its regional role." In the two earlier conflicts with China (1962) and Pakistan (1965), "the myth of Indian primacy stood completely shattered. This led to considerable questioning on the part of India's neighbors regarding the reliability of Indian defense guarantees. If India could not protect itself how could it protect others? . . . . The concept of 'Subcontinental security' lost its persuasiveness and viability. As a result the sixties witnessed the erosion of India security stakes in the neighboring states."[39]

The victory over Pakistan in 1971 somewhat redeemed the situation by dividing Pakistan in half, but in the minds of India's more hawkish strategists the need for firmness remained. Many routinely criticized the Simla agreement for being too generous with Pakistan and complained that India had made a serious mistake by indicating, on more than one occasion, its willingness to compromise and reach a settlement with Pakistan on the basis of the ceasefire line being converted into the new international border between the two countries. Some strategists, such as the influential K. Subrahmanyam, have taken Indian governments to task over the years for yielding to American trade pressures and pressures on India's nuclear program. Subrahmanyam has argued that India needed to build up its own defense industry, which would enable it to respond to pressures from the United States or China by engaging in its own sale of missiles and advanced military technology. The threat was repeated in 1999, when one of India's leading military scientists, A. P. J. Kalam, urged India to get into the business of missile sales in order to break up the "monopolies" of the dominant powers and their unfair regulating mechanisms, such as the Missile Technology Control Regime.[40] Some have even viewed the 1988–90 "peacekeeping" operation in Sri Lanka, which turned into a military catastrophe, as a success, because it demonstrated that "India has evolved a 'will to act' to preserve its vital national interests."[41]

India moved from a strategy of having force supplement diplomacy to having force substitute for diplomacy, even though Indira Gandhi regularly attacked the concept of deterrence as an amoral Western idea. As chapter 5 shows, in the 1980s India began to use its military capability proactively, even preemptively. This led to a period of strategic activism that came to a crashing halt in 1990. The debate over using force has continued, however, and has been extended to *nuclear weapons,* not only as an instrument of diplomacy and deterrence but also as items to actually be used.[42] This debate, summarized in chapter 6, led to an Indian nuclear program, but one without clear purpose or direction.

After the pivotal year of 1989–90, the utility of force as an instrument of Indian power underwent a major reexamination. Its weaknesses became evident when India suffered a string of inconclusive or disastrous minor military adventures, Soviet diplomatic and military support began to weaken, India had a crisis with a newly nuclear Pakistan over Kashmir, and both the Punjab and Kashmir became submerged in low-intensity conflict. Indians were forced to accept a more toned down use of military power. Nevertheless, military power as a symbol of state power remains politically important for New Delhi, as seen by India's response to Pakistan's military probe in Kargil in 1999 with a costly and highly publicized counterattack. This move turned an initial tactical failure into an international and domestic political triumph.

### Conciliatory India

Some in the core strategic community agree with the realist-hawks that India is a great power and even support the limited use of force. But they question strategies of defense-led economic development, a boastful military profile, and too-quick intervention in the affairs of neighbors. They would prefer to deal with Pakistan and China by territorial compromise and negotiation, displaying military power only to supplement diplomacy. Those who hold this position suggest that the nuclear program be deferred or limited and have been marginally more inclined to accept a limited outside role in regional affairs.

The liberal wing of the foreign policy establishment also envisions a peaceful change in the politics of India's neighbors and a subsequent mellowing of their attitude toward New Delhi. They are Wilsonians, although in the case of Kashmir they would reject Wilson's belief in self-determination. Even some of the liberal/idealists have been eager to protect minorities in neighboring states (especially those with Indian connections). George Fernandes, for example, a long-time labor leader and member of the Socialist International and former minister of defense, remained an outspoken critic of the Chinese government's policies in Tibet and of the Burmese government even after he joined the BJP-led coalition in 1998.

While much of the military would fall into the realist/realpolitik camp, the armed services have a solid appreciation of India's vulnerabilities as a budding military power. A recent generation of officers was strongly affected by the way in which the armed forces, especially the army, were overextended in confrontations with Pakistan, China, and the military intervention in Sri Lanka. A number of eminent retired senior officers have spoken and written publicly in favor of "peace and disarmament" in South Asia.[43] Others have written scathingly about incompetent management of India's various wars and conflicts.[44] On the issue of India-Pakistan relations, Lieutenant General M. L. Chibber concluded that reconciliation between India and Pakistan was more compelling than among the nations of Europe or the Middle East.[45] While he discusses the hawkish proposals of some of his fellow officers, and the very real attitudinal and institutional obstacles to India-Pakistan normalization, Chibber and other officers believe that a nuclearized South Asia, with high levels of defense spending, is both risky and unnecessary.

However, even Chibber argues that while India must behave responsibly, Pakistan will have to give up its obsession with parity with India and scale back its demands on Kashmir. He quotes approvingly the observation by G. Parthasarathy, a former adviser to Indira Gandhi, that an India-Pakistan reconciliation is like trying to treat two patients whose only disease is an allergy to each other.[46]

## Didactic India

Whether a realist or idealist, almost every member of the Indian strategic community thinks that India's inherent greatness as a power is itself a valuable diplomatic asset, and that others must become cognizant of the moral quality of Indian foreign and strategic policy. Furthermore, some would argue, misguided or critical American or European policies toward India merely indicate that its representatives have failed to forcefully present the Indian case. The country's official ambassadors, for example, are expected to present a cross section of Indian culture and to build people-to-people contacts, especially among Indian émigrés. It should be possible to persuade foreign officials of the wisdom and moral correctness of the Indian position, say, by stating the Indian case and supplementing political arguments with information about India's great civilization, its cultural and economic accomplishments, and its democratic orientation (the latter directed toward the Western democracies).[47]

Many Indians cite ignorance as the reason why the United States and others interfere in South Asia or otherwise threaten Indian regional dominance. Americans, in particular, do not (some Indians would snidely say cannot) appreciate India's potential, civilization, or culture. Thus educational and cultural diplomacy—aspects of India's civilizational power—are important ways of persuading other powers of India's inherent strength and of the foolishness of trying to confront India in its own region. This kind of diplomacy includes festivals of India, attempts by overseas Indian populations (especially in America) to influence foreign policy, and attempts to directly manipulate foreign public opinion in Western democracies.[48] According to K. Subrahmanyam, India needs to expand contacts with the American defense community and encourage the Indian business community and other resident Indians to help make its case. The same approach can be used with India's neighbors, the people of South Asia, who are predisposed to India in any case because of their common culture.

Since the end of the 1970s, this projection of Indian culture has taken a militaristic turn. India's considerable scientific and defense capabilities and its armed forces are becoming symbols of the capacity to produce the most modern artifacts of modern civilization: aircraft, tanks, missiles, and nuclear weapons. This is especially clear from names given to military equipment, such as the Agni missile and the Arjun tank, names drawn from Sanskrit or Indian traditions that show the world that Indian science and industry can make "sophisticated" systems. Such weapons are important not only as a means of maintaining military balances but also as a representation to others—and to Indians themselves—of Indian civilizational accomplishments in this area of modern technology.

## Diversity in Diversity

Terms such as "nonaligned," "the Indira Doctrine," and "Gandhian" do not come close to capturing the range of strategic opinions held by the Indian foreign policy community. Nor do they reflect the new perspectives on war, peace, and India's role in the world. Indian thought is both idealist and realist, Gandhian and Machiavellian, and individuals who hold such views can be found across the spectrum. Indeed, many hold such seemingly incompatible views simultaneously. According to George Tanham, India may not even have a national strategy: it is a great state characterized by the absence of one.[49]

Yet these very inconsistencies, these self-doubts, and diverse opinions reflect a diversity of internal interests, geography, and ideology resembling that of other great world powers. Nehru remains a pivotal figure in Indian foreign policy because he anticipated and reflected the hawkish-dovish, aggressive-moderate, forceful-diplomatic, moralistic-realist policy approaches. India is puzzling to outsiders precisely because there may not be much unity on crucial issues, whether it is the war with China, the incursion into Sri Lanka, the nuclear program, or relations with Pakistan. Not only are many voices heard but sometimes, many policies are pursued. Furthermore, Indian policy will be increasingly influenced by domestic political events that are sometimes beyond New Delhi's control. Nehru's invasion of Goa, the aggressive posture with China and the intervention in Sri Lanka were all prompted by domestic pressures, not a larger vision of India as a moderate and restrained power. This interaction between foreign policy priorities and domestic pressures will always be a factor in shaping Indian policy. The episode with Sri Lanka reveals that India could muster the "will to act," but also that any political authority in India will have difficulty building a national consensus for the use of military forces outside the boundaries of the country.

Yet there is consensus on two important strategic issues. First, the country is considered a status quo power with a natural right to dominate its region, but other than producing rhetorical flourishes, it does not—perhaps because it realistically cannot—extend its military or economic power very far. India's hawks recognize this. Second, India's tradition combines idealist and realist elements. Even the hawks accept that India first achieved international stature through the leadership of Mahatma Gandhi and Jawaharlal Nehru, and not that of the militant Subhas Chandra Bose or the Hindu Mahasabha. India was respected in the West, and in much of the non-Western world, as a state that took a principled stand against the use of force and in favor of negotiation and compromise as a way of settling international disputes. For the hawks, however, the moment has come for a renewed emphasis on the use of force: force not only provides status but also contributes to economic development because of the respect and deference that gravitates to a strong country. For the doves and moderates, economic development and social change come first, with an emphasis on India's liberal traditions.

The Indian strategic community is an elite divided against itself and within itself. These divisions do not fall along neat regional, cultural, economic, or professional lines. Even the military is sensitive to the demands of development, and the leading advocates of nuclear weapons do not wear uniforms.

The present diversity in strategic perspectives will be exacerbated by two trends: the introduction of new military technologies into the Subcontinent (especially nuclear weapons and ballistic missiles), and the difficulty of maneuvering in a world of many kinds of states without an overarching global ordering principle. Some officials may be tempted to abandon India's traditional aversion to alliances and learn to cope in a unipolar world, as many countries are doing. Others, such as the current BJP-dominated coalition, will attempt to please everyone by forming a "natural alliance" with some countries (such as the United States), and "strategic partnerships" with others (such as Russia) while trying to remain engaged with China. Whatever the case, India will have to overhaul its creaky decisionmaking system and encourage the circulation of ideas in the corridors of power, and it will have to adjust its policies along many dimensions in the face of continued disagreement over priorities and emphasis. Underlying all the disagreement, however, is the belief that India will, and should, become increasingly engaged in the world. Even BJP foreign policy intellectuals subscribe to Nehru's claim that India is one of the great states of the world, not just the legitimate and acknowledged hegemon of South Asia, and they may be more willing to use force—or at least to use force for its symbolic payoffs—to ensure that this claim is acknowledged by other major states.

Whether India veers toward the greater use of force, toward a more conciliatory approach, or toward a mixed policy, its decision will be justified in terms of the broad principles that help hold this pluralist, secular, former colonial state together. There is widespread agreement that its policies should promote anticolonialism; the vision of a just, equitable, and nonnuclear world; antiracism, democracy, and economic justice; and national dignity. Drawing on India's rich nationalist tradition, many argue that India, and Indian values, are nonthreatening to other societies. But Indians can also draw from a tradition of hard realist thought derived from the Kautilyan side of their civilizational legacy, from the example of the British (who, after all, raised "divide and rule" to an art), and observations of how other major powers behave. All of these traditions are deeply embedded in the strategic elite's consciousness, and a policy initiative that combines them is likely to receive both elite and popular support. After all, Indians, like everyone else, want to do well by doing good.

# THREE  *"The India That Can't Say Yes"*

$F$OR MANY FOREIGN OFFICIALS, dealing with New Delhi can be a frustrating experience. Western diplomats were for many years put off by India's flexible nonalignment, which for a time was a pretext for a close relationship with the Soviet Union. They were also irritated by the style of Indian diplomats. While professional and competent, they seemed compelled to lecture their British or American counterparts on the evils of the cold war, the moral superiority of India's policies, or the greatness of its civilization.

To its smaller neighbors, India presented a different face. Government officials in the smaller South Asian states tell stories about the insensitivity and arrogance of Indian diplomats, soldiers, government officials, and even businessmen. Pakistan finds that dealing with New Delhi can even be a dangerous experience, as the two countries have regularly harassed (and at times beaten up) each other's officials. As for Beijing, the 1987 question of one Chinese official, asked half in jest, half seriously, "Why are the Indians so 'inscrutable'?" reflected his puzzlement with what is seen as an unrealistic Indian combination of arrogance and poverty. Only Moscow seems to have gotten along well with New Delhi.

## Antecedents

India inherited a fully established state-empire from the Raj. Although predominately British, the administrative and governmental structure had Mughal, Persian, Hindu, and even some Chinese elements.[1] There

was *also* a separate tradition of statecraft as practiced by th...
Hindu Sikh and Muslim princely states, and different element...
nationalist movement.

The Raj was not formally an independent entity, however, e...
though India was a founding member of the United Nations.[2] Th...
British who governed India were part of a larger imperial policy apparatus that included Whitehall, the British Parliament, and the British military. During World War II, because of its financial and technical support
for preparations in India, even the United States had a say in India-
related strategic and foreign policy decisions. Gandhi, among others,
referred to the "British-American" strategy for India.

Even before independence, Indians were actively engaged in foreign
policy and military affairs. The Indian National Congress took positions
on global issues in the 1920s, and both it and the Muslim League had
overseas lobbies actively campaigning for independence.[3] Congress had
advocates in Washington, in addition to its high-profile operation in
Britain, led by Krishna Menon. The present-day competition between
the Indian and Pakistani embassies in capitals around the world has its
antecedents in this rivalry between the Congress party and the Muslim
League.

Indians were also involved in the Raj's security policy. By the end of
World War II, half of the army's officers were Indian (although the most
senior officer was only a brigadier).[4] A select group of civilians were
involved in high policy, both as servants of the Raj and as its critics. As
for the former, Indians were a key component of the Indian Political Service, a group of elite officers drawn from the Indian Civil Service (ICS)
and the military for duty as representatives both to the hundreds of
princely states and to posts all around India, ranging from the Persian
Gulf to Tibet and Southeast Asia.[5] Before independence, half of the
members of the elite ICS were Indians.[6] It played a significant role in fiscal policy, including the defense budget, and the articulation of British-
Indian policies.[7] After independence the ICS was restructured as the
Indian Administrative Service (IAS).

Indian critics of the Raj's foreign and security policies included a
number of distinguished Indian politicians, such as Jawaharlal Nehru's
father, Motilal Nehru, Mohammed Ali Jinnah, and the two outstanding
constitutionalist politicians, H. N. Kunzru, and Tej Bajadur Sapru.
Established in 1935, the Legislative Assembly provided a formal channel for criticism and advice, and a forum for vigorous and informed

foreign policy and defense budgets. Retired British officials
nitted that they were often hard-pressed by their Indian inter-
rs.

nus India achieved independence with an experienced community of
vil servants, soldiers, and politicians to implement its policies. Other
than replacing the Indian Political Service with the Indian Foreign Service (IFS), and moving to Indianize the domestic civil services and the
officer corps, the postindependence period saw no major institutional
changes. Yet the foreign policy process was transformed, coming under
the complete control of Jawaharlal Nehru, who dominated the process
for seventeen years, exerting an authority denied even to British
viceroys. His policies and administrative style were influential for
another generation. Not until fifty-three years after independence has
there been a critical reexamination of the process by which India defines
and pursues its strategic interests.

## Independence and a Prime Minister–Centered System

India's foreign and security policy process does not differ markedly from
the systems of other parliamentary democracies. It has the full comple-
ment of institutions: a foreign ministry, a defense ministry, intelligence
services, and armed services, most of them coordinated by the prime
minister and the cabinet. However, India has several important features
that set it apart and create a distinct Indian diplomatic style.

The Constitution of India confers upon the president the nominal
position of commander in chief, but in actuality the prime minister and
the cabinet dominate foreign policymaking, as is the case in other parliamentary democracies. Their authority derives from a parliamentary
majority. Parliament votes the defense and foreign affairs budgets annually, and individual members or parties may compel the government to
respond to questions or even enter into cursory debate. Parliament has
little voice in the routine conduct of foreign policy, however, and need
not be consulted prior to or during a crisis. It does not even have a role
in the declaration of war, nor is its consent necessary to ratify a treaty.[8]
The guiding principle is that the prime minister is the leader of the
majority party, and a parliamentary vote would be redundant. This system can be flexible, as in 1999 when the BJP dominated a coalition that
had lost a vote of confidence and yet prosecuted a war in Kargil as a
caretaker government.

During Nehru's tenure as prime minister and foreign minister (1947–64), Parliament played a very limited role in shaping foreign and defense policy. Even though Nehru encouraged debate on foreign policy issues, few politically strong figures could challenge him on the floor of Parliament. He kept his cabinet well informed and regularly wrote to and consulted with the various state chief ministers (almost all of whom were members of Congress), even though they played no constitutional role in foreign policy. Nehru recognized early on that India's states were intimately involved in relations with the country's neighbors. He also saw such consultations as an essential part of the democratic process, and his own eloquent foreign policy speeches were designed to educate broader publics. Nevertheless, on a few occasions, particularly toward the end of his life, Nehru was successfully challenged on foreign policy matters. One proposal (devised by Krishna Menon) that part of India's territory be exchanged with China was vetoed by the venerated member of Congress Pandit Govind Vallabh Pant, then home minister, who threatened to bring down Nehru's government if any Indian territory was traded away.[9]

Nehru was a one-man policy planning staff and coordinator, as well as the source of major initiatives that put India on the world's diplomatic map. His interest in foreign policy long predated independence. Nehru had traveled widely in the 1930s, visiting the Soviet Union and a number of European states, but never the United States. His idealism balanced his realism, and he projected an image of India that still lingers. There was no need for institutional development in the foreign policy community when Nehru combined both expertise and political power. In the area of foreign policy as well as other spheres, he has been compared to a banyan tree, which provides shade for those who shelter under it but in the long run stunts their growth.

After the trauma of the 1962 war with China, a period of hard realism set in, and Nehru's reputation as well as his health declined steadily.[10] Following Nehru's death, Parliament's role in foreign policy was further whittled down, and India began moving toward the de facto presidentialization of the political system and the further centralization of the foreign policy process.[11] The Prime Minister's Office (PMO) was strengthened under Nehru's successor, Lal Bahadur Shastri, as much for domestic as for foreign policy reasons. The PMO also assumed many policy and coordination functions previously carried out by various ministries.

Indira Gandhi and Rajiv Gandhi, Parliament lost whatever Nehru had allowed. Indira Gandhi sharply curtailed dissent within the Congress party and altered the constitution to ensure the prime minister's dominance over the president. Although Rajiv Gandhi had made gestures toward running an "open" government, he continued the policy of secrecy and nondisclosure that characterized all Indian governments since 1947. Even the controversy over the billion-dollar artillery purchase from the Swedish firm of Bofors became a political issue because of the press, not because of Parliament. The sensational bribery scandal of early 2001 that resulted in the resignation of Minister of Defense George Fernandes, the firing of a number of senior officers and bureaucrats, and the dismissal of the president of the BJP was triggered by an undercover probe by the investigative journalist website, Tehelka.com.[12]

Since 1989, when Rajiv's prime ministership ended, India has seen a long succession of weaker governments that have either depended on "outside" support to stay in office (Narasimha Rao's Congress government of 1991–96) or were coalitions (the Janata-led government of V. P. Singh, and subsequent governments headed by Deve Gowda, Inder Gujral, and Atal Behari Vajpayee three times).

P. V. Narasimha Rao, who served as prime minister from 1991 to 1996, did not command a majority and governed with the consent of other parties. Rao had been Indira Gandhi's foreign minister and had more experience in foreign policy matters than anyone in his government on the opposition benches or within the bureaucracy. He instituted several parliamentary reforms, among them the establishment (in 1992) of multiparty parliamentary standing committees. Organized by subject, these committees include both opposition and government members of Parliament (MPs) and are chaired by a senior opposition member. Unlike the parliamentary consultative committees, chaired by the relevant government minister, the standing committees have the power to ask government officials to testify, and several have produced serious studies on a range of foreign and security policy issues, including nuclear policy.[13] These committees and their publications resemble those of the foreign and defense affairs committees of the U.S. Congress. Though powerless, they did provide opposition (and Congress) MPs with an entry into the foreign policy debate. India's new diplomacy, shaped by the BJP, was foreshadowed by standing committee reports, especially those chaired by Jaswant Singh.

Most of the recent coalition governments have lacked the strength and stability of the Congress governments of the Nehru-Gandhi era. The United Front government failed to win solid majorities and was often unable to control its own coalition partners. This led to a continuous search for new allies to replace defectors and produced notably weak governments. In these circumstances, any issue, including foreign policy, could bring a government down. Each of the coalition governments of the 1990s fell because alliance partners defected. It took the BJP-led coalition that swept to victory in 1998 to put together an apparently stable government.

## The Foreign and Security Policy Establishment

In the early 1960s Paul Appleby, a leading American public administration expert, characterized India as one of the dozen best-administered countries in the world.[14] At that time, Indian foreign policy had a global reach: Delhi was active in the United Nations, it was courted by both East and West, and it was a leader of the nonaligned movement. Not a little of India's preeminence was due to its competent administration, which was seen as being capable of undertaking the tasks of both domestic economic and social reform and global political leadership, while providing highly professional officials for secondment to many international organizations, including the United Nations.

India's foreign policy and security bureaucracy include the IFS, the IAS, and a number of intelligence agencies, as well as the armed services and paramilitary forces. These bureaucracies are different in many ways from many other Asian, African, and Latin American systems. At the highest levels, foreign and security policy processes are dominated by civilians who are generally free of corruption, even if modestly compensated.[15] Senior civil servants pride themselves on their social status, bureaucratic control, and policy influence, not their material wealth. They have an almost puritanical view of the decisionmaking process and are wary of the corrupting power of money. Private corporations and foreign governments are viewed with deep suspicion. The best and the most influential civil servants see themselves as islands of honesty and rectitude in a sea of graft, as prudent men (and a few women) upholding a 200-year tradition of distinguished public service.

The foreign and security policy processes are still dominated by the civilian bureaucracy, which is not so surprising since India has been characterized as a civilization in the possession of a bureaucracy.[16] After weathering populist attacks and its own internecine warfare, the "steel frame" of the British Raj has rusted a bit, but it remains supreme.[17] While the professional foreign service has on occasion yielded pride of place to the Prime Minister's Office and India's external intelligence service, the Research and Analysis Wing (RAW), and even (recently) India's defense scientists, the Ministry of External Affairs (MEA), staffed by the IFS, still dominates.[18] Defense matters fall under the purview of the IAS cadre assigned to the Ministry of Defense and various defense facilities, and fiscal policy is largely shaped by IAS officials on assignment to the Finance and Commerce ministries.[19] India's civilian bureaucrats exert greater influence than their American counterparts; in this regard they are more like their British and French counterparts.

## India's Foreign Office

In the eyes of other governments, India's Foreign Service is thoroughly professional, with an unusually high number of brilliant officers, but it is a persistent underachiever. By contrast, Pakistan's foreign service is smaller in size and range than the IFS but is considered extremely effective when dealing with a few key places: the United States, China, and several Islamic and Middle Eastern countries. This reflects Pakistan's consistent and long-standing foreign policy priorities: its primary focus is India, and it engages intensely with only three or four major states and the Islamic world.

India has instead pursued a global diplomacy. It has always played a strong role in the United Nations, and it was a cofounder of the Non-Aligned Movement. During its long quasi alliance with the Soviet Union, it sought good relations with Cuba, many Eastern European states, and other Soviet allies. Its subsequent dependence on the Soviet Union for weapons led it into a close military and supply relationship with a number of other recipients of Soviet hardware, such as Iraq (India trained the Iraqi Air Force in the 1970s). India was also a major interlocutor during the cold war, and because of its original commitment to decolonization and anti-imperialism, it has maintained close and active relations with many states in Africa, Latin America, and Asia. For example, dozens of African National Congress cadres received training in the Indian Foreign Service Training Institute in the early 1990s, in the expectation that they would join the foreign service of a transformed

South Africa. New Delhi is certainly one of the major diplomatic centers of the world, with more than 140 accredited missions and posts, and its foreign office is kept busy managing a wide range of strategic and diplomatic contacts.

Having preserved the British-developed "file" system, Indian ministries also excel when it comes to retrieving and documenting past policies. All of the different divisional records of a particular issue or negotiation are kept in a single file; each official who deals with the issue adds his or her own annotation to the file. Thus officials who are new to the issue have a comprehensive record of both India's position and that of other states. When dealing with India, states that do not have a good recordkeeping system (such as the United States) are at a decided disadvantage. Even junior officials in India or those new to an office have access to the complete negotiating record, whereas their counterparts (especially Americans) depend on an institutional memory that may reach back only a few years. This surprises Indians, who erroneously believe that Washington has a master record system in which everything of importance is "on the computer," available for instant recall.

In the abstract, India's extensive global contacts and global diplomacy should serve it well in the post–cold war world. For a number of reasons, though, the foreign policy and security bureaucracy have found it difficult to make the adjustment. The recent incoherence of India's political system is partly to blame—it is hard to conduct a consistent or effective foreign policy when governments change so rapidly—but internal organization and the bureaucracy are also responsible for the underachievement.

First, a separate bureaucracy—the IAS-dominated Home Ministry—sets the MEA's "rules of organization." Thus it is difficult to develop interagency working groups or devise new procedures even within the MEA to handle a changing international environment.[20] Second, there is little, if any, cross-posting between the IAS and the IFS, and virtually no lateral entry into the foreign service from the military, other bureaucracies, or academia. Nor does the MEA have the expertise, let alone the authority, to integrate military factors into larger, strategic decisions. Its great international expertise has been in disarmament, and latterly, arms control (even here, the division is understaffed and ill-prepared, given India's assertion of leadership and the growing importance and complexity of arms control negotiations). Since who controls the files controls the policy, the MEA has dominated arms control policy for fifty years, while other bureaucracies jealously guard their own policy turf.

This problem is not confined to the MEA. Few in the upper reaches of Indian politics or the civilian bureaucracy have a military or diplomatic background and there is a strong tradition—stemming from Gandhi's nonviolence and Nehru's policy imprint—of downplaying military and strategic concerns in favor of economic and social issues. Jaswant Singh, minister of external affairs in the post-1998 Vajpayee government, is one exception, and he left the army when he was only a captain. Arun Singh, one of India's most informed civilians and a former minister of state for defense, never served in the armed forces, nor did K. C. Pant, a relative newcomer to the BJP and an ardent proponent of nuclear weapons for twenty-five years, who was a Congress minister of defense under Mrs. Gandhi.

Like the broader society that it serves, the Indian Foreign Service has its factions; some officers are more dovish, for example, and some more hawkish. However, the IFS is unrepresentative in two ways, and to some extent this reduces its political influence within the Indian system. First, unlike the IAS, it is Delhi-centric in its outlook. The IFS is a "central" service; the IAS is an "all-India service" (like the Indian Police Service). The latter services have deep roots in the states and districts and officers routinely move between the center and the states during their careers. Second, the IFS, as a bureaucracy, is inherently conservative. Because of its strong memory of the past, the IFS has had difficulty adjusting to rapid changes in the international system over the past decade. Contemporary senior ambassadors and officials received their training and formative political experience under Congress governments in the 1960s and 1970s, which consistently taught that the United States was a hostile power whereas the Soviet Union was a friendly and reliable state.

For the most part, the IFS has been dominated by those who see the need to be "firm" with neighbors and distant powers alike, while the conciliatory faction has grown weaker. In the view of the hawks, India needs to maintain its dignity, should not yield to pressure, and should not allow its smaller neighbors to take advantage of its good will (or seek alliances with outsiders). The Indira Doctrine asserting India's regional primacy, the absorption of Sikkim, the Bangladesh operation (and earlier the invasion and occupation of Goa) are cited as evidence of the good results that flow from being tough. This more assertive position foundered in Sri Lanka in the late 1980s. Despite overwhelming military power, the disinterest of other major states, and popular support at home, India could not decisively influence events, in part because the security and foreign policy bureaucracies were working at cross-purposes.

Conciliationists, on the other hand, point to the success of post-Partition agreements with Pakistan on a variety of refugee, transit, and trade matters (culminating in the important 1960 Indus-Waters Treaty, which distributed the common water resources of the two states along their western border), and various trade, water, refugee, and transit agreements with India's smaller neighbors. Another success, they say, was Atal Behari Vajpayee's "bus diplomacy" with Pakistan and Inder Gujral's "doctrine," which mended relations with some of India's smaller neighbors. This position would hold that as the larger power, India has responsibility for taking the initiative and beginning a dialogue with its neighbors.[21] This perspective founders on Pakistan, where intractable differences remain. While the Lahore-Delhi bus still plies, it does so in the shadow of the Kargil war.

### The IAS and the Ministry of Defense

The Ministry of Defense, dominated by the Indian Administrative Service, presents a mixed picture. The great strength of the average IAS officer is a broad background and diverse experience. The IAS is better placed than the IFS to relate domestic political, economic, and social factors to India's external security policies. The IAS has produced a few world-class defense managers and strategic thinkers, but as a bureaucracy, the Ministry of Defense still lacks both expertise and continuity.[22] It is almost entirely staffed by officials who have never served abroad for any period of time. Its cadres have neither the training, education, nor expertise to offer politicians informed advice on defense-related issues or to serve as constructive partners for the military in decisions concerning weapons acquisition, strategy, and planning. Furthermore, many of the activities of the Defense Ministry are still narrowly regulated by officers on detachment from the Ministry of Finance. Finance Ministry officers have a mandate to track defense expenditures, and Ministry of Defense officials (and the military) tell apocryphal stories of queries concerning "excessive" use of ammunition and supplies during times of war or armed confrontation.

There is also rivalry between the IFS and the IAS, and little coordination between the two, especially in areas of planning, strategy, and weapons procurement.[23] Being the older and "senior" bureaucracy, with deep domestic roots, the IAS professes to have a better understanding of India's needs than foreign service officers privately referred to as dilettantes who do not know their own country. The MEA thinks it knows the strategic picture and has a better sense of how foreigners approach India. The IFS feels hobbled by the IAS and other functionaries, whom it derides as "former managers of fertilizer factories." Similar bureaucratic rivalries occur in other states, of course, but these can be particularly damaging in India, which has few coordinating mechanisms for addressing these rivalries.

## The Intelligence Services

As befits a country whose ancient strategic text, the *Arthashastra*, devotes three chapters to espionage, India has a number of domestic and foreign intelligence services. Because of their large number, plus inevitable overlap between domestic and foreign intelligence, politicians are easily misinformed about the effectiveness of these services or the scale and direction of threats to the state (or the political leadership). At the same time, these competing and overlapping services act as checks and balances on one another.

Since 1963 the intelligence services have theoretically been coordinated by a Joint Intelligence Committee, although at least two—the Research and Intelligence Wing and the Intelligence Bureau (IB)—report directly to the prime minister.[24] The IB has deep roots in the British Raj, while RAW was created in the 1960s with assistance from the U.S. Central Intelligence Agency.

The distinctive features of India's intelligence cluster are its admixture of domestic and foreign intelligence, its lack of public and parliamentary accountability, and the possibility of unprofessional analysis and implementation. Domestic and foreign intelligence inevitably become intertwined in India, since so many of its neighbors are either suspected of hostile actions against its territory or could be used as a base for such actions by distant powers. The temptation to deploy intelligence resources to Bangladesh, Sri Lanka and Nepal, let alone Pakistan and China, is overwhelming and probably necessary. Yet such operations can be at cross-purposes with Indian diplomacy. The classic case, still fresh in the memories of both the IFS and the Indian military, involved Research and Intelligence operations in Sri Lanka in the 1980s. The bureau's earlier contacts with the Liberation Tigers of Tamil Eelam (LTTE) were kept from the military and even from some of the civilians who were negotiating with the Sri Lankan government, with disastrous military and diplomatic results. More recently, the Kargil conflict revealed great weaknesses in the way India gathers and coordinates intelligence. Former intelligence officers have even criticized the government inquiry into Indian actions during the crisis as being unduly harsh.[25]

## The Military's Anomalous Role

The most remarkable fact about the decisionmaking process is that the military plays almost no role in it. This is not to say that military factors (whether in terms of hardware or strategy) are not considered. Rather, in no other middle or great power is the military's advice so detached from political and strategic decisions. This applies with particular force to India's nuclear decisions, including nuclear policy, even though successive service chiefs have staked a claim on managing and delivering nuclear weapons.

After carefully observing Pakistan during the 1950s, Nehru and other leading Indian politicians concluded that the military takeover there was connected with Pakistan's alliance with the United States and might serve as a model for India's generals. When rumors of a possible coup in India began circulating, Nehru's friend and long-time associate, Krishna Menon, was brought in as minister of defense. The Indian political leadership has also been wary of military-to-military ties between the Indian armed forces and those of other states, notably the United States. Even routine contacts are strictly controlled. Indian civilian politicians and bureaucrats fear that their own generals might catch the coup virus from Pakistani counterparts and view with suspicion suggestions for military-to-military dialogues between India and Pakistan.[26] Modest India-U.S. military exercises and dialogues conducted before U.S. sanctions were imposed in 1998 raised similar political anxieties. There is no more politically sensitive issue for the core civilian strategic elite.

The Indian armed services regard this civilian control with mixed feelings. On the one hand, they are acutely aware of the pitfalls of military rule, especially in view of the sad examples of Pakistan and Bangladesh nearby. On the other hand, they do not have confidence in civilian expertise, they sometimes resent civilian style, and they are envious of the somewhat greater promotion and career opportunities available in the IAS.[27]

An important exception to the military's subdued role was General K. Sundarji's participation in the triumvirate that shaped policy during the brief spell of strategic activism from 1986 to 1989 (the other two key participants were the prime minister, Rajiv Gandhi, and Rajiv's adviser, Minister of State for Defense Arun Singh). So great was the resentment against Sundarji's influence in both the army and the civilian bureaucracy that no officer with his innovative mind and strategic ambition has been appointed to the position of army chief since then.

Still, the armed forces have had a growing influence on policy in the past ten years. Recent Indian governments have grown increasingly dependent upon the army for the maintenance of law and order. With weapons purchases now more costly and controversial, military expertise has also become a necessary part of the evaluation process.[28] The armed forces themselves have been causing problems: a number of Sikh units mutinied after the Sikhs' most holy shrine, the Golden Temple, was occupied by the Indian Army in 1984. And in several highly publicized cases, the military has voiced objections to its deteriorating budget and the heavy hand of politicians and civilian bureaucrats in its affairs.

From 1989 to 1998 the percentage of GDP spent on defense dropped from 3.6 percent (1986) to 2.5 percent (1992). This was due in large part to the struggling economy, demands for social and developmental investment, and a general political disinterest in security issues after the activism of Rajiv's prime ministership, although some funds were also being diverted into the growth of a rudimentary nuclear capability.[29] With a newly attractive private sector and the prospect of a dangerous posting for most army officers, recruitment, retention, weapons acquisition, and readiness have all suffered at a time when the commitments of the armed forces have increased. Current resources and policy are making it particularly difficult for the army to play a larger role in domestic security or nuclear preparedness. All of this has made the military less attractive to the "best and the brightest" young men, although there is a small core of able officers. Even here, those who rise to the top will find themselves tied down by a number of organizational and political restrictions.

The Indian system also has problems with long-term planning. MEA's Policy Planning Division has atrophied, and the armed forces find it difficult to make long-range plans because of the great turnover of political leadership in the past fifteen years and uncertainty over defense budgets and weapons acquisition strategies. There is a mechanism for defense coordination, the defense planning staff, but it serves under the chief of the army staff, and has no real power. Recently, the government has proposed the creation of a fourth "chief"—a chief of the defense staff, along the lines found in virtually every other major state. Such an officer could preside over genuine interservice coordination and provide expert, integrated, military advice to the political leadership.

The rapid growth and influence of the intelligence agencies (especially Research and Intelligence) have also affected strategic and long-term planning. These may have analytical and operational responsibilities, but the secretive nature of their programs makes them unwilling participants in any planning exercises. The Foreign Office was excluded from the planning for the exercise that led to the 1987 Brasstacks crisis, and only later, after the crisis had ended, was it given the task of "mopping up" and working out joint communiqués and statements.

A number of other groups, both official and unofficial, make intermittent contributions to the policy process, but scientists are the ones receiving the most acclaim, especially because of their role in the 1998 tests, the development of missiles, and the design and production of various weapons. The 1998 tests were carried out in secrecy by a handful of scientists drawn from the Defense Research and Development Organization and the Indian Atomic Energy Commission, assisted by special units detached from the Indian Army.[30]

Despite this new status, scientists do not yet have a place at the decisionmaking table. Few of them have a firm grasp of nuclear strategy, military affairs, or the operational requirements of combat-ready weapons. Even fewer understand the international politics surrounding nuclear weapons beyond a simplistic view that a strong (that is, nuclear) India will receive the deference that is its due. Those who are in the limelight may experience the fate of A. P. J. Kalam, a prominent scientist of recent years who in 1999 was "kicked upstairs," that is, promoted, to the position of scientific adviser to the prime minister. Shortly afterward, the budget for the Defense Research and Development Organization, which had failed to deliver a number of important projects, was cut, while the overall defense budget was increased by 28 percent.[31]

Although certain scientists may have strong ties to politicians (who after all must still approve their budget requests) and some have been feted as home-grown geniuses (a dig at the many Indian scientists who have gone overseas to work in the United States and other Western countries), the IAS is unlikely to make room for them in the Ministry of Defense. Nor will the IFS allow scientists to encroach upon its own international arms control turf. If the recent experience of both Pakistan and India is anything to go by, however, scientists can clearly play a public role. Some have already acquired considerable power and resources. Given the bureaucracy's inability to evaluate their work independently and the impossibility of nongovernmental experts seeing what they do, scientists will in all likelihood continue to develop more advanced versions of the weapons that they have already produced. They are competing not against Pakistan or China as much as against their own dream of self-sufficiency, in an open-ended arms race with themselves.

## Other Diplomacies

For most of its history, India allowed economic diplomacy to be dominated by government bureaucrats who negotiated for economic aid from foreign donors or who represented the country's large number of state-owned enterprises. Until 1991, the Union government controlled most of these enterprises, and the states were not allowed to deal directly with foreign investors or aid donors. Added to this were massive bureaucratic obstacles designed to control, if not discourage, foreign investment in India. These enterprises were also a source of campaign finance and thus provided incentives to the political parties.

With the advent of economic liberalization and the privatization of government corporations, this system has become dysfunctional. Managers who were once part of the civil service now find it difficult to compete abroad on the basis of quality and price, let alone adjust to market forces. Even so, India's private firms are beginning to make their way in the world. A few have established a major overseas presence. The Birlas, for instance, are among the top ten businesses in Thailand, and the Tata group has created a Tata of America and bought Tetley Tea in Great Britain. Two Indian business organizations have a worldwide network of offices, the Federation of Indian Chambers of Commerce and Industry (FICCI) and the Confederation of Indian Industries (CII). The latter is especially active, and its representatives seek to build support for India in several important countries. In the United States, CII has enabled American journalists, academics, and members of Congress to travel to India.

Despite these changes, India remains ten to fifteen years behind states that were its economic peers in the 1960s. Korea, Taiwan, Malaysia, and China all have far more active economic diplomacy, with close coordination between government and private sectors. Change is taking place in India, but very slowly and grudgingly. It is especially difficult to break the old habit of leaving diplomacy to the government or of beginning negotiations by saying "no," and to loosen the grip of well-entrenched bureaucracies. But change must come soon because a foreign policy establishment that has spent much of its fifty years in making a case for aid to India may not have the temperament to make the case for investment in India.

India also conducts an extensive, albeit erratic, cultural and information diplomacy. Two assumptions have been constant here: that India's civilization has considerable power to persuade others; and that if South Asia were allowed to reach a natural balance between India and its neighbors, there would be regional peace.[32] Nevertheless, the operation of India's official cultural diplomacy leaves much to be desired. The chief instrument for this diplomacy, the Indian Council for Cultural Relations, is run like a government department and lacks both the freedom and the credibility of counterpart organizations elsewhere, such as the British Council, the Goethe Foundation, or the Japan Foundation.[33] India's relations with foreign scholars who wish to visit or study in India have often been disappointing. Besides an excessive suspicion that such scholars are somehow subverting the Indian political and social order, India has at times used its academic and information programs to "punish" other states. The most self-defeating example of this was the denial of access to all but a handful of American scholars after the 1971 war over Bangladesh, in retaliation, according to Indian officials, for U.S. policy during the war. India's cultural policy, modeled on that of the Soviet Union for a number of years, limited the entry of foreign scholars to those working on innocuous historical and cultural subjects. This barred a whole generation of American scholars from learning more about India, sometimes creating hostility in a community that had been very pro-Indian.

## The "Influentials"

Surprisingly, but perhaps because of the closed-door nature of India's bureaucracy, India has in recent years developed one of the best-informed and most active unofficial security communities to be found between Israel and Japan. This increasingly influential community is centered in New Delhi and a few other cities. It includes journalists, a few politicians, members of various think tanks, retired generals and diplomats, and academics. Although a few of these individuals are more comfortable in Indian languages, English remains the primary medium for thinking and writing on strategic issues. Because of the crushing power of India's national security bureaucracies, which until recently discouraged informed public debate on virtually all security and foreign policy issues of consequence, this foreign and security policy community has had a long gestation.[34]

However, the philosophy of "We have the files, therefore you cannot speak about these issues" is breaking down, and a new relationship between informed political and strategic elites and the government is evolving. To some extent, this was bound to happen because the establishment's baroque system of decisionmaking and strategic planning, while it imposes a degree of consistency on Indian policy, is a drawback in an era of rapid international change. Having perfected the art of nondiplomacy, India could not say yes or no, which is not enough for either the politicians or the larger strategic community.

Furthermore, it is even harder to arrive at consistent policy than it was in the Nehru-Indira-Rajiv years. Under Nehru, the foreign policy bureaucracy could defer to a single, authoritative source. Under his daughter (and to some extent, Rajiv), policy was shaped by the prime minister, with the close cooperation of a kitchen cabinet and the bureaucracy. However, in an era of coalition and weak governments, with a bureaucracy that has been inflexible and slow to adjust to post–cold war realities, informed publics have become more demanding. In addition, the bureaucracy, loath to share its power and influence, finds it useful to expand its consultative mechanism.

This new interest in outside expert opinion is reflected in the activities of the National Security Advisory Board (NSAB), established in 1999 in the wake of the nuclear tests by the BJP-led coalition. Consisting of a dozen respected journalists, academics, and former officials, and divided into several working groups, the NSAB has been asked to prepare working papers on a variety of subjects, including terrorism, domestic security, and nuclear policy.

It is unclear whether the NSAB will be a source of new ideas and how the government will receive its advice. Its members are unpaid and do not have access to classified material. Some of them may well be co-opted by the government. The first NSAB (1998–2000) featured a number of strong-willed members, renowned for their independence. Many of the most outspoken members seem to have been removed since the BJP government won reelection in 1999.

Members of the nonofficial Indian strategic community look to the United States as a model because of its panoply of think tanks, reliance on the talents of academics and journalists, and efforts to make diverse opinions available to the government.[35] Critics of India's hitherto closed policy process recognize that the IFC and IAS are strongly opposed to consultation and a role for outsiders because they do not wish to share their influence and access to the politicians, or to let outsiders catch sight of their mistakes and vulnerabilities. All the same, the trend is toward a more open system. A number of new, nongovernmental think tanks have been started in the past five years, many of them led by retired officials and politicians of great stature and expertise. The op-ed pages and editorials of the major newspapers now carry commentary on key strategic subjects, and the quality of these pieces is high, often providing sound policy suggestions for the Indian government.[36] Many retired military officers and diplomats have been active in this community. The expansion of television services has created a new and lucrative market for their skills. All of the major Indian television channels (including those broadcast regionally) carry regular commentaries and analysis on foreign and strategic policy issues. The Kargil conflict, India's first "television war," greatly increased public interest in security matters.

### Beyond Delhi

India's foreign and security policy process will open even wider when budding regional perspectives on these matters are better articulated. Research centers in Chennai (Madras), Mumbai (Bombay), and Calcutta now conscientiously offer Southern, Western, and Eastern viewpoints on a range of issues.[37] Some Indian universities, especially in Chennai, Pune, and Calcutta, are moving in this direction as well. The new regional parties are slowly developing working relationships with these centers, and, when they enter into a government, this will mean fresh policy perspectives.

### Successes

Despite its infirmities—some of them due to the lingering effects of an antiquated policy process, others to the chronic shortage of funds—Indian diplomacy has scored many successes. When given time, a clear objective, and the opportunity to draw on a wide range of assets, the system is capable of notable accomplishments such as the 1971 diplomatic, strategic, and military initiative of Indira Gandhi that resulted in the eventual destruction of the old Pakistan and the creation of Bangladesh. This entire operation was coordinated by the Prime Minister's Office. A few years later, Sikkim was absorbed into India in another combined operation that made good use of India's intelligence, political, and military resources. Another success was achieved by the relatively weak Janata government: in 1990–91 it managed to quietly improvise the withdrawal of 100,000 Indian citizens from Iraq and Kuwait and then played a marginal role on the side of the UN coalition, despite its long-standing strategic ties to Baghdad. New Delhi allowed coalition aircraft to refuel on its territory until this activity was discovered and publicized by the press.

However, India's most important diplomatic accomplishments have been negative ones, achieved through its power to veto the initiatives of other states, as in the case of Kashmir. For many years Indian officials have stymied outside diplomatic involvement. In the 1950s, Krishna Menon became a national hero for his several marathon UN speeches on the subject. These contributed mightily to India's reputation as a country that knows how to say "no" frequently and vocally. This reputation was strengthened during the negotiations over the Comprehensive Test Ban Treaty (CTBT) in 1996. Although it was an early sponsor of a CTBT, India objected to some of the language in the treaty; some also argued that signing it would inexorably lead to the elimination of India's nuclear option. Indian diplomats managed to shift Delhi's position on the CTBT, taking a "principled" stand on an issue that was unpopular at home. Defying the United States, Japan, and other major countries, New Delhi stood up to considerable pressure. Another diplomatic stratagem might have deflected the criticism, but in this case the Indian strategic community appeared not only willing, but also eager, to run against the sentiments of the major powers, despite the economic and political costs incurred by this policy.

## Negotiating Styles: "Getting to No"

If India becomes a more important state in the world, then its interlocutors will have to gain a more comprehensive understanding of how India negotiates.[38] They will find, for example, that India tends to employ four kinds of strategies in negotiating with the West, especially the United States.

First, Indian negotiators are intent on establishing the moral and political equality of the two sides. Just as the Chinese try to establish a set of agreed-upon principles before negotiations can proceed, Indians tacitly (and sometimes explicitly) try to get their Western counterpart to agree to the principle of equality, usually via a series of arguments over often seemingly irrelevant issues. If the other side refuses to accommodate Indian sensitivities, then negotiations will not go smoothly (they may not go well for other reasons, of course). On one recent occasion, negotiations never started because a senior Ministry of Defense official felt that his American counterpart was of insufficient rank, even though that official was the decisionmaker responsible for the particular issue to be discussed. The Soviet Union had considerable success in negotiating with New Delhi, partly because it was willing to treat India as a "major" power, whatever its private views.

Second, Indians are patient negotiators who will wait until the terms improve. They rarely feel pressed to reach an agreement because of domestic politics or bureaucratic compulsions; indeed, the Indian system is agreement averse. Indian diplomats do not put their careers at risk by failing to reach an agreement. Even in the case of arms purchases, Indians will drag out negotiations in the hope that prices will fall or terms will soften. Privately, Indian officials pride themselves on "pulling a fast one" over foreigners, even when they are at a disadvantage. Delays also give Indian negotiators an opportunity to shop around with other countries. In 1987, for example, while negotiating with the United States for a Cray supercomputer, the Indian government opened parallel negotiations with Japan. Since Tokyo then consulted with Washington concerning the security restraints that were to be placed on the computer, the Indians delayed the purchase by many months, raising suspicions in both countries concerning their motives.

Third, Indian officials tend to negotiate for information. Indian officials and businessmen see negotiations as a cheap way of gaining information about the market, about particular items and technologies, and about the state of negotiations between rivals (especially Pakistan) and potential sellers. This practice is so common that it has contributed significantly to India's notoriety as a negotiating partner.

Fourth, in dealing with the United States and other major countries, Indians can draw on a vast factual base and have a much better institutional memory than their American counterparts. Current Indian officials have had considerable experience in dealing with the United States, in their view one of the major states of the world. Few Americans know as much about the convoluted history of U.S.-Indian negotiations over arms sales, economic assistance, rupee devaluation, or technology transfer. By way of example, during a Sino-Indian border crisis in 1987, American officials at all levels were simply unaware of the factual and technical implications of the crisis, including past American support for the Indian position on the dispute.

## Negotiating with the United States

In the view of some Americans, the Indian negotiating style consists of one stage in which Indian negotiators attempt to establish their moral superiority over their American counterparts. Few U.S.-Indian negotiations have ever gone much further. Most American negotiators are so taken aback by what they perceive as Indian arrogance that they find it difficult to engage in lengthy and complicated negotiations with New Delhi. Indeed, the Indian style is a deterrent to negotiations. Many American officials hate to deal with the Indians compared, say, with Pakistanis, Chinese, or Europeans. The United States and other countries must try to understand the reasons for this Indian diplomatic style if they are to successfully engage India.

When negotiating with Americans, Indian officials work from a complex set of assumptions and their own understanding of history. Like many other former colonial states, India sees in Washington something of the inherited aspirations of former colonial rulers and is determined to show that it is no longer subject to the whims and desires of former colonial masters. Despite their deep pride in their nation's national and civilizational history, Indian officials who have served overseas and who are more acutely aware of the failings of the Indian system compared with the systems of Korea, Taiwan, Malaysia, and even China are also embarrassed by India's poverty.

All of this gives rise to a defensive arrogance and acute sensitivity to real and perceived slights. The first and second generation of Indian leaders, including senior officials and bureaucrats, also considered the United States a racist country comparable to South Africa in the way it treated minorities, especially African-Americans. The few Indians who visited the United States sometimes encountered racial discrimination, and these events became part of the Indian elite's understanding of the United States. In the 1960s the second question Indians would ask an American visitor was "Why does the United States discriminate against Negroes?" (the first was "Why does the United States support the military dictatorship of Pakistan?").[39] Many in the IAS and IFS are particularly sensitive because of their upper-caste and upper-class origins. These officials tend to regard themselves as the guardians of Indian nationhood; many of them have cut their ties with provincial power centers and draw their status and influence from allegiance to the idea of a strong and powerful India dominating the South Asian scene. Some Indians are also still afflicted with a residual left-wing anti-Americanism, inherited from the British upper class, nurtured by the Indian left, and sanctioned by the eighteen-year de facto alliance with the Soviet Union.

Indian negotiating style, especially with the West, differs markedly from that of Pakistan, despite their similar culture. Whereas India seems to relish "getting to no," Pakistan is brilliant at "getting to maybe," rarely agreeing, but never rejecting initiatives coming from the major powers. Pakistani officials are invariably more polite and cooperative, especially to Westerners, at least in ordinary negotiations. They portray Pakistan as a long-lost friend of the West, especially the United States, and one of their stock lines, particularly effective in contrast to India's willful independence, is that Pakistan has been let down by its friends: after all, it was the "most allied of allies" in the past. Even the personal treatment meted out to visitors is strikingly different; whereas a midlevel official will be greeted by his or her exact counterpart in India, negotiations in Pakistan are likely to take place with very senior officials, often bypassing the Ministry of Foreign Affairs. India's MEA has tight control over foreign negotiations; they are rarely, and with difficulty, bypassed by politicians. In Pakistan the security establishment, led by the army, has a veto over all important treaties, especially those involving security issues.

### Regional Negotiations

India's regional neighbors see another face, that of the heir to the British regional system. Indian regional ambassadors and high commissioners are often given considerable operational responsibility and a strong voice in policymaking. These ambassadors and high commissioners try to overwhelm most of India's neighbors with the sheer weight of Indian culture, technology, and economic capabilities. For Nepal, Bangladesh, Sri Lanka, and Bhutan, India is a superpower, and Indian officials expect these states to be suitably deferential. Of course, the smaller regional states use deference as a tactic in dealing with Indians and try to avoid open confrontation. Indian links to dissident or opposition groups in many neighboring countries are used skillfully in negotiations with those states. Indian officials and diplomats hold a number of "cards," in the form of ethnic, economic, or political pressure points—the Sindhi card, the tribal card, the Tamil card, the trade and export cards, and so forth—which they frequently play.

Pakistan is a special regional case (see chapter 7). Distrust between the two countries is usually so high that serious negotiations can only be conducted at the most senior political level. However, Indian leaders are wary of arrangements with a Pakistani leadership that they consider insincere (in the case of the military regimes) or unable to sell an agreement at home (in the case of weak politicians such as Benazir Bhutto or Nawaz Sharif). From the Indian perspective, negotiations with Pakistan will always be difficult.

## Negotiating with Beijing and Moscow

Because it is so culturally different from India, China presents a special problem for Indian negotiators and policymakers. Apart from a handful of Sinologists, Indian officials have enormous difficulty understanding Beijing. Stereotypes abound concerning the "inscrutable," arrogant, and self-centered Chinese. What particularly galls Indian officials is China's contempt for India's position in the region, in Asia, and in the world.

India's relationship with the former Soviet Union and Russia has been more complex. In negotiating the large number of contracts and arms purchases from the Soviet Union, Indians found Moscow tough. Yet even questionable deals became politically palatable because the Russians were silent about the terms of a deal once it was completed. Because of the generally positive Soviet profile in India, the captive Soviet propaganda apparatus, and strong Soviet influence in the press and among Indian intelligentsia, an Indian official could negotiate even a somewhat unfavorable agreement with Moscow and avoid political criticism at home.

Overall, Indians saw themselves as superior to their somewhat backward and inflexible Soviet counterparts and believed that they controlled the relationship. Soviet officials were steady, reliable partners. The Indo-Soviet link worked to India's advantage because Indians were too smart and the country too big and too complex for the Soviet Union to "capture" in the way it brought Afghanistan under Soviet control. Indians knew how to dance with the Russian bear and not get their toes stepped on.

The collapse of the Soviet Union has led to a new diplomacy. The barter-like arrangements have given way to payment in hard currency and the special strategic relationship has evaporated. Russia sells advanced military hardware to India's rival, China, and some of the successor states, such as the Ukraine, have sold advanced military equipment, such as tanks, to Pakistan.

## A Diplomacy in Transition

For many decades, Indian diplomacy was directed by a small group of bureaucrats working with the prime minister. Nehru dominated the process during his sixteen-year tenure, while Indira Gandhi brought in her own personal advisers—a kitchen cabinet—but she also worked closely with the IFS. The short-lived Janata government did not change the pattern, relying heavily on the IFS. By contrast, Rajiv practiced a highly personal and active regional and global diplomacy, even firing one hapless foreign secretary without explanation.

Since 1989 all governments—coalitions of one sort or another—have had to face the reality that foreign policy is yet another issue that might bring them down. Although "bipartisanship" or consultation has grown over the past decade, it is still a rare occurrence; parties in power have no desire to reveal too much about their stratagems to those who would depose them. The BJP's foreign policy has been a success because it has been able to keep foreign policy out of coalition politics and has shared the decisionmaking process with some critical allies, most notably the former minister of defense, George Fernandes. The party has made concessions on many issues, but few in the area of foreign policy. In turn, Fernandes toned down his earlier open advocacy of Tibetan causes and a strong anti-China attitude, demonstrating that a coalition government can run an effective and innovative foreign policy.

Although India is clearly able to conduct foreign relations with competence and even brilliance under such difficult circumstances, its diplomatic and strategic planning processes do not maximize its assets. The decisionmaking system requires a thorough overhaul. There has been considerable talk of introducing a new and efficient system for nearly two decades, but to do so India will have to overcome the power of entrenched bureaucratic interests, the marginalization of the armed forces, and the overwhelming demands of domestic politics. The BJP-led coalition has introduced a few changes, which might point to future reforms. One was the creation of the National Security Advisory Board in 1999. Its first study produced the "Draft Nuclear Doctrine" (see chapter 6), but the exercise seems to have been more of a public relations gesture than a serious attempt to develop a new nuclear doctrine, and the government itself has neither accepted nor rejected the draft as government policy. Other studies now under way may be more fruitful and less controversial, as there is general agreement on the need to improve defense planning, better coordinate the military and civilians, and modernize India's higher defense foreign policy and training establishments. The hard decisions will be to create a true chairman of the Indian Joint Chiefs, a professional soldier who can offer informed judgment on security issues, and a National Security Council staff and secretariat that will perform some vital coordination and planning activities. Beyond this, India's system of higher military and strategic education needs to be overhauled and professionalized.

Given the decline in the standing of the IFS, the lack of other expertise, and the rise of new players in the process—especially the scientists—the rest of the world will have to get used to an Indian government that finds it difficult to negotiate except from the very top and even then may be unable to carry the negotiating process to fruition. Internal bureaucratic, party, and parliamentary politics can suddenly transform the political environment, disrupting negotiations and removing key people. This also makes it difficult for the Indian government to engage in medium- or long-range planning. An expansion of ad hoc and temporary arrangements should also be expected, including the induction of more expert outsiders.

Rapid domestic political instability would ordinarily favor the permanent bureaucracy, but the IFS cannot be expected to assume a larger role in the process. Its strategic vision is reactionary and defensive, and it lacks political clout. Although it is envied by its bureaucratic rivals, it does not have economic expertise, and with India's diplomacy becoming more complex and diverse, it is losing large areas of responsibility. The IFS's technical expertise is poor in other areas as well, now that the intelligence agencies, scientists, and, on occasion, outside consultants and advisers are playing a greater role. India's corporate and commercial interests are beginning to exert themselves, both domestically (as lobbyists) and abroad. Only the military remains marginalized, although the new minister of defense, Jaswant Singh (who retains the Foreign Ministry portfolio), may accept a greater voice for the generals.

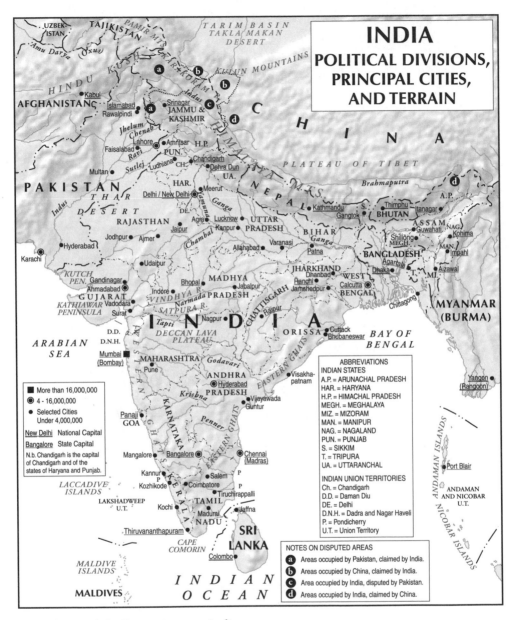

Figure 4-1. Contemporary India

FOUR    *The Domestic*
*Dimension*

INDIA'S INTERNAL WEAKNESSES have long been regarded as its distinguishing quality. In the 1950s American policymakers viewed Indian domestic politics as a critical battleground in the larger war against communism. As a result, India "had" to be built up to withstand the threat from the Soviet Union and Communist China. Fearing that hungry people would be attracted to communism, Americans sent massive shipments of food, and, more creatively, helped India build competence in agricultural and scientific research. In the 1960s, India "had" to be encouraged to adopt family planning and birth control policies lest its vast population outstrip its resources and create new instabilities. Other vulnerabilities included the gross inequalities of the caste system, India's regional and linguistic-based separatist movements, and the desperate plight of many Indian girls and women (of the 12 million baby girls born each year, one-quarter die by the age of fifteen). In recent years, there has been evidence of corruption and administrative mismanagement on a very large scale.[1]

Of India's weaknesses, the economy has been singled out as a critical problem.[2] Given India's expanding population, it is difficult to see how a slow-paced economy could generate the resources needed to support a growing population, let alone a modern military establishment. Although India was an economic giant alongside its smaller neighbors, its overall share of the world economy remained about 1 to 1.5 percent in terms of GNP (4–5 percent in terms of purchasing power parity, PPP), even as it moved toward becoming the world's most populous state.

93

Members of the strategic community argued for decades that India was far superior in its economic competence, political maturity, and social stability to any of the smaller Southeast or East Asian states, or to any state in Africa or the Middle East, even if it was not quite up to some American and Soviet standards. Today, India's vulnerabilities are viewed more realistically, especially after a series of shocks over the past twenty years forced a more honest appraisal of India's domestic setbacks. These shocks include the growth of the Asian tigers and China's demonstrable lead over India in manufacturing and exports (both of which were a surprise to the socialist-inclined Nehruvian generation and its successor), an increase in domestic instability and violence (epitomized by the assassinations of Indira Gandhi, Rajiv Gandhi, and dozens of lesser political figures as well as large-scale religious and caste riots in major cities), the breakdown of Congress's domination of the center and most of the states, the 1991 balance of payment crisis, a series of unstable national coalition governments, and the center's frequent takeover of state governments.

This chapter offers a snapshot of India caught in the midst of profound social and political change. It first shows the "eternal" India—a state that was easy to govern but difficult to change—and then the domestic revolutions that might affect India's emergence as a major power.[3]

## Unchanging India

During the years of Jawaharlal Nehru's high-profile diplomacy, India stood for something. India seemed the exception among third world countries, in that domestic considerations appeared to play a small role in shaping Indian diplomacy. Closer examination reveals that this was not the case. Economic, ideological, federal, and domestic ethnic and religious considerations were quietly important in shaping Indian policy.[4] Nehru and his colleagues believed that nonalignment would prevent India from becoming entangled in larger global conflicts and thus shield the fragile Indian economy from outside forces as it erected a modern infrastructure. Nonalignment would also keep the ideological battles of the superpowers away from India. New Delhi's close relations with many Arab states and its limited ties to Israel were shaped by the supposed sensitivities of India's large Muslim population, and relations with Sri Lanka and East Pakistan/Bangladesh were strongly influenced by the corresponding ethnic or linguistic groups in India (Tamils and Bengalis).[5]

India's economic policies were dominated more by New Delhi's bureaucrats and influential left-leaning economists than by the business and industrial community. "License Raj," a vast system of national and state-level licenses and quotas, allowed the government to enforce policies of statism and economic autarky. Nehru dampened the spirit of private enterprise and profit, favoring social engineering and economic egalitarianism. The government-centered economic strategy elevated officials to positions for which they were unqualified. The generalist Indian Administrative Service ran (or supervised) many government industries and undertakings. Its administrative talents were admirable, but it lacked an entrepreneurial tradition and was insular in its outlook.

Foreign aid programs were important for various developmental schemes, but these were almost all government-to-government activities. Foundations operating in India channeled most of their support through government entities. On balance, India's economic performance during the Nehru years was not bad. At 3.5 percent annually, its growth was three times as high as it had been under the British in the first half of the century. Only later did the East Asian Tigers demonstrate that 3.5 percent growth was slow rather than fast, but by that time India's planners "had become knowledge-proof."[6]

As for center-state relations, although India has a federal structure, the term "federal" does not appear in the Indian constitution, and India has in practice long been a unitary state as far as governance is concerned.[7] Major policy initiatives and the bulk of the financing have come from the center, with the states scrambling to implement policies developed in New Delhi. For the 80 percent of Indian citizens who lived in India's 500 largely rural districts, the penetration of the state was still weak. India was efficiently but loosely administered, with the district collectors and magistrates holding enormous power in their hands. The bureaucracy shared its power with elected officials, but the latter remained dependent upon them in many ways. The situation in most states resembled an Indian version of the British television parody of bureaucracy, "Yes, Minister," with the people's representatives holding nominal power, but the civil and police bureaucracies holding real power, and doing a fine job of it.

Social mobilization in India was very slow in some regions and states (North India), faster in others (Kerala, Tamil Nadu, and West Bengal), but most Indian cities and the countryside looked much the same in 1970 as they had in 1947, only more crowded. In the 1960s, foreign economic advisers and academics joked that the Indian countryside was "seething with apathy." The Indian economy provided enough wealth to satisfy the demands of most politically enfranchised groups, and the prospect of even a small stake in the system limited the growth of revolutionary movements. Nevertheless, some southern states experienced dramatic social changes in the 1950s as a result of their demand for linguistically unified states and the establishment of quota systems for certain Hindu castes. The most stable part of the country was the "cow belt," the northern states of Uttar Pradesh, Bihar, and Madhya Pradesh. Terrorism and violent separatist movements were rare and easily dealt with. For the most part these tended to be located in politically marginal and underpopulated regions such as the northeast.

On the question of India's identity, there was general agreement on a few important principles. India was a secular state that needed a strong government at the center to protect minority rights, build the economy, and rein in "fissiparous tendencies." The dominant external ideological influence on India was British-derived socialism, with a strong Fabian tinge. Foreign states having a religious orientation, including Pakistan and Israel, were thought to be dangerous models for the multiethnic, multireligious India. (The Indian Congress had long opposed the creation of a separate Jewish homeland, recognizing that such a state would be a precedent for a Muslim Pakistan; this policy carried over into the postindependence period.)

The presence of strong political leaders and a dominant political party also contributed to India's stable domestic political order. The Congress-dominated nationalist movement had created a pantheon of heroes who defeated the British Empire, created the world's largest democracy, and set India upon a secular, democratic, quasi-socialist course that seemed destined to lead it to true greatness. Indians could justifiably boast of giants such as the Nehrus—father and son— Mahatma Gandhi, Maulana Azad, and Sardar Patel, all prominent Congress figures. There were other heroes, but these were not to be found in the main gallery: Subhas Chandra Bose (who had joined the Axis powers during World War II in an attempt to liberate India by force), B. R. Ambedkar (the leading untouchable figure in modern India and the chief author of the constitution), Jayaprakash Narayan (a former socialist turned Gandhian), and Veer Savarkar (the founder of the Hindu Maha-

sabha). They were in the second rank compared with the more
tic" Congress greats.

According to Indians and foreign observers alike, India's one
dominant system—the "Congress system"—conferred great advan.
on a developing country. Congress governed at the center and in mos
the states, providing overall political stability. It was also a power.
symbol of national unity. At the same time, India could also take th.
high moral ground because it was a true democracy with a high voting
turnout, freedom of speech and movement, and the freest elections in
the non-Western world, even though these freedoms did not always
extend to all parts of the country.

Disputes over national policies were sorted out within the Congress
party. On foreign policy matters, the strategic community supported a
"consensus" policy, which was easy to achieve given Congress's dominance. When the first generation of leaders began to pass from the
scene, Indian stability appeared to be ensured, and Congress moved
away from one-party dominance toward one-family dominance, as
Nehru, followed by his daughter and then his grandson, seemed proof
that India remained in secure hands.

Lastly, democratic government in India was long regarded as some
kind of miracle. India challenged the assumption that only rich countries
could be democracies, or that the only way a large, poor state could
become wealthy was by brutal, forced industrialization or capitalism
uninhibited by a social conscience. Every time the Indian electorate went
to the polls, it was said to be the largest peaceful event in human history.
Although the "Emergency" of 1975–77 clouded this picture, two subsequent national elections (1977 and 1980) seemed to confirm India's special relationship with democracy and suggested that democratic elections would produce strong, stable governments at the center.

## India's New Revolutions

These policies and assumptions have all been challenged in the past fifteen years. One by one, the images of a stable, orderly, peaceful, and
progressive India have given way to a series of interacting social, political, and economic revolutions.[8] Since the late 1980s, India has become a
"revolutionary state" experiencing political, social, and economic
upheaval. The West Indian–British author V. S. Naipaul has called this
process "A Million Mutinies Now."[9] These are not so much "bloody

revolutions" as "bleeding revolutions." As Indian anthropologist M. N. Srinivas has observed, "Indians are actually living in a revolution, although it is not always recognized by many of them nor, for that matter, by the outside world."[10]

These revolutions include the bursting forth of hitherto quiescent groups, usually from low castes, with demands for ethnic and linguistic autonomy, a changed center-state relationship, a transformed Indian diaspora, and a direct challenge to India's secular order. On top of this, the global information revolution is spreading throughout the country. All of this has occurred at a time when nearby regional conflicts are spilling into India, and Delhi's foreign policy, loosened from its non-aligned moorings, is more than ever a function of these profound domestic economic, political, and social revolutions.

## The (Very) Gradual Economic Revolution

The most recent of these "revolutions" has been in the realm of economics. It was launched by Manmohan Singh, finance minister in the Narasimha Rao government in 1991, and triggered by a severe foreign currency crisis. India's state-dominated economic infrastructure is yielding gradually to private Indian and international investment and a market economy.[11] This has led to demands for greater access to international capital, a reexamination of Indian labor legislation, the removal of barriers to foreign direct investment, and the general expansion of contacts between Indian firms, foreign firms, and nonresident Indians. Most Indians now accept the idea that the government should assist, not retard, the growth of businesses, especially those that seek to operate abroad, and should foster the growth of lively stock exchanges.

These policy changes are all the more poignant and problematic because they were sharply debated and rejected more than thirty years ago when the Swatantra ("Freedom") party proposed them in the late 1950s. Swatantra, which was centered in Bombay, India's financial and industrial center, was ultimately submerged by the left-populist wave generated under Indira Gandhi's rule and was branded as unprogressive, pro-American, and anti-Indian. This opened up the political terrain to Congress's right, which was subsequently occupied by the Jana Sangh and its successor, the BJP.

India's economic revolution can be said to be moving at a walking pace. Both Indira Gandhi and Rajiv Gandhi had made weak gestures in the direction of liberalization by imposing somewhat fewer restrictions on the capital repatriation of foreign companies, allowing them expanded ownership in Indian subsidiaries and taking preliminary steps toward streamlined project approval. Even the success stories coming out of Southeast and East Asia during the 1980s had little impact. By 1990 India was still a quasi-command, bureaucratized economy, burdened with heavy state subsidies for the industrial sector, sometimes in the name of national security or autarky. The Congress party had moved toward a quasi-socialist economic philosophy. At the Avadi session of the Congress party back in January 1955, it declared that Indian economic planning should aim toward the establishment of a socialistic pattern of society, moving India toward the creation of a welfare state without the productive capacity required to sustain one.

To the giant, inward-gazing India, the economic growth of other states—including the "Tigers" of Southeast Asia (Malaysia, Singapore, Thailand, Indonesia), South Korea, and even China—seemed irrelevant. One pretext after another was hauled out to explain why India could not or did not need to change. There were alleged cultural reasons for the success of others, they had succumbed to foreign economic domination, or they were not democracies, as was India. China's economic policy was derided as leading to dependence on the West and Japan. Two examples of many show how India sacrificed an early lead on the altar of a statist, doctrinaire, and politicized economic policy, which drew its inspiration from the Soviet model and its leadership from rank amateurs.

By the end of World War II, India had acquired the fundamentals of an aircraft industry, including a modern repair and manufacturing facility and an Indian-owned airline. During the war, the United States had developed a major repair facility at Hindustan Air Limited (HAL), in Bangalore. It was designed to overhaul and repair a wide range of American and British aircraft in service throughout South and Southeast Asia. HAL grew rapidly and at one point began to manufacture light aircraft and parts. It remained a state-owned corporation, primarily because of its military applications.

Most of HAL's major military projects have been overambitious failures. Driven by Nehru's philosophy of self-reliance, plus a desire to strengthen India's nonaligned ties, New Delhi collaborated with Egypt in building a modern jet fighter, the HF-24 (Marut). Expatriate German designers (including Kurt Tank of Messerschmidt fame) helped design the plane, while India built its airframe and Egypt its engine. Only one squadron ever went into service, underpowered and highly dangerous: the plane killed several Indian test pilots. This fiasco was replicated twenty years later, when India attempted to build a Light Combat Aircraft, drawing upon technical assistance from American and other Western firms. This plane has also gone over budget, is at least ten years late, and if ever produced in numbers will probably be obsolete. In the meantime, India found itself utterly dependent upon the Soviet Union, eventually turning its air force into a predominantly Soviet-equipped service, relying largely upon the Soviet Union for critical parts and replacements. Yet Delhi was prohibited from servicing other air forces flying Soviet equipment, and there was no transfer of Soviet design or manufacturing technology to India.[12]

HAL could have linked up with foreign aircraft manufacturing firms, but the latter were wary of the Indian government's policies on investment and foreign control. The only significant contracts with Western aerospace firms were for assembling aircraft from kits and parts, with a minimal transfer of design and manufacturing skills. By the late 1990s, when HAL was given greater autonomy and was offering equity in its operations, foreign companies such as Boeing and Northrop had doubts about the quality of Indian management and thought it risky to become associated with a still-inefficient operation.

As for its civilian air services, India's first international airline, Tata Airlines, was founded before independence in 1932 by J. R. D. Tata, the head of India's second largest private industrial house. Renamed Air-India in 1946, it became the world's first all-jet airline in the 1960s and was an original purchaser of the wide-body Boeing 747. By then it had been taken over by the government and run as a quasi-autonomous government department, but it was still able to help Singapore, Malaysia, and other countries start up their own national airlines. When the Tatas were removed from the management of the airline, it failed to remain competitive, in part because of incompetent management and inefficiency (it has the largest ratio of employees to aircraft of any airline in the world). It has been unable to compete with the very airlines it had helped establish, let alone the major carriers of Europe and America. The Indian government is now debating how and when the airline should be privatized. Ironically, the airline's value lies not so much in its aircraft and personnel, but in the more than seventy international routes that the airline has the right to fly but does not service (today it flies to only nineteen destinations, whereas ten years ago it flew to thirty-two).[13]

The Air-India story was more than matched by the fiasco of India's major domestic airline, Indian Airlines, which had been cobbled together by the forced merger of several private regional airlines after independence. Indian Airlines had a monopoly of domestic services until the early 1990s but was even less efficient than Air-India. It is still subject to the whim of government bureaucrats and politicians in the matter of routes, schedules, safety, and the purchase of equipment. It was and remains too small, with its fares kept artificially low despite widespread demand at a higher price point. The government is attempting to privatize Indian Airlines, but its equipment and bloated staff make it unattractive to most buyers.

The inefficiency of the government bureaucracies that are responsible for the construction, maintenance, and safety of India's airports and aircraft, as well as the regulation of air safety, have further hampered both Indian Airlines and Air-India. Indian airports rank among the most dangerous, and Indian Airlines has the dubious honor of being the "most hijacked" airline in the world. Only after the December 1999 Kathmandu-Kandahar hijacking did the government order air marshals to fly on selected routes.

The real obstacles to the development of either an indigenous aircraft industry or the maintenance of an internationally competitive airline are ideological, not economic. The Indian government defined airlines as an essential, national service and placed them under the thumb of bureaucrats instead of experts. The government officials who ran India's major aircraft manufacture and repair facility and supervised its major airline were well-intentioned generalists who had to conform to an ideologically framed measure of success. These overmanned and inefficient entities lost money on a regular basis. Deficits were made up by the Indian taxpayer; the result was a missed opportunity. India never built up a Brazil-like capability to produce aircraft that might have earned precious foreign exchange, nor did it develop airlines—as did Singapore and Malaysia—that were consistently profitable.

Although Indira Gandhi and Rajiv Gandhi made token gestures in the direction of economic liberalization, real change was imposed upon India by the force of circumstances in the form of the balance of payments crisis in 1991. Its foreign exchange reserves had bottomed out, and the Reserve Bank of India had to secretly fly gold to London to maintain the country's credit. Since then, a consensus has developed for a more market-friendly economy. This now encompasses the encouragement of foreign and private investment and the dismantling of selected state-run enterprises. However, as Indian economic journalist Swaminathan S. Anklesaria Aiyar wryly notes, the "consensus" includes the continuation of politically popular subsidies, worker-friendly labor laws, the maintenance of sick industries, and an effort to adapt the market economy to replace the kickbacks that will be lost if sick state enterprises are closed down.[14] India's sagging infrastructure, especially the telecommunications, transportation, and power sectors, has simultaneously limited the inflow of foreign investment and hobbled economic growth. The major success story, the software industry, boasts that it does not have to rely upon the national telecommunications or power grids and has remained unregulated by the Indian government.

Such obstacles aside, India as a whole has successfully overcome its "Hindu rate of growth"—the sardonic term coined by the late Raj Krishna, one of India's most distinguished economists. Under Nehru, the economy grew at a rate of 3.5 percent a year, twice as fast as the 1.3 percent averaged during the first half of the century under the Raj and faster than Britain's own growth rate during its industrial revolution.[15] Over the past five years, growth has hovered around 5 to 6 percent. In 1999, the Indian economy had among the world's fastest growth rates (6 percent). Indians talk confidently of reaching 7 to 8 percent. If the country sustains the pace of its reforms and moves to the next phase, its national income could double in a decade. India's 1998 GNP of $420 billion was the world's eleventh largest; its GNP measured at purchasing power parity was $1,660 billion, the world's fifth largest, behind the United States, China, Japan, and Germany.

However, this rapid growth has been uneven. Some states have done extremely well, whereas others have lagged behind. Furthermore, the disparity in growth rates has widened, from a factor of 2 in the 1980s, to well over 3.5 in the 1990s, with Bihar growing at only 2.7 percent and Gujarat growing the fastest, at 9.6 percent.[16] Many factors appear to be involved—including specific state histories, external and internal investment, levels of corruption, natural endowment, and literacy and educational levels—although economists do not yet fully understand why some are moving ahead faster than others.[17]

India's new economic boom has been stronger in services than in manufacturing, which reflects overall global trends.[18] India's software industry has a foothold in many advanced countries, especially the United States, and software exports have grown at an astonishing annual rate of 50 percent for several years. They could grow from the current $4 billion to $50 billion by 2008 and reach $100 billion soon afterward, with more than half of that in exports.[19] Three Indian software companies are now listed on the NASDAQ exchange, and one of these, Infosys Technologies, has a market capitalization of $19 billion. So far, information technology is the one area that the Indian government has not tried to regulate, and it is doubtful whether any government in New Delhi will want to interfere with an industry that has been so productive at home and so effective in spreading a positive image of India abroad.

While foreign firms operating in India still complain about red tape and protectionism, they see India as a $100 billion investment market, especially in the power, road, and infrastructure sectors. Foreign firms are also drawing on India's highly trained, English-speaking educated elite (at the present rate, India will soon be the world's largest English-speaking country). After some teething problems, outsiders are learning how to do business in India. Even the much maligned Indian bureaucracy has been praised by foreign executives for providing stability and balance in a decade of political turmoil.

India's new approach to economic growth has varied implications for foreign policy.[20] On the one hand, some hawks believe that this new growth can provide the material means for a more powerful India. They relish a substantial increase in pay, improved service conditions, and better training and equipment. On the other hand, many politicians and economists are concerned that a more active foreign policy might discourage investment, bring down sanctions on the Indian government, or lead to a repeat of earlier disasters.

The facts of Indian poverty are undeniable and remain both a moral issue and a political embarrassment to any Indian government. Yet the Indian economy continued to expand at 6.1 percent a year between 1990 and 1998.[21] As India's population growth rate levels off, its identity may no longer be overdefined by its poverty. India is likely to surpass Pakistan in per capita income in several years, which will further strengthen its regional position.[22]

A growing economy, coupled with an expected decline in birth rates, will add teeth to a foreign policy that has been long on rhetoric but short on resources. The question facing India may not be *whether* more money can be put in the service of security and foreign policy, but how to ensure its efficient use. As discussed in chapter 3, India lacks an integrated system for allocating resources; decisions in this sphere remain in the hands of the civilian bureaucracy, except when a particular lobby is able to attract the attention of powerful politicians. Because of the antipathy toward the private sector, the defense science establishment has been sheltered from competition, and the exaggerated requirements of secrecy have screened it from effective cost-benefit analyses. This sector remains highly bureaucratized, leaving Indian science and technology lumbering along under the aegis of vast and inefficient national laboratories and entities that have stifled innovation. This is especially true in the area where science and security overlap: "In no major country, other than in India, is the bulk of the defense R&D effort directed autonomously by a scientific organization. In other countries, the participation of the military services and the production agencies is huge at every level of R&D."[23] In India the defense science sector is seen as an easy way to jump over intermediate technologies and provide instant international and domestic status. Yet India has not produced a single Nobel Prize winner for science, and the military science establishment does not even draw upon the better civilian institutions. Their graduates usually prefer to seek employment overseas.[24]

India's lone security-related economic and technical success has been in the area of missile development and related space launch vehicles and satellites. Drawing upon the experience of other states, as well as India's own civilian missile program, defense scientists have been able to fabricate and launch several types of missiles. Although greeted with skepticism by the Indian armed forces, they have had a major political impact in the region and in India's relations with the United States. It may be that the high quality of Indian basic science will overcome the failings in manufacturing techniques in the custom manufacture and launch of space vehicles. However, more and more of these programs are falling into the hands of India's "official" defense science sector, which combines a bureaucratic structure with an inflated faith in the power of science as a cure for India's economic, technological, and social problems, as well as its security. The most prominent spokesman for this position is the current science adviser to the prime minister, the charismatic A. P. J. Kalam. Kalam has frequently argued that Indian defense science provides the model for the rest of Indian society. One of Kalam's boasts is that India has the ability to design a "state-of-the-art" ABM system, an ICBM, and a supersonic earth-orbiting plane "if adequate funds are made available for the project."[25] Similar boasts are regularly heard from India's nuclear establishment. Yet India's Defense Research and Development Organization (DRDO) cannot produce a modern aircraft or tank, and some now doubt that the May 1998 nuclear tests were as successful as claimed or that India has more nuclear weapons than Pakistan.[26]

Indian economic reforms, the so-called first wave, are still in their infancy. So far, they have concentrated on improving the climate for foreign investors, making it easier for Indian firms to compete abroad, shedding a few of the most inefficient of state-owned enterprises, and encouraging competition in hitherto sacrosanct areas such as power generation, public infrastructure, and telecommunications. These efforts have received wide support and have benefited some Indians. But the next wave of reform—breaking up the vast majority of state enterprises, opening up economic sectors hitherto reserved for "small-scale" industries (which have been unable to meet foreign demands for high-quality, mass-produced goods, especially in textiles), creating a more fluid labor market, challenging the power of the Indian unions, and allowing the further expansion of foreign investment—will all pinch. The tradition of lifelong employment guaranteed by the state runs deep, and many sick enterprises are kept alive for political reasons or because the government fears the wrath of the unions. Unless it moves carefully, the BJP led coalition could invite a political backlash from workers, managers, and owners in these sectors.

Surprisingly, some of the greatest problems may arise in the software and computer industry. India's information technology (IT) industries have the potential to lead Indian growth and improve productivity throughout the economy. According to some observers, however, IT could also become an "enclave" industry, benefiting foreign companies and the rest of the world, with only a marginal or indirect impact upon India itself.[27] This could repeat a historical pattern of some 1,500 years ago that benefited the entire world but bypassed India itself when Indian mathematicians created the decimal system. They and many astronomers then emigrated to Baghdad, the "Silicon Valley" of that era; their ideas eventually passed from the Arab world to the West, where the decimal system replaced roman numerals.[28] Today, there is some risk that Indian achievements in software development will aid the rest of the world but not India: Indian-developed software is widely used in the world's banks, but Indian banks cannot take advantage of it. Indian-developed information management systems are used in ports and terminals around the world to speed shipments and ensure reliability, but the Indian infrastructure is so backward that they remain among the most inefficient in the world, and Indian businesses (and labor unions) resist the introduction of modern procedures that would threaten their inefficient but personally profitable operations or make it possible to reduce the level of corruption. Ironically, Indian soldiers who fought against the Pakistan Army in the frozen heights of Kargil were equipped with obsolete field telephones, while the Pakistanis had sophisticated satellite phones based on technology developed by Indian software engineers and programmers in the West.[29]

Although there will be bumps in the road ahead, most predictions regarding the Indian economy remain upbeat. In terms of risk, India ranks in the middle of the ninety-three "emerging markets," just behind China and ahead of Mexico, South Africa, Turkey, Brazil, Nigeria, and Indonesia, and well ahead of Pakistan and Russia, the world's riskiest economy.[30] In four or five years, the Indian economy will likely be growing at a rate of 7 percent annually, bringing it just behind the United States, China, and Japan.[31] Such growth may give the government considerably more "discretionary" funds for defense as well as developmental purposes. But the allocation of this money will depend as much on politics as economics and will be shaped by the demands of the Indian states and India's population for a greater share of the pie.

### Federalizing India: Are the Parts Greater Than the Whole?

The Indian constitution established a unitary political system making the center responsible for defense and foreign policy, and giving the states presumptive authority over law and order, education, and social policies. In practice, the balance of power has always tilted toward the center, which is able to reorganize, create, or eliminate the states as it wishes, and can impose "President's Rule" upon states with some ease. Within this constitutional framework, however, the federalizing process is well under way and constitutes a major change in the Indian political order. Some of the largest and most unwieldy states are "losing" territory, as three new states were created in 2000 out of parts of Uttar Pradesh, Bihar, and Madhya Pradesh. This movement of power to the states, and perhaps the creation of many new, and smaller states, has implications for India's role in the region and its relations with other countries.

For many years the dominant intellectual argument in India was that a strong, powerful center was necessary to keep India secure. It would have a unifying ideology, a centrally planned economy, and a powerful military force, giving it the capacity to deal both with its neighbors and with the wider world. As Rajni Kothari noted in 1989, "The idea that societies have to be organized around the authority of a centralized state, incorporated and legitimized by a set of institutions, is one to which India has tried to respond and is still trying to respond." Nevertheless, Kothari and many others came to believe, especially after the rule of Indira Gandhi, that while this brought about a "certain measure of power" and a new sense of purpose, the idea of a strong Indian state overrode and undermined the many diverse identities of which India was composed.[32]

India's federal revolution was brought about by at least four factors. First, the Congress party itself underwent transformation after Nehru's death in 1964. Congress fell under the control of a group of powerful state political leaders who had acquired the nickname "the Syndicate." Its members were influential because they were able to dominate their Pradesh (state) Congress parties through inner-party elections; they did not need New Delhi to prop them up. This situation changed radically when Indira Gandhi, who had been made prime minister by the Syndicate, methodically destroyed their power. She replaced chief ministers suspected of disloyalty, practicing a divide-and-rule strategy to the point where none were secure without her blessing. Eventually, the circle around her was reduced to a few trusted advisers and relatives, including her sons Sanjay and Rajiv. The end result was a Congress party that was seemingly more powerful—chief ministers could be made and unmade at a moment's notice—but it was no longer a vigorous and competitive party.

Second, this centralization of power within Congress coincided with an eighteen-month "Emergency" (during 1975–77) that brought autocracy to India. The Emergency contributed to a resurgence of regional parties. Dissident Congress party leaders who had been rejected by New Delhi but who still had a strong base in the states sometimes formed these state parties.[33] Many of these former members of Congress joined with various left and regional parties to claim power at the center in the Janata government of 1978–80, and then in 1991, as allies of P. V. Narasimha Rao's Congress government, and finally in the United Front governments of 1996–98. The two subsequent BJP-led coalition governments were also dependent upon state political parties.

Third, an opposition party—the BJP—developed a strategy that allowed it to expand its base from a few enclaves in the Hindi-heartland (Northern and Central India) to much of Western India and even the south. Although handicapped by its reputation as an extremist, ideologically driven, pro-Hindu party dominated by upper castes, the BJP managed to highlight issues that were broadly attractive and that expanded its caste and regional base. Although not outstanding, the BJP's success at governance has been no worse than that of some of the Congress governments it displaced, and the party is now attempting to develop a cadre of parliamentarians and consultants who are experts on a wide range of issues. While its ideology has repelled some, the lure of power has attracted many intellectuals and journalists to its ranks. Most important, the BJP has learned how to function as the dominant member of a coalition, accommodating its partners when required, acquiring new ones when necessary.[34] If the Congress party should ever adopt a similar flexibility, it stands a good chance of regaining power in many of the states and even the center.

Fourth, India's federal revolution has been made possible by the existence of strong regional traditions that in some states predate the Mughals and the British and go back to a time when they were powers in their own right.[35] When state boundaries were drawn up after independence, some large linguistic communities found themselves divided. Other groups (such as the Sikhs) pressed for a state in which they would make up the majority. The state reorganization of 1956 created Andhra Pradesh, Madras, Maharashtra, Karnataka, and Gujarat, each linguistically drawn. Subsequently, states were created in the northeast to give Mizos, Nagas, and others their own states, and Haryana was carved out of Punjab, giving Sikhs a more dominant role (but not quite a majority) in the latter state. The Congress party oversaw and took advantage of these changes by forming Congress governments in most of the newly created states, but state-based parties have supplanted these in many instances. The year 1989 was critical. It brought to an end the long era of Congress's dominance and introduced government-by-coalition at the center.[36] Both an increase in turnout and the number of political parties contributed to Congress's decline, but these factors are also likely to restrict the growth of the BJP. Turnout used to be well under 50 percent; it is now in the range of 57–62 percent.[37] In the 1950s India had one dominant party, Congress, and fifteen or so minor parties. By the 1990s there were over forty parties. Both the BJP and the regional parties have gained at the expense of the Congress, but they are locked in an uneasy embrace as they try to maintain a government at the center. Every government in New Delhi since then has been a coalition, or has been dependent upon outside parties to stay in power. Further, there appears to be little chance that future governments will return to the one-party dominant pattern.

The BJP is unlikely to achieve the same level of domination that Congress had in the 1950s and 1960s when it could pull in three-fourths of the Lok Sabha seats with 48 percent of the votes. The BJP has been able to manage a quarter of the popular vote in the 1990s, about the same as Congress, which gave them 179 seats in 1998 and 182 in 1999. Its seats were mainly in the north and west, and without the Telugu Desam and the AIADMK, for instance, it would not have been able to form the National Democratic Alliance government in 1999. Even a small player such as West Bengal's All India Trinamool Congress (which won 9 seats in 1999) can make or break a government. The future looks set for more coalitions.

A new wave of state creation began in 2000, as a result of the BJP's pledges when it was in opposition. Three new states were created. One (Uttaranchal) was carved out of the giant Uttar Pradesh, a second (Chattisgarh) comprises much of Bihar's tribal belt, and a third (Jharkhand) is made up of a number of Madhya Pradesh's tribal regions. The prospects for these new states are uneven; Chattisgarh will do well because it has rich mineral resources, and Bihar's civil servants are rushing to join it, but there is some risk that the creation of still more states will only result in a dramatic increase in the number of political parties without a corresponding improvement in the quality of government.[38]

India's approximately forty political parties are found mostly at the state level and there are at least seven national parties.[39] The latter are roughly distributed in three shifting alliances. One is dominated by Congress, another by the BJP, and a third by the "left" parties, including Janata. All but three or four of these forty parties have their power in a single state.[40] This has led to a political process at the center in which instability has been the norm for over ten years: except for Congress (1991–96), every central government since 1989 has fallen prematurely because of a breakdown in the ruling coalition. State-level parties have determined election outcomes as well as the fate of coalitions, turning the tables in Indian politics. As Philip Oldenberg has observed, "Thirty years ago state politics was a picture of coalition governments of convenience collapsing with alarming rapidity, forcing frequent elections with parties emerging and dying and splitting and merging. Now states display a remarkable pattern of stability."[41] Many states now have two-party (or stable two-coalition) or three-party systems; the outcome of this state-level coalition politics determines what coalitions are available for national elections. Indian state politics was always a matter of bargaining and horse-trading; now the mastery of this art shapes central governments as well.

In this, there is no difference between the Congress and the BJP. The latter has systematically abandoned its larger ideological and policy goals at the center in order to stay in power. In the 1998 BJP government, the party toned down every election plank except that of going nuclear.[42] In the second government, elected in 1999, it worked out a major compromise with its National Democratic Alliance partners at Chennai in December 1999. The "Chennai declaration," endorsed by senior BJP leaders, yielded on such contentious issues as the construction of a Hindu temple devoted to Lord Rama at Ayodhya and refined its policies of cultural nationalism.[43] These concessions have not prevented the BJP from pursuing its social and ideological policies more aggressively in states such as Uttar Pradesh and Gujarat, where it is the governing party.

Most of India's state-based parties are opposed to Delhi's heavy hand. From their perspective, the government of India should be just strong enough to carry out minimum security needs and provide financial support to state development plans; most would also prefer greater freedom to directly negotiate foreign economic, cultural, and even political ties. In 2000 some state leaders threatened to pull out of the BJP coalition if the government did not restore cuts in revenue to the states as recommended by the Eleventh Finance Commission (which quadrennially determines allocations to the states). They failed, but the issue runs to the heart of the federal question.[44]

State-based parties—such as the Communist parties in West Bengal and Kerala and some BJP state leaders—are even more wary of India's centralized national security apparatus and the use of the Indian Army and paramilitary forces to maintain law and order in the states. They all remember the many occasions on which Congress governments in Delhi, especially during Indira Gandhi's prime ministership, brought down state governments on the pretext that they were unable to ensure law and order. At the same time, many state parties want Delhi's support in dealing with a Bangladesh, Nepal, or Sri Lanka in such matters as water resources, trade, migration, and the treatment of particular ethnic, religious, or linguistic groups. Although these regional political forces have shared interests and remain dependent on the center for subsidies and investments, they generally want to be left alone.

The leaders of most of the state-based parties have only the vaguest understanding of complex national security issues. Their attention is focused on relations with New Delhi (and often a nearby South Asian neighbor). South Indians are less intensely concerned with India's policies toward Pakistan, China, Bangladesh, or Nepal, although television and press coverage of the 1999 Kargil conflict stirred patriotic and nationalist feelings even in the southern states. North Indians who are absorbed into Pakistan care little about the Bangladeshis streaming into Assam and Tripura; Biharis and Bengalis are concerned about Nepal, not "north-south" or disarmament issues.

No state illustrates the transformation of India's politics better than Andhra Pradesh. The largest of the southern states, with a population of 72 million (in 1996), Andhra is not a wealthy state and has been beset by tribal and revolutionary protest movements for decades.[45] In response to demands for a linguistically homogeneous state, the Telugu speakers of India—some found in the former princely state of Hyderabad, some in the Madras Presidency of British India, and the rest in other states—were brought together in Andhra Pradesh by the linguistic reorganization of 1956. Andhra's political leadership went through three successive phases, beginning with domination by the Congress party, which lasted for over twenty years. Powerful "organizational men," such as P. V. Narasimha Rao, a chief minister who was a devoted ally of Indira Gandhi and who served as prime minister from 1991 to 1996, worked within the Congress party to influence Delhi's policies, relying on a coalition of high and mid-castes and a well-oiled party bureaucracy.

Congress was displaced by a purely state-based party, the Telugu Desam, founded by the charismatic actor-turned-politician, N. T. Rama Rao. "NTR" combined political savvy, caste politics, and the divinity-by-association of an actor who had played Hindu gods in hundreds of roles. Rao was uninterested in foreign and security matters, but this did not prevent him from speaking about them. On one day he would proudly trace the origin of nuclear weapons back to the Vedas, and on the next, eloquently condemn nuclear weapons as barbaric devices of mass destruction, demanding that they be wiped from the face of the earth.

Andhra, still in the political forefront, is now undergoing another transformation under NTR's son-in-law, Chandrababu Naidu, who assumed power upon his father-in-law's death. Naidu favors an efficient, results-oriented approach to governance, styling himself as the "CEO" of Andhra Pradesh.[46] The Congress model was rigidly structured and reliant upon the state bureaucracy; NTR's model had a touch of Hollywood and Ronald Reagan, while Chandrababu Naidu's has blended Microsoft and Singapore, taking advantage of the fact that Telugus had an early interest in software and computers and thus giving the neighboring state of Karnataka a run for its bytes and bits (he nicknamed the state capital, Hyderabad, "Cyberabad").[47] Naidu has sent missions from Andhra Pradesh to several countries, including Pakistan, there hoping to take advantage of the fact that many Karachites who migrated from Hyderabad to Karachi over the years have retained ties to Andhra. Though Naidu is a mediocre speaker and lacks the charismatic qualities of his father-in-law, he has impressed leaders in other states with his results-oriented leadership, favoring strong international ties, which led to his victory in the 1999 election. His Telugu Desam also became the second largest party in the BJP coalition and persuaded the BJP to moderate its election platform and abandon its most provocative planks.

## Still a Strong State, When Necessary

Although the states have become economically and politically more important, the union government retains the capacity to acquire, organize, and apply the full resources of a continent-sized country to any particular region. The central civil services (the army, the police, and the Indian Administrative Service) and sister services, such as the Indian Police Service, constitute the institutionalized memory of the Indian Union. The IAS and the IPS have especially strong ties to the state governments (they are organized around state cadres and rotate back and forth between Delhi and their home state). They have a clear, if somewhat formulaic, understanding of what it takes to deal with a militant, violent, or separatist movement.[48] In its crudest form, the strategy at both the state and national levels is, in the words of a senior IPS officer, to "hit them over the head with a hammer, then teach them to play the piano," which means apply massive (and sometimes brutal) force to contain any group that proclaims that it wants to leave the Union, but after that deal with the leadership politically in whatever way is necessary. This is most evident in the northeast, where yesterday's student radicals have become today's members of government and have their hands full trying to cope with their revolutionary successors.[49]

The key element in India's strategy is accommodation: the Indian government will accede somewhat to the demands put forth by even the most extreme separatist groups once the latter acknowledge the sovereign authority of the government of India. In many instances, political patronage has grown out of the barrel of a gun that has been laid aside for electoral politics. Much political violence, even in the name of separatism, stems from the failure of democratic politics to accommodate separatist or violent groups soon enough. At the height of the Khalistan movement, for example, most Sikhs in India were not as interested in a separate state as they were in obtaining justice.[50] This is also true of the separatist movement in Kashmir. It had Kashmiri rather than Islamic roots and would not have burst into armed opposition in 1989 had Kashmir been treated more fairly in the preceding years.[51]

The pressure and co-option strategy has been successful because of two interrelated factors: India's physical vastness and the inability of separatist movements to work together. These movements have usually occurred at different times in different regions of the country, often for different reasons. This enables the government to apply massive resources to counteract each. Although India appears to be in perpetual chaos and there has been a substantial increase in social and political violence, the major separatist threats have been regularly spaced (the Tamils in the 1950s, the Nagas in the 1960s, the Mizos in the 1960s and 1970s, the Sikhs in the 1980s, and the Kashmiris in the 1990s). If dissident and separatist groups were able to mount simultaneous attacks on different parts of India, then some might succeed, but this seems improbable.

The Indian federal system is a metastable structure. The center has lost some of its strength at the same time that (and partly because) the states are growing more coherent. Yet the political chaos is more apparent than real. If anything, the federal revolution that began in 1989 has provided new opportunities for growth, social reform, and political participation at the state level. It has also turned far more attention to forging a consensus and developing interparty coordination on a wide range of economic, social, and foreign policy issues. To reiterate, India's federal revolution is real, but it is grinding away slowly.

## The Social Revolution

India's federal revolution is closely related to what Indian intellectuals have referred to as a "social churning" and, as already mentioned, what V. S. Naipaul has termed "A Million Mutinies Now."[52] This social revolution pits middle and low castes and India's many tribes against one another and against once-dominant high castes in a sometimes violent struggle for power.

Violence in rural India falls into two broad categories: "traditional" conflict instigated by high castes attempting to control the poorest and most backward castes and tribes (sometimes with the connivance of the police), and conflict instigated by the poor resisting high-caste domination. In these conflicts poor Muslims behave like another caste, and much "religious" conflict in rural and urban India has less to do with faith than with social class, although Hindu-Muslim violence produces larger ideological waves and has an impact on foreign policy.

This ongoing social revolution is weakening the Indian caste system, one of history's most hierarchically organized social systems. It is a revolution dictated by the logic of democratic politics and bears some resemblance to the revolution that accompanied the Civil Rights movement in the United States.[53] It began slowly, sparked by British determination to put certain tribes and "untouchable" castes under state protection. These groups, known as "scheduled castes and tribes," came to the attention of Mahatma Gandhi as he steered the Congress party on a course of radical social reform.[54] Gandhi felt that the scheduled castes, which he termed "Harijans," or "Children of God," had to be elevated socially before India would be worthy of independence.[55] Gandhi's concerns were embedded in the Indian constitution, which technically makes the practice of untouchability illegal. Laws were passed that created the most elaborate system of quotas and reservations of any democracy in the world. During the 1970s these laws brought relief from official discrimination to a whole generation of untouchable and low-caste Indians (and tribal groups). In the 1980s, these individuals organized into increasingly militant movements, many operating independently of other political parties and known as Dalits.[56]

The Dalits took as their father figure not Gandhi, but B. R. Ambedkar, a leading American-trained untouchable, the chief author of the Indian constitution, and a convert to Buddhism from Hinduism. During the 1990s the Dalits and low castes, as well as Muslims (who tend to be

among the poorest of Indians), broke from Congress and assumed a share of power in an increasing number of states. A similar process took place among India's tribal population, which in a few states in the northeast has come to power, displacing caste Hindus or Muslims.

These movements have often faced strong opposition. In states such as Uttar Pradesh, which has a large and oppressed Dalit population, statues of Ambedkar have replaced those of Nehru and Gandhi, and their desecration (by high castes) frequently precipitates riots, or worse. High castes have resisted the emergence of middle castes, which in turn have resented the emergence of untouchables, scheduled castes, Harijans, Dalits, and poor Muslims. The poor Muslims, although not eligible for the quotas and reservations directed against the inequalities implicit in the Hindu caste system, had been part of the Congress coalition. Conflicts between Hindus and the newly assertive tribal populations frequently had religious overtones, since many of the latter were converts to Christianity.

Evidence from those states whose internal social revolutions are well advanced (Tamil Nadu and Andhra Pradesh in the south and West Bengal in the north) suggests that this highly stressful and often-violent period evolves in a certain pattern. First, new groups stake their claim to political power, challenging the existing political order. Second, the dissatisfied (or outnumbered) may seek help from their internal and external diasporas. In some instances (Punjab, Nagaland, and Kashmir), dissenting groups seek help from foreign countries. This cross-border assistance may flow in the other direction as well. Perhaps the most important example occurred in Tamil Nadu, where populist Tamil nationalists vied with one another to support terrorist or separatist groups in Sri Lanka. In turn, Tamil Tiger hit squads were used in Tamil Nadu politics to settle old scores. The politics of Tamil Nadu, Sri Lanka, and New Delhi became tragically intertwined, contributing in part to the assassination of Rajiv Gandhi while he was campaigning in Tamil Nadu.

These social revolutions have contributed to greater violence and insecurity among high and low castes alike. At times this has created a fertile environment for organized crime syndicates, complete with Godfathers and Mafias carrying light weapons and organized into private "senas" or armies. In some states, it is difficult to separate the politicians from the criminals; in others, the police are under the sway of high and middle castes and are used to hunt down and kill low-caste or tribal leaders in what are euphemistically called "police encounters."

Thus India's social churning has come at a price. From the mid-1980s on, many of India's most important states, sometimes referred to as a group under the title BIMARU (Bihar, Madhya Pradesh, Rajasthan, and Uttar Pradesh (all parts of the conservative "Cow Belt") have become extremely violent and unstable.[57] Bihar, Uttar Pradesh, and Orissa together account for half of India's poor.[58] According to one recent report, more than 200 of India's 535 districts are experiencing insurgency, ethnic conflict, extremism, caste clashes, and other crises. Of the 69 districts in the northeast, 48 are affected by insurgency and ethnic violence.[59] India's cities no longer resemble the orderly cantonment-dominated British–Indian metropoles so much as the corrupt, violent, machine-dominated cities of nineteenth-century Britain or early-twentieth-century America.

These social revolutions have contributed to the general increase in police violence and illegal detentions. The New York–based Freedom House used to rate India as a "free" country (except for the years of Indira Gandhi's Emergency). Yet since 1991 the ranking has slipped to "partly free" because of the Kashmir uprising and the brutal methods used to suppress separatist movements in the northeast. Kashmir itself has a rating of 6.0, "not free," while India as an aggregate had a rating of partly free, although in 1998–99 that reverted to free. These are admittedly crude measures, but are in line with the view of many foreign and Indian observers.[60]

While there has been a great increase in the state's coercive power over the past fifteen years, it has not kept up with the increase in social violence. In many areas the police themselves have become co-opted by criminals, who wield considerable political influence. As a result, paramilitary forces, which now approach the army in size, perform basic police functions while the army is forced to carry out tasks more appropriate to the paramilitary forces. India badly needs a thoroughgoing transformation of its police and paramilitary forces. The former, once a proud service, remain a "top-down" instrument of state power (they were originally modeled after the Royal Irish Constabulary); the latter could also be reduced in size if they were more professional and had a clearer mission.

## The Transformed Diaspora

There are two major categories of overseas Indians: persons of Indian origin (PIOs) and nonresident Indians (NRIs). Together, PIOs and NRIs

number some 20 million people; after the overseas Chinese, they constitute the second largest diaspora in the world.[61] The largest community,
made up almost entirely of PIOs, is in Malaysia, with more than 1.7
million people. Other large communities reside in the United States (1.5
million), Saudi Arabia (1.3 million), the United Arab Emirates (1.2 million), and Great Britain (1 million), and there are substantial communities in Mauritius, Canada, Fiji, Burma, Bahrain, and Tanzania.

The PIOs derive largely from the days when India was a great source
of labor throughout the British Empire, after Britain ended its own slave
trade in the early nineteenth century. Millions of desperately poor Indians emigrated to Fiji, the West Indies, East Africa, Ceylon, Malaya, and
other British colonies to work in mines and on plantations. They often
went as bonded laborers living in conditions that were not much better
than slavery. In many cases, they were tended to by Indian professionals
(doctors, businessmen, and lawyers such as Gandhi, who began his law
career in South Africa). During the 1950s, there was substantial Indian
migration to the United Kingdom, where Indians filled the service sectors of British society.

The diaspora of the past three decades, which has produced several
million nonresident Indians, is quite different. By the 1970s the Indian
educational system began to produce trained physicians, engineers, and
scientists in greater numbers than the Indian economy could absorb.
The highly bureaucratic and rigid organization of many Indian institutions, plus policies of reverse discrimination, were also a powerful disin-
centive for many to remain in India or to return if they were abroad.
They constitute India's new, rich diaspora, and most of it has landed in
the United States.

About 25 percent of the graduating classes of the four prestigious
Indian Institutes of Technology go to the United States. About half of all
Indian scientists trained in the United States stay there on a semiperma-
nent basis.[62] The result has been an Indian presence in the United States
that is unmatched in its economic standing, social status, and, increasingly, political influence by any other recent immigrant group. In several
areas, such as computers, engineering, and advanced research, Indian-
American talent may well exceed the talent available in India itself.
More than 40 percent of new start-ups in Silicon Valley are owned by
Indian Americans. Many major American aerospace companies have
large numbers of engineers and scientists from India. Boeing's vice president for exports is an aerospace engineer of Indian origin. Two of the

principal executives in the recent merger between USAir and United Airlines are Indian-Americans. Officials of Northrop once mused that they could build an Indian light combat aircraft more cheaply and better simply by using their own Indian-American employees than by collaborating with India's Hindustan Aircraft.

## The Revitalizing Revolution

India is now in the throes of a challenge to one of the foundations of Nehruvian India, a secular or civil nationalism. This has come under attack from the Hindu revitalist movement, frequently described in the Western press as "Hindu fundamentalists" or "Hindu nationalists." However, the term "revitalist" best captures the thrust of India's new Hindu-oriented politics, epitomized by the BJP-RSS combine and other members of the Hindu "Parivar" or family.[63] It is not a return to an earlier era or even to fundamentalism—the strict adherence to religious or social texts—but seeks to use the state and modern technology to energize or revitalize values that are perceived to have been prominent in the past. According to India's revitalists, these were submerged in the Nehruvian era, which the BJP regards as catering to special, minority pressures rather than the desires and interests of India's Hindu majority.

India's long-standing revitalist revolution was one of the alternative visions of India that emerged in the Nationalist movement. The Congress party was the "mainstream," favoring a secular state, albeit one that would have the state managing and supporting religious institutions (a practice of the British, who regulated Hindu temples, Muslim mosques, Sikh gurdwaras, and Christian churches). Only a secular state could bring economic prosperity, political stability, and moral grandeur to India. The Congress welcomed Muslims into its fold, and many important Indian Muslim politicians were Congress party members.[64]

But Congress was not unchallenged, and there were other competing visions of India. One was that of the Muslim League, which favored a separate state for Indian Muslims. The Muslim League did help establish Pakistan, a separate homeland for Indian Muslims, and the very existence of Pakistan constitutes a continuing rejection of Congress's secular ideology. The other alternative to Congress was the Hindu Mahasabha, which favored a special role for Hindus in an independent India.

The Mahasabha shared many views with Congress. One was that Indians—or Hindus—have been weak and have allowed others to invade their country, steal their property, and rule them with impunity. This was an important theme in Gandhi's political philosophy, and his great genius was his nonviolent resistance to evil, a strategy that would both restore the self-esteem of Indians and build a new and positive relationship with the former antagonist.

While Gandhi's militant nonviolence was widely supported in theory if not always in practice, others responded differently to the dilemma of Hindu and Indian weakness. India has a strong tradition of terrorism, and such figures as Bhagat Singh have become folk heroes (he was a young Sikh hanged for the bombing death of a British policeman). Swami Dyanand praised violence as a cathartic act and gave it an explicitly Hindu tinge. Subsequently, Nehru's great rival, Subhas Chandra Bose, while a secularist, also stressed the virtue of force as an instrument of policy.

The Jana Sangh was the Hindu Mahasabha's political successor. The Jana Sangh contested elections at the state and national level. It was particularly strong in several northern states and among refugees from Pakistan. However, the spiritual backbone of the Jana Sangh was provided by an ostensibly nonpolitical organization, the Rashtriya Swayamsevak Sangh. The RSS's founder, K. B. Hegdewar, believed that Hindu Dharma (destiny) was sick, and in need of reform. He created "shakas" (training camps) to instill discipline, pride, and a martial spirit into RSS members. Most senior leaders of the Jana Sangh have been RSS members. When the Jana Sangh merged with other parties to form the Janata party in 1978, a major issue was the continuing membership of its politicians and cadres in the RSS. When the Janata experiment collapsed, the "political" side of the movement achieved expression in the Bharatiya Janata party (Indian People's party). Although as recently as the 1980 election, the BJP had won only two parliamentary seats, it had strong cadres in many states and could count on the support of the RSS and a growing number of "Sangh Parivar" (brother) organizations. The BJP steadily expanded from its north and west strongholds and its high-caste base, often exploiting Hindu-Muslim riots as way of recruiting new members.

The BJP and its Parivar (family) argue that India is composed of an essentially Hindu society. Therefore the state should reflect the values and ambitions of the Hindus, just as western states reflect the values and ambitions of their Christian population, the Muslim states reflect Islam, and Israel embodies the values and aspirations of Jews. The Hindu revitalists argue that India must act in the world as a *Hindu* civilization-state.[65] Non-Hindus are welcome to live in India, but only if they accept the fundamentally Hindu nature of the country.

The BJP's breakthrough came in 1990, when the party chairman, L. K. Advani, completed a circumambulation of India in a "Rath Yatra," echoing both Gandhi's marches and traditional pilgrimages.[66] This triggered over 300 riots. These were surpassed by the massive communal riots that followed the destruction of the Babri Masjid in December 1992 by the BJP, the VHP, the Bajrang Dal, and the Shiv Sena, the Maharashtra ally of the BJP. These were India's worst-ever riots after Partition, with thousands of deaths, often under gruesome circumstances.[67]

The Parivar's activities have included attacks on Christians. Indeed, in recent years these have increased dramatically, whereas Hindu-Muslim violence has declined, for a number of practical reasons. In areas where the BJP is in power, it does not want to see law and order degraded, particularly because of the possibility that anti-Muslim riots could push Muslim voters back into the Congress party. While Christian voters are numerically inconsequential (except in Kerala, parts of the northeast, and Goa), the assault against them is based on the same argument as that against Muslims: their religion is that of a foreign civilization that came to India to conquer, plunder, and convert. Unlike Jews and Parsis, who migrated to India in small numbers and who have lived without incident for many hundreds of years, Muslims and Christians are seen as a potential fifth column working on behalf of Christian and Muslim countries. In recent years there have been shocking acts of violence against Indian Christians and foreign missionaries, such as the murder of an Australian missionary and his sons who were burned alive in 1999.

The Sangh Parivar's ideological revolution has also produced a struggle for control over Indian educational and cultural institutions. The BJP and the Parivar have attempted to rectify what they see as a distorted view of Indian history and an improper neglect of some aspects of Indian culture. This struggle is especially important in states such as Gujarat where the BJP commands a majority. In such circumstances, the BJP and its affiliated organizations can experiment more freely by placing constraints on Hindu-Muslim marriages, check the activities of Christian missionaries, attack missionary and convent schools, and rewrite school textbooks according to party ideology. In Gujarat, permission was given (but then retracted, because of protests from other parties, including the BJP's coalition partners) to allow government employees to join the RSS, breaking a long-standing prohibition of membership in what the Congress party had defined as an extremist organization (the RSS has been banned intermittently over the years).[68] However, the BJP may have suffered because of this policy (and because of the attempt by its political ally, the extremist Shiv Sena, to expand its operations from Maharashtra into the urban areas of Gujarat). The BJP suffered heavily in local elections held in October 2000, despite a split in Gujarat's Congress party.[69]

The revitalist revolution shows no sign of abating. Social and caste tensions, the stresses of rapid and uneven economic growth, and the erosion of traditional caste norms spur it on. Support for militant nationalist parties, especially the BJP, has been accelerated by televised coverage of the Kargil war and the December 1999 hijacking of an Indian Airlines plane by militant Islamicists from Kathmandu to Kandahar (by way of India, Pakistan, and the Gulf). These have intensified the sense of India under siege and the need for a militant response to domestic and foreign threats, both important themes of the BJP, the RSS, and members of the Parivar.

Yet several factors temper the rise of militant nationalism in Indian politics. First, the growth of powerful state parties has created (and reflects) a loyalty to regional traditions and ambitions. Of the state parties, only the BJP's Maharashtran ally, the Shiv Sena, shares its militancy, which also means that it competes with the BJP for the same type of voter. Other state parties have worked with the BJP in alliances at the center but are wary of its growth in their own states and have forced a watering-down of much of the BJP's national cultural agenda. The BJP is compelled by its radical elements and the Parivar to take extreme positions, but in the last six years it has been pulled back to the Indian center by the logic of coalition politics and the need to meet the test of elections.

The acquisition of political power has created tension within the BJP and between it and its Parivar supporters. Party members who do not have an RSS background (such as Jaswant Singh, or K. C. Pant) are considered suspect. To the true believer, they represent a dilution of party and Parivar values. Only the presence of the widely respected Atal Behari Vajpayee has averted open conflict. Ironically, such events as Kargil and the 1999 hijacking have further polarized the Parivar. The Kargil war was masterfully reinterpreted as a great victory for India, and the BJP took full credit for the "success" in throwing the Pakistanis out. The hijacking could not be seen as anything but a humiliating defeat for India and for the party that proclaimed that it would restore Hindu and Indian pride. The most prominent spokesman for the hard-line view, L. K. Advani, proclaimed the outcome of the hijacking a success for the Indian people (because only one Indian hostage was killed), but a defeat for the BJP. The party had always urged a tough line of no bargaining when dealing with terrorists and hijackers, but here a BJP-dominated government and a BJP minister (Jaswant Singh) were forced into humiliating concessions to save the lives of Indian passengers, many of whom fit the profile of typical BJP supporters (middle-class, urban Hindus). These tensions will continue, although the BJP seems to be better able than Congress to manage such differences and avoid fatal splits in the party. BJP functionaries argue that their success in managing coalitions can be traced to their long history as an opposition party—hence they understand the psychology of the "outsider"—and to the traditions of the party, especially the skill of such leaders as S. P. Mookerjee, who founded the BJP's precursor party, the Jana Sangh, in 1951.[70]

Finally, the actual policies pursued by the BJP at the center and in the states reveal that the party has no magic formula for governance. Communal riots, which are tolerable when one is in opposition, are unacceptable while one is in office. The BJP cannot afford to have India's 110 million Muslims view the party as their sworn enemy.[71] Good relations with Pakistan, with the United States, and China and sound economic policies demand that ideology be tempered by pragmatism. As the party has learned in national, state, and by-elections from 1996 to 2000, it does not yet have the strength wielded by Congress in the 1950s and 1960s; it is not yet automatically India's "first" political party.

It is unlikely that the Indian revitalist revolution will achieve victory. Instead, the BJP and its Parivar allies will retain an important but not decisive position in Indian politics. Like Likud in Israel, or the Christian right in the United States, it can count on the fervent support of its cadres. Nevertheless, to maintain its hold on power, the BJP must temper its policies, work in coalitions, and, inevitably, run the risk of disillusioning its core supporters.

## India as a Revolutionary State

South Asian specialists tend to preface their answer to questions about Indian society and politics with the caveat, "Well, it depends." In an era of unprecedented domestic change "it depends" even more. India is a paradox, a seemingly impoverished country racked by political instability, yet it is also a rich and powerful country, especially when viewed from the perspective of its smaller neighbors or in terms of gross measures of economic and military capability.

While distance tends to magnify capabilities and vulnerabilities, making the task of understanding India more difficult, there is no doubt that it is in the throes of a series of belated social, economic, political, and ideological revolutions of unprecedented magnitude. These affect its economic prospects, its federal structure, its social order, and its very identity. The economic and social revolutions are far advanced and unstoppable. The shift in power between the union and state governments (the federal revolution) was unplanned and unexpected and was largely a function of the decay in Congress and the concomitant rise in state parties, although it was hastened by the onset of an economic crisis in the early 1990s. India's ideological revolution, which pits intellectual against intellectual, party against party, and one vision of India against another could move in any of several directions. Together, these revolutions are changing the face of India and will inevitably have a complex and diverse impact on India's status as a great or emerging power. Three general points may be made about them.

First, they have been amplified and intensified by the rapid expansion of electronic communications over the past eight years. This has been a revolution in its own right. In 1991 India had one feeble state television channel; by the end of the decade it had become a major base for a half-dozen Indian and Asian television networks, several of which cover thirty to forty countries. While these networks have taken full advantage of India's powerful film industry, they have also relied heavily on India's English-speaking elite for commentators, analysts, and reporters. Cable television and satellite systems brought new images to India, and there are now two news networks broadcasting twenty-four hours to the country. Indians can also view broadcasts from America (CNN), Britain (BBC), and Pakistan (Pakistan Television). The four elections of the 1990s were covered intensively by television in English and many regional languages, and the Kargil conflict of 1999 was India's first televised war; later that year the Kandahar hijacking was India's first televised hijacking.

By the end of the decade, the Internet had begun to play a significant role in India's politics. It enabled the diaspora to keep current with, and participate in, developments in India. The "net" also became another battleground between India and Pakistan, and between the government of India and many private human rights, environmental, and social reform groups that were quick to take advantage of it.[72] The main Indian political parties all have active web sites, as do various interests (ranging from human rights groups to the armed forces), most of the Indian states, and the regional political parties. India is now newly accessible to the world, but also newly vulnerable to the worldwide flow of ideas and information.

Second, while some of these revolutions have been accompanied by violence, most have been contained within India's democratic framework, and *the ballot box is seen as the arbiter of legitimacy.* Democracy is not a goal in its own right, but a method for improving what is inevitably an imperfect and unjust society. The fact that India has seen the repeated transformation of revolutionary movements into evolutionary movements suggests that the present social tensions, violence, and disorder will eventually subside. Two regions of India, Assam in the northeast and Punjab in the northwest, were at one time seemingly hopelessly bogged down in terrorism, maldevelopment, corruption, and violence. Today both states are normal, and Punjab is thriving with beauty parlors and software schools as the new "sunrise" industry of the state.[73] Authoritarianism is no longer relied on, as it was under Indira Gandhi. The economically weak lower and backward castes understand that their power depends on their numbers, and they are enthusiastic supporters of democracy. The upper castes and classes of some states that have been the object of reverse discrimination (especially Tamil Nadu and Bengal) have not argued for the imposition of a totalitarian government but have often voted with their feet, reestablishing themselves in the state capital, moving to New Delhi, or migrating.

Third, these revolutions are spread unevenly across India. Some states remain backward and poor, while others have experienced phenomenal growth in income, literacy, voter participation, and good government. India must not be seen as an undifferentiated whole, but as a continent-sized country comparable in diversity and social development to a Europe: it has the criminal politics of a Sicily and the enlightened democracy of a Sweden. The mass media, popular entertainment, and many shared cultural elements hold India together, as do the IAS, the civil and military bureaucracies, and most of the political parties. They all differ over the direction India should take, but there is little fear that a significant separatist movement will arise in the near or medium term or that India will somehow splinter into its constituent parts.

Finally, these revolutions have taken place at a moment in history when India's external political and strategic environment was unusually fluid and increasingly unpredictable. It has been difficult enough for the Indian strategic and political community to grasp these changes, but they have also had to factor in domestic developments of unprecedented magnitude. It is no wonder that there is widespread consensus among the strategic community that India's security problems stem as much from domestic sources as from abroad. It is beyond the scope of this book to attempt to predict the outcome of these revolutions. Like an unruly troika, they pull India in different directions.

To summarize, a few general observations can be made about the effect of these revolutions on India's possible role as a great power.

—There will be unsettling violence in the environment in which policy decisions are made; New Delhi itself is turning from a garden city into an unpleasant, crowded, and polluted megalopolis; the sense of physical unease and danger has been greatly enhanced by sensational television coverage of riots, hijackings, and border wars.

—Indian foreign policy managers will continue to be sensitive to ethnic, religious minorities; this is fundamental to management of the Indian system, because in the new Indian politics, there are many more "veto" groups linked to smaller state and national parties that may be part of a national coalition.

—The Indian states will continue to grow in power, especially in the economic sphere, but they will not displace the center. Indeed, some of them will be challenged, and balanced, by new states created out of distinctive regions, offering the chance for a "fresh start" for such regions as the hill areas of Uttar Pradesh (now formed into Uttarkhand) or the tribal belt of Bihar, which has become the state of Chattisgarh.

—India's historical north-south division—roughly along the Vindyas, and separating the primarily Hindi-speaking belt from the rest of the country—is no longer the only important national division. There is a growing gap between the richest and most rapidly developing states and the poorest and most backward ones. Some of the fastest-growing states are in the south, but Punjab and West Bengal have shown remarkable growth, and some of the newer states can be expected to move ahead quickly.

—The Indian diaspora will play a greater role in key countries, especially the United States; it will develop closer links to India itself, and the Indian government will view it as a political and economic asset.

—The rapid changes in the Indian party structure and the rise of coalition government have made it impossible to pretend that there is a consensus on Indian foreign policy. New mechanisms of consultation and consensus building have yet to be worked out. Attitudes on many specific issues, such as nuclear weapons, remain fragmented.

The many Indian revolutions now under way may not all succeed, but not so many of them are likely to fail or go awry that India will become a problem because of its weaknesses rather than its potential strengths. In a world of imploding and dividing states, this is important. India should be given more credit for its generally peaceful revolutionary process. This should be factored into the moral intangibles that contribute to a balanced estimate of India's strengths and weaknesses. The complexity of these revolutions also ensures that India will not move about the international stage in a swift, highly aggressive manner. Rather, it will continue to have difficulty choosing its direction and maintaining a consistent course. India cannot become a tiger, but it may be a still lumbering but more efficient elephant.

## FIVE

*India as a Military Power*

FOR A STATE THAT ACHIEVED its independence by peaceful means and often proclaimed its commitment to the peaceful resolution of disputes, India has had a large number of armed conflicts. These include four wars with Pakistan, one with China, numerous border skirmishes with each, and several military interventions in smaller neighbors. Moreover, much of India's large army and almost all of its paramilitary forces (which alone number nearly a million men) are devoted to checking the many separatist movements that have cropped up. In addition, India has on several occasions used its military power outside of its immediate neighborhood, either by itself or in concert with other powers. There have been several UN peacekeeping operations, and India demonstrated a formidable airlift capability when it transferred more than 100,000 Indian citizens from Iraq and Kuwait just before the start of the Gulf War in 1991. This chapter offers an overview of the development of India's present military establishment (excluding the nuclear program, which will be examined in chapter 6), its use of military power in several wars, and a series of crises, some of which had nuclear overtones. While the recent Kargil crisis may lead to cosmetic changes in defense policy, it is not likely to fundamentally change either India's continental outlook or its cautious strategic style.

## Defense as Development: 1947–62

The origins of postwar security policy can be traced to the pre-independence views of Indian nationalist politicians rather than guidelines followed by British strategists responsible for India's defense right up to 1947. The British conducted an active diplomacy in all of India's neighbors and during World War II accepted significant American military assistance. This turned India into a major arms producer and a base for military operations in China, Southeast Asia, and the Persian Gulf.

However, free India's two most important leaders, Mahatma Gandhi and Jawaharlal Nehru, had reservations about the use of force. Gandhi admired the armed forces for their discipline, but rejected their use when other paths (nonviolence) were available. Gandhi and the Indian nationalists preferred to go to jail rather than support either the war effort or armed insurrection. In the first important application of what was later to be termed "nonalignment," Gandhi did not want the Japanese to win, but neither would he support the Allied war effort.

India's first prime minister, Jawaharlal Nehru, brought to the office a strong distaste for armed forces and things military. He wrote scathingly of the soldier, "bred in a different atmosphere, where authority reigns and criticism is not tolerated. So he resents the advice of others, and, when he errs, errs thoroughly and persists in error. For him the chin is more important than the mind or brain."[1] Piling on the ridicule, Nehru wrote of the military man who, "stiffening to attention, drops his humanity and, acting as an automaton, shoots and kills inoffensive and harmless persons who have done him no ill."[2]

Believing, too, that the Indian Army had been a tool of the Raj, and thus was not to be trusted, Nehru not surprisingly focused most of India's postwar energies on building state power, but not state military power.[3] He took seriously his own statements about the priority of internal economic development, so defense budgets remained stagnant. Nehru and most of his peers were cautious about pursuing policies that exceeded India's limited military capabilities. India had more than enough military power to fight Pakistan to a standstill in 1948, to overwhelm the Nizam of Hyderabad's forces the same year, and to overrun the weakly defended Portuguese colonies of Goa, Daman, and Diu in 1961. For Nehru's generation, this was enough. Nehru and his confidants saw defense spending as detrimental to both economic growth and civilian dominance. It was the erection of a strong industrial and economic infrastructure, not the acquisition of arms, that would be critical to India's long-term independence. Nehru's stewardship was an economist's and planner's heaven. Indian defense planning was virtually nonexistent, an afterthought, once the Soviet-inspired five-year plans were implemented.[4]

During World War II, however, India became a major military power, with American assistance. The U.S. and British governments determined that India could be an important source of cheap and trained manpower and a base from which to pursue the war against Japan. A 1942 mission led by Henry Grady, later the first U.S. ambassador to India, developed a plan that turned India into a significant arms producer.[5]

Taking a comprehensive view of the problem, the Grady mission argued that India could not become a major military power without changes in its economic policy. Since Britain was unable to spare equipment, expertise, or raw materials, it was proposed, and eventually accepted, that the United States would help India expand production lines and manufacture or assemble a number of military systems.

The American-supported and funded defense production effort inaugurated a process of backward linkage that tied the requirements of defense production to India's overall economic strategy. It also "involved the United States in the industrial exploitation of the subcontinent for a war effort to which the future leaders of India had refused to give their support."[6] While on the one hand many American politicians, including President Franklin D. Roosevelt, strongly favored Indian independence, the nationalists, especially Nehru, were fearful of American dominance of this critical sector. Even though the Indian armed forces had war-surplus American equipment, Delhi continued to rely on Britain for defense technology and expertise and eventually purchased a number of second-tier British systems, including Canberra bombers (still operational in 2001 in a reconnaissance role), Centurion tanks, and surplus World War II British vessels.

It took the growing tensions with China and the 1958 coup in Pakistan to persuade the government to reconsider its overall security policy. Nehru appointed his confidant, V. K. Krishna Menon, as minister of defense to bring about greater military self-reliance.[7] There was new emphasis on indigenous production and licensing, rather than the purchase of complete systems from foreign suppliers, and—despite Nehru's contempt for the "merchants of death"—an effort was made to market these weapons abroad. Thirty-five years later, the Indian government is pursuing the same policy, although conditions are even less favorable for the growth of an independent Indian arms industry.

Nehru not only disliked the armed forces, he distrusted them. One of Menon's tasks was to help control the generals: Nehru had been shocked by developments in Pakistan, when its army seized power. There were also rumors of military dissatisfaction in India, and one army chief, K. S. Thimayya, eventually resigned. No evidence has ever been produced to support these rumors, but Nehru wanted a trusted friend to head up the Ministry of Defense and keep watch over the generals.

Neither Nehru nor Menon attempted to develop a coherent security doctrine. The strategy of "nonalignment" was designed to avoid conflict, not to anticipate and prepare for it. Nehru was not interested in military policy, and none of his advisers had any experience in military and security matters before Partition (as noted in chapter 3, the highest-ranking Indian officer in 1947 was a brigadier). They were content to keep control over the military—and over strategic policy—through decisions on individual weapons, and even then their answer was usually "no."

## India's Strategic Framework

Despite this distaste for security and defense policy, India did inherit a number of security concepts from the British, most notably the defense of the Himalayas. These ideas were retained as India signed security treaties with Nepal and Bhutan (and later absorbed Sikkim). Only the British role in Tibet was liquidated, a gesture toward China that earned Nehru little goodwill. The following postindependence treaties formalized and consolidated earlier British-Indian ties with smaller neighbors.[8]

—The 1949 Indo-Bhutan Treaty of Friendship required Bhutan to be guided by the government of India in its external relations; while Bhutan sees this as binding only with respect to matters concerning India's interests, the Indian interpretation is that the treaty restricts Bhutan's relations with other states more broadly.

—The 1950 Indo-Sikkim Treaty of Peace kept Sikkim a protectorate of India with autonomy in internal affairs, but the defense of Sikkim was India's responsibility.

—The 1950 Indo-Nepal Treaty of Peace and Friendship and Treaty (for) Trade and Commerce replaced a 1923 treaty that had been a "standstill agreement" from 1947. Article 2 requires that each state inform the other of "serious friction . . . with any neighboring state likely to cause breach (of) friendship between the two governments." Article 5 granted Nepal permission to import arms "from or through" India. This became an agreement to make India the sole supplier of arms.

—Treaty of Friendship with Burma, 1951.

—India-Ceylon agreement on immigration, 1954 (and 1964).

Thus India assumed the Raj's strategic commitment to all but one of its South Asian neighbors. The exception, of course, was Pakistan. Until 1954, India did not consider Pakistan a serious military threat. Most of the Indian leadership, including Nehru, expected Pakistan to collapse and return to the fold. Not until 1954, when America agreed to supply Pakistan with modern arms and forged an alliance relationship was Pakistan perceived as a threat. The earlier conflict in Kashmir was seen in India as purely defensive and limited; India even allowed the United Nations to play a major role in its resolution, first bringing the dispute to the Security Council in 1948, and then, after the UN mandated cease-fire on January 1, 1949, allowing UN observers to be stationed along both sides of the cease-fire line.

Except for waging a limited war in Kashmir in the early years after independence (1947–48), India employed force only for domestic reasons. The armed forces were used to absorb the princely state of Hyderabad (1948) and to invade and absorb Portugal's Indian colonies, most notably Goa (1961). The Goa invasion, which angered the United States and other North Atlantic Treaty Organization (NATO) allies of Portugal, was prompted in part by Menon's desire to boost his political fortunes in a forthcoming election (Menon represented the Bombay South constituency, which had a number of Goans).

The mountainous border with China in the Himalayas was inactive in the 1950s, in the sense that Indians could not conceive of a major conflict with China. However, domestic pressures and incompetent diplomacy contributed to an eventual confrontation with China, a confrontation for which India was ill-prepared and which produced a military and foreign policy catastrophe that still shadows India-China relations.[9] Nehru and Krishna Menon had believed that the Chinese were bluffing and were poorly informed about Chinese strategic policies and style. They thought that India could play a game of high-altitude checkers along the border, placing troops in front of and behind Chinese posts (thirty years later, a probe testing the Chinese in the same area was whimsically named "Exercise Checkerboard" by General K. Sundarji). After underplaying the border conflict, the Indian leadership began to exploit it to whip up public opinion. Eventually, India could not retreat militarily because it could not retreat politically.

Guided by Menon and a number of unqualified generals, Nehru miscalculated seriously, triggering a Chinese attack across the vague and contested line separating the two armies. The Indians were so poorly prepared and badly led that Chinese forces (the PLA) advanced much further than even they had expected. Ultimately, and embarrassingly for the Indians, the Chinese unilaterally withdrew to the line they had offered as a compromise and India had refused to accept.

The confrontation also led to a closer relationship with the United States, then searching for allies to contain Red China. Earlier, India had acquired substantial amounts of surplus World War II American weapons.[10] After the India-China war, Washington and Delhi engaged in close cooperation, including intelligence sharing. For several years afterward Washington provided $80 million in grant military aid and sold India a number of advanced but largely defensive systems. This angered Pakistan without convincing India that the United States was a firm supporter. India wanted the United States to provide weapons without qualification, but Washington was reluctant to do so. It insisted that whatever equipment it provided was not to be used on the frontier with Pakistan. Washington refused to supply advanced F-104 fighters but was willing to equip a number of mountain divisions, provide air defense technology, engage in joint exercises, and help India improve its antiquated defense budgeting and planning process, introducing the idea of a rolling five-year defense plan. Simultaneously, Washington prodded India and Pakistan to deal with the Kashmir dispute, the third and last U.S. effort to resolve the Kashmir dispute. There was no direct linkage between military assistance and progress on Kashmir.

On the Subcontinent itself, the frontier with East Pakistan was never militarized, and a purely defensive strategy was adopted toward West Pakistan. The Indian Army was still a small force in the late 1950s. At sea, no naval threat was envisaged as long as Britain maintained a presence in the Far East, and there was close cooperation between the Royal Navy and the tiny Indian fleet.

India's forces have also taken part in several UN peacekeeping operations. New Delhi contributed an infantry battalion to UN operations in the Gaza Strip from 1956 onward. A much larger contingent of the Indian Army and Air Force served in the Congo in 1961. Smaller groups of often no more than a dozen Indian military personnel were involved in UN monitoring and peacekeeping exercises in Korea (1953), Indochina (1954), Lebanon (1958), Angola (1988), and along the Iran-Iraq border.

India sent 900 troops to Rwanda in 1994. The Indian Army and Air Force also played a role in peacekeeping in Somalia in 1993–94, suffering a dozen fatalities; the navy ferried these troops to and from Somalia, and in 1999 there was a large contingent of Indian forces as part of the UN peacekeeping operation in Sierra Leone. Indian officers have been prominent in these and other UN operations: Major General Inderjit Rikhye served as a military adviser to the United Nations for many years (subsequently cofounding the International Peace Academy), and recently Lieutenant General Satish Nambiar headed UNPROFOR in Bosnia.

However, some of these peacekeeping operations revealed that Indian forces do not always operate smoothly in the context of a multinational force. Nambiar quit UNPROFOR in anger, and after the Indian head of the Sierra Leone operation criticized his Nigerian colleagues, India withdrew its entire peacekeeping force from Sierra Leone. It may be that the background and training of Indian officers make it hard for them to work within a coalition framework, although there is no question as to the quality and bravery of the forces under their command.

## Expansion and Defeat of Pakistan: 1962–71

The embarrassing defeat by China in October 1962 led to the formulation of an Indian strategic doctrine and the partial transformation of the Indian security apparatus. It was determined that the Indian armed forces would have to be reorganized and newly equipped, and that India would have to plan for a two-front conflict. Therefore its strategy could not be purely defensive. Like the Israelis, Indians knew they could not afford to be bled in a defensive war on one front and still expect to defeat a major enemy on the other. Attitudes toward defense spending and development also changed radically. Leading Indian strategists argued not only that increased defense spending was necessary for military security, but that it made a positive contribution to economic development.[11] A defense-led strategy of economic growth would improve India's R&D sector and speed up the arrival of defense autarchy (even if it temporarily increased dependence upon foreign suppliers and technologies). This strategy of defense-led growth has been pursued most effectively in the electronics industry and in some fields of metallurgy and heavy forging. However, the approach was never tried in the aircraft industry, and the civilian nuclear program (begun in the mid-1940s) was always ahead of any military applications, although it did provide a base on which the military nuclear program was quickly erected.

From 1963 to 1965 there was a burst of military cooperation with the West. Commonwealth and U.S. air force units conducted exercises with the air force in India; the defense planning process was influenced by American thinking and a large American military mission took up residence in Delhi. Plans were also drawn up to provide India with substantial technical and material support to modernize its armed services, with the British taking responsibility for the navy and the United States for air and ground forces.

Indian military power thus grew rapidly after 1963. This was a factor in Pakistan's decision to probe the Indians in Kutch, a swampy region on the western India-Pakistan border in the first months of 1965. Then with tribal proxies and Pakistan Army soldiers in mufti, it attempted the seizure of Kashmir in August 1965.[12] Foreign Minister Zulfiqar Ali Bhutto had persuaded the usually cautious President Ayub Khan that it was better to move militarily against India before it grew too powerful and would be impervious to Pakistan's views on Kashmir. India's response was not confined to Kashmir, however, and New Delhi expanded the war across the international frontier in the west, leading to full-scale armor and infantry engagements, although neither side moved in the east. The war resulted in a military standoff. Neither army performed well, and B. C. Chakravorty's official history (still suppressed) is scathing in its discussion of Indian generalship and the quality of Indian political leadership.

The 1965 war also provided the occasion for Washington and London to suspend the military aid and sales programs to both India and Pakistan. The U.S. Congress was especially incensed at the sight of two aid recipients deploying their American-supplied weapons against each other. President Lyndon Johnson was less concerned with South Asia than with the growing conflict in Vietnam, and his secretary of state, Dean Rusk, did not view India in the same positive light as had John F. Kennedy.

By 1971, even without full American cooperation, the reconstruction of India's armed forces had been completed and a major change in outlook had occurred. Dieter Braun, a leading West German analyst, observed the difference in outlook between 1963 and 1971: "Under Nehru, India pursued a globally oriented foreign policy with an eye on the power blocs of East and West and usually at a careful distance from them," but under Indira Gandhi priorities were changed and by the time

Bangladesh emerged, if not earlier, "the consolidation and protection of its dominating position in its own sub-region, along with the elimination of Pakistan's long-standing claim to the greatest possible parity with India, in particular, had become the primary goal."[13]

While Indira Gandhi was a nationalist, like her father she was also more insecure in dealing with the rest of the world and had a greater willingness to link military force and political power.[14] Her deprecation of the liberal idealism of her father and her emphasis on strength in dealing with smaller neighbors and superpowers alike struck a powerful response in the Indian political and military community. She remains the most militaristic politician ever to become prime minister in her willingness to resort to force both abroad and at home.[15]

Mrs. Gandhi led the Indian military to victory over Pakistan in December 1971. After an eight-month buildup, Indian forces crushed an outnumbered Pakistan Army contingent in East Pakistan.[16] The Indians skillfully orchestrated public diplomacy and events on the ground to make the intervention appear to be both just and necessary. India was in this case fortunate in its enemy: the Pakistani leadership contributed greatly to India's military and diplomatic success by its incoherent military strategy, inept public diplomacy, and brutality toward civilians in Pakistan's East Wing.

There was no serious fighting on India's western border with Pakistan, despite U.S. concern on that score. It would have been difficult for India to mount successful attacks in the west as long as the Pakistan Army retained its basic integrity. The battles fought there (especially along the Punjab/Kashmir front) showed the Indian Army at its most cautious.

The war in East Pakistan revealed another characteristic of Indian strategic policy, namely, a reluctance to commit significant orders or policies to paper. Even though the Indian defeat of the Pakistan Army seemed to be well planned, in fact no orders were actually issued for the capture of the capital of East Pakistan, Dhaka. It was later revealed that a senior Indian general took it upon himself to make the decision.[17] India's nuclear program has similarly been approved at each stage without formal written authorization, each prime minister making an ad hoc, verbal decision regarding nuclear policy (which gave scientists wide latitude in interpreting policy).

During the 1971 war, as in 1965, India had also been subjected to verbal warnings from China. Since the memory of the 1962 defeat was still fresh, there was some apprehension about what Beijing might do. Because the final Indian invasion of East Bengal was delayed until the winter season, however, there was no prospect of a ground attack by China across the frozen Himalayas.

Far more disturbing to the Indian leadership were the movements of the aircraft carrier *Enterprise*. The ship skirted the southern edge of the Bay of Bengal while heading westward and never came near the scene of fighting, remaining south of Sri Lanka. Nevertheless, its maneuvers had a profound impact on civilian policymakers and the Indian armed forces, especially the hitherto quiescent navy. What Richard Nixon and Henry Kissinger intended as a political gesture to an already defeated Pakistan and a new partner, China, lives on in Indian history as a symbolic demonstration of U.S. hostility to India. The fact that the *Enterprise* had in 1962 sailed into the Bay of Bengal on a mission in support of India against China was forgotten; the gambit was thereafter seen as the harbinger of an American strategy of encircling India. Furthermore, it was seen as an implicit nuclear threat (the *Enterprise* presumably carried nuclear weapons) and stimulated Indian interest in both strengthening seaward defense and acquiring a nuclear deterrent.[18] Its dramatic appearance on the strategic scene influenced an entire generation of Indian civilians and shaped Indian naval and nuclear strategy thereafter.

However, a few strategists saw the 1971 war as only a limited triumph. Pakistani morale was shattered but its armed forces were intact. Indian military analysts cautioned against a revival of Pakistani power. Leading Indian strategists, such as Inder Malhotra, D. K. Palit, and K. Subrahmanyam, tried to persuade a disinterested public that the old strategic doctrine had to be expanded in accordance with India's new status.[19] Their views were summarized by Verghese Koithara, then a young naval officer and later the author of a major study of Indian security policy. Koithara argued that India's security objectives had to include (a) the ability to fight China to a standstill in a nonnuclear war, (b) the means to inflict a quick and decisive defeat on Pakistan, and (c) the power to dissuade any nation along the Indian Ocean rimland—including the United States—from allying itself actively with either Pakistan or China.[20]

## From Dominance to Insignificance? 1972–80

After 1972 Indian diplomacy moved to consolidate its regionally dominant position earned by force of arms in 1972. India signed a further round of treaties with its smaller neighbors, the most important one being with Bangladesh, the former East Pakistan. Sikkim, a protectorate of India, was absorbed into the Indian Union after a staged demonstration of support for India in Gangtok, the capital. These treaties seemed to ensure India's regional predominance.

—In 1971 India signed the Trade and Transit Treaty with Nepal.

—The Indo-Bangladesh Treaty of Friendship, Cooperation and Peace was signed in 1972 (duration: twenty-five years). Article 8 stated that no military alliances could be joined that were directed at the other party, Article 9 that the territory of one state could not be used to threaten the other, and Article 10 that no assistance would be provided to third parties engaged in conflict with the other state. If there was a military attack, there were to be consultations to "eliminate" the threat. This treaty was subsequently renewed, and additional treaties regarding a shared power grid, trade, telecommunications, civilian nuclear technology, and cultural exchanges were quickly signed.

—Sikkim became an Associated State of the Union of India, 1974.

—On December 12, 1996, India and Bangladesh at last signed a thirty-year agreement on the sharing of the Ganga waters. A committee of experts was established and a joint commission created to oversee the implementation of the treaty, which allocated waters between India and Bangladesh during the dry season (when Bangladesh needed the water the most) and the rainy season.

—Separate trade and transit agreements were reached with Nepal, 1979.

The victory over Pakistan seemed to be decisive, as noted by Canadian-Indian scholar Baldev Raj Nayar: "The war in South Asia in 1971 resulted in a major restructuring of power in the region, raising India to a position of preeminence in the subcontinent and consequently making it an important middle power."[21] However, the Indian armed forces concluded that more weapons and a tougher posture were needed to guard against the rapid buildup of forces on India's land and sea borders. The *Enterprise* episode revealed how quickly the United States could change its policies, one year supporting India against China and only a few years later supporting both China and Pakistan against India. The *Enterprise,* as much as anything else, led to India's version of the Monroe doctrine, the "Indira Doctrine."[22]

The Indira Doctrine represented a tough, uncompromising attitude toward neighbors, large and small. Two principles were laid down: no foreign power should be allowed to cross the crest of the Himalayas, and India would consider the presence or influence of an external power in the region as adverse to its interests, unless that power recognized Indian predominance. In light of India's impotence during the Soviet invasion of Afghanistan, the latter now seems peculiarly optimistic. Also optimistic was the assumption that India could by itself gather enough power to keep outside states from exerting "influence" in South Asia. The United States could advance a Monroe Doctrine because it was far from the center of European power and could count on the tacit support of the Royal Navy. India was in a dangerous neighborhood: it did not have the power to keep others from interfering in the region. It hoped to rely on the Soviet Union to keep other major powers at a distance, but the USSR was itself indirectly responsible for a greatly expanded Chinese and American presence in and near South Asia when it invaded and occupied Afghanistan in December 1979.

The Indian public embraced the Indira Doctrine, although there was a feeling that with Soviet support, India need not rush to strengthen its military capabilities. However, the naval buildup did begin in earnest, largely with Soviet assistance. India delayed purchasing an advanced-strike aircraft to replace its aging Canberra bombers, although it did acquire twin-engine Jaguars in 1979, after a long debate as to whether the expense was necessary and whether India could make do with an upgraded MiG-21 (a single-engine interceptor). One reason the Indians chose the Jaguar was that it was one of the few available aircraft that would be capable of delivering an early-generation nuclear bomb.

The detonation of a nuclear device, ostensibly a "peaceful nuclear explosion," in 1974 appeared to confirm Delhi's premier regional position, since it demonstrated that India could become a nuclear weapons state if it wished to. However, Indira Gandhi's rule was soon challenged in court and on the streets, and she plunged India into a domestic "Emergency," her euphemism for a personalized dictatorship. Debate on military and foreign policy issues ground to a halt. It was not until early 1977 and the installation of the Janata government that the Indian strategic community returned to the question of security. It was clear that the international environment was changing, but to India's disadvantage. From Delhi's perspective, the most troubling new developments involved events in Pakistan, Iran, and China.

While Pakistan had begun to rearm after its 1971 defeat, Indians believed that they could deal with Zulfikar Ali Bhutto, who had emerged as Pakistan's undisputed leader after the armed forces were discredited for their handling of the war. When Bhutto was jailed in 1977 and the army assumed power, the reaction in India was extremely hostile. The working assumption of most Indian strategists is that Pakistan's generals are more anti-Indian than its civilians. Bhutto's fall was thought to be a threat to the bilateral process for resolving differences between him and Mrs. Gandhi that had been agreed to at Simla in 1972. The Indian elite seemed uninterested in Bhutto's efforts to acquire a nuclear weapon and were aware of—but discounted—his success in rearming Pakistan with Chinese and French weapons. The return of the Pakistan Army revived that country's image as India's major strategic enemy.

To the west, the fall of the Shah threatened a newly crafted Indo-Iranian strategic link and the continued steady supply of oil. The Iranian revolution had direct, domestic implications for Indian politics: there are more than 140 million Indian Muslims, and India has always been a center of Shi'ia thought.[23] New Delhi scrambled to open up ties to the new Islamic government. However, New Delhi had developed a close relationship with secular Iraq, with which it shared several weapons systems of Soviet origin, and Indian Air Force teams were sent to train the Iraqi Air Force. The Shah's fall also brought a large American fleet into the Indian Ocean and led to the establishment of a major facility on the island of Diego Garcia. From Delhi's perspective, this was seen as still another hostile act by the United States, and for more than ten years Diego Garcia was a contentious issue between India, the United States, and Great Britain, which had leased the island to America.

Further westward, the decisive Israeli victories over various Arab ground and air forces in the 1973 war raised questions about the quality of Soviet military systems; by this time, about 70 percent of the Indian Air Force was Soviet-equipped, and most of its armor was from the Soviet Union. The demonstrable superiority of American over Soviet equipment was one major reason for renewed Indian interest in gaining access to Western military technology in the 1980s.

When China became Pakistan's main arms supplier after 1965, its relations with India remained cool. This gradually began to change after the Janata party came to power in 1977, and there was a major attempt to resolve the Sino-Indian border dispute. This effort collapsed (showing, perhaps, how weak the incentive for normalization was on both sides) when China invaded Vietnam. That invasion reminded New Delhi of India's own 1962 humiliation. The impact was amplified because

Atal Behari Vajpayee, the Indian foreign minister, happened to be in Beijing at the time and was trying to mediate between China and Vietnam. Vajpayee was pursuing an innovative and expansive—but non-Nehruvian—foreign policy that was to anticipate his foreign policy approach when he became prime minister in 1998.

Relations with the United States were also strained owing to Washington's insistence that New Delhi adhere to provisions of the 1978 Nuclear Non-Proliferation Act and open all its nuclear facilities to international inspection. Indian suspicions deepened when New Delhi learned more about the covert Pakistani nuclear program. Many Indians concluded that Washington was trying to disarm Delhi and look the other way while China armed Islamabad, another example of the "tripartite" axis against India.

Yet India's relations with its long-standing supporter, the Soviet Union, were also strained. On nuclear matters, the Soviet side was no more helpful than the American; its government was also pursuing an independent policy toward China, and despite assurances from the Kremlin gerontocracy, Moscow was becoming an embarrassing ally, with forays into Africa, the Middle East, and, finally, Afghanistan.

For India, the Soviet invasion of Afghanistan was a political calamity. It occurred during a change of government in Delhi and the initial Indian response, by the outgoing Janata government and the incoming Congress government (led again by Indira Gandhi) was badly managed. Delhi had not been informed in advance by the Russians. The Indian government could only stand by, hoping for a quick withdrawal. When this failed to materialize, India concluded that it could play no role in the dispute other than to issue pious statements about noninterference in the affairs of Afghanistan, statements that never named the Soviet Union and could also be interpreted as referring to the Mujahiddin, supported by Pakistan, China, the United States, and other powers.

However, the conflict would not leave India alone. When military support for Pakistan began to pour in (just as news about advances in the Pakistani nuclear program became more credible), New Delhi considered, but dismissed, the possibility of dramatic action against Islamabad. In effect, it sat out the Afghan war, doing nothing one way or another to significantly influence its outcome. With the exception of Exercise Brasstacks (1987), Delhi refrained from overt pressure on Islamabad, although it may have covertly assisted dissident Pakistanis, especially in the rebellious provinces of Sind and Baluchistan.

## Changing Assumptions: 1980–84

In the early 1980s Indians embarked on still another major national security debate. Beset by internal problems, with severe resource constraints, and unsure about the behavior of friends and enemies alike, India felt politically adrift and feared that it had lost its military edge. The Indian strategic community was increasingly concerned with the isolation of its own country, the reemergence of Pakistan, and the uncertain role that the United States and China might play in any future India-Pakistan war. In the 1970s Indians had proudly asserted their regional dominance; now a series of unexpected events toppled India from its position as the only South Asian power that counted.

The reexamination of India's regional role failed to produce a new consensus. There were still very different views on how to deal with old and new military and strategic threats. There were also others who advocated the vigorous pursuit of India's rightful regional and global role, a major rearmament program, and the exercise of the nuclear option. There were those who shied away from large arms levels on the grounds that India could not afford the cost. Some in this group wanted to pursue Indian interests through conciliation and diplomacy. Others felt that Indian interests could be advanced by an even closer relationship with the Soviet Union.

The first group came to dominate defense and security policymaking for most of the 1980s. Indira Gandhi—despite her strictures against deterrence—favored the harder line, but without severing the Soviet tie.[24] A 1983 volume edited by Ambassador U. S. Bajpai, a retired senior Ministry of External Affairs official, updated the consensus in light of the Soviet invasion of Afghanistan, renewed American arms sales to Pakistan, and the prospects of a Pakistani bomb. This report—and those of other seminars held in various Indian universities and research centers—both informed and influenced the broader Indian security community.[25] Its members argued that India could, and should, assume a more proactive security posture. The relationship with the Soviet Union would provide an anchor and serve to deter both Chinese and American meddling. At this time the Kremlin was fighting a war against Afghan guerrillas, who were serving as both American and Pakistani proxies. The general belief among Indian strategists was that the Soviet Union was thus dependent upon India, and that India could extract even more and better equipment from the Russians. In any case, India could not allow the revival of Pakistani power or the growth of a Pakistan-China-America axis. Here the Soviet Union was a natural ally. This relationship, so important to India psychologically, diplomatically, and militarily, merits a closer look.

## The Soviet Link

The platform for India's new activism was an expansion of the relationship with the Soviet Union that had dated back to the 1950s. Moscow originally attempted to compete with the West by providing India with steel mills, assistance to heavy industry, and educational and cultural exchange programs. In 1962, about the time of the India-China war, it began providing significant assistance to India's defense establishment in the form of high-altitude helicopters and a MiG-21 factory. The motives for both sides were fairly straightforward. Geostrategically, the tie with Moscow enabled New Delhi to counter the Chinese, who were actively assisting Pakistan by the 1960s, and Soviet assistance lessened Indian dependence upon the West. The relationship was generally compatible in human terms: economic and social differences between the two countries were not as great as those between India and some advanced western states.

The military connection with the Soviet Union was part of a larger strategic alignment. Moscow provided a veto in the United Nations on Kashmir, the arms program was linked to Indian domestic politics, and an entire generation of Indian officials, scholars, journalists, and politicians grew up with the belief that the Soviet Union was a true "friend" and the United States was at best unfriendly. For its part, the Soviet Union provided India with massive supplies of modern weapons as India became the world's largest arms importer in the 1980s.

Even though this equipment had been designed within the context of Soviet military doctrine and tactics, India adapted it to South Asian circumstances. Indian military thinking remained based on British and American doctrines. The Indian Army never adopted Soviet armor tactics, nor did the Indian Air Force reorganize the air defense system along Soviet lines (as had Iraq and Yugoslavia).

The Soviet link made it possible for a society with a slow-growing economy to maintain a fairly advanced military establishment. India paid for Soviet weapons through a variety of innovative arrangements. Instead of demanding hard currency, the Kremlin worked out many long-term deals, with terms of payment similar to those of other socialist and developing countries, by which India would get military equipment and spare parts in exchange for goods manufactured in India. Thus India became a supplier of many light industrial products and a wide variety of consumer goods to the Soviet Union. Photocopying machines, refrigerators, and television sets manufactured in India under license from Western and Japanese sources were shipped to the Soviet Union, along with shoes and clothing of all varieties. In return, India received MiGs, tanks, and ships.

This arrangement, while seemingly beneficial to both sides, had its problems for New Delhi. First, the Soviet Union, while providing assembly lines and spare parts, never allowed India to sell its Soviet-originating but India-manufactured arms on the international market, depriving India of a valuable source of hard currency. The Soviet Union also prohibited the sale of spare parts to other Soviet arms recipients, blocking India from a closer military relationship with such countries as Egypt and Iraq, also recipients of Soviet weaponry.

Second, the large flow of Soviet equipment reduced the incentive for India to develop its own weapons or to seek other sources. The Kremlin was eager to keep India as a customer and frequently undercut other potential arms providers by lowering the price on Soviet systems or providing more advanced technology. The Soviet Union built up a powerful lobby among Indian bureaucrats and politicians through this relationship, with the result that the earlier policy of defense self-reliance was abandoned. All during this period the Indian defense laboratories boasted of their accomplishments and promised newer and better weapons based on Indian designs. Very few of these promises were kept.

Consequently, India never became the kind of significant arms exporter that early defense planners had foreseen. There are both moral and practical dimensions to this problem. Nehruvian liberalism remains strong enough to view arms sales as something associated with the "merchants of death," and Parliament has often criticized Indian governments for allowing such sales, even inadvertently, to states that were not close to New Delhi. More practically, India has not produced the kind or quality of weapons that are internationally competitive, even in the non-Western world. Recent Indian arms exports are valued at only $5 million—compared with China's $600 million and even Iran's $80 million.[26]

Third, the Soviet relationship made Western suppliers wary of supplying technology to a country (in the 1970s and 1980s) that was perceived as a Soviet ally. The fact that Western intelligence services had access to Soviet equipment provided to India did not inspire confidence in the Indians' ability to protect Western technology from Soviet eyes.

Fourth, the dependency relationship with the Soviet Union corrupted both the Indian economy and its political system. The companies that provided manufactured goods and other products to the USSR were assured of long-term contracts and could afford to produce in quantity, setting up huge production runs for the Soviet market as well as the Indian one. However, the USSR did not demand high quality, and the companies that produced these goods fell further below international standards of excellence. Goods made for the USSR could only be sold to the choice-less Indian consumer. Furthermore, some of these companies were directed to channel part of their profits into the coffers of the Congress party. In the 1970s and 1980s, while railing against the "foreign hand," Congress was hip-deep in Soviet and East European money that was used to finance its electoral campaigns.

Finally, some Soviet weapons had technical problems. Many turned out to be second-rate, and India had to ship some components (such as aircraft engines) back to the Soviet Union for repair or reconditioning. Because of Soviet reluctance to share technology and the limited Indian capability to reverse-engineer Soviet products (both out of a fear of alienating the Kremlin and the lack of Indian engineering skills), India had the weapons, but not the expertise or the capabilities, to produce them.

In the end, India paid a high price for its Soviet relationship. When the Soviet Union disappeared, so did its arms export establishment. India had to reconstruct the manufacturing process in the former Soviet republics, tracking down the origin of each component of its own weapons systems. Some manufacturers had gone out of business, others had sold their inventory to Western companies, and still others insisted on a costly renegotiation. Indian defense experts prowled the factories of Russia, Ukraine, and other states in search of spares and machinery. The result was a serious degradation of Indian military readiness that lasted through much of the 1990s.

To summarize, Indian security policy was transformed between 1962 and 1982. It moved from a defense and strategic policy based on one specific enemy, Pakistan, to one based on two enemies (1963–72), then to an attempt, during the 1970s, to acquire a capacity to engage any external enemy. After 1962, India moved from a defense dependent upon diplomacy to a diplomacy strengthened by a strong defense. During these years India also shifted from a narrowly conceived strategy of pure defense to one of "offensive defense" verging on preemption; from a vague, still-theoretical nuclear option to the grudging encouragement of a secret weapons program; from the view that defense and development are contradictory, to the view that they are complementary; from a policy of expanding and contracting armed forces to meet individual crises, to one of continual modernization within fixed budgetary limits; from separate service planning to limited interservice cooperation; from a policy of limited and balanced reliance on outside weapons suppliers to one of high dependency on a single source.

## Four Crises and an Intervention: 1984–90

The debate over Indian military strategy led to an unprecedented six years of Indian military activism that began even before Mrs. Gandhi's assassination in November 1984. She had always kept a skeptical and restraining hand on the exercise of power, unless (as in East Pakistan) she felt there was no alternative. After her triumphal return to power in January 1980 (a week after the Soviet invasion of Afghanistan), however, she turned hawkish. From her perspective, the forces that had conspired against India ten years earlier—the United States, China, and Pakistan—were again unified. They were colluding to keep India from assuming its natural position as a great power in Asia and the dominant power in South Asia. Furthermore, a full-fledged insurrection had begun in Punjab, and there was strong evidence that Pakistani intelligence agencies were supporting the separatist Khalistan movement.

Successively, she began to use Indian intelligence services to provide covert support for several Tamil groups in Sri Lanka (especially after the 1983 anti-Tamil riots). That year she authorized an integrated guided missile development program that eventually led to the Agni, the Prithvi, and other missiles. Mrs. Gandhi also authorized Operation Bluestar (the 1984 occupation of the Sikhs' Golden Temple) and certainly approved the Siachin military operation. She also presided over an enormous arms buildup, including massive purchases from the Soviet Union. Indira Gandhi was pursuing a policy of regional dominance that featured the use (or threat of use) of military power and a substantial increase in Indian defense spending: the defense budget more than doubled, from $4.09 billion in 1980 to $9.89 billion in 1988–89.[27]

Although much less experienced in politics than his mother, Rajiv Gandhi continued this activism. In 1987 there was a massive game of brinkmanship with the Pakistanis on the plains of the Punjab and Rajasthan (Exercise Brasstacks), a challenge to the Chinese PLA in the northeast (Exercise Checkerboard), and an airlift (Operation Poonali) and ground intervention in the beleaguered northern region of Sri Lanka (Operations Pawan and Ravana). Other than the five wars that India has fought, the 1984–90 period was the high-water mark of Indian military activity. This activism took place under Congress and non-Congress governments, strong and weak leaders, and it involved Pakistan, China, and Sri Lanka.

### Siachin, Brasstacks, and Checkerboard

In 1984 the northern area commander, Lieutenant General M. L. Chibber, moved units of the Indian Army across the Siachin Glacier, occupying posts that had been earlier controlled by the Pakistan Army.[28] This led to a Pakistani response, some heavy fighting, and an eventual stalemate over control of the glacier. The glacier is located in an area where the "Line of Control" (the former cease-fire line) had not been demarcated or even agreed upon. Pakistan has claimed that this was an egregious violation of the Simla accord. India denied the charge, defending its interpretation of the Simla text.

For Delhi, Siachin was a chance to conduct a military operation that would surprise and embarrass Pakistan, much the way India was surprised and embarrassed by China's occupation of parts of Ladakh and the Northeast Frontier Agency in the late 1950s. Although undertaken during Mrs. Gandhi's prime ministership, the Siachin Glacier conflict anticipated larger Indian initiatives three years later. Moreover, just as it seemed to echo earlier "games" with the Chinese before 1962, it anticipated a major Pakistani initiative in Kargil (just southwest of Siachin) in 1999. Siachin has cost the lives of perhaps a thousand Indian and Pakistani soldiers, largely because of frostbite and high-altitude sickness, not actual combat.[29] Attempts to settle this dispute between "two bald men over a comb" have routinely failed.

The same spirit that led to the occupation of Siachin was evident later in the decade when India mounted a major military exercise, Brasstacks, that led to a second crisis. In the early 1980s Indian military and civilian strategists agreed that they were once again in a good position to use force—or at least the threat of force—to their strategic advantage. Large quantities of Soviet-designed and Indian-manufactured weapons were being produced, and those that could not be built or assembled in India were imported. The Soviet Union, bogged down in Afghanistan, looked to India as a friend that might open a "second front" to Pakistan's southwest, especially since India was angry with Pakistan because of the latter's support for a Sikh separatist movement in the Punjab that advocated an independent Sikh state, Khalistan. India assumed that Pakistan itself was vulnerable: Islamabad had been receiving significant American and Chinese support, but Washington had refused to give it security guarantees in the event of a Pakistan-India war. For some Indians, there was a sense of "now or never" regarding Islamabad. According to many newspaper accounts (and comments by some senators and members of Congress upset with American policy), Pakistan's nuclear program was coming close to fruition; the Soviet Union, indebted to India as long as it was in Afghanistan, might neutralize the Americans; Pakistan itself was waging a war along its northwestern frontier and had not yet fully integrated its considerable new American equipment.

In 1986 India launched Phase I of Exercise Brasstacks. This multistage exercise was to last for four months. Its stated purpose was to test several organizational and military innovations. There were also parallel air and naval exercises. Brasstacks, conceived by the American-trained head of the army, General K. Sundarji, with the support of Arun Singh, minister of state for defense and a close friend of Rajiv Gandhi, featured the largest armored exercises ever held in the Subcontinent. Sundarji was a politician's general, and Arun Singh was a general's politician. They understood and worked well together, and both had a close relationship with Rajiv. Although not an "operation," Brasstacks was an open-ended attempt to probe Pakistan's defenses as well as the response from its allies, especially the United States and China.[30] It represented the last opportunity that India had for a major conventional war with Pakistan before the latter went nuclear.

At the height of the exercise India assembled massive ground and air forces pointed toward the direction of the India-Pakistan border in Rajasthan. However, Pakistan moved its forces in the direction of India's then-troubled Punjab. The calculation was that even if New Delhi could cut Pakistan in half by an armored thrust across the border in Rajasthan, it might lose parts of Punjab and possibly road access to the disputed state of Kashmir. The Indians blinked, and Brasstacks ended without a shot being fired. The Indians, under international pressure, wound up the training exercise (which had been converted midway into a military operation).[31] The crisis was formally defused when President Zia ul-Haq flew to India to attend an India-Pakistan cricket match. Brasstacks did lead to the weaponization of both countries' nuclear programs. The next India-Pakistan crisis, three years later, was to have stronger nuclear overtones.

Paralleling Brasstacks, the Indian Army conceived of a second exercise, this one on the India-China border. Code-named Checkerboard, it was the brainchild of General Sundarji. The name derived from the checkerboard-like deployment pattern of Indian and Chinese troops just before the 1962 war. According to those who worked with him, General Sundarji excelled in developing these scenarios, and planning for Checkerboard was carried out simultaneously with the unfolding of Brasstacks. In mid-1986 there was also a Chinese intrusion at Sumdorong Chu at the India-Bhutan-Arunachal Pradesh junction near Thagla Ridge, a disputed portion of the Line of Actual Control. The Indian Army quickly reinforced the surrounding areas, and a skirmish seemed highly possible for some time. However, the scare caused by Brasstacks and the intrusion suggested caution, with the result that most of Exercise Checkerboard was called off, although some map exercises took place in the first half of 1987. Checkerboard was planned by Sundarji in the same spirit as Brasstacks, as an experiment in armed diplomacy. Delhi wanted to probe the response of the Chinese to a limited border dispute and may have been interested in the response of China's superpower "friend," the United States, and its own quasi ally, the Soviet Union. However, both Washington and Moscow urged restraint upon India, which may have been another reason for Checkerboard's early termination.

### An Expedition to Sri Lanka

Twenty miles from the southern Indian state of Tamil Nadu, directly across the Palk Straits, a Tamil insurrectionary movement was at this time growing in Sri Lanka (about 3 million or 18 percent of the Sri Lankan population are ethnic Tamils; there are about 60 million Tamils in Tamil Nadu). Various Sri Lankan Tamil groups had received support and training from India's intelligence agencies and private support from Tamil Nadu, where some of Congress's political partners were openly supporting a Tamil separatist movement in Sri Lanka.

New Delhi could neither ignore the activities of Tamils on both sides of the water nor could it openly admit parentage. The result was a policy of drift and miscalculation, which ultimately led to a catastrophic Indian military intervention in late 1987 when the Indian Air Force undertook a number of overflights of Sri Lanka to resupply the beleaguered Tamils in the northern part of the island. After this demonstration of power—there was also a threatened sealift—the Indian intervention was formally legitimized in an agreement between Prime Minister Rajiv Gandhi and Sri Lankan president J. R. Jayawardena to place an Indian peacekeeping force (IPKF) in northern Sri Lanka. The agreement had several appended letters that constrained the foreign use of Trincomalee port, foreign assistance to Sri Lanka, and foreign broadcasts beamed from the island. Shortly afterward, Indian forces mounted an air-drop of "relief" supplies over the beleaguered Tamil-dominated portion of the island, then occupied the northern districts in a vain attempt to impose a peace and disarm the Tamil insurrectionaries. However, Rajiv was tricked: the Sri Lankan Army withdrew to fight a Sinhala terrorist movement in the south, leaving the Indians alone to take on the Liberation Tigers of Tamil Eelam (LTTE). The Indian Army was bogged down in someone else's civil war, suffered heavy casualties, and was withdrawn in humiliation in early 1990.

The Sri Lanka intervention was another case of "civilian militarism," with the lead being taken by Indian diplomats and intelligence agencies that had been deeply implicated in the Tamil separatist movement since 1983, and perhaps earlier. The proactive Indian high commissioner in Colombo (J. N. Dixit), referred to privately by Sri Lankans as "The Viceroy," had encouraged intervention while promising the Indian Army an easy victory. India's foreign intelligence service, the Research and Analysis Wing, was deeply involved in Sri Lankan politics, and indeed had trained the very LTTE that the army had been sent to disarm. The Tigers first turned their guns on their Tamil rivals, and then, after eliminating them, waged a successful guerrilla war against the Indian Army. Senior and junior officers alike blamed Sundarji for allowing the army to be used (or abused) by civilians who had not even told the army of their own earlier meddling through RAW on the island.[32] The mood of the Indian Army swiftly changed from one of optimistic adventurism to something akin to the "Vietnam Syndrome" apparent in the American military after 1974. Sri Lanka was India's Vietnam, or perhaps its Afghanistan, and it was not until the Kargil operation, nine years later, that the army regained its self-confidence as well as the public's esteem.

## The 1990 Crisis

In January–May 1990, an overextended India became embroiled in a crisis composed of several nearly simultaneous subcrises: an uprising in Kashmir, substantial Pakistani involvement in the Kashmir insurrection, politically fragile governments in both New Delhi and Islamabad, and nuclear threats emanating from Islamabad.[33] Pakistan, led by its new army chief, General Aslam Beg, used a putative nuclear capability as an umbrella to protect its assistance to the Kashmiris.[34] The newly elected Indian government led by V. P. Singh considered, but rejected, attacks on training camps in the Pakistan-administered regions of Kashmir (and perhaps the rest of Pakistan itself). At one point, Indian leaders believed they were threatened with a nuclear strike by a Pakistani emissary, and the crisis was severe enough to bring a high-level American team to the region urging calm and dialogue. India had not initiated this crisis, and its behavior, in contrast to that in Siachin and Brasstacks, was cautious and defensive. One important consequence of the 1990 crisis was that the rest of the world began to look more carefully at India and Pakistan as two states that were war- and crisis-prone and likely to be in possession of nuclear weapons.

## Explaining Indian Military Activity

After 1971, and before the Kargil operation, the Indian military was very active, but its only successful operation was the occupation of the capital of the Maldives in 1988.[35] Why did India flex its military muscles after 1984? There were many reasons.

First and foremost, the personalities of Indira Gandhi, alternatively arrogant and defensive, and her son and successor, Rajiv, a "modern" but inexperienced leader, propelled India into situations where restraint or prudence might have better served Indian interests. During her second term in office, Indira had grown suspicious, to the point of paranoia, and felt that the world was encircling India and that New Delhi was justified in using force to maintain India's regional dominance. She had, of course, successfully defeated the Pakistanis and defied the Americans in 1971.

Rajiv was a technocrat, but a political innocent. He did not share the obsessions of his mother, but his security team included some innovative strategic thinkers. General K. Sundarji tried to push the Indian Army (and with it, the other services) into the information age while Arun Singh was one of India's most forceful military managers. One or the other, or both, were at the center of the Brasstacks, Checkerboard, and Sri Lanka operations. With their departure and Rajiv's loss at the polls, India retreated from confrontational strategies, even canceling scheduled maneuvers along the Pakistan border in 1989.

Several domestic reasons account for the activism. The Sri Lankan intervention was laced through with party political calculations, both under Mrs. Gandhi's regime and that of her son. The Congress party had developed an alliance with the Tamil Nadu party, the DMK, which was deeply enmeshed in Sri Lankan politics, having established (or tolerated) a support network in the state for expatriate Tamil groups.

But by 1988–89 it was apparent that Pakistan could not be frightened or tricked into a war, that the Chinese were willing to meet threat with counterthreat, and that both the United States and the fast-disappearing Soviet Union were uninterested in supporting an Indian regional adventure. The disaster in Sri Lanka signaled the end to this period of military activism. Ironically, one of the consequences of this six-year spell of activity was that India had acquired the reputation of a "great power," or at least of a militarily strong state. This perception was embodied in the cover of the Asian edition of *Time* magazine. Senior Indian naval analysts groaned when they saw its picture of the Indian Navy at sea and its lead article describing "Super India."[36] The article, plus the growth of the Indian Navy in the previous eight years, alarmed many of India's neighbors and created false expectations that India would emerge as an Asian naval power as well as South Asia's dominant power. In reality, the navy was still underfunded and dependent upon outside technology, the air force was totally dependent on outside suppliers, and the army had been traumatized by the Sri Lanka operation. None of the Indian military services could carry out more than one or two of their main missions. It seemed that while India was the only regional nation of potential strategic reach, it had become essentially inward-looking and regionally focused.[37]

## Collapse and Crises: 1990–99

The failure of the Sri Lanka intervention, coming on top of a series of strategic misadventures, plunged India into another strategic debate, this time against a backdrop of failed activism and impending loss of India's superpower patron. The United States, seen as India's superpower adversary, not only did not decline—as many had predicted—but was still interventionist, as the Gulf War (and later, Kosovo) had shown. It could assemble an effective strategic coalition, and its weapons could easily defeat Soviet equipment. Pakistan, rather than fading away, had become a nuclear weapons state (even though many Indians still doubted Islamabad's capabilities to produce a nuclear weapon), and it was openly supporting the Kashmir uprising. Finally, the era of strong central governments had come to an end at home.

Above all, India had entered a period of economic stagnation that punctured any dreams of becoming a major military power. The armed forces suffered the largest cut ever in the defense budget. After rising consistently for five years in the period 1984–89, from 9.9 percent of total government expenditure to 10.3 percent, India's defense budgets were cut in the next four years, dropping from 4 percent of GDP in 1986 to 2.44 percent by 1993–94. The high defense expenditures of the 1980s contributed to large government fiscal deficits and had an adverse effect on India's balance of payments: in a 1993 report, the head of India's Reserve Bank attributed the balance of payments crisis in part to arms imports during the late 1980s.[38]

Reductions in military expenditure became an important goal of India's policymakers in the 1990s. Until 1999, such a policy appeared reasonable as well as necessary. Pakistan was also in a state of economic decline, and it was widely believed that there would be no military crisis in the Subcontinent if the two states were near-nuclear or (after 1998) declared weapons states. Changes in military doctrine and cuts in force structure and recruitment appeared inevitable, given the serious economic situation.[39]

Nine years after the crisis of 1990, Pakistan again took the initiative, feeding large numbers of "militants" (most of whom were Pakistan Army regulars) across the Line of Control (LOC) in the Kargil region of Kashmir. Planning for the incursion extended back several years, but the first positions on the Indian side of the LOC were probably occupied in April 1999.

The 1990 crisis took place with the knowledge that India might go nuclear; Kargil occurred after both had tested nuclear weapons, had declared themselves to be nuclear weapons states, and were beginning to formulate nuclear doctrine. The invasion came at a particularly difficult moment for New Delhi: the BJP-led coalition government had just fallen and ruled in a caretaker status. As in 1965 and 1990, Pakistan's calculation was that the Indian response would be indecisive; certainly, as in these earlier cases, the Pakistani goal was to internationalize the Kashmir issue, and there is evidence that Kargil was launched in part to embarrass the Pakistani prime minister, Nawaz Sharif, because of his meddling in army politics (he had just forced out an army chief) and his soft attitude toward the Indians and on Kashmir.[40]

The Indian response was quite different from that in 1990. The government managed to persuade several countries, especially the United States, that Pakistan had taken the initiative. India argued (and Washington agreed) that the Kargil operation was especially provocative because Kargil had taken place shortly after Prime Minister Sharif and his Indian counterpart, Atal Behari Vajpayee, had held a successful summit at Lahore. The reaction in India, even under a caretaker government, was massive and intense. The Pakistani incursion was seen as a betrayal, a "stab in the back." Feelings ran as high as they had in the 1962 conflict with China, except that in 1999 there was no military humiliation, and there was a widespread belief that the Pakistanis could, and eventually would, be pushed back across the Line of Control.

Despite several threats to broaden the fighting, the Kargil crisis was limited to Kashmir, and to the area where the Pakistani incursion across the LOC had taken place. On both sides, the respective governments quieted voices urging a nuclear response, or the broadening of the conflict. The Kargil crisis showed that India (and Pakistan) had a knack for maneuvering along, but not quite over, the precipice of war.

Although Kargil did not represent a turning point in Indian foreign policy, it certainly led to a major reconsideration of almost all strategic policies. Inadvertently, inept Pakistani decisions again made it possible for India to deploy its considerable diplomatic resources as well as a courageous and bloody counterattack, turning Pakistan's clever military gambit into a political defeat. As in 1971, India demonstrated considerable skill at shaping the strategic and diplomatic framework of a conflict: Pakistan may have achieved tactical military surprise at Kargil, but India won the strategic political battle.

## India as a Military Power

Britain ceased to be a great power when it lost India's manpower and territorial base. Even though it took over these resources, free India did not take a place in the front ranks of states. The self-denying policies of Nehru, including his reluctance to join with another major power (such as the United States) to develop India's military potential, plus his unwillingness to challenge the Chinese in Tibet, set India on an essentially defensive and reactive path. This policy was acceptable in political terms because it was based on the assumption that economic growth was paramount and would produce a bigger base for Indian military power. The defense and security policymaking structure that Nehru put in place and that remains virtually unchanged discouraged both expert military advice and a broad consideration of defense and military options. India's postindependence experience in the strategic use of military power can be summarized in four points.

First, Indian strategic policy has largely been responsive to major external events. On the whole, India has been a status quo power. While Nehru's vision of a great but unmilitary state declined after the 1962 war, it remains influential, especially among civilians. Indians can be persistent but have so far not displayed the ruthlessness (or consistency of purpose) found in some other states. Although defense was a high priority for a time (1962–73), surpassing even development programs, Indians remain skeptical—or at least divided—about the virtues of military power.

Second, as capabilities have increased, Delhi has moved—usually ponderously, but effectively—to exploit opportunities or to respond to new developments. This was demonstrated fully in the 1971 invasion of East Pakistan. More recently, the intervention in Sri Lanka shows that Indians have come to think in terms of a three-front capability, and the intervention in the Maldives and the massive evacuation of civilians from the Gulf in 1990 show a capability for rapid response. These operations would not have been technically possible fifteen years ago. However, the standstill in military acquisition, the need to concentrate on domestic insurgencies, and the loss of the Soviet ally suggest that five years from now the range of Indian capabilities may not be any greater than today. Moreover, within that range, India is capable of effective action, as Kargil demonstrated. Kargil also showed that India has begun to coordinate airpower and ground forces, and effectively deploy India's considerable diplomatic machine.

Third, strategic policy has always been deeply influenced by domestic political events. Nehru's invasion of Goa and his Himalayan adventure against China were both partly a response to domestic pressures; they certainly did not conform to his larger vision of India as a moderate and restrained power. Similarly, India's meddling and ultimate intervention in Sri Lanka was triggered in part by Congress party ambitions in Tamil Nadu.

Outside powers also continue to play an important role in Indian strategic calculations, especially when they are perceived to have links to troublesome neighbors. In this, the United States, various Islamic states, and China are singled out. All have been seen as supporting Pakistan, inflating its power to the point where Islamabad can think of challenging India. In addition, some Indians conclude, the only explanation for this strategy is that the United States and Pakistan's other friends really want to undercut and weaken India. The supportive American response to Indian policies in the 1999 Kargil crisis moderated this feeling somewhat, but suspicion of the United States still remains very deep, despite recent assertions that the United States and India are "natural allies."[41] The preferred Indian world is one of several great powers, not a sole superpower plus the rest. India will continue to see American power as essentially constraining if it is not totally supportive.

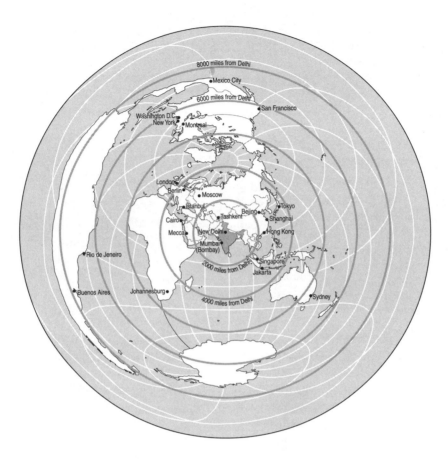

Great circle distances from New Delhi (in miles) to selected major cities

| | | | | | |
|---|---|---|---|---|---|
| Mumbai (Bombay) | 730 | Jakarta | 3130 | New York | 7300 |
| Bejing | 2350 | Johannesburg | 4940 | Paris | 4090 |
| Berlin | 3625 | London | 4185 | San Francisco | 7690 |
| Buenos Aires | 9815 | Mecca | 2390 | Singapore | 2580 |
| Cairo | 2735 | Mexico City | 9030 | Sydney | 6480 |
| Hong Kong | 2345 | Montreal | 6990 | Taskent | 1050 |
| Istanbul | 2835 | Moscow | 2700 | Tokyo | 3640 |

*Figure 6-1. Great Circle Distances from New Delhi*

| SIX | *India as a*
|     | *Nuclear Power*

MOST, BUT NOT ALL, of the world's major powers are nuclear weapons states. Most, but not all, of the world's nuclear weapons states are major powers. Four of the G-8 states are nuclear weapons states, as are all five of the permanent members of the UN Security Council. India is not a member of the G-8 or the Security Council. It has joined the ranks of the nuclear powers, but whether this will speed up its movement to great-power status remains to be seen. This chapter examines India's evolution from a nuclear-abstaining state to a threshold state, and in 1998 to a self-declared nuclear weapons state that has tested nuclear weapons but is not yet a nuclear weapons power in the broadest sense of the term.

### The Slow March to Nuclear Weapons

The Indian program began even before India achieved its independence, largely through the efforts of Homi J. Bhabha.[1] Studying in Britain first as an engineer and then as a theoretical physicist, Bhabha probably heard about the Manhattan project from fellow students and teachers but was turned down for sensitive work, possibly because of his "colonial" status. After he returned to India, Bhabha turned to research on cosmic rays. Then in 1944, using his considerable reputation, his contacts with the government of Bombay, and his family ties, he established the institution that became known as the Tata Institute of Fundamental Research.

Bhabha and other Indian scientists persuaded Jawaharlal Nehru that nuclear energy was an area where India had a comparative advantage. It had both the nuclear scientists and vast deposits of thorium, a potential source of fissile material. India could even become an exporter of nuclear raw materials (there was a global search at that time for valuable uranium deposits). This fit in well with Nehru's interest in science and in energy and security autarky, and his belief that the scientific community could speed up India's development by decades. The atom, in its peaceful guise, would enable India to go from dung power to nuclear power in a single step. He proclaimed India's new dams and power stations modern "temples" and set out to create one of the best science training systems in the non-Western world. For many years, Indian science was considered among the finest in Asia, although it has lagged behind the other major Asian states with large science establishments, such as Japan and China, in applying theoretical scientific knowledge to practical activities.

The Indian Atomic Energy Commission (AEC) was created shortly after independence, about the same time that India opted for a strategy of self-reliance in producing military equipment. With Bhabha as its first chairman, India embarked upon an extensive program of civilian nuclear research. However, the program always had room for a military project: the legislation that established the AEC in 1948 contained stringent controls on the release of nuclear information (these could then be justified in terms of security, but were later used to shield the program from public scrutiny). These laws were further tightened in a 1962 revision of the Atomic Energy Act.

Before India could achieve self-reliance in all areas of nuclear energy, an infrastructure had to be painstakingly built, and that required foreign help. A British-designed research reactor (APSARA) was constructed in 1956; a second research reactor (CIRUS) was provided by Canada and went critical in 1960. This reactor would figure in the 1974 nuclear test that led to the suspension of Canadian nuclear cooperation.

By the time China exploded a nuclear device at the Lop Nor test site in Sinkiang on October 16, 1964, India possessed advanced nuclear research and power programs and had even begun exporting radioactive material. This program included an enrichment facility that had a production rate of about 8 kilograms of plutonium per year, enough for at least one nuclear weapon. Although dependent upon foreign sources for early reactors, heavy water, and enriched uranium, India achieved autonomy in some areas of design and construction. Autonomy was not only a goal but became a necessity after 1974, when most Western nuclear assistance was terminated.

From its inception, "going nuclear" seemed to be less a technical question than a political one. By 1964–65 Bhabha and his team had moved India to the point where they could seriously consider becoming a nuclear weapons state (Bhabha claimed in a conversation in February, 1965, that India could go nuclear within eighteen months).[2] Thus politics, economics, and morality, rather than technology, were the uppermost issues when the first major public debate over nuclear weapons took place in the wake of the Chinese explosion.

### India's First Nuclear Debate

No other country has ever engaged in as lengthy, wide-ranging, and intensive debates as India did before it crossed the various nuclear thresholds. These thresholds included building, testing, and weaponizing a nuclear device; declaring it to the world; and developing a nuclear doctrine. The order of these steps is not immutable; Indians have been talking about doctrine for over thirty-six years, beginning immediately after China's first test in 1964. Nuclear doctrine and strategy again took the stage in 1968, when India was pressed to sign the Nuclear Non-Proliferation Treaty (NPT). Although these two events produced extended public discussion, neither resulted in a nuclear device, let alone the declaration of a nuclear capability.

These two early national debates involved most of the leading Indian political, scientific, and strategic figures of their era. Nuclear weapons were a new issue, one that commanded the attention of the entire political community for the six months after the first Chinese test.[3] During meetings of the All-India Congress Committee and an annual session of the party in Durgapur, West Bengal, nuclear weapons were the central foreign policy issue. Outside the Congress, other political parties staked out their positions: the communists and some socialists opposed nuclear weapons, the Jana Sangh, the forerunner of the Bharatiya Janata party, was the first party to openly favor them.[4]

Nehru died in May 1964, six months before the Chinese test, but both Bhabha and the chief opponent of the nuclear weapons program, V. K. Krishna Menon, participated in the debate, the former supplying proponents of a nuclear weapons program with information about the ease of building an Indian bomb and the modest cost.[5] The politically discredited Menon was passionately antibomb. These sessions set forth the positions and arguments that were to dominate the Indian debate for nearly twenty years.

The 1964–65 debate was oriented entirely toward China. While it was widely assumed that India retained its conventional lead over Pakistan, this was hardly the case with China. After India's humiliating defeat of 1962, the addition of nuclear weapons to the Chinese arsenal was seen as a grave strategic challenge. Anti-Chinese feelings were particularly strong among politicians in northern India. K. C. Pant, later to become an influential politician in Congress (and in the 1990s a member of the BJP), gave his maiden public speech at the session in Durgapur, arguing for the immediate development of nuclear weapons to meet the Chinese challenge, a position he was to hold for the next thirty-five years. In response, Menon sneeringly termed it "Bhabha's notes," indicating his contempt for both Pant and the AEC chairman.[6]

Next to the Chinese challenge, with its implications for Indian pride, national dignity, and revenge, cost was the most important consideration in this early nuclear debate. There were wildly different estimates of the economic burden of a nuclear program. A number of influential Indians, including the civilian bureaucracy, were convinced that India could not sustain a nuclear program coming on top of the massive rearmament after the 1962 war with China. Even though India had received considerable military assistance and grant aid from the United States and the Soviet Union provided a MiG-21 factory, there was concern that high defense spending would derail the five-year plans. At the other extreme, a few early hawks argued that nuclear weapons could solve India's security problems and still permit a reduction in defense expenditure—echoing the Western position that nuclear weapons permitted "more bang for a buck" with an indigenous version: "more rumble for a rupee."

The *military* dimensions of an Indian nuclear program figured only marginally because few Indians understood either the physical effects or the military use of nuclear weapons. After twenty years of condemning the nuclear powers and still under the influence of Gandhian and Nehruvian moral precepts, the Indian establishment was ill-equipped to deal with such concepts as compellence, limited nuclear war, or deterrence. One leading politician, indicating the space between his thumb and forefinger, asked a visitor whether a nuclear weapon could be made "this small" and fired from a rifle. The Indian Army, disgraced by its performance during the 1962 war, was not heard from on the subject; the Indian Air Force, not deployed during the China war, was similarly silent. Both services could take comfort in the fact that Beijing had, at best, a primitive first-generation nuclear weapon and no effective delivery systems. Homi Bhabha, who was familiar with Western notions of deterrence, argued publicly and privately that India must either secure an "umbrella" or security guarantee from the major nuclear weapons states, or pursue an Indian bomb. Some thought the United States and Great Britain might provide such an umbrella, and the Indian government sounded both states out on such an arrangement after the Chinese tests.

Moral considerations were another important component of the debate. India's nuclear policy had always been influenced by two powerful ideological themes: Nehruvian internationalism and Gandhian nonviolence. Under Nehru, India had taken the lead in calling for the suspension of nuclear testing, the ending of the nuclear arms race, and the abolition of nuclear weapons. Nehru had a strong distaste for these weapons, and he ordered the compilation of the world's first unclassified study of their effects, published in 1958.[7] This study offered a careful discussion of the physical consequences of a nuclear explosion, including prompt and delayed effects and nuclear fallout. Homi Bhabha was "associated" with the study, prepared by the Defense Science Organization.

In the first edition, Nehru wrote movingly: "We now have to face death on a colossal scale and, what is much worse, the genetic effects of these explosions on the present and future generations. Before this prospect, the other problems that face us in this world become relatively unimportant. But even without war we have what are called nuclear test explosions which, in some measure, spread this evil thing over large parts of the world." In the forward to a second edition (published to coincide with the UN Conference on the Peaceful Uses of Atomic Energy), Nehru added: "These peaceful uses will only prosper if they are divorced from the idea of war. There can be no doubt that people all over the world passionately desire some agreement among those who control these frightful engines of destruction, to put an end to the fear that haunts humanity." Even after his death in 1964, Nehru's practical and moral arguments against nuclear weapons remained powerful. Yet, as his successors pointed out, he had approved a reprocessing facility that could—and ultimately did—produce the fissile material for the very weapon he had railed against.

The 1964–65 nuclear debate also included a few notable proponents of "Gandhian" views. These included Morarji Desai (then finance minister and a former chief minister of Bombay, and subsequently prime minister in the 1979 Janata government), and J. P. Narayan, one of the most prominent and revered non-Congress figures, who was to lead the national uprising against Indira Gandhi that prompted her to impose the 1975–77 Emergency. Led by Morarji and "J. P.," the Gandhians were unqualifiedly opposed to nuclear weapons. Their numbers were small, but they were a powerful reminder of a cherished tradition.

## The NPT and the Second Debate

Four years later, a second debate focused on whether India should sign the NPT. This time the pressure came not from China, but from the West, Japan, and even the Soviet Union. Signing the NPT would not only foreclose the nuclear option, but also commit the nuclear weapon states to pursue "effective measures relating to the cessation of the nuclear arms race at an early date and to nuclear disarmament."[8] This had been a long-standing goal of the Indian government. Furthermore, the NPT held out the promise of civilian nuclear technology to signatories that renounced nuclear weapons, but in practice this would only be the case when they allowed full-scope inspections of their nuclear facilities.

However, much had happened in the years since the 1964–65 nuclear debate. India had fought an inconclusive war with Pakistan, the United States had lost interest in the Subcontinent, and Indian domestic politics were adrift. The Chinese threat seemed to have receded: one minister of defense declared that India had nothing to fear from a Chinese missile carrying a nuclear weapon as it would "pass over" India on its way to targets elsewhere.

The Indian government faced a difficult choice. India had grown accustomed to an environment that included a nuclear threat still seen exclusively as coming from China. However, the United States had quit the Subcontinent, and the Soviet tie had yet to mature. India sought, but was unable to obtain from either the United States or the Soviet Union, firm security guarantees against a nuclear threat from China. Again, India postponed a decision. It declined to join the NPT but did nothing to undercut it. To justify this position, Indian officials developed the concept of a "discriminatory" international nuclear order. The "discriminatory" or "have/have not" theme was an expression of nationalism and had little impact on the nuclear weapons states, even as it became an irrefutable position in Indian political terms. It was set before the Eighteen Nation Disarmament Commission by Ambassador V. C. Trivedi, the Indian representative, in words that made explicit the Indian view that discrimination and racism were still being used to oppress the poorest states of the world:

> The civil nuclear Powers can tolerate a nuclear weapon apartheid, but not an atomic apartheid in their economic and peaceful development. . . . The Indian delegation does not deny that the technology involved in the production of a nuclear weapon is the same as the technology which produces a peaceful nuclear device, . . . [but] technology in itself is not evil. Dynamite was originally meant for military use. . . . That does not mean that only the poor and developing nations should be denied all technology for fear they may use it for military purposes.[9]

In reality, India's scientists advised the policy community that the civilian infrastructure was secure enough to proceed on its own and that Western assistance was unnecessary. However, Delhi was willing to meet the NPT halfway, and it pledged to do nothing to prevent the treaty from coming into force, nor would it engage in nuclear trafficking to other potential nuclear weapons states.

## The Nuclear Option

The debates of 1964–65 and 1968–69 left India in a characteristically ambiguous position. On the surface, it pursued a policy of keeping open the decision to develop a military nuclear program, not foreclosing the "option." This was a way of deferring a weaponization decision that might prove to be politically risky, unpopular, or unnecessary. In fact, the "option" was itself an uneasy compromise between three groups.

The first were the nuclear abolitionists, flatly opposed to nuclear weapons in principle and in practice. For them, the "option" was a way of holding off the hawks. As far as they were concerned, the option meant "never." With the attrition of the Gandhians, and the weakening of the Nehruvian opposition to nuclear weapons, this group declined over the next decade.

A second group, the nuclear hawks, were also willing to support a nuclear option strategy. They knew that India was deficient in many technologies and that it could not hope to field an impressive Chinese-scale military program quickly. Electronics and missiles suffered grave weaknesses, and without actual nuclear tests, there was no proven bomb design. They knew that if they waited, the cost of a nuclear weapon would go down, as long as basic research continued. Their support for the option strategy was *tactical*; they envisioned a full-fledged nuclear-capable India at some point, but not soon.

The third group consisted of analysts and military figures who were "contingent" hawks. They did not see India going nuclear soon, unless new strategic/political threats appeared, such as a revived conflict with China or another unspecified crisis. At such a moment, they said, India could declare itself to be a nuclear weapons state or conduct nuclear tests and announce its new status to the world.

In the 1960s there seemed to be little reason to make such an important decision. The option strategy worked well and was reiterated by Indira Gandhi after the 1974 Indian test, which was known to insiders as a weapons test but portrayed to the world as a "peaceful nuclear explosion," or PNE. She also reiterated India's interest in a global approach to nuclear disarmament, and its rejection of the NPT on the grounds that it was "discriminatory." When India demonstrated that it had mastered some of the relevant technologies, it gained respect, if not admiration, for its accomplishments. As a contemporaneous view noted, this left open several possibilities. India could have continued the PNE program, gathering data and building a missile capability, or it could have moved to a staged deployment of nuclear weapons, beginning with a "defensive" capability limited to the Himalayas and simultaneously declaring a no-first-use policy.[10] Instead, Delhi did nothing. The weapons program was put on hold as the country entered a period of domestic political chaos, culminating in the 1975–77 Emergency, a non-Congress government (led by bomb opponent Morarji Desai), and the return of Indira Gandhi in 1980.

Work on the Indian weapons program continued quietly, both in the laboratories and in the realm of strategic thinking, kept alive by a small team of scientists with little support from the politicians. The 1974 test did not yield much useful data, but the weapons team continued to perfect that design and began work on others. These efforts moved very slowly. The political community was content with the idea that moving toward the development of a weapon or conducting another test was not a national priority.

### Developing Doctrine

Simultaneously, a few Indian strategists were exploring the development of nuclear doctrine. This had to be done stealthily, since the government still rejected nuclear weapons. These efforts fell into two broad categories: extending the "option" strategy through the adoption of a "nonweaponized" deterrent, and developing the theoretical justification for a declared but limited nuclear force.

Could India receive the political and strategic benefits from a bomb without actually declaring itself to be a nuclear weapons state? Several Indians argued that deterrence would work if India had a bomb in the basement. "Recessed" deterrence, a term popularized by Jasjit Singh (the director of India's official think tank, the Institute for Defence Studies and Analyses, IDSA), or "nonweaponized deterrence" (a term coined by the American nuclear expert, George Perkovich), asserted that an undeclared nuclear weapon, whether assembled or not, provided a security umbrella in the unlikely case that another power threatened India with nuclear weapons. If such a threat arose, India could "weaponize," thereby neutralizing the threat. Weaponization might involve assembling a few last components and mounting a nuclear device on one of India's fighter-bombers. Until that moment, there was no need to declare India a nuclear weapons state.

These concepts attempted to deal with an unpleasant development. Without actually testing or declaring itself to be a nuclear weapons state, Pakistan was clandestinely acquiring a nuclear capability. It had made veiled (and not-so-veiled) threats in 1987 and 1990, and the Indian security community was trying to figure out a way to respond without either embarking upon a large public program or leaving the country at risk. Thus India now faced both a China threat—which it had lived with since 1964—and a Pakistan threat.

As doctrine, "recessed deterrence" posed many problems:

—The threat might materialize before India could weaponize, and it might have to accept a delay between threat and response. It might even have to accept a delay between a nuclear strike and a retaliatory counterattack. A clever enemy might send a threatening message along with the first nuclear salvo, warning against further strikes if India were to retaliate.

—The recessed deterrent strategy was also militarily primitive. Did India have the aircraft to deliver a retaliatory strike in the face of an alerted opposition? Did it have weapons that could be safely and reliably delivered? There had only been a single test, and that was of a first-generation weapon; this imposed certain weight and size requirements, but India had only a limited number of planes that could haul such a bomb (these were primarily British Jaguars, which were slow and vulnerable to an alerted air defense).

—Did India have a command and control system in place should an enemy attack wipe out senior political leaders? If authority was delegated to the Indian Air Force or to other services, what was the risk of accidental or unauthorized launch?

—An Indian retaliatory strike could not reach China and would have no relevance whatsoever against a threat from a truly major nuclear power (the United States), except perhaps to attack Diego Garcia or a nearby American fleet.

—Recessed deterrence carried no status or prestige: it was not going to attract the attention of the major powers and generate the respect that many Indian leaders felt was their due.

Those who wanted a true military nuclear capability therefore argued that recessed deterrence was a ruse. It served the interests of those foreign powers that wanted to keep India from achieving full nuclear capability—it was, in effect, an extended "option" strategy—and, above all, did not address the growing nuclear threat from across India's borders.

## Beyond the Option

Before the advent of the BJP in 1998, Indian governments discouraged nuclear strategizing and refused to acknowledge that there was a nuclear weapons program. With the partial exception of Rajiv, most clung to the belief that by not going nuclear India could still have an impact on the global nuclear debate, or that it did not need nuclear weapons at all and that maintaining the option to weaponize was sufficient. It would allow India to meet any emergency by the rapid development of a nuclear weapon. As noted, such a threat was expected to come from China, Pakistan, or even the United States. India's option

had become a "contingent" option; it is ironic that a few years later the "foreign threat" that contributed to the decision to weaponize was a treaty that banned nuclear tests.

In the 1980s a handful of Indians took it upon themselves to develop a nuclear strategy, or doctrine. They worked with some of the more prominent nongovernmental strategists. Chief among these was the former civil servant, K. Subrahmanyam, for many years a major source of ideas, books, and articles on nuclear issues and nuclear weapons "guru" to a generation of Indian scholars and journalists.[11] Subrahmanyam had a close ally in General K. Sundarji, one of the few Indian officers who had thought seriously about nuclear weapons and strategy.[12] Sundarji organized the first serious quasi-official study of nuclear doctrine.[13] In it, the relevant states were identified as "A," "B," and "C." A number of civilian and military strategists—including serving officers—were asked to comment (by mail) on the scenario, which was, as Subrahmanyam himself noted, a thinly disguised India-Pakistan-China situation. Most, but not all, of the contributors favored a limited nuclear program.

In 1988 Sundarji contributed to a government study commissioned by Arun Singh (Rajiv Gandhi's minister of state for defense).[14] It contained a "threat assessment"—which ranked nuclear and nonnuclear threats to India—persuasive enough to win widespread support. These threats were primarily from China and Pakistan, but also from the United States or some other outside power that might want to intrude on India's natural sphere of influence.

Pakistan could be dealt with by a small nuclear force. All India needed was a rudimentary capability to destroy high-value Pakistani targets. This would be enough to deter Pakistani threats to Indian cities and restrict any conflict to conventional arms where India was believed to have a substantial advantage. When coupled with a declaration of "no first use," Sundarji, Subrahmanyam, and others believed that the threat from Pakistan could readily be neutralized. As followers of Kenneth Waltz's benign view of nuclear proliferation, they felt that an Indian bomb would stabilize the regional military situation, allowing India's larger economy and cultural superiority to prevail in the broader competition between the two states. The acquisition of nuclear weapons, they added, tended to make states more cautious and conservative in their diplomacy. They vehemently disputed the Western criticism that nuclear weapons for the "third world" were more dangerous than nuclear proliferation elsewhere.

China was a more difficult challenge. The combination of a border dispute, a long-term perceived strategic rivalry, and the desire to avenge the humiliation of 1962 made Beijing a serious long-term threat for the mainstream "hawk." The problem was that India could not soon match China's conventional or nuclear forces. The answer was to slowly develop a missile capability that could reach a few Chinese urban targets. This, plus a tactical nuclear capability in the Himalayas, would suffice. Such a capability would, en passant, be more than adequate to deal with Pakistan.[15]

The third threat, that of a major outside power interfering in South Asia, was more problematic. An Indian missile force could not soon reach the United States nor were there important allies or American bases nearby, with the exception of Diego Garcia in the Indian Ocean. Fending off the Americans was a political rather than a military task, although it was widely believed that Washington would be dissuaded from intervening in a region having active nuclear weapons states.

Finally, two powerful political arguments, deeply anchored in Indian values and goals, favored an Indian nuclear program. Viewed separately, they seemed contradictory. On the one hand, nuclear weapons were considered a shameful badge worn by the great powers of the cold war. This position, first and best expressed by Jawaharlal Nehru, concluded that India would demonstrate its global leadership by rising above and attempting to end the global nuclear arms race. Nuclear weapons were evil, they had been dropped on a defenseless and defeated Asian state; India was to be the great power that renounced this perverted concept of a great power.

At the other extreme, some saw a positive link between India's nuclear weapons and great power status. These included the militant Hindu nationalists such as the Jana Sangh (the BJP's precursor), but also secular nationalists like the north Indian socialist, and Nehru's nemesis, Ram Manohar Lohia. Lohia was a populist and greatly influenced George Fernandes, who was to become minister of defense in the BJP coalition that tested nuclear weapons in 1998. These groups favored nuclear weapons because they demonstrated Indian civilizational superiority by the acquisition of the most advanced form of military power known to mankind. They assured their followers that with India's inherent civilizational greatness, such weapons would only be used for peaceful and defensive purposes (a prominent theme in recent official statements). Thus if anti-bomb Indians felt that India could demonstrate its

superiority by renouncing nuclear weapons, the bomb lobby felt that India could demonstrate its superiority by acquiring them.

For thirty years, the nuclear option obscured the differences between these very different positions. The hawks could be assured that work would continue on the bomb, the doves could hope that diplomatic progress would make the bomb unnecessary. Then, in a clever synthesis in the 1970s, the positions were merged by a number of former diplomats and officials, led by K. Subrahmanyam. Like many of his generation, Subrahmanyam respected Nehru's commitment to a democratic, secular state but felt that Nehru had been too weak and pliable and bore some of the responsibility for both the disaster of 1962 and India's failure to deal decisively with Pakistan (and Kashmir) at an early stage. More recently, he tried to make the case that Mahatma Gandhi would have favored nuclear weapons.[16]

Subrahmanyam's formula, developed twenty-five years ago, is now widely accepted: India would acquire nuclear weapons in order to pressure the nuclear "haves" to disarm and to protect itself against nuclear blackmail. Indians could thus have their nuclear cake and eat it: the Indian bomb would be an instrument of resistance to the blackmail tactics of the nuclear weapons states while affirming India's concern with the welfare of all nations. The Indian program could be justified on the grounds of morality and realpolitik, idealism, and self-interest.

This logic could also be applied to the various schemes for disarmament proposed by the superpowers and other nuclear weapons states (such as the NPT and eventually the CTBT). If nuclear weapons were evil, then the so called disarmament plans of the nuclear weapons states (whose hands were dirtied by their use and threat of use of nuclear weapons) were also evil, and as such could be opposed on moral grounds—conveniently leaving open the possibility of a morally sound Indian nuclear program.

Thus the bomb lobby appropriated the original moral impetus against nuclear weapons that dominated Indian thinking from 1947. The new synthesis combined idealism and self-interest: by going nuclear, India could not only enhance its military position in relation to potential enemies, but it could put pressure on the hypocritical nuclear weapons states and hasten the day of complete and global disarmament.

This position won some support in India in the late 1980s, but there were still powerful reasons to do nothing. Subrahmanyam wrote and spoke regularly on the nuclear issue, but his arguments went largely ignored until several developments made the "build the bomb to end the bomb" synthesis more persuasive.

## From the Second to the Third Debates

India emerged from the 1971 war with Pakistan as South Asia's dominant power. Three years later, the May 1974 Pokhran test demonstrated Delhi's nuclear potential. However, an unsettled domestic political order plus an unwillingness to press the advantage over Pakistan turned India away from the nuclear option. But neither China nor Pakistan was standing still, and by 1979 Beijing had put its economic house in order and was actively assisting Pakistan's nuclear program. This was known to some elements of the Indian government, although some Indian nuclear scientists, who had experienced considerable difficulty themselves in developing a weapon (the first test was far smaller than had been predicted), were skeptical of Pakistan's nuclear capability.

China's assistance to Islamabad was accompanied by a revival of the United States-Pakistan partnership after the Soviet invasion of Afghanistan on Christmas Eve 1979. Washington was willing to overlook Islamabad's program, and the Carter administration lifted its economic and military sanctions against Islamabad.

Suddenly India was relegated to the back bench in South Asia. From a position of supreme dominance in 1971, it had fallen to strategic and nuclear irrelevance in 1981 and to a lower strategic level than Pakistan and China. The United States, which had moved closer to both of India's adversaries, appeared to be an additional threat, and the notion that the United States planned to encircle and contain India gained wide acceptance.

In response, New Delhi increased its dependence on Moscow, embarking upon the largest conventional arms-buying spree in the Subcontinent's history. Indira Gandhi considered, but rejected, the idea of a nuclear test in 1983. There is also evidence that Delhi contemplated direct action against Pakistan's uranium enrichment site at Kahuta in the mid-1980s, and it is very likely that the 1987 Brasstacks crisis was conceived in part to provide cover for an attack on Pakistan before its nuclear program reached fruition.[17] In 1984–87 India also made an attempt to "wean" the United States away from Pakistan. This was mirrored by an American attempt to wean India away from the USSR and led to a brief conjunction of policies, if not of strategic objectives.

India's response to a worsening strategic position was not to build and deploy a nuclear weapon, but to meet the challenge through political and conventional military instruments. There was some movement toward the United States, and Rajiv made a successful visit to Washington in 1985, but no progress took place on the nuclear front, while the Pakistan program was moving steadily ahead.

## The Third and Fourth Debates: Comprehensive but Flawed

In 1988 the nuclear weapons states gave a cool response to Rajiv Gandhi's "Action Plan" for phased global and regional nuclear disarmament. This scheme represented a change in Indian policy, as it proposed disarmament steps at the regional as well as the global level; earlier Indian positions insisted on global disarmament before regional issues could be tackled. Rajiv's gambit was not taken seriously by American officials who never bothered to test his sincerity. Amid increasing evidence of nuclear activity in Pakistan, Rajiv authorized the Defense Research and Development Organization to restart the nuclear program in cooperation with the Indian Atomic Energy Commission.[18] This step led to a third major national debate on nuclear policy. In 1964 this debate was seemingly precipitated by a worsening strategic situation; this time the debate was propelled by the West's demand that India and Pakistan sign the Comprehensive Test Ban Treaty (CTBT).

Publicly the Indian government continued to deny its interest in nuclear weapons, and as late as 1996 official statements noted: "We do not believe that the acquisition of nuclear weapons is essential for [India's] national security."[19] Privately, the nuclear hawks in the Indian government—including some in the nuclear establishment—worked with outsiders (journalists, members of think tanks, and a few parliamentarians) to weaken public support for the do-nothing nuclear option strategy. The ensuing debate began under a Congress government, continued during the Janata interregnum, and was concluded under a BJP-led coalition, when India stepped across the two separate nuclear thresholds of testing and declaration in May 1998.

### A More Threatening but Ambiguous Environment

When the third national debate on nuclear weapons began, a key theme of those who pressed for an Indian bomb was India's worsening strategic position. On closer inspection, however, the situation in the years and months before the decision to test was a more complicated one of ebb and flow rather than a sharp deterioration. If a disadvantaged security position alone had been a critical factor, then India should have tested much earlier than 1998.[20]

The late 1980s saw a new enthusiasm for India's strategic position in the world. The Soviet withdrawal from Afghanistan raised the prospect that the United States might lessen its support for Pakistan. Many Indian strategists believed that Washington itself would begin to decline and that Japan, the "emerging superstate," would be Asia's emergent dominant power, eventually supplanting the United States.

The prospect of such a new Asian order was not worrisome for India. Since most Indian strategists held that New Delhi was (potentially) one of the four or five great states of the world, its true emergence would come about through a combination of its own movement from the status of middle power to great power and the decline of the superpowers. The Soviet Union had gone, and "declinist" theorists—Japanese, Chinese, British, and American—found a ready audience in India. The superpowers were in retreat from Asia in general and India's South Asia in particular.

Nuclear weapons were not vital to this scenario. Japan was not a nuclear weapons state, the Soviet Union was in decay, and the United States was thought to be weakened by economic problems and the cold war. If Indians later argued that nuclear weapons were the "currency" of international politics, few Indians believed this at the moment that the nuclear weapon states were fading and nonnuclear Japan was rising.

India's optimistic scenario never materialized. The United States did not decline, and Japan showed no interest in a special relationship with New Delhi. India wound up with the worst of all worlds: a continuing of the China-Pakistan nuclear tie, no new Asian partners, the collapse of the Soviet Union, and a burgeoning domestic insecurity problem, abetted by a Pakistan that after 1990 had to be treated as if it were a nuclear weapons state.

## Treaties, Politics, and the Fourth Round, 1995–97

These strategic concerns—some genuine, some exaggerated—were enough to move Indian public opinion (and several governments) to treat nuclear weapons as a serious strategic option at last. A number of

Indian officials and strategists who were either agnostic or opposed to an Indian nuclear weapons program became "contingent hawks." That is, they would favor weaponization (vaguely defined) if India's strategic situation worsened. Still, this gradual shift in elite and public opinion alone would not have pushed India into a nuclear test had the advocates of immediate weaponization not been bolstered by two unlikely developments: the diplomacy surrounding the extension of the NPT and the accession to power of a political party that was enthusiastically pro-bomb.

When the NPT went into force in 1970, it contained provisions for a review conference every five years, and after twenty-five years, a determination as to whether it would be extended further. Although not a signatory, India rejected such an extension, hoping that the treaty might be modified in several ways. In May 1995, however, the treaty was extended indefinitely with surprising ease, and Indians who followed these issues were alarmed by the prospect of growing international support for an arms control treaty that targeted particular capacities. In India's case, there was no opposition to a test ban per se, but the nuclear establishment strongly opposed any treaty that threatened the nuclear option. Its members knew that the 1974 test was not a success, and fresh tests were required to improve the old design and to experiment with new ones.

Since India had been the first-ever state to propose a comprehensive test ban, the shifting Indian position was not taken very seriously by the new Clinton administration. Its highest priority was nonproliferation, and people saw India as a traditional supporter of a test ban. Yet, not without reason, many Indians saw the CTBT, as it eventually evolved, as part of a strategy that would permanently foreclose India's nuclear option. This belief was reinforced by the repeated statements of senior American officials that Washington's goal was to cap, reduce, *and then eliminate* India's and Pakistan's nuclear weapons capabilities, and the capabilities of other states that were not nuclear weapons signatories of the NPT. While the United States and Russia had succeeded in substantially reducing their nuclear arsenals, the Indian hawks were able to play upon the popular image in India of huge superpower arsenals; again, it was the "haves" versus the "have-nots," still a powerful theme in a highly nationalistic India.

One could not have proposed a more threatening formulation than "cap, reduce, and eliminate," as far as the Indian security community was concerned. The common ground had been to retain the option, not to exercise it or to abandon it. Incredibly, this American formulation continued even after the Indian tests, providing ironclad confirmation of the bomb lobby's depiction of a malign American policy.[21]

Unsurprisingly, the debate within India over the CTBT was framed by the Indian pro-bomb lobby in such a way that opposing the CTBT was taken to be a blow for Indian autonomy and a blow against American hegemonism. The anti-CTBT position thus encompassed right-wing and conservative militants, a traditional left-wing anti-American faction, and advocates of nonalignment. The latter two groups included many who did not want a bomb but who thought that opposing the CTBT was vital to protecting Indian security interests. The defining moment in the Indian debate came on June 20, 1996, when the United Front government authorized Arundhati Ghosh to publicly state in the Geneva negotiations over the CTBT that as far as India was concerned, "security" interests were a consideration and would be compromised by signing the treaty. This was a rare moment of candor, but it came too late to affect the treaty's end game. The major nuclear weapons states had worked out a number of compromises among themselves, and there was no interest in accommodating India.

The inadvertent consequence of U.S. policy can be seen in its effect on George Fernandes, who became minister of defense in the BJP-led government that finally decided to exercise the option. Fernandes came out of the left-wing trade union movement and had been vehemently antinuclear during his entire political career. He has stated that he remained opposed to the bomb "from Day One till the nineteenth of July, 1996," when the Lok Sabha began its debate over the CTBT.[22] For Fernandes, who was morally opposed to nuclear weapons, the pressures from the five nuclear "haves" was even more obnoxious. When the BJP leadership informed him of their decision to go ahead with the tests, he heartily concurred.

During the fourth phase of the Indian nuclear debate, positions against the West, especially the United States, hardened, and led to new alliances and partnerships in the Indian strategic community. Anti-American groups joined with antinuclear groups in opposing the CTBT. The latter included those who wanted to abolish all nuclear weapons and those who saw an Indian weapon or at least an option as useful in pressuring the West to come up with a serious comprehensive disarmament program. They joined the bomb lobby, which increased in number and outspokenness after 1990, and the security specialists, who saw the need to retain the capability of moving beyond the simple first-generation weapon that India was assumed to have designed. The CTBT debate had succeeded in doing what thirty years of insecurity and uncertainty had not: it united Indian opinion against a treaty that India had originally proposed. Yet this was a negative consensus: there was still no support *for* an Indian nuclear weapon. Most Indians who opposed the CTBT were not in favor of either a declaration of nuclear weapons status or nuclear testing.

### Domestic Politics: Necessary, Not Sufficient

Obviously, the turn of the wheel that brought the BJP into power briefly in May 1996 and then again in 1998 was critical to the final decision to test and declare India to be a nuclear weapons state. It certainly was not a sufficient condition but might have been a necessary one, at least as far as the declaration (as opposed to a nuclear test) was concerned. At least two previous Indian prime ministers had considered a test—it took considerable American diplomatic pressure to prevent P. V. Narasimha Rao from testing in December 1995—and at least one (Inder Gujral) thought that India should have gone nuclear many years earlier, although he did not give the order when he was prime minister from 1997 to 1998.[23]

More broadly, the Indian political process had undergone a major change. Earlier nuclear decisions were tightly held, even though they were intensely debated. What changed in the 1990s was the political context in which these decisions were made. Four prime ministers (Nehru, Shastri, Indira Gandhi, and Rajiv Gandhi) were secure in their positions because they had a clear parliamentary majority. Except for Indira Gandhi in her first term as prime minister, none of them faced a severe internal challenge or could be defeated at the polls or in an internal party struggle over a nuclear decision.

With the advent of weak coalition governments in the 1990s, a challenge to the government on foreign policy was possible from outside as well as from within the dominant party. This occurred during Narasimha Rao's prime ministership (May 1991 to March 1996). Though he was widely respected as a shrewd manager of Indian foreign policy (he had been Indira Gandhi's foreign minister for a number of years), Rao had little popular support and governed with the support of only non-Congress parties. The subsequent Janata-led coalition was even more precarious, and both Deve Gowda and Inder Gujral headed governments resting on the tepid support of disparate coalition partners. None of these partners were as vehemently pro-bomb as the BJP, but during this period the BJP was picking up new members from Congress and other parties, and some of them were nuclear hawks.

By this time, the nuclear weapons program had come to be seen as an important symbol of Indian nationhood and identity. Advocates of an Indian bomb saw it as a way of projecting an image of a scientifically adept, multicultural people, capable of achieving great things with a minimum of resources. Originally, this symbolism was attached to the civilian nuclear program, and its leadership often boasted of the way in which Indian talent and innovativeness thrived in spite of Western economic sanctions and technology restraint regimes. Indians of all religions—Hindus, Muslims, and Sikhs—and of all regions—from Tamil Nadu to Kashmir—contributed to the effort. The underlying message was that no single Indian state was capable of such a project, and only by working together behind New Delhi's leadership could the diverse peoples of India accomplish such great deeds.[24] Because the program is civilian, it is a reminder to the military (and the Indian public) that Indian civilians still reign supreme.

Opposing the CTBT was also an act of nonviolent resistance to the West. The dovish Inder Gujral had structured the debate over the CTBT so that India presented itself as a moral authority on strategic and nuclear issues and openly challenged the West to punish it. As Gujral said in one of his speeches, Indians were proud of their willingness to address these great moral issues and would not mind—it even welcomed—the consequences.[25]

Building on this sentiment, the bomb hawks argued that India's overall position was so desperate and India had been "pushed around" so much that active defiance was called for. Echoing Gandhi, some bomb advocates claimed that the supine Indian had to take a stand against foreign arrogance. Mere noncooperation would not do. A bomb would symbolize both India's self-reliance and its defiance and lead to a place at the strategic high table of international politics. Arguing that since the UN's "Perm 5" each had nuclear weapons, India could join that "club" if it, too, acquired them. The net result of these impassioned debates over nuclearization and the CTBT was that both elite and public opinion toward an Indian nuclear program gradually shifted.[26]

To summarize, India's strategic environment grew both more complex and dangerous after 1990, the medium-range political calculations seemed to have made it easier to reach a decision to go nuclear, and there was a general movement away from opposition to nuclear weapons per se and a growth of militant nuclearism. Nuclearization now seemed capable of solving a wide range of national, cultural, and strategic problems. These created an environment in which the decision to go nuclear was domestically permissible and perhaps politically essential for those on the Indian right.

While the cost of a bomb was a major consideration in the 1964 Indian debate, it had ceased to be so by 1998. By then the financial burden of developing a nuclear weapon was diminished because of major investments already made in the nuclear and missile programs over the years. Indeed, when the civilian power program failed, the weapons program was seen as a means of sustaining the infrastructure for an eventually expanded civilian program. The limited economic reforms initiated after 1991 seemed to suggest the money would be there if the nuclear option were exercised. Indian hawks argued that the country could bear the economic costs (including likely sanctions) that might be imposed.

By the time of the BJP's second tour in office in 1998, the ground had been prepared for a change in policy. There was widespread support for any decision that would preserve the option and maintain Indian pride and independence. Yet there was still no serious discussion of what a nuclear test would mean in terms of Indian strategic interests or the military implications of being a nuclear weapons state, or of India's relations with other major powers, including the United States. Indeed, it was widely agreed that the bomb would improve relations with China, the United States, and even Pakistan. It would put India on a "level playing field" with China, forcing Beijing to negotiate seriously over the resolution of the long-contested border; it would certify that India was the dominant power compared with Pakistan, might persuade the Pakistanis to be less provocative in Kashmir, and would impress the Americans with India's determination to assert itself in the world.

The election of 1998 brought the most pro-nuclear party, the BJP, to power. The BJP's forerunner, the Jana Sangh, was the only party that for many years favored an overt, declared Indian nuclear weapon.[27] The BJP had tried to test in May 1996 but quit office before anything could be done. Two years later, the strategic and political reasons for testing were equally powerful, but there was an additional domestic calculation. In order to stay in power, the BJP had negotiated away all but one of its most important electoral planks.[28] Only the bomb was left. The BJP leadership also believed that it had to test quickly because this would be one of the few major accomplishments it could hold up to voters in the event of an election. Though it lost power after thirteen months, the fact that the party had at last "nuclearized" India was an important component of its foreign policy manifesto.

The inner circle of the BJP who knew of the impending tests carefully prepared the ground. On April 6, 1998, Pakistan tested a Chinese-supplied medium-range missile, the Ghauri. While one participant in the decision has claimed that this test and accompanying bellicose rhetoric from Pakistan constituted "claims from the other side of a war," it was only one in a series of provocations offered up by each side and does not quite square up with the government's post-test insistence that the tests were carried out because of its concerns about Beijing rather than Islamabad.[29] Just before the test, George Fernandes (the defense minister) gave a speech attacking Beijing for its aggressive policies, and his remarks were not refuted by the government of India.

The government also mounted a disinformation campaign designed to allay American concerns about a possible test (the test site was being closely monitored by American satellites). As late as May 1998, U.S. officials and other visitors were reassured that there would be no test until the BJP convened a National Security Council and conducted a general strategic assessment. Only then would it consider a weapons test. The BJP's foreign policy adviser, Ambassador N. N. Jha, stated in Colombo on May 7 that India might just go ahead and declare itself a nuclear weapons state but would *not* test. Defense Minister Fernandes might have known of the tests by then, but it is not clear that Ambassador Jha did.

## After the Tests: A Nuclear Conundrum

On May 11 and 13, 1998, India claimed to have detonated five nuclear devices and simultaneously declared that it was a nuclear weapons state but made no statements about the deployment of its nuclear arsenal. There followed a series of strong reactions from around the world, and still another debate within India, this one being more problematic than any of its predecessors.

The reaction from the West and China was hostile. The United States, surprised because its intelligence services had been unable to warn the president of a test and angered by the Indian disinformation program, invoked a number of sanctions, many of which were lifted by late 2000, when Prime Minister Vajpayee reciprocated President Clinton's March 2000 visit. Other countries—especially Japan, Australia, and Canada—also kept sanctions on India through 2000. China intensified the reexamination of its Southwest Asia policy and the implications of having nuclear India as a neighbor. Beijing claimed to have been especially upset because the Indians had implied that the tests were necessary because of the security threat emanating from Beijing, and Indian diplomacy scrambled to undo the damage in India-China relations in the following months. As for Pakistan, it responded by claiming that it had detonated six nuclear weapons on May 28 and 30 (thus equaling India's total number of explosions (if one counts the solo 1974 test), and Islamabad continued its highly publicized missile testing in competition with New Delhi.

## The Fifth Debate: What Kind of Nuclear State?

Indian strategic thought had been glued together by the option policy, but it was a political not a strategic innovation that allowed Indians to reach a rough consensus on nuclear weapons. The only party that did not accept the option—the BJP—smashed it.

The initial Indian response to the tests was surprise and delight. Politicians and the press hailed the tests as a great strategic and scientific accomplishment, although mastering the technical aspects of simple nuclear weapons was not a difficult task. Design teams in the Bhabha Atomic Research Center (BARC), along with scientists from the Defense Research and Development Organization (DRDO), had been working toward a test for ten years (once the order was given in 1989 by Rajiv Gandhi to have an unassembled nuclear weapon). This work built on the 1974 test and benefited from a considerable amount of public information about the physics of nuclear weapons. Indian designers also had access to high-performance computers and knew that certain configurations would work. The Indian team worked on several systems: a refinement of the 1974 plutonium bomb, components of a thermonuclear design, and perhaps tactical/battlefield weapons. Little is known about these tests, although there has been considerable controversy as to whether they were successful or not.

The Indian public moved on to other issues, especially the precarious coalition politics that was to bring down the BJP-led government less than a year after the tests. Before the government fell, however, it commissioned the "Draft Nuclear Doctrine," written by the newly created National Security Advisory Board for the National Security Council.[30]

The NSAB was to produce a draft doctrine for the government's consideration. Since the committee had only advisory standing and none of its members had security clearances (some were working journalists, which suggested a serious conflict of interest), their work was regarded with some skepticism. Not all views were represented on the NSAB; its members bickered publicly, and a number of the original members were removed when the group was reconstituted in early 2000.

The document produced by the NSAB was a catchall, designed to please many important interests and still make some claim to originality. It embraced the idea of "minimum" deterrence: just enough to dissuade an unnamed adversary from launching a nuclear attack on India. Perhaps the doctrine's most important argument was that India need not engage in an arms race with its likely opponents: a small force would be sufficient. Nevertheless, this minimum deterrent would require a "triad" of air, ground, and sea-delivered weapons to ensure the survivability of an Indian nuclear force. The Draft Nuclear Doctrine also declared that India should adapt a declaratory policy of "no first use" against other nuclear weapons states and "no use" against nonnuclear states. It also called for progress on global disarmament.

No sooner had the draft been issued than it was attacked from the still-strong antinuclear community and by a few hawkish strategists on the grounds that it did not go far enough or was inconsistent. In the view of many former serving officers, it was motivated more by politics than strategy. Even the government dissociated itself from the draft, and Foreign Minister Jaswant Singh modified at least one of its positions.[31]

The draft was the focal point for Indian and foreign debate over the Indian nuclear program, but it could not settle the major questions concerning the Indian nuclear program. The tests seemingly ended forever the option strategy and tenuously set India on the path of nuclear weaponization. "Seemingly" and "tenuously" are necessary qualifications because three years later there is still no consensus on the meaning of weaponization, the status of the Indian weapons program remains in doubt, and the Draft Nuclear Doctrine seems to have intensified the confusion about the way in which nuclear weapons might be fitted into Indian grand strategy. These questions and more have led to a new nuclear debate in India. The debate was triggered by the draft, but it has moved beyond the issues raised in that report. The fifth phase of India's extended nuclear debate promises to be more extensive, more serious, and more consequential than any other. At this point, the supporters of the earlier option strategy are divided. Indeed, all of India is less united on the nuclear question than it has been for fifty years, and a grand debate, reminiscent of India's first (1964–65) struggle with the idea of being a nuclear weapons state, has begun.

## The Players in the Emerging Debate

Participants in the current Indian debate over the nuclear program fall into four main camps.[32] Three support it: the rejectionists, pragmatists, and maximalists. One still opposes it: this group includes traditional antinuclear groups and the remnants of the Gandhian movement.

Nuclear *rejectionists* oppose all nuclear weapons but see an Indian nuclear program as providing leverage that would force the international community to agree to equitable elimination. This position, popularized by Subrahmanyam and others ten years earlier, rejects "unequal" discriminatory treaties such as the NPT and even the CTBT. The most visible advocate of this position in recent years has been India's former ambassador to the United Nations, Arundhati Ghosh, although even the Draft Nuclear Doctrine supports an Indian nuclear program as a means of bringing about global nuclear disarmament.

Another group, though labeled nuclear "hawks, are now self-styled pragmatists who essentially echo the government's policies. A number of them, including the indefatigable K. Subrahmanyam, served on the National Security Advisory Board. He and others shifted their position from support of a "recessed" deterrent (that is, an undeclared nuclear capability) to overt weaponization, primarily to deter a nuclear attack by another nuclear weapons state.[33] They also believe that the tests enhanced India's international status. This group argues for a "minimum" deterrent variously defined, the limited deployment of nuclear weapons, caps on programs, the de-mating of warhead and delivery system, and a declaration of no-first use.[34] It strongly believes in the utility of uncertainty and the power of ambiguity. They do not believe that a nuclear war will ever be fought in South Asia and argue that the existence of nuclear weapons will keep a large-scale conventional war from ever again occurring in the region. One of their leading political figures is Jaswant Singh, who became foreign minister in the 1998 BJP government. In a comprehensive study of Indian defense policy, published immediately after the tests, Singh noted: "There is an inescapable conclusion to be drawn about the nuclear reality: of recognizing both the deterrent factor of such weapons and, paradoxically, their actual nonusability in conflict."[35] The pragmatists are generally opposed to the development of tactical nuclear weapons but would also seek to use the Indian program to persuade existing nuclear weapons states to eliminate or reduce their nuclear arsenals. In their opinion, the primary threat to India comes from Pakistan and China, but they also believe a limited capability is needed to deter extraregional powers from meddling in South Asia. They view the Indian program as exceptional: autonomous in its technology, superior in its morality (because of self-imposed restraints on the development and deployment of nuclear weapons), and strategically sophisticated.

The primary concerns of the nuclear *pragmatists* are the operational and strategic difficulties associated with India going nuclear. For this reason, several influential military thinkers in the group have argued that the decision to go nuclear was premature. Like most government officials and the new "moderates," the pragmatists think that, given its strategic and military position, India needs only a limited nuclear capability. Moreover, because of critical technical and doctrinal problems, not to mention economic ones, the tests might have come too soon. These must be solved before India's nuclear program will be able to improve Indian security. Lieutenant General (retired) V. Raghavan, and civilian strategists such as P. R. Chari all agree that the tests have hurt India's standing in the international community and have solved few security problems. Raghavan, one of India's noted military thinkers, wrote skeptically before the tests (and regretfully after them) of the argument that India would be better off with a declared nuclear capability. He distinguished between a "soft" or ambiguous nuclear deterrent and a "hard" one. He concluded that, on balance, India's security was adequately protected by a "soft" or unannounced deterrent, and that a declaration of nuclear status would unnecessarily complicate strategic and military planning. A tested and militarized nuclear weapons capability would place India on the Western path of large nuclear arsenals, tempting others to introduce ever new nuclear and missile technologies into India's zone of primary strategic interests: "India would have then truly joined the nuclear and missile race" and would still have a significant conventional defense burden.[36]

The position of nuclear *maximalists* mirrors some of the doctrinal and strategic practices developed in the United States, except they believe nuclear weapons (and other forms of military power) are important to India's economic development and political status. The leading theoretician of this group is Bharat Karnad, who has had extensive exposure to Western thinking on nuclear doctrine.[37] Their core belief is that nuclear weapons are instruments of war, not merely symbolic totems. To maintain a credible deterrent (and all the political benefits that accrue to a nuclear weapons state), India will have to be prepared to move beyond the posture of deterrence advocated by the pragmatists to the ability to fight and win a nuclear war. Thus India needs an all-purpose nuclear weapons program, with continued testing and refinement of thermonuclear designs. Such a program will not hurt India's economic prospects, since the recent economic reforms will eventually cause the United States and other advanced states to treat India in the same favorable way that they have treated newly prosperous China.[38]

India, the maximalists add, must be prepared to face a combination of nuclear threats and threats that are less than total, perhaps requiring a tactical nuclear capability.[39] They explicitly reject the view that nuclear weapons are less moral than other types of weapons and disavow India's "Gandhian" and "Nehruvian" past.

One Indian strategic writer deserves special mention as he is a bridge between the moderates, the pragmatists, and the maximalists. In an insightful study of Indian nuclear policy, Rear-Admiral (retired) Raja Menon has set forth a basic proposal for achieving important military and political goals.[40] For years Menon was critical of nuclear ambiguity and was an early advocate of a nuclear weapon for India, but his study demonstrates the difficulty of the present Indian position. With limited funds, a weak command and control structure, and a complex nuclear environment, India is now in a "dumb" place, like a submarine that is neither on the surface (where it can fight) or deep below (where it can hide). Menon has outlined the requirements for a nuclear India but concludes that for some years it will lack an effective nuclear deterrent or a nuclear war-fighting capability, yet by going nuclear it has greatly increased the possibility that it will become the target of a nuclear-armed opponent.

Finally, there are the nuclear *rejectionists*.[41] Their influence, though much diminished today, still gives them some moral authority, most notably among the abolitionists and pragmatists. This group would include Gandhians, some communists, and members of the liberal anti-nuclear movement, including Kanti P. Bajpai, Achin Vanaik, and some noted Indian writers such as Arundati Roy and a few retired military officers, including Admiral B. R. Nanda.

Since 1998, the Indian strategic community has been subjected to a crash course in nuclear weapons, nuclear technology, and doctrine. Until then, Indians knew little about these devices, despite the missionary work of advocates of nuclear weapons over the years. Thus India's most recent nuclear debate has been as inconclusive as earlier ones. There is still no national consensus; there is still strong opposition to the bomb and some concern that having tested, India may be less rather than more secure. Difficult questions also remain concerning the technical and engineering foundation of the missile program that might produce a delivery system.

## Nuclear Weapons and Indian Security

The Indian tests and the declaration of nuclear status were undoubtedly triggered by a change of government. It is possible that a United Front or a Congress government might have tested without declaring India a nuclear weapons state, or even declared without testing. The BJP both tested and declared, raising important questions concerning India's relations with Pakistan, China, and the United States.

### Pakistan as a Nuclear Adversary

Many Indian strategists and scientists have long held Pakistan's nuclear program in low esteem and thus were surprised by its claim to have tested six nuclear devices. Despite the nuclear crisis with Islamabad in 1990 and the first Bush administration's inability to legally certify that Pakistan did not possess a nuclear weapon, Pakistan's nuclear capabilities have been underestimated. Interestingly, India's hawks have always underplayed the nuclear aspects of these crises, preferring instead to emphasize the long-range threat to India from China's nuclear capabilities. There was no concerted Indian campaign against Chinese nuclear and missile assistance to Islamabad, although the connection had been well established by the mid-1980s. Instead, Delhi sought to normalize its relations with Beijing. At best, it thought Pakistan was highly dependent on outside technical assistance and had produced only a few kilograms of enriched uranium. Not only did the tests take Delhi by surprise, but China's revived support for Pakistan and reduced American pressure on Islamabad seemed to benefit Pakistan far more than its own nuclear tests helped India. Nor is there any evidence that an Indian nuclear program has lessened Pakistan's support for insurgents in Kashmir.

After months of mixed signals, the BJP government embarked on a diplomacy of accommodation. This had been anticipated twenty years earlier, when Atal Behari Vajpayee was the Janata party's foreign minister. His continuing interest in good relations with Islamabad was dramatically evident in the "bus diplomacy" Vajpayee employed when he let it be known that he would accept an invitation from Pakistan's prime minister, Nawaz Sharif, to journey to Lahore when interstate bus service was restored in February 1999. Vajpayee did so, and the two used the opportunity to sign an agreement (the Lahore Declaration) aimed mostly at easing U.S. concerns about the new regional nuclear situation. Prenotification of missile tests, new hot lines and further discussions of confidence-building measures (CBMs) were all agreed upon, although India failed to get Pakistan to adhere to a no-first-use agreement.[42]

This, coupled with continuing control of the nuclear program by the military—especially the Pakistan Army—raises important questions for India. While India does not fear an initial Pakistani conventional attack, the converse is not true. For several years, Pakistani military advisers have been thinking about ways to use the small nuclear arsenal in a tactical mode. They have developed an "escalation ladder" that would allow for the graduated use of nuclear weapons, from demonstration tests, to using nuclear land mines (on Pakistani territory), to tactical battlefield use up to city-busting attacks on Delhi or Bombay.[43] Indian nuclear theorists such as General Sundarji and IDSA Director Jasjit Singh have declared that India had no need for tactical nuclear weapons (against Pakistan), but Delhi may yet be forced to consider the development of a tactical arsenal or delivery systems that would deliver small nuclear weapons in a tactical mode.

The question of how nuclear doctrine should be shaped in relation to Pakistan was subsequently examined in a postmortem review of the Kargil war.[44] While the report argued that the 1998 tests had no role in Pakistan's incursion in Kargil, the evidence it cited is based either entirely on Indian interpretations of decisions made in Islamabad or on conjecture. In fact, Pakistani officers, interviewed both before and after Kargil, were pleased with the Indian tests, because they saw them as an act of frustration, not self-confidence. The Kargil report asserted that Pakistan intended to pressure India in Kashmir even before the Pokhran tests, and that the tests alone did not give the Pakistanis the idea of using a nuclear capability as an "umbrella" under which they could reopen the Kashmir issue.[45] The conclusion reflects a profound misunderstanding of Pakistani strategic thinking, which was not that dissimilar from that of Homi Bhabha thirty years earlier, or of military experts anywhere in the world: that there is an important difference (at least in the minds of the Pakistanis) between a theoretical nuclear capability and a proven capability. If one has the latter (at least in the case of Pakistan), then bolder steps are possible, and greater risks can be run. The Indian tests—followed by the Pakistani series—made the two states strategic equals (in the minds of the Pakistan Army) and provided an opening for the more hawkish among them to take advantage of India's inadequate apparatus, the latter being amply documented by the Kargil report itself.

Given Pakistan's domestic political problems and the Kargil crisis of May-June 1999, India's nuclear pragmatists may have to revise their optimism about a "normal" relationship with Pakistan. If Pakistan should deteriorate further as a coherent state, then India, more than any other country, will be faced with the problem of nuclear terrorism and rogue nuclear operations from Pakistan. The security of India in relation to Pakistan depends not on the quality of the *Indian* nuclear force or the rationality of an *Indian* decisionmaking system, but on the integrity of *Pakistan's* chain of command. Indian lives and security ultimately rest on the calculations of the least reliable link, the least informed decisionmaker, the most extremist general, and the most rabidly anti-Indian politician, who find themselves in Pakistan's decisionmaking system. Deterrence must work not only with a rational, sympathetic adversary, but also with irrational and hostile decisionmakers on the other side, which is why states that begin by relying on a strategy of deterrence come back again to strategies based on defense.

## India and Beijing's Bomb

The Chinese response to the Indian tests was extremely negative, not least because the Indian government originally justified the tests in terms of a Chinese nuclear and strategic threat. Some retired Indian officials criticized the tests as premature and unnecessarily alarming to Beijing.[46]

On the other hand, India's program for building missiles that could reach China has been criticized as inadequate by the Indian maximalists.[47] India now has to make hard choices regarding the development and deployment of different kinds of China-oriented weapons and their accompanying strategies.

One such weapon is a missile that will reach high-value Chinese targets that could deliver the thermonuclear device claimed to have been tested in 1998. If India embarks upon this course (the cost of deploying and developing such a system is very high), Indian strategists will have to be assured that their own missile force and nuclear-capable aircraft are secure against a Chinese first strike. Even if a disarming first strike from Pakistan seems unlikely and a deterrent against Islamabad would be credible, there is less assurance on both counts in the case of Beijing.

Some Indian strategists have suggested that the Chinese "threat" can only be met by a seaborne nuclear capability, preferably one mounted on a nuclear-powered submarine with ballistic missile capability. The costs of such a system would be steep, but nuclear experts, especially those with ties to the navy, see this as the only way to maintain a secure second strike capability against China, emulating American, British, Russian, Chinese, and French "triads" that include missile, air-deliverable, and sea-launch capabilities.

The Indian nuclear weapons program also raises questions concerning the tranquility of the vast disputed India-China land border. Either India or China could conclude that the introduction of tactical nuclear weapons along the Himalayas, or in the disputed Aksai Chin area of Ladakh, would be to their advantage. In this context even a small nuclear weapon could have a significant military and psychological impact and, if it were a ground burst, a catastrophic environmental one. Besides air or ground bursts on military formations, either side could deploy nuclear land mines, or use enhanced radiation weapons. These are thought to be in the Chinese inventory and may have been tested by India.[48] Such weapons blur the distinction between "tactical" and "strategic," and if deployed on one's own territory—or territory claimed as one's own—they blur the distinction between using a weapon offensively and defensively. Although the subject was first raised in the Indian media as long ago as 1965, there has been no extended discussion of the military value of tactical nuclear weapons or their place in an escalation "ladder" should India again confront China in the Himalayas.

## *The United States: Nuclear Threat or Ally?*

The contemplated use of nuclear weapons to keep outside powers from intervening in a regional dispute, while a popular idea among the Indian strategic community, raises serious questions. Indian strategists still speak with passion about the role the *Enterprise* played in 1971. Indian hawks have argued that an Indian nuclear capability would be able to deter Americans from intervening in a matter of vital importance to New Delhi: it should be able to attack a flotilla imposing a critical blockade on India by using subkiloton nuclear weapons, for example, and should have accurate sea- and air-launched missiles to prevent a U.S.-led Kosovo-like operation from ever being mounted in South Asia.[49]

India has several ways of deterring an American attack or making Washington think twice about intervening in a matter vital to India. One would be to launch a direct attack on an interventionary force; the other would be to threaten the United States itself. At present, India lacks the capability to target and destroy an American naval force, although it might launch satellites that would give it such a capability. There had been some discussion, even before the 1998 test, of developing a seaborne capability that could target American cities, en passant deterring the Chinese.[50]

However, such a system would be hopelessly expensive and at risk to advanced American defenses. The development and deployment of such a force would be regarded as a hostile act by the United States and bring India within still another set of nuclear crosshairs. For the moment, such plans remain in the realm of fantasy, but they circulate as credible analysis of Indian strategic requirements and offer some insight into the diversity, if not the quality, of Indian strategic thought. Finally, India could consider an attack on an important U.S. facility within Indian missile range, the British-owned island of Diego Garcia. Only 1,200 miles from South India, it is an important transit point for American forces deployed in the Persian Gulf and was vital for the air war against Iraq. Diego Garcia could be hit by Indian missiles.

## The Indian Nuclear Program: Looking Ahead

Indian decisions on nuclear matters will affect the kind of state that India becomes, its security, and the stability of Asia through their impact on (1) the interaction of the Indian nuclear program with those of other states, (2) the development of a command and control structure compatible with India's democratic system and its unique civil-military relationship, (3) the risks—and costs—of a nuclear war, (4) future nuclear proliferation, and (5) the reconciliation of nuclear policy with deeply held Indian values.

## India and the Emerging Asian Nuclear System

India and Pakistan are situated in a part of the world that already has many nuclear states and several nuclear aspirants. Because India's nuclear pragmatists had Waltzian assumptions about the connection between proliferation and rationality—that the possession of nuclear weapons was a stabilizing and relaxing act—little thought has been given to the interaction of an Indian nuclear program with other regional programs besides those of Pakistan and China. However, because of the ease with which nuclear weapons can be delivered by missiles and the spread of missile technology of ever-increasing range, a "nuclear *proliferation* chain" (much discussed in the 1970s and 1980s) is being transformed into an interactive, multinational, nuclear *weapons* chain stretching from Israel to North Korea, and perhaps beyond.[51]

In India, maximalist hawks and "moderate" pragmatists see two ready-made nuclear threats (China and Pakistan) and one distant threat (the United States). China, in turn, has three known nuclear threats: Russia, the United States, and now India (and possibly Taiwan, and in the future perhaps Korea and Japan). Pakistan, whose nuclear program has been entirely India-oriented, raises serious questions for Israel, especially if Islamabad should change its policies and decide to share nuclear technology with states that are hostile to Israel, such as Iraq. Saudi Arabia has no nuclear infrastructure, but it does have actual enemies, both in the Gulf and in its mind, it possesses old Chinese medium-range missiles, and it has a close ideological and financial relationship to Pakistan. Pakistan itself could soon have a nuclear neighbor to its west, Iran. While Pakistan and Iran have not been hostile, they have had serious policy differences on such matters as Afghanistan and the treatment of Shi'ia minorities in Pakistan. Finally, both Iran and Iraq seek nuclear weapons to deter each other. There the next ten years holds the prospect of a complex of nuclear weapons states stretching from Israel to North Korea. While they will not necessarily be contiguous, all may have missiles capable of reaching at least two other nuclear weapons states.

Because missile strikes among these states would have virtually no early warning and because it will be very difficult to detect *where* such strikes came from, many of these states, including India, are doubly vulnerable in a way that enormously complicates command and control decisions and nuclear strategy. India must now calculate whether it can withstand a threat from two (or more) of its potential adversaries, deterring not only Pakistan or China, but also a combination of the two and perhaps other states. It must also calculate the response to a surprise attack from an unidentified state. To do this it must be certain that a missile (or other form of attack) comes from a particular quarter. It is imaginable that an adversary (or a terrorist) will disguise a nuclear attack to make it appear to have come from another state entirely. In the 1950s this problem was identified as "catalytic war" since a third party was able to trigger a nuclear war between two major adversaries.[52] At that time, the third party was thought to be China, and the major nuclear powers the United States and the Soviet Union. Because of the multiplicity of nuclear weapons states, current and prospective, India will have to ensure that it is neither the object of a superior nuclear alliance nor the subject of the machinations of such a third party.

## Command and Control and Decisionmaking

After the 1998 Indian and Pakistani tests, Washington demanded that these two states develop a nuclear strategy and demonstrate that they had effective command and control arrangements. The request generated some irritation in India, which had always prided itself on strong civilian control and had kept its nuclear program entirely in civilian hands for many years. Above all, the question seemed to imply that Indians (and Pakistanis) were not responsible members of the nuclear club.

The request was neither frivolous nor patronizing, although it may have been premature. The United States and every other major power, as well as India's neighbors, now have a legitimate interest in the safety and security of Indian nuclear systems. A number of countries, especially the United States, have found that newly developed nuclear systems are especially unstable. In South Asia, two nuclear weapons states were born at the same time in circumstances that were reminiscent of the birth of the Chinese system, when Moscow apparently requested, and Washington considered, a surprise disarming attack on Chinese nuclear facilities.

Beyond the technical difficulty of controlling nuclear weapons, exacerbated by the large number of nuclear rivals (at least as seen from New Delhi), there are special problems affecting India's command and control system, the implementation of whatever doctrine is developed, and the integration of nuclear weapons with India's overall political and military strategy. These include the tight civilian control over the military and the consequences for India of even a "small" nuclear war or terrorist attack.

The total domination of civilians in India has important implications for nuclear doctrine and war fighting. As a matter of policy, the military has not played much of a role in developing nuclear doctrine or strategy. One exception to this was General Sundarji; another was Major General D. K. Palit, who had written a 1966 study on strategy that included a chapter on nuclear strategy.[53] This was reprinted more than thirty years later, with a new introduction by the author. Palit noted that the "chiefs of staff—however relegated to the wings they might have been in the past in matters of national security formulations—will now have to be drawn into the deliberations of policymaking bodies in order to make their due contributions to nuclear war planning."[54] As Palit acknowledges, India's political leaders would prefer that nuclear weapons be kept away from the control of military commanders, but India would have to "adapt existing strategic and tactical doctrines to meet a possible future situation where our political leaders and the Government decide that nuclear weapons may actually have to be used to win a war."[55]

However, there is little evidence that the Indian government has expanded military participation in its nuclear deliberations, let alone created a system that would put the armed forces in the position of making a decision to use nuclear weapons.[56] Nevertheless, the requirements of nuclear war, whether or not a state adopts a no-first-use policy, are such that at some level the military will be put in charge of nuclear weapons and may have to decide how they will be used if communication with political authorities is disrupted or the chain of command is broken. The problem becomes more difficult if a country adopts a policy of launch under warning or launch under attack without predelegation of launch authority. Then India will require a fairly widely dispersed *civilian* authority, with perhaps more than one civilian authorized to make a launch decision. Would such a civilian be fully briefed about the choices open to him or her? Would this include the president as well as the prime minister? Can India develop a secure communications link between the civilian center of power and various military commanders? What if no senior civilians are able to communicate with force commanders? No wonder one Indian official has been quoted as saying that in the absence of an institutionalized doctrine for fighting a nuclear war and a workable nuclear command structure, South Asia is one of the world's most volatile flashpoints, "especially so in the absence of agreed language and grammar of nuclear responses."[57]

These difficulties are faced by every nuclear weapons state, but India's choices are made acute by the high barrier between civilian and military. Becoming a nuclear weapons power will erode this barrier, not only because of the difficulty of communicating authoritatively during or after a nuclear war, but because very few Indian prime ministers, and even fewer presidents, have had the kind of military/strategic background to equip them to make these kinds of decisions quickly.[58] India's major strategic and military crises (Brasstacks, 1990, Kargil, and various border skirmishes with both China and Pakistan) indicate that on several occasions the Indian armed forces, despite civilian control, have exceeded their authority or have misled civilians about the strategic situation. In one case (the Indian Peacekeeping Force in Sri Lanka), the military itself was misled by a civilian intelligence agency.

The task of developing doctrine and managing control over nuclear weapons will be compounded by two other factors, neither unique to India but perhaps more severe there than in most other nuclear weapons states. The first is the difficulty of balancing between the requirements of secrecy and the requirements of deterrence. All nuclear weapons states must keep their vital national security secrets to themselves, but all must, to some extent, reveal how their systems operate, both to reassure the rest of the world that they are in safe hands, but also to persuade opponents that they have a deterrent capability. However, the Indian nuclear program has been shielded less from foreign eyes than from the Indian public.[59] The problem may be that Indians are too good at keeping secrets and that in a crisis an insecure or uninformed opponent will conclude that New Delhi has plans, technologies, or capabilities that have not been revealed and thereby be led to consider a first strike. Future Indian governments will have to strike a balance between keeping secrets and allowing outsiders a glimpse of their capabilities.

Command and control arrangements will be complicated by the difficulty of developing a system that will be "safe" against a variety of terrorist threats and false alarms. Because of the very low quality of India's civilian nuclear program, it may be difficult to tell the difference between a terrorist (either homegrown or foreign) attack on such a facility and a foreign military attack or a nuclear accident. The reactors in Mumbai (Bombay) are within reach of Pakistan aircraft and missiles, as are reactors in North India. Several have already had severe safety problems; the Indian government will have to be able to detect the difference between a hostile foreign attack, a domestic terrorist act, and an accident.

## The Risks—and Costs—of War

With a few exceptions—mostly among the small antinuclear movement in India—the actual costs of a nuclear war have not been the subject of public debate, or probably, government calculations. This is almost entirely because those who dominated the Indian nuclear debate for twenty-five years have argued that a nuclear war was unlikely. Indeed, they argued that nuclear wars occur when one side has nuclear weapons and the other does not (Hiroshima), or when nuclear adversaries are foolishly racing with each other and engage in reckless decisions to widely deploy nuclear weapons and put them in the hands of low-level officials or allies. The example most often cited is the United States, which allowed its allies to fly nuclear weapons on their aircraft and once had large numbers of tactical weapons dispersed near potential battlefields. Therefore the consequences of a nuclear war have not been a subject of widespread interest in India, because the risk of nuclear war is thought to be low.

An objective assessment must include both costs and risks. A strategy of pure deterrence theoretically reduces risk but may be insensitive to levels of destruction and may actually seek to *increase* the destructiveness of a nuclear exchange (to a potential adversary, and even to one's own side) to ensure that the potential enemy thinks twice. Furthermore, extended deterrence—the belief that nuclear weapons will have an impact on deterrence calculations at lower levels of conflict, such as conventional war—suggests a different calculation of risk and loss if it should fail to deter conflict at a low level. At that point, the choice may involve escalating back up to nuclear weapons or issuing nuclear threats. If force has already been used, then both sides will be at a heightened state of preparedness.

Most Indian strategists are familiar with such calculations but have not thought much about consequences. A few studies have tried to present a rough picture of the effects of a nuclear war. The most comprehensive, based on publicly available data, posits three levels of nuclear war and thus a range of outcomes. At a minimum, India and Pakistan would suffer casualties of about half a million deaths each in a limited attack restricted to military facilities; at a maximum, about 17.5 million Pakistanis and 29.4 million Indians would be killed in a city-busting attack involving megaton-sized weapons (these figures are for 1990 population projections and assume that India and Pakistan had megaton-sized weapons).[60]

It is also doubtful that India and Pakistan have good estimates of how many nuclear weapons the other possesses. Guesses based on presumed reprocessing or enrichment facilities may be misleading. It could be that neither country has turned fissile material into metal and metal into warheads, let alone mating warheads to delivery systems. Such ambiguity has consequences in tranquil times and may be dangerous in a crisis. Each side may assume that the other is unable to escalate or has used all of its nuclear forces, or is preparing to strike first because of limited nuclear arsenals. In the absence of better information and the presence of adequate fissile material, this tends to drive the relationship in the direction of a classic arms race. The situation is further complicated when China's nuclear arsenal is factored in. Pakistan might see this as helping to deter India, but India might see it as a good reason to go to war against the weaker state (Pakistan) sooner, rather than later.

## India and Future Proliferation

The Indian strategic community—whether self-proclaimed pragmatists or nuclear maximalists—has not yet come to grips with the possibility that India might yet provide nuclear weapons, missiles, and other advanced technologies to other states. Again, the debate has been dominated by the hawks-turned-pragmatists, who have stressed that it has been irresponsible of other powers to share these technologies.

Yet India's own history, and that of the spread of nuclear weapons and missiles, suggests that India—or Pakistan—might become a significant exporter of sensitive technologies. For many years, India tried to become an arms exporter. Its defense industry was built with the expectation that surplus capacity would be diverted to foreign sales, thus earning valuable foreign exchange for the purchase of systems and parts not made in India. However, several considerations inhibited this policy, including the moral objection to such sales as well as India's dependence on foreign technology and the pleasure of foreign technology suppliers.

Thus a policy of restraint on arms sales made necessity a virtue. This attitude seems to be changing in certain sectors, and India's civilian space industry has been actively pursuing customers. Certain civilian systems, such as the Polar Space Launch Vehicle, have components such as solid propellant technology with military applications.

Strategic benefits may also flow from nuclear exports, sales, or the sharing of technology. India has for years complained about Chinese sales of advanced technology to Pakistan. This is believed to include missiles, missile designs, and nuclear technology. North Korea has also sold advanced technologies to Pakistan. It may be that a future Indian government will find attractive the notion of using its own sales as counterleverage over such providers. Thus sales or assistance to Taiwan, or to South Korea, would make the point sharply and might even provoke the Japanese into escaping from the American nuclear umbrella. Rather than condemning the spread of nuclear weapons, a future Indian government may well assist it, especially if the maximalists should win the current debate. From their perspective, arming such states would not threaten India but would provide countervailing power along China's periphery and would enhance Indian leverage over the United States.

### The Moral Dimension

Having declared that it possesses nuclear weapons, the Indian political community now has to grapple with what may be the most difficult of all aspects of this move: reconciling its own deeply held values and beliefs about nuclear weapons with the operational implications of being a nuclear power. Morality and nuclear policy intersect in several areas.

One of the major reasons why the BJP and many secular Indians supported a nuclear weapons program was to destroy the image of India as a "Gandhian" or nonviolent country.[61] More practically, the BJP sought to undo Nehru's legacy, with its emphasis on disarmament, peace talks, and its special opposition to nuclear weapons. By supporting the very weapons that the Congress party of Nehru and Gandhi had for so long opposed, the BJP was attempting to redefine India's political identity along new lines. The BJP, and some members of the Indian security community, have been able to argue that even Gandhi would have approved of an Indian nuclear weapon on the grounds that it will be used to restrain the nuclear weapons of others.

Nevertheless, just as India was never entirely "Gandhian," it has not entirely rejected the Mahatma. Gandhi's political appeal rested on his assertion of Indian pride and dignity. He argued that Indians had a special obligation to resist evil by nonviolent means if at all possible, but by violent means if necessary. The greatest sin for Gandhi was to yield to evil or to collaborate with it by doing nothing. If the development of an Indian nuclear weapon fails to provide security for India against putative threats from Pakistan, China, the United States, or another quarter, then enthusiasm for its development and deployment will wane. The nuclear advocates will have to continually jack up the external threat in order to win support for additions to the nuclear program and make the argument that there was no other way to resist this international "evil." Furthermore, if nonnuclear threats continue—whether in the form of international pressure, terrorism, conventional conflict, and so forth— then Indians will have to examine the relevance of nuclear weapons to threats that must be "resisted," in Gandhian terms, but that seem impermeable to nuclear weapons.

Not only are nuclear weapons irrelevant to such threats, but Indians may find their own nuclear decisions have led to an acceleration of nuclear weapons in their neighborhood, as well as among the major nuclear weapons powers. This has not only practical implications, as discussed earlier, but also moral ones. New Delhi had for many years been opposed to treaties and regimes that were regarded as "discriminatory," yet it now finds itself at the epicenter of nuclear proliferation. Should it ignore the process? Should it join with other nuclear weapons states and signatories of the Nuclear Non-Proliferation Treaty in a concerted effort to prevent further proliferation? Or should it accelerate the breakdown of the international nuclear and missile regimes? There is a tension between India's acquisition of nuclear weapons and its long-standing support of the international arms control and disarmament process.

To conclude, there is a profound difference between the highly secretive, closed process of becoming a nuclear weapons state and the highly public implications of doing so. If India remains a democracy, the latter will eventually become an object of intense debate as the Indian public, especially in its major cities, becomes aware of the threats it now lives under and the consequences of even a small nuclear war. Although the hawks were able to manipulate the debate in favor of "going nuclear," they may be unable to control it after the first major nuclear accident or the first nuclear crisis that involves India. Then other perspectives will reemerge. India's antinuclear movement is weak but has strong international support and is bolstered by the growth of global environmental movements. Many in the business community are wary of a nuclear India, widely seen as "bad for business": the decline in foreign direct investment and worldwide criticism of the Indian nuclear program may not be causally related, but they happened at the same time.

India has discovered that testing a nuclear weapon and declaring oneself such a state are technically and politically easy steps to take. It must now decide whether it will be a major nuclear weapons state, whether it will maintain a very modest force, or whether—like Brazil, Argentina, South Africa, and other states—it might want to eliminate its nuclear capability some day. All of these choices are still open, which is why the nuclear program will continue to receive the close attention of other countries. Whether this attention alone makes India a "great" or major power is doubtful. While nuclear weapons are clearly instruments of national prestige, India's trophy bomb will not impress other major powers with its military utility, nor does it seem to have much relevance to India's major security challenges, including those from China and Pakistan, its two nearest nuclear neighbors. India should be regarded as a great state, not because it has become a modest nuclear power, but in spite of this.

## SEVEN

*India and Pakistan*

PAKISTAN IS THE ONLY South Asian state that contests India's regional dominance. This chapter offers an overview of this relationship and Indian strategies for coping with Pakistan and the Kashmir issue, which is the focal point of the India-Pakistan dispute. If India fails to "solve" or better manage its relationship with Pakistan, its wider strategic role is likely to remain circumscribed, as India's net military power will remain the sum of its own capabilities minus those of Pakistan, as the latter are directed largely toward the diminution of Delhi.

## A Paired-Minority Conflict

The origins of the India-Pakistan conflict have been traced to many sources: the cupidity of the British in their failed management of the partition; the deeply rooted antagonisms between the Subcontinent's major religious communities, Hindus and Muslims; the struggle for control over Kashmir; Kashmir's importance to the national identities of both states; and the greed or personal shortsightedness of leaders on both sides of the border. Particularly important were Nehru's romance with Kashmir and his Brahminical arrogance (the Pakistani interpretation), on one side, and Mohammed Ali Jinnah's vanity, shortsightedness, and religious zeal, on the other (the Indian interpretation). These and other factors all play a role, but the conflict is greater than the sum of its parts.

The world's most intractable disputes are psychological paired-minority conflicts. Such conflicts are rooted in perceptions held by important groups on both sides—even those that are not a numerical minority and may even be a majority—that they are the threatened, weaker party, under attack from the other side.[1] Paired-minority conflicts are most often found within states, but some occur at the state level, such as that between Israel and some of its Arab neighbors. Another state-level paired-minority conflict is that between Iraq and Iran; Iraq fears the larger (and ideologically threatening) Iran, which in turn sees Iraq as the spearhead of a hostile Arab world. South Africa and Northern Ireland are two other sites of such conflicts, and in South Asia, Sri Lanka has a paired-minority conflict between its small Tamil population and the Sinhalese.[2]

These extremely persistent conflicts seem to draw their energy from an inexhaustible supply of distrust. As a result, it is difficult for one side to offer reassuring concessions or compromise on even trivial issues, since doing so might confirm one's own weakness and invite further demands. Nevertheless, leaders entrapped in such conflicts resist compromise when they have the advantage, believing that as the stronger side they can bend the other party to its will. As if they were on a teeter-totter, the two sides take turns in playing the role of advantaged/disadvantaged. They may briefly achieve equality, but their state of dynamic imbalance inhibits the prospect of long-term negotiations.

These paired-minority conflicts are also morally energized. Politics takes place where the search for justice overlaps with the pursuit of power. In South Asia, conflict, goaded by a sense of injustice, is legitimized because it seems to be the only way to protect the threatened group. In addition, the group sees itself as threatened because it is morally or materially *superior*. Even past defeats and current weaknesses are "explained" by one's own virtues, which invite the envy of others. Another prominent feature is a distrust of those who advocate compromise, whether outsiders or citizens of one's own state. The former may be fickle; they may shift their support to the other side for one reason or another.

*Time* is a critical component of these conflicts. Often, one or both parties are looking ahead to a moment when they can achieve some special advantage or when the other side will collapse. Do long-term demographic trends, real or imagined, appear to be threatening? Is the country, or one's group, acquiring some special advantage in terms of technology, alliances, or economics that will change one's relative position of power in the future? In brief, does the calendar work for or against one side or the other? If either believes that time is not on its side, the conflict is unlikely to be resolved.

## Indian Insecurity

One of the puzzles of India-Pakistan relations is not why the smaller Pakistan feels encircled and threatened, but why the larger India does. It would seem that India, seven times more populous than Pakistan and five times larger, would be more secure, especially since it defeated Pakistan in 1971. This is not the case, and Pakistan remains deeply embedded in Indian thinking. Historical, strategic, ideological, and domestic reasons all play a role in India's obsession with Pakistan, and Pakistan's concern with India.

### Generations and Chosen Traumas

The first generation of leaders in both states—the founding fathers, Gandhi, Patel, Jinnah, and Nehru—were devoted to achieving independence and building new states and nations. With the exception of Gandhi, they did not believe that partition would lead to conflict between India and Pakistan. On the Indian side, some expected Pakistan to collapse but did not see the need to hasten that collapse through war. On the Pakistani side, Jinnah hoped that the two countries would have good relations; he expected a multireligious Pakistan to be counterpoised against a predominantly Hindu India, with both possessing significant minorities whose presence would serve as hostage to good relations.[3]

A second generation of Indian and Pakistani leaders was unprepared to solve the problems created by partition. Nothing in their experience had led them to place reconciliation ahead of their own political advantage. They reached a number of agreements that cleaned up the debris of partition, and there were trade and transit treaties, hotlines, and other confidence-building measures installed as early as the 1950s. At the rate they were moving, India and Pakistan were headed toward an uneasy truce.

For India, what set the second generation apart from its predecessors was the defeat by China in 1962; for Pakistan, it was the division of the country by India in 1971. The ten-year difference is important: Indians are further into reconsidering their great humiliation than are Pakistanis, although the rise of China as a major economic power has rekindled old anti-Chinese fears in New Delhi.

In each case, the other side denies the seriousness of the other's grievances and doubts the sincerity of the other's claim.[4] In 1962 Ayub Khan stated his skepticism that there was a real India–China conflict, and Pakistanis still belittle Indian obsessions with Beijing. Indians seemed to assume that Pakistanis have more or less forgotten the events of 1971 and cannot understand why Pakistani officials remain suspicious when New Delhi professes its good intentions.

These two conflicts had profound domestic consequences, not a small matter in a democracy. No Indian politicians have admitted publicly that the Indian case against China is flawed or suggested that there should be a territorial exchange. No Pakistanis can publicly talk about a settlement of Kashmir short of a plebiscite and accession lest they be attacked for being pro-Indian and anti-Islamic.

Each trauma led directly to the consideration of nuclear weapons and the further militarization of the respective countries. In India's case, the lesson of 1962 was that only military power counts and that Nehru's faith in diplomacy without the backing of firepower was disastrously naive. The linkage between the shock of 1971 and the nuclear option is even tighter in Pakistan, and for Zulfiqar Ali Bhutto a nuclear weapon had the added attraction of enabling him to reduce the power of the army. Ironically, Pakistan has wound up with both a nuclear program and a politically powerful army.

### Traditions: New and Invented

While many Hindu and Islamic traditions suggest ways of reducing differences and ameliorating conflict, each also has elements that contribute to the idea of what Elias Canetti terms a war-crowd.[5] Indians and Pakistanis draw selectively from their own traditions and point to those on the other side that seem to "prove" the other intends to conquer and dominate. For example, Pakistanis like to cite the *Arthashastra* as "proof" that the Indian/Hindu approach to statecraft emphasizes subversion, espionage, and deceit.[6] For their part, Indian strategists, especially on the Hindu nationalist end of the spectrum, emphasize those aspects of Islamic teachings that portray a world divided between believers and unbelievers and suggest the former are obliged to convert the latter.

While Pakistani ideologues see the spread of Islam to South Asia as having purged and reformed the unbelievers, Indians read this history as reinforcing the notion of a comprehensive civilizational and cultural threat to India. When the Muslims arrived, India was militarily weaker, but morally greater. India's riches and treasures attracted outside predators, who despite their momentary technical or military superiority, lacked the deeper moral qualities of an old and established civilization. The first predators were the Islamic invaders; these in turn betrayed India and failed to protect it from the subsequent wave of Western conquerors. In the history of Islam and Christianity in India, Hindus were the odd men out.

Indians also see Pakistan as an important example of neo-imperialism, meaning that when neighbors (that is, Pakistan) are allied to powerful intruders (such as Britain, the United States, or China), their domestic politics and their foreign policies become distorted.[7] The U.S.-Pakistan alliance is widely believed to have militarized Pakistani politics and foreign policy through the connection between the Pakistan Army and the United States, making it impossible for Delhi to come to an accommodation with Islamabad over Kashmir. Most Indians also believe that Pakistan compounded the error by allowing its territory to be used for the objectives of the cold war alliance, introducing a superpower into the region. The American tie is also seen as encouraging Pakistan to challenge the rightfully dominant regional power by providing the advanced weapons that enabled Pakistan to attack India in 1965. The preferred Indian solution to such a distortion of the natural regional power structure is for the international community to recognize dominant regional powers that are benign, accommodating, and liberal rather than allow either a global hegemon or adjacent powers to meddle in a region.

Pakistan is seen as an essential element in a shifting alliance against New Delhi composed of the West, Islam, China, and other hostile states. Another focus of attention in recent years has been the extremist Islamic forces led by Pakistan, with China as a silent partner. Like Samuel P. Huntington, many in the strategic community see a grand alliance between Islamic and "Confucian" civilization. The ring of states around India provides a ready-made image of encirclement, of threat from all directions. As naval theoreticians are quick to point out, both the Arabs and the Europeans, and—thirty years ago—the USS *Enterprise*, all came by sea.

The threat from Pakistan, Islam, China, and the West is attributed to jealousy of India: outsiders want to cut it down to size. India's sense of weakness, of vulnerability, is contrasted with its "proper" status as a great power, stemming from its unique civilization and history. It is India's very diversity, long regarded as a virtue, that offers a tempting target for Pakistan, the Islamic world, and others. Even its minorities (tribal groups, Sikhs, Christians, and Muslims) are a potential fifth column, awaiting foreign exploitation.

### Pakistan as an Incomplete State

The very nature of the Pakistani state is said to pose a threat to India. According to a 1982–83 survey of India's security problems, the "Pakistan factor" looms large for reasons related to the state's many shortcomings.[8] These include Pakistan's limited cultural and civilizational inheritance, its military dictatorship, theocratic identity, unworkable unitary system of government (as opposed to India's flexible federalism), the imposition of Urdu on an unwilling population, the alienation of Pakistan's rulers from their people, Islamabad's support of "reactionary" regimes in West Asia (India identified its interests with the "progressive" segments of Arab nationalism, such as Saddam's Iraq), its dependency on foreign aid, and the failure to develop a strong economic base. This perspective has enjoyed a renaissance in the ten years since Pakistan began open support for the separatist and terrorist movements that emerged in Indian-administered Kashmir.[9]

Pakistan is a threat also because it still claims that Partition was imperfectly carried out, it harbors some revanchist notions toward India's Muslim population, and it falsely accuses India of wanting to undo Pakistan. Thus Pakistan still wishes to claim Kashmir and even to upset the integrity and unity of India itself.[10] Because Pakistan continues to adhere to the theory that brought it into existence—the notion that the Subcontinent was divided between two nations, one Hindu, one Muslim—and because it purports to speak on behalf of Indian Muslims, Pakistan's very identity is "a threat to India's integrity."[11] More recently, Pakistan has served as the base for Islamic "jihadists" who seek not only the liberation of Kashmir, but also the liberation of all of India's Muslims.

### The Pakistani Perspective

Pakistani leaders see themselves as even more threatened than their Indian counterparts but better able to withstand the challenge than the much larger and more powerful India.[12] Its leaders have a profound distrust of New Delhi, and the latter's reassurances that India "accepts" the existence of Pakistan are not taken seriously.

The dominant explanation of regional conflict held by Pakistan's strategic community is that from the first day of independence there has been a concerted Indian attempt to crush their state. This original trauma was refreshed and deepened by the loss of East Pakistan in 1971. Many Pakistanis now see their state as threatened by an increasingly Hindu and extremist India, motivated by a desire for religious revenge and a missionary-like zeal to extend its influence to the furthest reaches of South Asia and neighboring areas. There is also a strand of Pakistani thinking that draws on the army's tradition of geopolitics, rather than the two-nation theory or ideology to explain the conflict between India and Pakistan.[13]

Like Israel, Pakistan was founded by a people who felt persecuted when living as a minority, and even though they possess their own states (which are based on religious identity), both remain under threat from powerful enemies. In both cases, an original partition demonstrated the hostility of neighbors, and subsequent wars showed that these neighbors remained hostile. Pakistan and Israel have also followed parallel strategic policies. Both sought an entangling alliance with various outside powers (at various times, Britain, France, China, and the United States), both ultimately concluded that outsiders could not be trusted in a moment of extreme crisis, and this led them to develop nuclear weapons.

Further complicating India-Pakistan relations is the 1971 defeat, a great blow to the Pakistan Army, which has governed Pakistan for more than half of its existence. Thus to achieve a normal relationship with Pakistan, India must not only influence the former's public opinion; it must also change the institutionalized distrust of India found in the army. The chances of this happening are very slim.

Another source of Pakistani hostility to India is the Indian claim that Pakistan needs the India threat to maintain its own unity. This argument has an element of truth: distrust of India and the Kashmir conflict do serve as a national rallying cry for Pakistanis, and thus as a device for smoothing over differences between Pakistan's dominant province, Punjab, and the smaller provinces of Baluchistan, Sind, and the Northwest Frontier.[14] India-as-an-enemy is also useful to distract the Pakistani public from other concerns, such as social inequality, sectarian (Sunni-

Shi'ia) conflict, and the distinct absence of social progress in many sectors of Pakistani society. These factors explain Pakistan's fear of India in part. A still more contentious issue between the two states is Kashmir.

## Strategies in a Paired-Minority Conflict

States or groups that see themselves as threatened minorities have at least eight strategies to cope with the situation. In the abstract, these include fleeing the relationship, either physically or psychologically; demonizing the opponent; assimilation (joining the dominant power); accommodation (living as a weaker state by yielding to, or compromising with, the dominant power); changing the behavior or perception of the enemy state (by people-to-people diplomacy, persuasion, or bribery); using outsiders to redress the balance of power; and finally, changing the balance of power by war or other means (such as increasing one's economy or population faster than the other side). Over the past fifty years, India and Pakistan, not to mention third parties, have contemplated each of these strategies.

### Fleeing the Relationship

India and Pakistan, created as a "homeland" for Indian Muslims, have tried to flee their relationship several times. The first instance was a physical escape; the others symbolic, psychological, and strategic flight.

The key West Pakistani leaders came from North India, Delhi, and Bombay; the key East Pakistani leaders were Bengali Muslims. Most of the state's founders were secular politicians worried about being outnumbered in democratic India, where Hindus would have a controlling majority. They had no interest in creating a theocratic state but favored a tolerant Muslim majority state where Hindus, Sikhs, and Christians would live as contented minorities.[15] Indeed, some Islamist groups such as the Jamaat-i-Islami originally opposed the creation of Pakistan on the grounds that Islam could not be contained within a single state.

Intermittently, India has pursued a policy of psychologically escaping the relationship with Pakistan by the "look East" policy, or by ignoring Pakistan, simply refusing to engage in serious negotiations with it. The late Sisir Gupta used to privately argue that India might well encourage Pakistan's ambitions to be a Middle Eastern country, if that would temper Islamabad's obsession with India.[16]

Demonization is another way of escaping a relationship. If the leaders of the other country are evil, misguided, or corrupt, then there is no need to talk to them. Indeed, dialogue with such a country, or its leaders, is immoral and dangerous. For many Indians, Mohammed Ali Jinnah, the founder of Pakistan, has long personified the misguided, evil leader who challenged India's civilizational unity with his two-nation theory, began the militarization of Pakistan by seeking arms from the West, and in a cold, undemocratic, and jealous spirit whipped up hatred and fear of India.[17] His successors, largely military officers, are thought to lack even Jinnah's leadership qualities and the moral authority to place their country on a stable footing. Many Hindus believe that Pakistanis are insecure because most were converts to Islam from Hinduism, and their new faith creates additional problems for India because Islam is seen as a religion that is notably illiberal.[18] A former director of military intelligence of the Indian Army has traced the "psychological" origins of the India-Pakistan dispute directly to Pakistan's leaders: they carved Pakistan out of India, their hatred of India has permitted them to become "the plaything of external forces," and they are content to be dominated by the military. In sum: "There is no doubt that the troubles of India and Pakistan are basically of the making of the leadership. In the last 41 years the leadership of one country has consistently fanned popular hatred and suspicion and pursued it as an instrument of policy."[19] Today, Indian diplomats despair of negotiating with Pakistan, a chronically weak state under the control of the most anti-Indian elements, most notably the military, the intelligence services, and the maulvis (Islamic teachers).

Pakistan's image of the Indian leadership is no less hostile. An important component of Pakistan's founding ideology was that Muslims could not trust the "crafty" Hindus, who still suffered from an inferiority complex.[20] While Gandhi and Jinnah were once respected rivals, their successors in both states lacked even professional respect for each other.

Although many on both sides would like to flee the relationship, some Indians hope that Pakistan will someday rejoin India. Indeed, most of India's past leaders assumed that the Pakistan experiment would fail and that the state would come back to the fold. However, Pakistan's leaders have never contemplated assimilation.

Indians no longer talk of Pakistan reintegrating into India, but there are widespread (if generally private) discussions about how India might establish friendly relations with successor states to present-day Pakistan.

Many Indians regard Bangladesh as an acceptable neighbor and believe that they could develop a similar relationship with a Sindhu Desh, Baluchistan, Northwest Frontier, and even a militarily diminished West Punjab. Bangladeshis may not like or love India, but they fear and respect Indian power and would not dream of challenging New Delhi the way that Pakistan has.

If Pakistan did not rejoin India, many Indians expected it to accommodate Indian power. However, Pakistani strategists view the accommodation of Nepal, Sri Lanka, Bhutan, and even Bangladesh as precisely the wrong model for Islamabad. These states have lost their freedom of action, they have been penetrated by Indian culture, and New Delhi has undue influence on their domestic politics, even intervening by force where necessary. By way of example, India absorbed Sikkim, intervened in Sri Lanka, and has a military presence in Bhutan. Because Pakistan is larger and more powerful than any of these states, many of its strategists contend, it does not need to accommodate India. This resistance to accommodation or compromise with India is especially powerful in the armed forces. Pakistan, its officers argue, may be smaller but it is not weaker. It is united by religion and a more martial spirit than India and need not lower its demands on India, especially in regard to Kashmir.

## Altering Perceptions

From time to time, outside countries, foundations, and private individuals have supported efforts to change the perceptions of Indians and Pakistanis and to promote better understanding between the two. Over the past ten years, at least 100 programs have attempted to bring together students, journalists, politicians, strategists, artists, intellectuals, and retired generals from both countries. Much of the goodwill created by such efforts was washed away by the hawkish television coverage of the Kargil war and the Indian Airlines hijacking in 1999.[21]

Most of the India-Pakistan dialogues intended to promote understanding wind up rehearsing old arguments, often for the sake of non–South Asian participants present. History is used—and abused—to emphasize the legitimacy of one's own side and the malign or misguided policies of the other. Such dialogues take the form of a duel between long-time adversaries, each knowing the moves of the other and the proper riposte to every assertion. Any discussion of how India can work out its differences with smaller neighbors is sooner or later likely to move upward to a discussion of civilizational differences with Pakistan (presumably incompatible ones), or downward to personality differences or the intractability of certain issues (nuclear proliferation, trade, water, and so forth), or laterally to the responsibility of outside powers for regional disputes.[22] Meetings between Indians and Pakistanis rarely last long enough to systematically discuss the differences between the two sides and how those differences might be ameliorated or accommodated.

The Indian and Pakistani governments have also tried to influence deeper perceptions across the border. Several Indian governments have undertaken major initiatives in an attempt to win over Pakistani opinion. This was especially the case with non-Congress governments, beginning in 1979 with the prime minister, Morarji Desai, and his foreign minister, Atal Behari Vajpayee. Subsequently, major initiatives were taken by Inder Kumar Gujral, both when he was foreign minister and then prime minister; Vajpayee undertook yet another goodwill mission when he traveled to Lahore in the spring of 1999 to meet with Prime Minister Nawaz Sharif in Lahore. These recent efforts seem to have failed dramatically, with the Lahore meeting discredited by the subsequent Kargil war and the Nawaz linkage destroyed by the army coup of October 1999. The Indian proponents of a conciliatory line toward Pakistan came under strong attack from both the opposition parties and more hawkish elements of the BJP itself. President Zia's "cricket diplomacy" of the late 1980s raised the prospect of a more forthcoming Pakistani policy. Nevertheless, Pakistan's two democratically elected prime ministers, Benazir Bhutto and Nawaz Sharif, both assumed a very hawkish policy toward India, especially after the 1989 uprising in Kashmir.

Several nonregional states and organizations have tried to promote India-Pakistan cooperation or dialogue. In the 1950s and 1960s, the United States wanted to broker a détente between the two states so that they might join in a common alliance against threats from the Soviet Union and Communist China. Considerable diplomatic energy was expended on these efforts, but their only result was to provide each with enhanced diplomatic leverage against the other, sometimes with ironic results. In 1949 Nehru had offered Pakistan a "no war" pact, but Pakistan did not respond. Then, in 1958, Ayub Khan offered India a "joint defense" agreement provided the Kashmir dispute was solved, after which Nehru again reiterated India's offer of a no war pact. Several years later, with the U.S.-Pakistan alliance revived after the Soviet occupation of Afghanistan, President Zia offered Delhi a "no war" proposal, flabbergasting the Indians. Of course, neither proposal was serious, their purpose being to impress outside powers of Indian (or Pakistani) sincerity.

Much the same can be said of recent proposals for the institution of confidence-building measures (hotlines, summits, dialogues, and various technical verification proposals) between the two countries. Outsiders regard such measures as no-risk, high-gain arrangements. In the India-Pakistan case, however, cooperation is seen as low-gain and high-risk. If cooperation fails, losses will be public and politically damaging; there might also be a multiplier effect in that the risk of conflict might increase if an active attempt at cooperation fails and if the costs of conflict are very high.

The South Asian Association for Regional Cooperation has provided a venue for meetings between Indian and Pakistani leaders and sponsors some cooperative projects on regional issues.[23] However, SAARC cannot deal with bilateral issues, and the smaller members are vulnerable to Indian pressure concerning the focus of SAARC initiatives. India has twice been able to force a postponement of its annual meetings when it was displeased with developments in Pakistan.

### Seeking Outside Allies

The most consistent policy in both states for over fifty years has been to seek outside allies against each other. Pakistan has enlisted several Arab states, Iran, the United States, China, and North Korea in its attempt to balance Indian power, but Washington, feeling uncomfortable in this role, has resisted Pakistan's efforts to extend the security umbrella to cover an attack by India. The Reagan administration drew the line at calling India a communist state, which would have invoked the 1959 agreement to take measures to defend Pakistan against communist aggression. The Chinese have been less restrained, and while no known treaty binds Pakistan and China together, Beijing has provided more military assistance to Pakistan than it has to any other state. Beijing saw its support for Pakistan as serving double duty, since a stronger Pakistan could counter the Soviet Union and resist Indian pressure. Yet China has moderated its support for Pakistan's claims to Kashmir and gradually normalized its relationship with India. After 1988 New Delhi itself saw an opportunity to weaken the Beijing-Islamabad tie by moving closer to China and lately has been circumspect in its criticism of Chinese policies in Tibet and elsewhere.

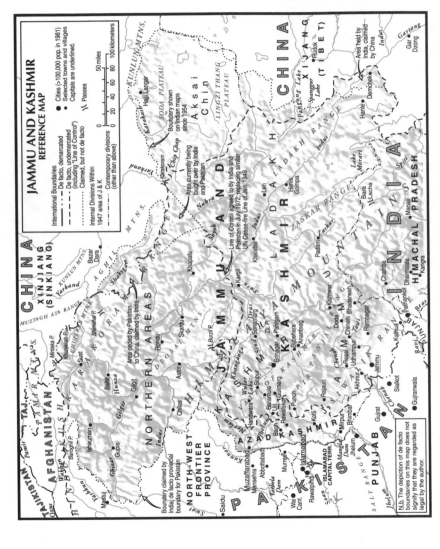

Figure 7-1. *Jammu and Kashmir*

India has also seen the Soviet Union as a major ally in its competition with Pakistan. The Soviet Union provided a veto in the United Nations, massive arms supplies, and general sympathy for New Delhi. However, this support was not directed so much against Pakistan as it was against China; when the Gorbachev government began to normalize relations with Beijing, its support for India gradually declined. These and the other activities are expected to continue indefinitely, with India and Pakistan seeking outside support against the other. This has been the dominant feature of Indian diplomacy for decades, and it is unlikely to change soon.

### Changing the Balance of Power

Both India and Pakistan have also attempted to use their armed forces to change their balance of power. The closest the two have come to a decisive turning point was in 1971, when the Indian Army secured the surrender of the Pakistan Army in East Pakistan. However, rather than pressing on to a decisive victory in the West—which would have been very costly and might have brought other states into the contest— India settled for a negotiated peace and the Simla agreement. Both the United States and China provided verbal support for Pakistan in 1970–71, but neither seemed prepared to take any direct action that would have prevented India from defeating the Pakistanis in East Pakistan.[24] A second opportunity came in 1987 during the Brasstacks crisis, when India had conventional superiority and Pakistan had not yet acquired a nuclear weapon.[25]

By 1990 both India and Pakistan had covertly exercised their nuclear options and seem to have concluded that the risk of escalation had reached a point where the fundamental balance between the two could not be achieved by force of arms. This did not prevent the discrete use of force, and Pakistan adopted a strategy of hitting at India through the support of separatist and terrorist forces, and in 1999 a low-level war in Kargil. As discussed in chapter 5, this now raises the prospect of escalation to nuclear war, but so far neither India nor Pakistan has advocated a *decisive* nuclear war.

## Kashmir: Territory and People

Kashmir is primarily a dispute about justice and people, although its territorial dimensions are complicated enough.[26] Like many intractable problems, it is hard to tell where domestic politics ends and foreign policy begins. Thus the dispute has become firmly wedged in the internal politics of both countries.

Territorial Kashmir, the former princely state of Jammu, consists of the Hindu-majority Jammu south of the Pir Panjal range of mountains that separates the Valley of Kashmir from the rest of India; the Buddhist-majority districts that compose Ladakh, which is the subject of a separate dispute between India and China—the latter in possession of some portions of Ladakh claimed by the Indian government; the Punjabi-influenced districts of Mirpur and Muzzafarabad (now part of what the Pakistanis call "Azad" or Free Kashmir and the Indians call "Pakistan Occupied Kashmir"); and the Northern Territories, consisting of Baltistan, Hunza, and the Gilgit Agency, sparsely settled, with a predominantly Muslim population. A portion of this northern region, north of the peak K-2, was ceded to China by Islamabad in an agreement reached on March 2, 1963.[27] In addition, there is the "Vale," or Valley of Kashmir centered on Srinagar (now called "Held Kashmir" by the Pakistan government). The Valley contains most of the state's population and resources and is the subregion most often equated with "Kashmir" in the minds of Indians and Pakistanis. Some states, such as Britain, dodge the sovereignty issue raised by these locutions and refer to them as "Indian-administered" and "Pakistan-administered" Kashmir, as appropriate.

These subregions have a different ethnic and religious composition. Jammu is about 66 percent Hindu and 30 percent Muslim; Ladakh is about 50–55 percent Buddhist and culturally linked to Tibetan Buddhism (although the Kargil district contains a substantial number of Shi'ite Muslims, as do the Northern Territories). The Valley is overwhelmingly (about 90 percent) Sunni Muslim, but the Hindu minority includes one of the most important Indian castes: the Kashmiri Brahmins (to which the Nehru family and many other senior Indian politicians and bureaucrats belong). There is also a significant non-Kashmiri Gujjar Muslim population in and near the Valley. Finally, Mirpur and Muzaffarabad are entirely Sunni Muslim, albeit with a strong Punjabi cultural influence.[28]

Territorial Kashmir has contributed to the overall dispute between India and Pakistan in several ways.[29] The military establishments on both sides of the border insist that control over Kashmir is critical to the defense of their respective countries. The Indian Army, echoing nineteenth-century British geopolitics, claims that giving up the mountains of Kashmir would expose the plains of Punjab and Haryana, and even Delhi, to foreign (in this case, Pakistani) attack. The Valley is strategically important because of the communication links that run through it to Ladakh and to Siachin, where the Indians and Pakistanis remain frozen in conflict. The threat to Kargil in 1999 was more serious than to Siachin, because it overlooked the already perilous road from Srinagar to Siachin and Leh.

Pakistan, by contrast, points out that for years the major roads to Kashmir led through what is now Pakistan and that the proximity of the capital, Islamabad, to Kashmir makes it vulnerable to an Indian offensive along the Jhelum River. Furthermore, Pakistanis argue, the inclusion of Kashmir would give it a strategic depth that Pakistan otherwise lacks.[30] While both countries are now nuclear, Pakistan's capability is "thinner." On the whole, however, Pakistan's choice of proxy war tactics since the late 1980s is dictated as much by the political hope of a Kashmiri uprising as it is the result of military necessity.

Kashmir is also the source of many vital South Asian rivers, including the Indus and the famous five rivers of the Punjab: the Jhelum, Chenab, Ravi, Beas, and Sutlej. In one of their major agreements, brokered by the World Bank in 1960, India and Pakistan agreed to a permanent division of the water through a series of dams and canals. This costly project left the land on both sides of the new international border more poorly irrigated than before, but at least the Indus Water treaty has been peacefully implemented.

The second "Kashmir," found in the minds of politicians, strategists, and scholars, is a place where national and subnational identities are ranged against each other.[31] The conflict in this Kashmir is as much a clash between identities, imagination, and history as it is a conflict over territory, resources, and peoples. Competing histories, strategies, and policies spring from these different images of self and other.

Pakistanis have long argued that the Kashmir problem stems from India's denial of justice to the Kashmiri people, by not allowing them to join Pakistan and by not accepting Pakistan's own legitimacy. If New Delhi were to pursue a just policy, then a peaceful solution to the Kashmir problem could be found.[32] For the Pakistanis, Kashmir remains the "unfinished business" of the 1947 Partition. Pakistan, the self-professed homeland for an oppressed and threatened Muslim minority in the Subcontinent, finds it difficult to leave a Muslim-majority region to a Hindu-majority state.

Indians, however, argue that Pakistan, a state defined and driven by its religion, is given to irredentist aspirations in Kashmir because it is unwilling to accept the fact of a secular India. Hence India sees no reason to turn over a Muslim majority region to a Muslim neighbor *just because* it is Muslim. The presence of this minority belies the need for Pakistan to exist at all (giving rise to the Pakistani assertion that Indians have never reconciled themselves to Pakistan).[33] Indians also point to Bangladesh as proof that Jinnah's call for a separate religion-based homeland for the Subcontinent's Muslims was untenable. In contrast, India's secularism, strengthened by the presence of a Muslim-majority state of Kashmir within India, proves that religion alone does not make a nation. Indians maintain that Kashmir cannot be resolved until Pakistanis alter their views on secularism. Of course, this would also require a change in the identity of Pakistan, a contentious subject in both states.

These same themes of dominance, hegemony, and identity are replicated within the state itself. The minority Buddhist Ladakhis would prefer to be governed directly from New Delhi, and (like their Shi'ia neighbors) fear being ruled from a government in Srinagar dominated by Sunni Muslims. In Jammu, much of the majority Hindu population has long been discontented with the special status lavished upon the Valley by the Union government in New Delhi. The small Kashmiri Pandit Brahmin community in the Valley is especially fearful. It has lost its privileged position within the administration of the state and much of its high status in academia and the professions. After the onset of militant Islamic protests, most of the Pandit community fled the Valley for Jammu and several Indian cities (especially New Delhi), where they live in wretched exile. Some of their representatives have demanded *Panun Kashmir,* a homeland for the tiny Brahmin community within Kashmir.

### Underlying Causes

The original Kashmir dispute arose because of a British failure of will and of imagination at the time Britain divided and quit India in 1947. The failure of *imagination* was reflected in the mechanism used to divide the princely states between India and Pakistan. Each ruler was to decide whether his state would accede to India or Pakistan. The British, Indians, and Pakistanis all agreed that a "third way," independence, was to be ruled out. Yet there was no way to ensure that each ruler would make a fair or reasonable decision, even though the British, the Indians, and the Pakistanis opposed the further partition of the Subcontinent. In the case of Kashmir, a Hindu ruler governed a largely Muslim population but was also considering independence.

The failure of *will* was evident in the hasty retreat from India by the British, who took their army with them, leaving the bewildered Indian and Pakistan armies behind. Had the date not been rushed forward, the partition of India could have been managed in a more orderly fashion. Instead, it was accompanied by horrific bloodshed, which embittered at least one generation on both sides of the new border, leaving a seemingly permanent legacy of hatred and revenge for future generations. While Indians and Pakistanis in regions distant from the frontier were less affected, the Pakistan Army was particularly traumatized. Most of its officers came from the newly divided Punjab or were migrants from northern India, and their desire to build a new army was partly motivated by the desire to settle old scores. Furthermore, the Pakistan Army was primarily India-oriented in its thinking, an attitude that has been passed down through four generations of Pakistani officers.

Leaders in both countries compounded the original problem when they turned Kashmir into a badge of their respective national identities. For Pakistan, which defined itself as a homeland for Indian Muslims, the existence of a Muslim majority area under "Hindu" Indian rule was grating; after all, Pakistan had been created to free Muslims from the tyranny of majority rule (and hence, from rule by the majority Hindu population). India, on the other hand, sought to include such predominantly Muslim regions to demonstrate the secular nature of the new Indian state. Since from their respective standpoints neither India nor Pakistan could be complete without Kashmir, this raised the stakes for both enormously.

Kashmir came to play a role in the domestic politics of both states. For Pakistani leaders, both civilian and military, Kashmir was a helpful diversion from the daunting task of nation building. There are also powerful Kashmiri-dominated constituencies in major Pakistani cities. On the Indian side, the small but influential Kashmiri Hindu community was overrepresented in the higher reaches of the Indian government, not least by the Nehru family, a Kashmiri Pandit clan that had migrated to Uttar Pradesh from the Valley.

Kashmir also acquired an unexpected military dimension. After Pakistan crossed the cease-fire line to set off the 1965 war, Kashmir became a strategic extension of the international border to the south. In addition, China holds substantial territory (in Ladakh) claimed by India, and New Delhi itself has made claims on regions historically subordinate to the rulers of Kashmir (Gilgit and Hunza) but now administered by Pakistan. From 1984 onward, advances in training and high-altitude warfare have turned the most inaccessible part of Kashmir—the Siachin Glacier—into a battleground, although more soldiers were killed by frostbite than bullets.[34] The recent limited war in Kargil raised the stakes considerably, as it was the first time that offensive airpower had been used between Indian and Pakistani forces since 1971.

Kashmir was also indirectly linked to the cold war and became an issue at about the same time the cold war got under way. Washington and Moscow armed India and Pakistan (often both at the same time), supporting one side or the other in various international fora, while the Soviet Union wielded the veto threat on behalf of India in the UN Security Council. However, the superpowers ultimately reached an understanding that they would not let the Kashmir conflict (or India-Pakistan tensions) affect their core strategic relationship.[35] Ironically, the process by which the cold war ended had an impact on Kashmir because the forces of democracy and nationalism that destroyed the Soviet Union and freed Eastern Europe were also at work in Kashmir.[36] In addition, Kashmir was affected by the liberation and revolutionary movements in the Islamic world, primarily Iran, Afghanistan, and most strikingly (since it was extensively covered by Indian and Pakistani television services), the Palestinian *Intifada*.

The Kashmir controversy has a contemporary dimension as well in the recent stirrings of a national self-determination movement among Kashmiri Muslims. Encouraged by neither India nor Pakistan, it had been present but muted for decades and burst into view in late 1989 after a spell of particularly bad Indian governance. Angry and resentful at their treatment by New Delhi, and not attracted to even a democratic Pakistan, younger Kashmiris especially looked to Afghanistan, Iran, the Middle East, and Eastern Europe for models, and to émigrés in America, Britain, and Canada for support. In an era when the international economy is changing fast (particularly with the advent of self-sustaining tourist destinations) and the prospect of the direct linkage of Central Asia to Kashmir looms large, the old argument that Kashmir cannot be economically self-sufficient unless it is attached to a major state has lost credibility. This movement for self-rule by a younger generation of Kashmiris was a reaction to decades of mismanagement, especially the manipulation of Kashmiri politics in the 1980s, first by Indira Gandhi and then by Rajiv Gandhi. They alternatively opposed and co-opted Farooq Abdullah, a weak carbon copy of his father, Sheikh Abdullah. By joining with Congress in 1987, Farooq provoked his own followers, who, after the rigged election of 1988, turned to Pakistan for assistance.

The separatist movement in Kashmir has been attributed to a combination of the slow and imperfect growth of political mobilization among the Valley Kashmiris, especially among the younger generations, plus the decay of Indian political institutions, or at least those dealing directly with Kashmir.[37] Kashmiris were mobilized too late too quickly and therefore imperfectly. "Kashmiriyat" (the refined amalgam of Hindu-Muslim culture that characterizes the Valley and surrounding areas) remains, but is not the rallying point for this mobilization.

This social revolution took India and Pakistan by surprise. Except for a handful of scholars and some administrators, few people understood its origins or its political implications.[38] Undoubtedly Pakistani support was provided—it was never hidden—and Pakistanis speak proudly of their assistance to the Kashmiris and their right to help the latter free themselves from an oppressive Indian state. However, Pakistan's role was not the decisive factor in starting the uprising, although a critical one in sustaining it.

## Strategic Implications

Kashmir's strategic and diplomatic importance has waxed and waned. While it was the central objective of the first two India-Pakistan wars (1948, 1965), it was not an issue of high priority for either state for twenty years, from the 1966 war until late 1989. Kashmir played no role in the 1971 war fought over the status of the separation of East Bengal from Pakistan. However, the Simla agreement seemed to offer a solution: defer a formal settlement and in the meantime improve India-Pakistan relations.

Since 1989 regional instability and regional nuclear programs have increased. Both are inextricably linked to Kashmir. Many Indian policy-makers believe that Pakistan intends to use its new nuclear capability to make a grab for Kashmir, since escalation to conventional war would be risky. They also point to the connections between the Afghan war and the training of Kashmiri militants, and thus American responsibility for India's Kashmir problem. The Indian logic is that if Washington had not lavishly supported extremist Muslim elements in Afghanistan, Kashmir would not have been radicalized. This ignores the large-scale supplies of weapons by both Iran and China, and above all, India's own misman-agement of Kashmiri politics, especially the imposition of corrupt gov-ernments and the absence of free elections.

The failure of diplomacy to resolve the Kashmir dispute is surprising, given the amount of international and regional attention paid to it, espe-cially after the 1948, 1962, and 1965 wars. In 1948 the United Nations became deeply involved; Kashmir is the oldest conflict inscribed in the body of UN resolutions and is certainly one of the most serious.[39] After the 1962 India-China war, there were intensive but fruitless American and British efforts to bridge the gap between Delhi and Islamabad. At the end of the 1965 war, the Soviet Union began acting as a regional peacemaker.[40] It did manage to promote a general peace treaty at Tashkent, but this could not prevent a civil and international war in 1970–71 over East Pakistan (Bangladesh).

For the most part, however, the great powers have been ineffective in trying to help address the Kashmir problem. Beyond their regional cold war patronage, the United States and the Soviet Union have played sig-nificant, often parallel and cooperative roles in the Subcontinent.[41] Over the years the United States has had considerable influence with both India and Pakistan, as has the Soviet Union. Though generally regarded as pro-Indian, Moscow has also helped Pakistan, even providing mili-tary assistance to Islamabad and brokering the 1966 Tashkent agree-ment. Yet neither superpower has been able to make a difference. This suggests that any outside power should step carefully if it seeks to end or even moderate this conflict.

Kashmir was important to Pakistan and India only insofar as it cre-ated concerns for their respective regional partners, yet both resisted being dragged into the Kashmir issue by those same partners. Con-versely, while Indians and Pakistanis have often based their regional strategies on outside support for their position on Kashmir, that support has been limited and constrained. As already mentioned, for years the Soviet Union automatically vetoed Kashmir-related resolutions in the United Nations and otherwise backed New Delhi diplomatically. The Pakistanis became more dependent on the United States for political and military support but could never get it to commit itself to firm security assurances against India, precisely because Washington was afraid of being sucked into a Kashmir conflict. Both Washington and Moscow made several inconclusive efforts to mediate the dispute or bring about its peaceful resolution but were wary of anything more. It took the 1990 crisis, with its nuclear dimension, to bring the United States back to the region, and then only briefly.

After India defeated Pakistan in 1971, it kept outsiders at a distance as it sought to reach a bilateral understanding with Pakistan. Mrs. Gandhi and Zulfiqar Ali Bhutto met in the Indian hill station of Simla in late June and early July 1972. There, after a long and complicated negotiation, they committed their countries to a bilateral settlement of all outstanding disputes. Presumably this included Kashmir, which was mentioned only in the last paragraph of the Simla Agreement. The text did not rule out mediation or multilateral diplomacy, if both sides agreed.

Ironically, divergent interpretations of Simla added another layer of distrust to the India-Pakistan discussions. While there is a formal text, the two leaders may have arrived at verbal agreements that have never been made public. According to most Indian accounts, Zulfiqar Ali Bhutto told Mrs. Gandhi that he was willing to settle the Kashmir dispute along the Line of Control, but could not do so for a while because he was still weak politically. Pakistani accounts claim that Bhutto did no such thing and that in any case the written agreement is what matters.[42] For India, Simla had supplanted the UN resolutions as a point of reference for resolving the Kashmir dispute. After all, Indian leaders reasoned, the two parties had pledged to work directly with one another, implicitly abandoning extraregional diplomacy. For Pakistan, Simla supplemented but did not replace the operative UN resolutions on Kashmir.

After the Simla Agreement, the Kashmir dispute seemed to subside. The Indian government began to view the Line of Control as a more or less permanent border, which did not prevent it from nibbling away at the Pakistani positions as in Siachin. For Pakistani diplomacy, the Simla Agreement did not replace the UN resolutions nor did the conversion of the cease-fire line into a Line of Control produce a permanent international border. Guided by these varied interpretations, both sides continued to press their respective claims whenever the opportunity arose. Yet for seventeen years those outside the region saw the Kashmir issue as either solved or on the way to resolution. Furthermore, other regional issues displaced Kashmir; the 1974 Indian nuclear test, Pakistan's covert nuclear weapons program, and the Soviet invasion of Afghanistan in December 1979. Between 1972 and 1994 India and Pakistan held forty-five bilateral meetings, only one of which was fully devoted to Kashmir.[43]

Since the uprising of 1989, the situation in Kashmir has reached a bloody stalemate. India continues to apply a mixture of pressure and inducement, organizing its own squads of former terrorists and sending them against the Pakistan-sponsored "freedom fighters." Numerous bomb blasts in major Indian and Pakistani cities, several unexplained railway wrecks, the occasional air hijacking, and miscellaneous acts of sabotage seem to be evidence of organized attempts to exploit local grievances and extract revenge. While Indian officials see a decline in "militancy," international human rights groups and independent observers report little change, and within Kashmir the death toll mounts. Most of the Kashmiri population remains alienated, whether they are the Pandits, many of whom have fled their homes, or the Valley Muslims, bitterly divided and increasingly terrorized by radical Islamic groups.

## Toward a Solution?

Over the years many solutions have been proposed for the Kashmir problem. These include partition along the Line of Control, "soft borders" between the two parts of Kashmir (pending a solution to the entire problem), a region-by-region plebiscite of Kashmiris, a referendum, UN trusteeship, sharing of the territory along the lines of the "Trieste" and "Andorra" models or a nominally sovereign territory controlled jointly by two states, revolutionary warfare, depopulation of Muslim Kashmiris and repopulation by Hindus from India, patience, good government, a revival of "human values," and doing nothing.[44]

The dispute has not been resolved because of at least three factors. First, over the long run, the cold war led the United States and the Soviet Union to see this dispute as part of the systemic East-West struggle. Second, both states have continued to pursue inflexible strategies. India's has gradually eroded Kashmir's special status under Article 370 of the Constitution of India, which grants the state a special status in the Indian Union. It also pretended that the problem was "solved" by the Simla Agreement. This dual strategy of no change within Kashmir and no discussion of the issue with Pakistan failed to prepare New Delhi for the events of the late 1980s. India rejected the political option, did not want to accommodate Kashmiri demands, excluded Pakistan from its Kashmir policy, and stubbornly opposed outside efforts to mediate the dispute. Yet New Delhi lacks the resources, the will, or a strategy to deal with the Kashmir problem unilaterally. Pakistan, on the other hand, has often resorted to force in attempting to wrest Kashmir from India, further alienating the Kashmiris themselves in 1947–48 and in 1965 and providing the Indian government with the perfect excuse to avoid negotiations. Third, the Kashmiris, while patently victims, have not been reluctant to exploit the situation. A significant number have sought independence from India *and* Pakistan. The two states disagree as to which should control Kashmir and the mechanism for determining Kashmiri sentiment, but they are unified in their opposition to an independent state. Thus the seemingly well-intentioned proposal, heard frequently from Americans and other outsiders, that Kashmiris should be "consulted" or have a voice in determining their own fate is unacceptable to both Islamabad and Delhi.

The Kashmir problem is so complicated that one is hard pressed to say how the parties involved might ever begin to resolve it. Like the Middle East peace process, it is surrounded by degrees of contentiousness. While the Valley Muslims complain that they are dominated by Indians, other Kashmiri groups, especially the Pandits and the largely Buddhist population of Ladakh, fear being dominated by Muslims. Thus a number of proposals have suggested separating the Valley from other regions (Azad Kashmir, Ladakh, Jammu) and allocating parts of Jammu and Kashmir to India and Pakistan, leaving to the end the intensely disputed Valley.

To further complicate the situation, there are different perspectives within India and Pakistan on Kashmir. During the height of the 1990 Kashmir crisis, the further one was from Delhi and Islamabad, the less passion there was about Kashmir. In Madras, Calcutta, Hyderabad (Deccan), and Bombay, Kashmir was, and is, considered New Delhi's obsession; in Karachi, Quetta, Peshawar, and Hyderabad (Sind), it is a secondary issue, for relations between these provinces and Islamabad and the Punjab come first.

Like proposals to resolve other complex disputes, such as those in the Middle East or China-Taiwan and the two Koreas, "solutions" to the Kashmir problem must operate on many levels. The examples of the Middle East, South Africa, and Ireland indicate that seemingly intractable disputes can be resolved, or ameliorated, through patience, outside encouragement, and, above all, a strategy that addresses the many dimensions of such disputes. If a strategy for Kashmir had begun in the early or mid-1980s, then some of the later crises might have been averted, and it would not now be seen as one of the world's nuclear flashpoints.

Any comprehensive solution to the Kashmir problem would involve many concessions and changes in the relationship between India and Pakistan and reforms within each state. In the case of India, it would require a change in the federal system. The military balance between India and Pakistan would have to be reexamined along with provisions that would prevent the two states from again turning to arms in Kashmir. Above all, Pakistan would have to make major concessions, and India might have to accept a Pakistani locus standi in Kashmir itself. Pakistan would also need an incentive to cooperate in such ameliorative measures, since its basic strategy is to draw outsiders into the region and to put pressure on India. In brief, India has to demonstrate to Pakistan not only that it would be willing to make significant concessions, but also be willing to pledge that if Pakistan ceased its support for Kashmiri separatists Delhi would not change its mind once the situation in the Valley had become more normal.

Doing nothing is likely to be the default option for Kashmir. It might be possible to ensure that the state does not trigger a larger war between the two countries. However, this would do little to address Kashmiri grievances or the widespread human rights violations in the state. Nor would it resolve the deeper conflict between India and Pakistan.

One of the major obstacles to finding a solution to the Kashmir tangle is the belief, on all sides of the dispute, that "*time* is on our side." Since the Kashmir problem has been mismanaged by two generations of Indians and Pakistanis (and Kashmiris have contributed their own share of errors of omission and commission), no one in South Asia, except perhaps the youngest age group, believes that the time has come for a solution since it will not be long before one side or the other regains the advantage. Moreover, both sides seem to assume that the other will not compromise unless confronted by superior force. "Punjab rules"—a zero-sum game with a club behind the back—appear to dominate India-Pakistan relations. The greater Kashmir problem is persuading both sides—and now the Kashmiris themselves (whose perception of how time will bring about an acceptable solution is not clear at all)—to examine their own deeper assumptions about how to bring the other to the bargaining table and reach an agreement.

## Resolution or Permanent Hostility?

A paired-minority conflict does not readily lend itself to the kind of sustained dialogue that leads to regional peace. But neither does it imply that war is likely. Other paired-minority conflicts have been moderated or appear on the road to resolution, or at least manageability. The debate surrounding Kashmir and relations with Pakistan is particularly intense in India (far more so than that in Pakistan), and no future can be absolutely ruled out.[45] Many Indians would like to draw the international boundary along the cease-fire line, with minor adjustments.[46] Pakistan rejects this idea, although it keeps cropping up in Indian discussions and in proposals by third parties.

On one hand, it is possible to envision a peace process that could resolve or ameliorate the core conflicts between India and Pakistan. Drawing on the experience of other regions, as well as South Asia's own history, such a process would require major policy changes on the part of India and Pakistan, as mentioned in the preceding section, and on the part of the most likely outside "facilitator" of such a process, the United States.[47]

However a regional peace now seems improbable, given the difficulty of arriving at political acceptance in both countries at the same time. India is highly critical of the two-nation theory, which it sees as Pakistan's sole reason for existing and also as a force that would encourage India's large Muslim population to promote separatist groups. At face value, the Indian argument suggests there can be no real peace process between India and Pakistan as long as either retains its identity. Any peace process is bound to fail if it does not recognize their core differences.

The obstacles to peace are even greater on the Pakistani side. The intellectual and political debate there is dominated by hard-liners and the military-security establishment, and moderate voices either go unheard or are routinely suppressed.

To complicate matters, the debate over Pakistani identity has moved well beyond the question of needing two nations in order to have a homeland for Indian Muslims. After the Punjabi-dominated military assumed power, Pakistan came to see itself as a fortress, a state (that happened to be Muslim) threatened by India. This was a Punjab-centric view of Pakistan. After the loss of East Bengal, Pakistanis turned toward Islam as a way of asserting a national identity. In the midst of a debate over their own national identity, Pakistanis agree on at least one point, the unremitting hostility of India.

Therefore India and Pakistan may not be able to arrive at a comprehensive peace without the help of an outside power or powers. The only outsider that could initiate such a process at this time would be the

United States, but since 1964 Washington has been reluctant to become deeply engaged in South Asian conflicts. Recent American studies have stopped well short of recommending a regional peace process, and there appears to be little interest in a large American role, although since the 1998 tests the United States has become more active behind the scenes, fearful that events might slip out of control in the region.

A more likely development is that steps will be taken to encourage India and Pakistan to accommodate one another and to reduce their conflict. Such measures have already been gaining support over the past fifteen years and in some quarters are seen as a prelude to a real peace agreement. The uprising in Kashmir and the nuclearization of India and Pakistan have stimulated this interest, as reflected in the expansion of "Track II" diplomacy as well as increasing research on ways to stabilize the India-Pakistan relationship, and various confidence-building measures. The goal of all these efforts is to increase regional cooperation and trust, and to moderate, if not transform, a relationship that seems to be based on fear, hatred, and distrust. These suggestions emphasize the gains and benefits that each side may reap from cooperation.

India and Pakistan have already agreed to a wide variety of confidence-building measures, including notification of troop movements and exercises and of the location of nuclear facilities, hotlines between military commanders, regular meetings between prime ministers, and restrictions on propaganda and other activities that might exacerbate India-Pakistan relations.[48] The best that can be said for these measures is that neither India nor Pakistan has yet boasted of breaking the arrangements. In times of crisis, most have simply ceased to function, and whatever "lessons" about cooperation have been learned seem to have evaporated. Nevertheless, there is a strong feeling in both countries that they can avoid major conflicts and that South Asia is not as unstable as outsiders believe.

One of India's Sandhurst-trained generals, D. K. Palit, once characterized India-Pakistan wars as "communal riots with armor." In many ways that was the case in the wars of 1947–48, 1965, and 1971, the Kargil war of 1999, and near wars in 1955, 1987, and 1990.[49] In the typical communal riot, each side views the riot as one episode in a protracted conflict that will be followed by a temporary truce. Both sides not only battle each other, but they keep one eye on outside forces (the police, the civilian administration, and politicians), who may or may not play favorites and who may or may not put a speedy end to the conflict.

During these armor-plated riots, both sides played heavily to an international audience, knowing that they lacked the resources (or, so far, the will) for a fight to the finish. As in the communal riot, the causes of conflict between the two states run deep, and wars are assumed to be as predictable as riots stemming from religious, linguistic, or caste differences.

However, the possibility that the India-Pakistan relationship might undergo a major transformation cannot be ruled out. Several scenarios suggest themselves, and though some of these seem far-fetched at the moment, all merit at least brief mention.

—Pakistan could collapse under the weight of its own contradictions and cease to exist in its present form, perhaps splitting into several states. This seems to be the pattern many Indian strategists foresee who expect the Kashmir problem to be solved in the same way that East and West Berlin were merged, the smaller simply ceasing to exist. Such a Pakistan might continue as a united state (few Indians would welcome the addition of a hundred million Muslims to the Indian union), but it certainly would not be able to stand up militarily and politically to Delhi.

—India could cause Pakistan to change its identity or cease to exist in its present form. One precedent is the creation of Bangladesh, an Islamic state that is unwilling to challenge India in any significant way. However, India could alter Pakistan's national identity by other means. Delhi could support dissident ethnic and linguistic groups in Pakistan, especially those that were less "Islamic" or less anti-Indian than the Punjab.

—Some RSS and Hindu ideologues believe that India's "civilizational pull" will triumph over the idea of Pakistan, and that Pakistanis will simply succumb to India's greater cultural and social power. They do not expect Pakistan to necessarily merge with India, although many Indians who hail from towns and villages that are now in Pakistan would like to see some parts of Sind and West Punjab reincorporated into India. This school is prepared to wait Pakistan out for decades and even generations, not just months or years.

—India might underestimate Pakistani nationalism and power and take some action that would lead Islamabad to actually use its nuclear weapons in a Masada-like last attempt to defend Pakistan, and if that fails, to bring India down with Pakistan by attacking India's cities.

—A no less dramatic transformation in the relationship could come about if Pakistan itself changed its priorities, putting development ahead of Kashmir, at least for a while. This would put India in the peculiar situation of a former enemy seeking peace. The question is whether India would or could respond in a positive fashion and be willing to negotiate a long-term settlement of the Kashmir dispute. After Kargil, this seems less likely.

—India could accept Pakistan's identity as an Islamic state. It could declare that it disagrees with this identity and that it rejects such a theory of religion-based statehood for itself. It could also point to the accomplishments of a secular democracy—and the general willingness of Muslim and other religious and ethnic minorities to live in such a state—but it could acknowledge that on this irreconcilable point Pakistanis have the right to continue to choose to live a different life. It could then move to cooperate on a whole range of shared economic, cultural, strategic, and political interests.

None of these extreme outcomes seem likely, but together they add up to a possibility that the India-Pakistan relationship could take a dramatic and even dangerous turn. Without some fundamental changes in India and Pakistan, the most likely future of this dispute will be a continuing stalemate, one of hesitant movements toward dialogue, punctuated by attempts on both sides to unilaterally press their advantage in Kashmir and in international fora. This is a conflict that Pakistan cannot win and India cannot lose, a true "hurting stalemate."

### India's Dilemma

Stalemate seems to be more attractive to each side than finding a solution. From the perspective of the Pakistan military, which has an absolute veto over any policy initiative regarding Kashmir, the ability to tie Indian forces down in Kashmir is an important consequence of the dispute; cynically, it could be said that Pakistan is willing to fight India to the last Kashmiri. As long as Pakistan sees itself as militarily disadvantaged, it will try to equalize the military balance by any means possible, even through the nuclear program or a strategy aimed at forcing India to divert important resources to a military front (Kashmir) where the terrain and political situation are in Pakistan's favor. For India, Kashmir has so many links to India's secular political order—especially the place of Muslims—that any settlement appearing to compromise this order is unacceptable. Clearly, Kashmir is linked to broader issues of the military balance between India and Pakistan, and the very identity of the two states, and while more could be done to ease the suffering of the Kashmiri people—a cease-fire and some drawdown of regular and paramilitary forces on the Indian side, and less support for extremists coming from the Pakistan side—no lasting settlement will be possible unless the two sides address these larger strategic and ideological concerns.

Until a few years ago, the prospect of a "failed" Pakistan did not greatly disturb India. In the face of Islamic extremism, Pakistan's acquisition of nuclear weapons, and the state's economic collapse, however, the thought of a failed Pakistan is worrying India more and more. Pakistan could spew out millions of refugees, it might accelerate the spread of nuclear weapons to hostile states and terrorist groups, and it could serve as a base for radical Islamic movements that target Indian Muslims. Strategically, a failed Pakistan might draw outside powers into the Subcontinent. Conversely, a more normal India-Pakistan relationship could help India assume a place among the major Asian and even global powers. It would not be a question, as it is now, of Indian power *minus* Pakistani power, but of an India free to exercise its influence over a much wider range, without the distraction—and the cost—of a conflict with a still-powerful Pakistan.

Indians need to fully debate their relationship with Pakistan. The problem is that events may outrun India's capability to understand them. In recent years there has been a summit, a war, and a coup in Pakistan in rapid succession. New Delhi may still seek agreement with Pakistan on Kashmir and other disputes. But the most important question one can ask of the relationship is not whether Indians or Pakistanis can be trusted to fulfill obligations incurred in agreements where they had little incentive to comply, but whether, under the influence of a pessimistic vision of the region's destiny, they can be trusted in cases where it *is* in their self-interest to comply.

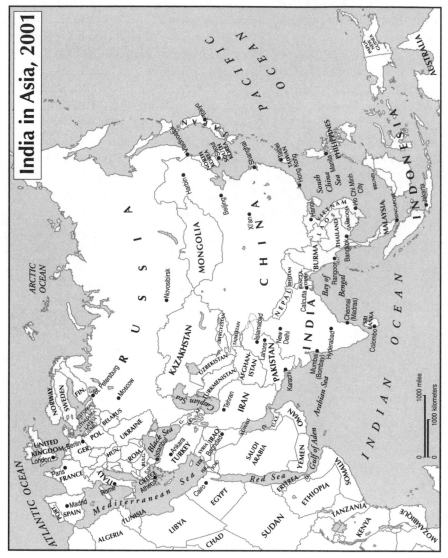

Figure 8-1. India in Asia

EIGHT    *India as an*
*Asian Power*

Before the cold war India was a major Asian power. The British used Indian assets to develop and control other colonies in a region that stretched from Africa to the Pacific Ocean. India provided troops for imperial expeditions to China, Tibet, and the Persian Gulf, and Indian soldiers fought on the Allied side during both world wars. It was from India that Britain and the United States were able to supply the Nationalists in China and roll back the Japanese from Southeast Asia. Naval bases at Trincomalee in Ceylon and at Bombay, Madras, and Vishakahapatnam in India were used for operations in the Indian Ocean, the Arabian Sea, and the Persian Gulf, while Indian air bases were used for movement from Europe to Southeast Asia and Australia and flights over the Himalayan "hump" to China. Vast numbers of Indians were recruited for the war effort, and with American assistance, India became an important defense production center.

Complementing this strategic role, millions of Indian émigrés in the Middle East, Africa (especially South Africa and East Africa), Southeast Asia, East Asia, and in other South Asian states constituted a diaspora that strengthened British control over parts of Africa and the Middle East. They also played an important part in the economies of British possessions in Southeast Asia, especially Malaya and Singapore, and the crown colony of Hong Kong. Indians were recruited as plantation workers and laborers in large numbers after the slave trade was outlawed in the 1840s. This first wave was followed by a significant flow of Indian professionals, including engineers of all varieties, civilian administrators, and architects, as well as lawyers, physicians, and a very influential business and commercial community.

Indians themselves looked forward to a new role for India in Asia after it achieved independence.[1] Subhas Chandra Bose had claimed that with Axis help, India could liberate other colonies and assume its role as a major Asian state, sharing power with Japan. The RSS saw India as having a "natural" role as the dominant power in a region stretching from the Persian Gulf to Southeast Asia. The Muslim League assumed that India would be partitioned and that the then-projected state of Pakistan would align with the West because of its location on the edge of West Asia. This view eventually led Pakistan into the Baghdad Pact (later CENTO). In addition, Pakistan joined the Southeast Asia Treaty Organization (SEATO) because of East Pakistan's strong links to Southeast Asia.

The Indian National Congress, opposed to the liberation model of Bose or the pro-Western strategy of Jinnah, was influenced largely by Nehru's vision of India as a great peace-promoting Asian state.[2] Asia was a single if variegated entity: bonds of culture and religion linked its component states, which had had good relations before the colonial era. Although India had inherited the Raj's strategic obligations, it would be a benign power, shunning conquest or domination. As the *first* Asian state to free itself from European domination, India had a responsibility to peacefully liberate other colonies and promote a regional framework of cooperation. It did, in fact, provide some assistance to the Indonesian revolution. As Asia's *largest* free state (China was in the throes of a civil war until 1949), India saw itself as the natural leader of this movement, and New Delhi developed links with the newly independent powers of Africa, the Middle East, and Asia, inviting a number of Asian leaders to the 1947 Asian Relations Conference held in New Delhi just before independence.

The cold war dashed these Indian expectations. As Indians saw it, the major colonial powers delayed their retreat when the United States stepped in to help its NATO allies (Britain, France, the Netherlands, and Belgium) regain control over their colonies. Even more threatening, the United States established close military ties with several countries in West Asia, Southeast Asia, and even South Asia. The provocative containment strategy of the United States and its allies, Indians have argued, was what drew the Soviet Union into the Middle East and Southeast Asia.

For more than forty years, Indian policy was devoted to the reduction of the American presence in Asia, not because India was anti-American (although some Indians could be so described), but because the U.S. presence made it difficult for India to extend its own influence. For reasons of policy and nationalism, India was unwilling to consider an alliance with the United States; it chose instead to maintain its ties with both superpowers, using its good relation with Moscow to balance out American and British power.

From Delhi's perspective, bringing Pakistan into the American orbit was the worst consequence of the cold war. While Western alliances with a large number of Asian and Middle Eastern states undercut Indian influence in these adjacent regions, the Pakistan alliance bolstered an enemy of India and brought the West into South Asia itself.

As the cold war wound down, Indians anticipated that the United States would withdraw from India's periphery, enabling New Delhi to emerge as the most important state in the Indian Ocean and Southern Asian region. However, two nearly simultaneous events laid low these hopes. The first was the 1991 Gulf War, which demonstrated that the United States could aggressively pursue its regional interests and was using its cold war alliances to entrench itself as the Gulf's police force. Second, the Soviet Union/Russia did not oppose the war and ended its support for Iraq, which (like India) was largely equipped with Soviet weapons. This presented an entirely new kind of challenge to India: a major and perceived unfriendly power was sitting astride its vital oil supplies; its own superpower quasi ally, the Soviet Union, was gone; and the United States showed little interest in a new relationship with New Delhi. The United States further expanded its economic and political ties with China, while extending its presence to the new states of Central Asia and continuing close ties with the major states of Southeast Asia.

These developments present three major challenges to New Delhi as it tries to shape a policy in the various subregions of Asia, including South Asia: to come to terms with American power in Asia, to rank India's priorities among the countries and regions that surround it; and to marshal adequate resources to protect Indian interests. This chapter examines how India has tried to manage these choices, and how it might cope with them in the near future. It also notes some special problems that grow out of the strategic rivalry between India and China. While all of India's smaller neighbors view New Delhi with a mixture of awe, admiration, and fear, the idea of India as a major power is a dubious proposition in Beijing, the Asian capital that matters the most for India.

## India's Inner Ring

Other than Pakistan and China, India's immediate neighbors include Bangladesh, the two Himalayan states of Nepal and Bhutan, and the two island states of Sri Lanka and the Maldives. These, plus Pakistan, are all members of the South Asian Association for Regional Cooperation, formed in 1985. In addition, Burma has a border with India, and Tajikistan is separated from the Pakistan-administered region of Jammu and Kashmir by a thin slice of Afghanistan. A third Himalayan state, Sikkim, had protectorate status but was incorporated into India in 1975. At one time, Bangladesh, Sri Lanka, and Burma were part of British India (Burma became a separate crown colony in 1937). Sri Lanka (Ceylon) was governed as an independent colony after the 1790s, and Bangladesh, the former East Pakistan, was separated from India at the time of Partition.

Owing to their weakness and location, Nepal, Bangladesh, and Sri Lanka are of special importance for New Delhi. Nepal and Bangladesh are among the poorest and least developed states in the world, and Nepal and Sri Lanka may be open to the influence of hostile powers and forces, including Pakistan, China, and radical Islam, although all three states have overlapping economic, political, and social ties with India. Bangladesh shares a language with the Indian state of West Bengal, Sri Lanka's Tamils have historical links to the Indian state of Tamil Nadu, and Nepalis, especially in the southern Terai region, have ties with north Indian society. India is also an important regional educational center, especially for Nepalis and Bangladeshis. Delhi has aid projects in Nepal, Bangladesh, and Sri Lanka and formal treaties with all three, some of which derive from agreements that predate independence.

Another small neighbor, the Maldives, is a small chain of islands that focuses on tourism. It depends on India for its basic security and is only forty minutes' flying time from Trivandrum. It called on New Delhi to intervene when it was attacked by mercenaries in 1988. In the case of Bhutan, Indian dominance is legitimized by treaty, and Delhi provides it with economic assistance and maintains a military training team in the country, paying for the salary and equipment of the Royal Bhutan Army.

Bhutan has less freedom of action than states within the American orbit such as Panama or Grenada.[3]

## Nepal

Nepal has a 1,000-mile open border with India and a 750-mile border with China to its north. For over 150 years Nepalis have described their position as a "yam between two boulders," although it has closer historic cultural, economic, and military ties with India than with China or Tibet. As Delhi sees it, Nepal is a critical buffer state, and Indian strategists worry that a weak or collapsing Nepal might provide China with opportunities for direct interference in South Asia. More recently, Indian officials have claimed that Nepal is a base for Pakistani intelligence operations, most notably the hijacking of an Indian Airline flight, seized after it departed from the Kathmandu airport on Christmas Day, 1999.

Although Nepal was never part of British India, India has deeper strategic interests in Nepal than in any other South Asian country. Nepal was integrated into India's defense system after it came to Britain's assistance during the Mutiny of 1857. The relationship was codified in a 1923 treaty between British India and Nepal, which in turn was "reiterated and revised" in the 1950 Treaty of Peace and Friendship between India and Nepal.[4] India continues the British practice of recruiting Gurkhas for the Indian Army and trains many of the higher ranks of Nepal's Army. There is also a substantial Nepali population in India, and Nepalis do not need official permission to seek employment in India.

The strategic stakes were elevated in 1950 when the People's Republic of China gained control of Tibet, which had been a buffer between India and China, thereby turning Nepal into a "front-line state." However, India's border dispute with China did not emerge for another five years; in the meantime, domestic changes in Nepal further complicated relations with India.

In 1947–48 following an anti-Rana uprising, the power of the ruling family, the Ranas, declined, and the influence of both Nepal's monarch and the popular democratic movement led by the Nepal National Congress (which had close ties to the Indian National Congress) increased. Thereafter India's position in Nepal became very complicated, especially when the monarchy began cultivating China to balance out the generally pro-Indian democratic forces. By the mid-1960s Nepal had distanced itself considerably from India and was pursuing its own version of non-alignment, to the point where China stated that it would come to Nepal's defense in case of any foreign threat, which could only mean India.[5] Nepal also tried to balance Indian influence by internationalizing itself by inviting diplomatic missions and aid programs from many states.[6]

Nepal's efforts to distance itself from India have had some surprising results. After India vetoed King Mahendra's idea of declaring Nepal a "zone of peace," the Bangladesh government developed plans for a *regional* structure, which eventually led to the creation of the South Asian Association for Regional Cooperation (SAARC) in 1985. India originally fought the idea, suspecting that a Pakistani hand was behind it, and has not allowed SAARC to handle any but the most innocuous matters. Twenty years later, in response to a Chinese sale of antiaircraft weapons to Kathmandu, Rajiv Gandhi closed India's borders with Nepal. The ensuing economic crisis inadvertently persuaded the monarchy to yield more power to democratic groups and the present parliament-dominated system.

India continues to influence Nepal's domestic politics. Indian officials are part of the Nepali political process and are not reluctant to inform their counterparts as to which policies might be perceived as hostile to India. To back them up, India has its largest foreign aid program in Nepal, an educational exchange program that has trained many of Nepal's leaders and a significant military presence near Nepal; of course, landlocked Nepal is dependent on India for almost all of its imports.

Indian experts on Nepal have been scathing about Delhi's diplomacy in that country, complaining of India's "diplomatic ineptitude," its insensitivity toward the democratic and nationalist aspirations of Nepalis, the lack of understanding of its leaders, and their "smallness, weakness, and inexperience."[7] Yet the overall record could have been much worse. India has so far prevented a significant foreign presence from establishing itself in Nepal, while Nepalis themselves remain closely linked to India through economics and culture: Nepal is a Hindu state. Furthermore, Nepal has certain assets that India desperately needs, namely, hydroelectric potential, and the joint management of Nepal's enormous water resources is vital to north India and Bangladesh. Hitherto, India has rejected an integrated, multistate approach to the water problem, preferring to deal with each of its neighbors on a bilateral basis.[8]

The liberalization of India's economy is likely to have significant implications for its relationship with Nepal. Kathmandu stands to benefit enormously from India's rapid growth and modernization, but economic growth will put new strains on Nepal's political system, and the temptation for India to manipulate different Nepali factions and parties will always remain. India would like to promote pro-democratic and pro-Indian forces but is wary of interfering in Nepal too blatantly. Meanwhile, an increased Chinese presence in Nepal and possible expansion of Pakistan's role in Nepal are seen as threatening.

## Bangladesh

India's relations with Bangladesh are complicated by the latter's turbulent domestic politics, its location, and the concern that other states might gain a foothold to India's disadvantage. It has one additional quality that sets it apart from India's other neighbors. Indians see Bangladesh as proof of the bankruptcy of the "two-nation theory," the ideological bedrock of the Pakistan movement. Bangladesh may pose many challenges to Indian diplomacy, but it represents one great accomplishment, the military defeat of Pakistan: if India can maintain cordial relations with the former East Pakistan, if the two states can work out their various political and economic differences, if Bangladesh can accept India's military primacy, then there remains a possibility that "new" Bangladeshes could be formed out of Pakistan, raising the prospect that India could emerge as the unchallenged power in South Asia.

Despite Bangladesh's strategic and ideological importance, relations with India have not been smooth. Like Nepal and Sri Lanka, Bangladesh feels it is taken for granted by New Delhi. It resents the proconsular style of some Indian officials and feels overwhelmed by India's vast economic capabilities. Senior Bangladeshi civil servants, diplomats, and army officers remember the "Pakistan days," when they were part of a larger and strategically important state.

Until recently, Delhi has resisted Bangladesh's attempts to be part of any larger international framework that might impinge upon its own regional dominance. This is especially true in the case of managing river waters that flow from India to Bangladesh. Bangladesh draws most of its water supply from two great rivers, the Ganges and the Brahmaputra, which are therefore vital for its very existence. Most of Bangladesh is culturally adapted to the seasonal flooding of these rivers. In the late

1970s the United States offered to fund a scheme to create an integrated river management system that included Bangladesh, Nepal, India, and possibly China (the Brahmaputra and some of the branches of the Ganges rise in Tibet). This idea was firmly rejected at the time, and it took another twenty years before progress was made on a partial scheme for the management of the Ganges.[9] In the interim, India proposed a canal across Bangladesh (along with greater access for India to its Northeast), but Bangladesh suspected that the Indians had been improperly diverting water all along and indignantly rejected this link. Eventually, the Gujral government signed a thirty-year agreement in 1996.

Because of the great increase in social violence and separatist movements in India's northeast, as well as conflict along India's border with Burma, Bangladesh's location and geography have also assumed strategic importance. Before Partition the entire Bengal Delta had an integrated river transportation system, at its upper reaches providing steamer service to India's northeast. This was curtailed after Partition and has never been revived. Meanwhile, separatist and autonomist movements gained increasing strength among the Nagas, Mizos, and other groups in India's northeast. India has deployed large numbers of troops to this region, either by air or by a circuitous northern railway route through a narrow corridor. India would like to see a rail route or other transit facility across Bangladesh, as well as the opening up of river traffic. Dhaka has resisted these requests, partly out of fear of being overwhelmed by India, but also because such access represents one of its few bargaining chips.

In the area of domestic politics, New Delhi was a strong supporter of Sheikh Mujib, the charismatic East Pakistani who led the Bangladesh independence movement. When Mujib was assassinated in a 1975 coup, India suspected the Bangladesh Army of being anti-Indian (some of its senior officers had served in the Pakistan Army). At one point, Indian strategists hypothesized that an aggressive Bangladesh might receive foreign support and join a Western-led encirclement of India. In recent years, India has demonstrated a clear preference for the Awami League, now headed by Mujib's daughter, Sheikh Hasina, over the Bangladesh National party (BNP), led by the widow of General Ziaur Rahman, who was himself assassinated when president. Furthermore, because Bangladesh is overwhelmingly Muslim, Indian strategists fear that it might harbor extremist anti-Hindu, anti-Indian Islamic groups, possibly with support from Pakistan.

Because of social and cultural ties, the domestic ethnic politics of one state often resonates in the other. While 12 percent of Bangladesh's population are Hindu (85 percent are Sunni Muslims) and communal relations are relatively harmonious, religious crises in either India or Bangladesh could lead Bangladeshi Hindus to move to India and, in some instances, Indian Muslims to Bangladesh. For economic reasons, Bangladeshis have migrated in large numbers to the underpopulated states of the northeast, especially Assam, a Hindu-majority state now in fear of acquiring a Muslim majority. Hundreds of thousands of Bangladeshis also attend Indian schools and colleges.

New Delhi still worries that outsiders will become involved in Bangladesh's affairs. There have been frequent newspaper accounts of Pakistani intelligence operations mounted from Bangladesh and of activities of radical anti-Indian and anti-Hindu Islamic groups. New Delhi is also concerned about possible American assistance to the Bangladesh Army. The latter has been very active in international peacekeeping operations, and American officials have considered such aid to enhance Bangladesh's capabilities. The worry for Indian strategists is not that this will encourage an attack from the minuscule and ill-equipped Bangladeshis, but that it might tilt the political balance within Bangladesh. Given the army's record of political involvement in the past and coup attempts as recently as 1998, this is not an unreasonable concern.

## Sri Lanka

Sri Lanka used to be regarded as the South Asian state most likely to achieve middle-income status and once sought membership in the Association of Southeast Asian Nations. Its strategic elite are largely educated in Britain, the United States, and other English-speaking countries. As an island state situated at an important Indian Ocean crossroad, it has a more varied and cosmopolitan population than Nepal or Bangladesh, with Muslim, Arab, Hindu, Buddhist, Chinese, Dutch, British, and other traditions contributing to a society of great diversity but increasing divisiveness.

The Sri Lankan economy was the first in South Asia to find a profitable niche in the new global economy. Besides producing tea, spices, gems, and other traditional products, Sri Lanka has become a major clothes exporter and could have been a significant player in light electronics. It has a literacy rate in the 90th percentile and one of the healthiest populations in Asia.[10] Being an island, Sri Lanka is psychologically more distant from India than either Nepal or Bangladesh. The dominant Sinhala community has few social or cultural ties to India. The more chauvinist members of the community see Sri Lanka as the beleaguered outpost of Buddhism in South Asia, holding off a resurgent Hindu majority, whose agents include the largely Hindu Tamil community.

Of India's South Asian neighbors, Sri Lanka is second only to Pakistan in its determination to be more than another small neighbor. In 1947 it was the first South Asian state to sign a defense agreement with a foreign power (Britain), and in the 1950s and 1960s it sought influence in the Pan-Asian and nonaligned movements. While sympathetic to India's aspirations, Sri Lanka did not want to be overshadowed by New Delhi.

This attempt to distance itself from India was entangled in the domestic politics of both states. The British had favored the Tamil community, which held a number of senior positions in the island's administrative and cultural systems, even though it accounted for only 18 percent of the population (a figure that includes the "Indian" Tamils, the more recent arrivals from India). Democracy in Sri Lanka made it possible for Sinhala chauvinism to emerge in full bloom, and the Sri Lankan government pressed New Delhi to make concessions regarding the repatriation of thousands of Tamil migrant workers (the "Indian" Tamils, who had migrated to Sri Lanka several generations ago to work on the plantations). This group did not include the "Sri Lankan" Tamils, largely found in the urban areas and the north and east, who trace their presence on the island back at least a thousand years. Sri Lanka's search for an independent role, and its fear that India could be a security threat, still rankles in New Delhi, where such views are seen as irrational and a contributing factor in Sri Lanka's own internal security problem.

Tragically, Sri Lanka has plunged into one of the world's most intractable civil conflicts, with India drawn in as a major player. The long-running conflict is between Sri Lanka's Tamils in the northern and eastern sections of the island and the Sinhala (and largely Buddhist) majority dominant elsewhere. This strife has made Colombo one of the world's most dangerous capitals and has transformed the Liberation Tigers of Tamil Eelam into a world-class terrorist/political movement. These factors, coupled with Sri Lanka's location and magnificent harbor facilities, make the island the most important of India's weaker neighbors.

Note, too, that the Tigers represent an ideological threat to India. Not only do they want to divide Sri Lanka into two states, they envision a homeland for the Tamil nation that would include the northern districts of Sri Lanka and the Tamil-speaking state of Tamil Nadu, in a Tamil version of the "two-nation" theory. Fortunately for New Delhi, Indian Tamils are now less interested in a greater Tamil state than they were thirty years ago, as most Indian Tamils prefer to be part of a larger India rather than a slightly expanded Tamil state.

The treatment of Sri Lanka's Tamils generated sympathy in Tamil Nadu and became an important human rights issue in Southern India. Until 1991 the Tigers (and other Sri Lankan Tamil groups) received direct support from the Indian Tamil community and were allowed to establish political offices and conduct fund-raising operations. There were also Tamil training bases in Tamil Nadu, winked at by the state and union governments. Though sympathy for the plight of the Sri Lankan Tamils remains, that for the Tigers diminished sharply after they carried out several assassinations in India, including that of Rajiv Gandhi in 1991.[11]

One of India's main concerns has been Sri Lanka's effort to bring in outsiders to help it cope with the threat from the Tigers. At one time or another Sri Lankans have turned to Pakistan, Israel, the United States, China, and Britain for help. India's response was twofold: it put pressure on Colombo to forestall outside support, and it offered to help Sri Lanka settle with the Tigers.

This policy led to an Indian military catastrophe second only to the 1962 loss to China. As a way of pressuring the Sri Lankan government to negotiate a peace settlement with moderate Tamils, New Delhi supported various Tamil extremist groups, notably the Tigers. The critical moment came in 1987, when India and Sri Lanka signed a bilateral treaty in which Sri Lanka acknowledged the security concerns of its powerful neighbor and accepted India's role as South Asia's dominant power. Both the United States and the Soviet Union approved the treaty, tacitly acknowledging India as the region's preeminent power.

Then, things went very wrong. Instead of surrendering their weapons to the Indian Peacekeeping Force (IPKF) the Tigers first turned them on their Tamil rivals and then on the surprised Indian soldiers. Over the next three years, Indian forces fought the Tigers in a bitter and unsuccessful war in the jungles of the north. The Indian Army eventually decamped from Sri Lanka in early 1990. To make matters worse, India's intervention led directly to a series of assassinations of Indian military and political figures by the Tamil Tigers. There is some suspicion that the Tigers provided support to other separatist and dissident groups in India; certainly, their signature remote-control explosive devices and suicide bomber attacks are emulated elsewhere, including Kashmir.

India's failure in Sri Lanka raised serious questions about New Delhi's ability to manage regional conflict and the way it might behave as the dominant power in South Asia. At first, India supported the Tamil separatists in order to pressure Colombo into meaningful concessions, but both underestimated the fanaticism of the Tigers and undercut a democratically elected (if very insensitive) government. Support for the Tigers was a calibrated attempt to apply force in a delicate situation; when things got out of hand, India was unable to apply *force majeure*, even though it sent several divisions to flush out the Tigers.

India's response to the failed intervention parallels that of the United States after its defeat in Vietnam or the Soviet Union after its pullout from Afghanistan. New Delhi washed its hands of the situation for a number of years, amid recriminations and much finger pointing. Without publicly encouraging it, New Delhi has tolerated some military and technical assistance to the Sri Lankan government in its long struggle with the Tigers; for several years it appeared as if the Sri Lankan Army might finally reduce the area under control of the Tigers, and offers of peace plans and negotiations satisfied India that the Sinhala-dominated leadership would not pursue a vengeful policy.

However, the Sri Lankan Army suffered a major setback in early 2000, and India was again confronted with a difficult situation. One option was to do nothing to affect the stalemate, which would have pleased the BJP's Tamil coalition partners. However, this might have led to a further radicalization of the Sri Lanka government, with militant Buddhists gaining ascendancy, possibly inviting some outside power to help it suppress the Tigers, and possibly leading to the partition of the island, with a flood of refugees pouring into India. A second possibility was to attempt to repeat the 1988 IPKF operation and use force to suppress and even eliminate the Tigers. This would have been a bloody effort and might have been beyond Indian capabilities. Third, India could have strengthened the capabilities of the Sri Lankan government to deal with the Tigers. This would have placed New Delhi on one side of a civil war, which would have put it at the mercy of Sinhala politics. A fourth option would have been to depart from past policy and sponsor a coalition of regional and outside powers to help Sri Lanka cope with the insurgency, while continuing peacemaking efforts. Such a coalition could have been sanctioned by the United Nations or SAARC, with India as the lead state, but with other South Asian states contributing their forces and expertise as well. The risk was that Pakistan and other states might have argued that Kashmir deserves the same kind of internationalization.

In the end, the BJP government has taken a prudent middle course, assisting the government indirectly (offering the services of former Indian officials with expertise in counterterrorism), offering humanitarian assistance, and restraining the Tigers' supporters. New Delhi has also quietly allowed other countries to assist Sri Lanka, but it is unlikely that it would tolerate direct foreign intervention. India is a great power that is wary of direct engagement but cannot allow the situation to deteriorate further.

For its part, the Sri Lankan government has introduced major changes in its own past policies and may allow New Delhi access to Trincomalee port, once a major Royal Navy base.[12] Whether this will prevent Sri Lanka's continued descent into chaos is another question. India was not responsible for the island's catastrophe; that was the primary responsibility of the Sinhala chauvinists who failed to offer concessions to a Tamil community that had legitimate concerns about the government's discriminatory policies, and of the extremist Tamil forces, notably the LTTE, which bring to South Asia a world-class fanaticism and willfulness.

## Regional Management Strategies

India has attempted to follow several strategies in its relations with Nepal, Bangladesh, and Sri Lanka: regional cooperation, political transformation, and coercion. However, a changing global economy and new developments in India itself suggest that the substance and the style of its regional diplomacy need to be reappraised.

Until 1981 India was uninterested in any meaningful South Asian regional grouping, preferring to deal with its smaller neighbors on a one-to-one basis. This contradicted India's enthusiastic participation in several global multilateral organizations, including the nonaligned movement (NAM) and the United Nations. India's cool approach to regionalism was implicitly challenged in 1981 when Bangladesh's President Ziaur Rahman proposed that a regional association be formed in South Asia.[13] After some hesitation, both Delhi and Islamabad came around to the idea, and SAARC was launched in 1985. Although bilateral issues were ruled out of bounds from the beginning, considerable attention has been given to South Asia's potential for economic, ecological, and cultural cooperation. This has not produced many substantive results. Perhaps the most useful activities sponsored by SAARC are the annual meetings of heads of government, which have, ironically (in view of the agreement to keep bilateral issues out of SAARC), been a good opportunity for India's and Pakistan's prime ministers to meet. Even these meetings were interrupted, for example, when the Indian government declared in late 1999 that it would not attend the forthcoming SAARC summit. The unstated reason was that this might confer legitimacy on the new Pakistani chief executive, General Pervaiz Musharraf.

Regionalism in South Asia cannot move beyond marginal issues, as long as India believes that multilateralism invites substantial risks. From Delhi's perspective, there is not yet enough congruence between India and its smaller neighbors (let alone Pakistan). Despite the common cultural heritage, Delhi thinks that regionalism cannot work if the Pakistan government remains overtly hostile and the leaders of the smaller states are not entirely sympathetic with Delhi's security interests. India's strategy has been to allow SAARC to function on minor matters, but to construct new regional associations based on economic ties. These exclude Pakistan but include some of India's other regional neighbors (see "Looking East," later in the chapter ). The hope is that India will benefit from regionalism without allowing Pakistan to benefit and will further isolate Pakistan from other South Asian states.

A second Indian strategy toward Nepal, Bangladesh, and Sri Lanka has been to make them more perfect neighbors. Indians tend to complain that the leaders of some of these states are undemocratic, corrupt, or authoritarian, and invariably and wrongly anti-Indian. Thus they cannot permit elections and the free expression of the popular will; instead, they lead astray an otherwise peaceful population. However, the "common man" in these has a long-term interest in good relations with India, and it is the leadership of these states that has betrayed this shared regional interest:[14] in Nepal, the Ranas and some of the kings; in Bangladesh, the army, with its residual ties to Pakistan (or the Mullah's connection to pan-Islamic movements); in Sri Lanka, a Sinhalese elite under foreign influence and heedless of Tamil minority rights or historic Tamil ties to India.

Indians also disagree as to the kind of state they want on their borders. The Nehruvian tradition placed great emphasis on encouraging secularism and democracy in the region. Yet democracy in Sri Lanka produced a Sinhala majority that whittled away Tamil minority rights. In Nepal, democracy has yielded a chaotic political system of dozens of political parties, some of them avowedly pro-Chinese. The view from New Delhi is that neighboring states are not yet completely formed, that they deny their own heritage (that is, a connection with India), and that their leaders wrongly attempt to distance their states from India. Since this situation is unlikely to change soon, New Delhi is reconciled to a degree of incoherence in its neighbors. This calls for continuous vigilance and, occasionally, more direct involvement in the affairs of its neighbors. Because it is more concerned with the foreign relations of these states than their form, India has been able to remain on good terms with regimes that it does not like, tolerating a touch of authoritarianism in Bangladesh, a monarchical system in Nepal, and a highly discriminatory Sinhala-dominated regime in Sri Lanka.

The humiliation in Sri Lanka made Indians wary of using military power in the smaller states, but the possibility of future intervention in Nepal, Sri Lanka, or Bangladesh cannot be ruled out. The goal of such intervention might be to shore up a weak but pro-Indian government, to preempt the intervention of another power, or to assist a neighbor in containing a separatist or other movement that threatened Indian interests. The first is more likely in Nepal, the precedent being the airlift of a number of Indian troops to the Maldives to save a government under attack from mercenary forces. The last option remains a possibility in Sri Lanka. However, given the serious military problems facing the Indian government from separatist movements in Kashmir and elsewhere, anything but a quick in-and-out operation is unlikely.

Though India is an old civilization, it is still a young state with much to learn about the use of force and its limits, as demonstrated by its relations with Bangladesh and Sri Lanka. The intervention in East Pakistan/Bangladesh was a notable success but led India to overestimate its capabilities. It is likely to continue less-than-visible security intervention in its most important neighbors, which will dissuade others from using force and hence will not require substantial Indian intervention. There is still a lingering opposition to external military interventions in general stemming from the anticolonial tradition and strengthened by the Sri Lanka experience. India's reluctance to intervene does not reflect pacifism or an unwillingness to use force and suffer casualties (both were abundant in the recent Kargil operation), but it does suggest that future operations on foreign territory will be carefully debated beforehand, with some assurance that India will have massive local military superiority over any likely foe.

### The Future of India's Region

There have been many attempts to characterize South Asia as a region. Barry Buzan and others have focused on the "security complex" between India and Pakistan. From the vantage point of Nepal, Bangladesh, and Sri Lanka, India's regional foreign policies have a domestic quality because of the intimate relationship between the societies of the region's states and their security concerns. One Indian scholar has whimsically compared the region to the caste system, with Brahmins at the top and other castes on lower rungs of the hierarchy.[15]

Another way of describing the region is to examine the degree of force used by the region's great power and the willingness to accept such intervention by the lesser state. By this measure, one can distinguish between dominance, primacy, and hegemony, dominance being a high degree of coercion and a low degree of acceptance, primacy being the opposite combination, and hegemony representing an intermediate proportion.[16] India sees itself as the *primary* South Asian state, but to its neighbors' view it is more like the regional *hegemon,* and even the regional *dominant* power.

With its new economic links to the outside world and the realization that South Asia, as a whole entity, has been left behind, even India is moving toward a more open and cooperative relationship with its neighbors, other than Pakistan. India's fear of the United States has declined in recent years; Israel (once derided as America's surrogate) has been accommodated in Sri Lanka and has established a close defense relationship with New Delhi. India wants to share the burden and the benefits of regional economic growth. The region may well be on the verge of a new spell of cooperation, which will allow international firms to operate on a regional basis with a more relaxed diplomatic style. India itself is changing, a welcome development for its neighbors because they stand to gain from the new economic policies.

## The Second Ring: Central, West, and Southeast Asia

If New Delhi's ability to develop and maintain a dominant position among its smaller neighbors appears mixed, then what of the next circle of states? India's neighbors have neighbors: Afghanistan, Iran, Central Asia, and the Gulf states. Somewhat further afield, but easily accessible by air and sea, are a number of other states in Africa, the Middle East, and Southeast Asia, all of which make up India's extended neighborhood.

These states and regions were part of the India-centered strategic system developed by the British; many of them had even earlier ties to India because they were the homeland of those who invaded the Indian Subcontinent, or in some cases were the object of Indian expansionism during the great era of South Indian empire-building in the eighth century A.D. In addition, many of these regions have an Indian diaspora that retains close links to the motherland.[17]

### *Africa*

India's links with Africa are varied, but most date from the colonial era. Indian merchants and professionals dot the continent, with concentrations in South Africa and other former British colonies. The armed forces of India, Nigeria, Ghana, and Kenya share a common British legacy, and Indian civilian and military institutions train a number of African officers and officials. Yet India is a marginal presence on the African continent. As one Indian expert noted, India's 1962 defeat by China undermined its position in world affairs, especially in the NAM and Africa: no one likes a loser.[18] India maintained a presence in Africa through small aid and training programs but could not compete with China and other major powers in this regard. However, it could trump Pakistan, as one Pakistani ambassador noted: "I could bring a singer, the Indians could bring a whole cultural troupe."[19]

One African state receives special attention from India: South Africa. Gandhi's early career in South Africa, plus the presence of a large Indian community, created important bonds there, and India was a long-standing supporter of the African National Congress (ANC), Africa's major multiracial political party. Before South Africa achieved independence, India's Foreign Service Institute trained well over fifty black South African cadres from the ANC, and India offered technical assistance to a state that was, in some respects, more advanced than itself. This attention has not produced significant results. South Africa is unwilling to side with India on the Kashmir issue and advanced an "Indian Ocean" initiative that seemed to challenge India's regional leadership. Most significantly, South Africa (which had terminated its own nuclear program and signed the Non-Proliferation Treaty) was publicly critical of India's nuclear tests.

India has not made significant economic inroads into Africa either, although a few of the larger Indian firms have ventures there, and a number of joint projects have been initiated in telecommunications, roads, and airport and rail construction. These, however, amount to very little—less than 5 percent—for either Africa or India.[20] Delhi's strategy has been to develop joint commissions with major African states to promote bilateral trade, investment, and technical assistance. In addition, has India courted many African states as a cofounder of the NAM and advanced an "Indian Ocean Zone of Peace" in a 1971 UN resolution as a way of keeping the superpowers away from the larger Indian Ocean area.

India's strategic interests in Africa are indirect and consist largely of balancing Pakistan and China and of winning a few more votes in the United Nations or in the now-defunct NAM. In the 1960s a more pressing issue was the fate of the large Indian community that was subject to political repression, economic confiscation, and, in the case of Uganda, physical expulsion. India could have protested, but it had no capacity to materially influence developments under Idi Amin, and Delhi could only watch while the Indian community was purged.[21]

### West Asia

No region on India's periphery has been as critical and as frustrating as the Middle East, which Indian diplomats refer to as West Asia/North Africa. India imports 50 percent of its oil from this region, almost all of it from Saudi Arabia, Kuwait, Iraq, and Iran.[22] This was once a region where British Indian influence was paramount; the old Indian Political Service, precursor to the Indian Foreign Service, had numerous posts in the Gulf and West Asia, and the Indian Army was an important presence. The Indian rupee was the dominant regional currency in the Gulf, and Karachi and Bombay were once important banking and commercial centers for Gulf enterprises.

To a large extent, the Raj conducted its diplomacy with the Middle East independently of London. The two regions had important cultural links, and India was a major source of innovative Islamic thought. Partition and the cold war changed India's strategic position in the Gulf. With the creation of Pakistan, India had a powerful Islamic rival competing for the same access, influence, and resources. The cold war brought in the United States—ultimately as an ally of Pakistan—and Indian diplomacy has struggled ever since to establish itself in the Middle East. During the cold war, Moscow and Washington competed in the region, providing a small opening for India to move among the strategic underbrush. New Delhi established close ties with a number of Middle Eastern states, notably Iraq and Egypt, which were more "secular" than other states in the region. Iraq was a major source of oil, and both Iran and Egypt were developed enough to provide markets for Indian finished products. India also supplied them with technical military assistance; India and Egypt cooperated on a joint fighter, and the Indian Air Force provided training to the Iraqi Air Force. Indian relations with Iran have also been cordial, whether under the Shah or the present regime. Soviet influence in the Middle East was not seen as detrimental to Indian interests, since the Soviet Union balanced the preponderant American and British presence there, a task that was beyond India's capabilities if it were to act alone.

However, the decline of Soviet influence in the Middle East—which Indian writers date from the 1967 Arab-Israeli war—left the United States as the dominant power, and American and Indian interests frequently clashed. Washington was critical of India's attempts to build a relationship with the revolutionary Iranian regime (which included the sale of a small research reactor) and of its military relationship with Iraq. In turn, as a staunch supporter of the Palestinians, India was critical of the Middle East peace process sponsored by the United States.

India took an interest in Arab-Israeli relations for several reasons. For one thing, it saw Israel as a "religious" state and thus an analogue to Pakistan, with its two-nation theory. For another, Indian Muslims were upset by the Arab-Israeli conflict. As a result, Delhi did not want to offend the "sensibilities" of a largely pro-Congress bloc by moving closer to Israel. This policy was reversed in 1992 by P. V. Narasimha Rao's Congress government when the two countries finally exchanged ambassadors, a change in policy that had been advocated by the BJP. Rao calculated that the dangers from Islamic extremism were so great that it was worth risking domestic Muslim opposition. In the end, there were no serious objections. Since then, Israel and India have cooperated closely on a number of high-technology defense and economic projects, and their trade has increased (from $200 million in 1992 to $600 million in 1996). The BJP-led coalition has been especially enthusiastic about this new tie with Israel.

There is also a direct relationship between developments in the Middle East and the South Asian balance of power. The Organization of Islamic Conference has been critical of India's policies in Kashmir, and a number of West Asian and Gulf states allowed their citizens to fight in Kashmir as part of a pan-Islamic jihadist movement. Furthermore, Islamabad has long seen itself as a West Asian power and maintains military and strategic ties with several Middle Eastern and Gulf powers. For a number of years, a Pakistani brigade was stationed in Saudi Arabia, Pakistani pilots are an important component of several Gulf and Middle Eastern air forces, and Pakistan sheltered its aircraft in Iran during its wars with India, giving it greater strategic depth. Some of these activities have generated considerable revenue for Pakistan. Theoretically, Islamabad could induct aircraft and other weapons from those states where Pakistanis serve as pilots, a contingency that the Indian Air Force has to plan for. Finally, Pakistan's nuclear program, while developed to meet the Indian threat, could enhance Islamabad's position in the Middle East and weaken India's should it decide to extend a security umbrella over such states as Saudi Arabia. This raises the prospect that the South Asian arms race could be extended to the Middle East, with nuclear weapons and conventional forces exchanged for hard currency and access to energy resources.

## Afghanistan and the Soviet Tie

On December 25, 1999, Indians awoke to the news that an Indian Airlines plane had been hijacked and forced to land at Kandahar, in the heart of Taliban-controlled Afghanistan. India had refused to recognize the Taliban government, and most Indians saw it as a fanatic, irresponsible supporter of revolutionary Islam. Many also thought the Taliban government was under the control of Pakistan (the hijacking had certainly been organized by extremist Islamic groups based in that country). Yet television coverage showed the Taliban in a favorable light, and the hijacking was peacefully resolved with the safe return of all but one of the passengers and crew members.[23] The incident generated enormous resentment against Pakistan, but the Afghan regime had performed credibly. The episode may have marked another turning point in India's convoluted relationship with Afghanistan.

Most Indians regarded Afghanistan as part of South Asia. Indian maps and the Ministry of External Affairs treat it as such. It is in Afghanistan that India played a classic balance-of-power game, supporting several Afghan regimes in their effort to maintain their distance from Pakistan. This was a dramatic reversal of traditional policy: under the British, Afghanistan was seen as a buffer state that shielded India from Russian, Soviet, and German pressure. For fifty years, India has used Afghanistan to counter Pakistan. Whether or not this was a conscious application of the *mandala,* it was a classic expression of realpolitik: India's enemy's enemy, Afghanistan, had become a friend.

Events since 1979 have undercut this strategy. When the Soviet Union crossed the Afghan border on Christmas Eve, 1979, one Indian partner occupied the territory of another, and Moscow had not even bothered to inform Delhi beforehand. India remained equivocal about this invasion for nearly ten years. It did not feel prompted to reconsider its basic assumptions about the Soviet Union. If anything, it hardened its attitude toward the United States.

During the cold war, the United States treated the Soviet Union as a deadly enemy (and caused difficulties by providing military aid to Pakistan), China condemned Moscow for its hegemony. By contrast, influential Indian strategists placed considerable store in "the countervailing force represented by the Soviet Union against imperialism and colonialism" and saw Moscow as a "factor for peace and stability."[24] India had become dependent on the Soviet Union for heavy industrial equipment and technologies. Moscow was also India's major supplier of modern arms and defense production facilities. Politically, the Soviet Union had been supportive of Delhi's regional policies, especially the invasion of East Pakistan; Moscow was extremely careful to avoid offending Indian sensibilities and had mastered the art of playing to Indian idealism. Indian publicists turned out a steady stream of paeans to the Indo-Soviet relationship, even as it began to crumble in the late 1980s.[25]

Strategically, good relations with the Soviet Union were "vital" to India and had to be "maintained despite doubts and differences arising out of Soviet policies in Afghanistan."[26] The damage that the Soviet occupation of Afghanistan caused to South Asia lay in the renewal of American aid to Pakistan, which in turn threatened the entire region because of the threat to India. Washington, not Moscow, became the object of Indian pressure and resentment. As a leading Indian strategist wrote at the time, "[T]he United States has much greater immediate capacity to influence developments in our neighborhood than the Soviet Union. Apart from . . . Indochina, the Soviet Union has very little direct or indirect authority in our smaller neighbors."[27]

For more than nine years Delhi placed such importance on the Soviet connection that nothing could be said or done that would jeopardize it. For another nine years India watched and waited, while Pakistan expanded its influence in Afghanistan, supporting first the various opposition and Islamic parties based in Peshawar and northern Pakistan, and then nurturing and backing the Taliban movement, which had its origins in the *madrassas* of Pakistan.

One of India's most important decisions in the next few years will be whether it reassesses its Afghanistan policy. Delhi could revert to an earlier policy and woo the Taliban, trying once again to turn Kabul against Islamabad. But the Taliban government is not a passive regime, has supported Islamic groups in Kashmir and beyond, and in 2001 it destroyed priceless historical Buddhist treasures. The new thinking in Delhi concerning the importance of having a buffer state is that now Afghanistan is the threat and Pakistan might be the buffer. India cannot allow revolutionary Islam to approach its borders, but it will have great difficulty influencing Afghanistan with a hostile Taliban regime installed in Kabul. While watching and waiting suits India's diplomatic style, if the Taliban should triumph in Afghanistan and spread its influence to Pakistan (or if Pakistan should gain control over the Taliban), India could be threatened by a revolutionary regime promulgating a dangerous religious message.

India has consulted closely with other states concerned about the Taliban. There is now a formal agreement with Russia to coordinate the operations of the two countries' "special services." This could mean mere information sharing, or it might be the prelude to coordinating an attempt to isolate the Taliban and sanction Pakistan in the United Nations and other fora. Such a policy might include a tougher embargo on travel to Afghanistan, support for the anti-Taliban Northern Alliance, and public disavowal of Pakistan as a state that supports terrorism. An effort of this kind would be effective only if it was backed by other concerned states such as Iran and could be seen as a way of checking the influence of the Taliban/Pakistan axis. Conversely, it might backfire and strengthen the Taliban, or lead Pakistan to expand its engagement in Afghanistan. In the meantime, the prospects for a much-needed gas pipeline to India through Afghanistan and Pakistan seem to be dimming.[28]

There is still a possibility that India will revert to its traditional balance-of-power strategy in Afghanistan. If the Taliban government is not dependent upon Pakistan or does not come to resent Pakistani "assistance" once it has secured power, Delhi might have an opening. The judgment of regional specialists varies, but some believe that Pakistan is overextended in Afghanistan. Certainly, the influential Pakistanis who think the Afghans would be "grateful" for Islamabad's help are mistaken. A Taliban regime that wants to be part of the wider world would seek support from many quarters, and it is not inconceivable that India could regain its once-substantial position in Kabul.

## Central Asia

Now that new states have emerged from the wreckage of the Soviet Union, the Commonwealth of Independent States (CIS) has been delinked from India's old ally, Russia, and reoriented toward the West. This central part of Asia is an oil- and gas-rich region, and New Delhi fears that Pakistan may move quickly to assert itself in what one leading Indian diplomat calls the "new region" stretching from Pakistan to Turkey and Kazakhstan to Iran and the Gulf.[29] This area contains much of the Muslim world, several militarily powerful states, and vast reserves of oil and natural gas. The geographical limit of such a grouping would stop at Pakistan's border with India. Of these states, India has focused on Uzbekistan, which shares Delhi's concern with Islamic extremism and which has a common border with four other Central Asian republics.[30]

Here, however, India has important strategic assets that Pakistan does not. Most of the CIS states do not stress their Muslim heritage as much as Pakistan does. Furthermore, fifty years of Soviet domination has tempered their Islamic zeal. This is one area where the India-Soviet connection has produced collateral benefits. Many Indian scholars and diplomats are familiar with the CIS states because of contacts during the cold war, whereas Pakistan has had little or no access to them. Indeed, many of these states fear Islamic extremism, and Pakistan is increasingly viewed as a state that supports radical and fundamentalist Islam. The cautious leaders of most of the CIS states (many of whom were former

Communists) have no interest in such a relationship and have been open to the United States, Turkey, and other outside powers. India finds itself competing not so much with Pakistan as with the West and even China. In this competition, it has turned to an old ally, Russia, which itself has residual influence in many of the Central Asian states. India and Russia are likely to continue cooperating on a range of policies, balancing Chinese influence in the region and also countering Islamic extremist elements flowing from Afghanistan, Pakistan, and Iran. On the latter issue, India and China have common interests, while India and the United States have come to see the spread of radical Islam as a new and threatening fact of life.

### Looking East

The states to India's east represent a third major cluster of neighbors.[31] The most important of these is Burma, once part of British India. Because of its Andaman Island territories (only 90 miles from Indonesia), India can also be considered part of Southeast Asia, although it makes no claims to be a Southeast Asian state and has limited strategic interests in the region, other than normal access. India has been granted "dialogue partner" status as a member of ASEAN, and in 1996 became a member of the ASEAN Regional Forum (ARF), a forum for dialogue, which includes all of the Southeast Asian states and other significant states such as the United States, Australia, Canada, the European Union, China, Japan, and Russia. India is welcome in the region as another (and nonthreatening) state, part of a mix of insiders and outsiders that Southeast Asian strategists hope will prevent any one power from dominating the region. However, India has not been admitted into the Asia-Pacific Economic Community (APEC), even though it qualifies in terms of its geographical location and its role in the Asia-Pacific economy. Japan is India's second largest trade partner, accounting for 5.3 percent of India's foreign trade (the United States, the largest, accounts for 14.54 percent). Southeast Asia as a whole (excluding oil imports) constitutes 17.18 percent of Indian trade. In addition, Delhi participates in APEC working groups on energy and technology.[32]

In 1992 Prime Minister P. V. Narasimha Rao instituted a "Look East" policy that continued to pursue India's interests in the security of Southeast Asia while instituting two significant changes: it reduced resistance to regional cooperation and committed itself to a new, more open economic policy. India has begun to explore new regional groupings, most of them linking parts of its own region to Southeast Asia. In June 1997, for example, it promoted a new organization, BIMSTEC (Bangladesh, India, Myanmar, Sri Lanka, and Thailand) in an attempt to link South Asia with two important Southeast Asian states. BIMSTEC's two major poles are India and Thailand. Indian officials saw it as a link to ASEAN and as a vehicle for promoting trade and tourism in the Bay of Bengal region. There is also talk of a Bay of Bengal community (BOB-COM), which would consist of SAARC minus Pakistan, but with the addition of Myanmar and Thailand.[33] When neither BIMSTEC nor BOBCOM seemed to catch fire, India floated the idea of still another cooperative forum with five of its eastern neighbors (Burma, Thailand, Laos, Cambodia, and Vietnam), called the Mekong-Ganga Cooperation scheme.[34] This group will emphasize tourism, culture, and education. It pointedly excludes China while emphasizing India's traditional cultural ties with these Southeast Asian states.

As already mentioned, Burma's importance stems in part from the long border it shares with India (and with Bangladesh) and from its earlier political ties with British India. In addition, Burma's first civilian leader, U Nu, was a close associate of Nehru and the Congress party and was very active in the NAM. India accepted U Nu's land reform efforts even though they deprived Indians of extensive holdings in the Irrawady Delta and forced many Indians out of Burma's civil bureaucracy.

Under Ne Win (1962–88), Burma sharply restricted Indians, transporting 100,000 (mostly Bengalis who had been employed in the Burmese government services) back to India. In view of Burma's nonaligned status, however, India was reluctant to try to balance Chinese influence in Burma (Burma had once paid tribute to Chinese emperors), but because of the 1962 loss to China, India lost stature in the eyes of Burmese leaders. If India was unable to defend itself, how could it counter Chinese power?[35] As one Indian analyst describes it, Burma's relationship with India in the postindependence period has been guided by its concerns over relations with Beijing, and the balance has slowly tilted in the direction of China.[36] Burma had nothing to gain by moving closer to India: "An Indian policy which had established that India's interest in Burma was largely benign in nature, had assured for itself a marginalised position in Burma's policy decisions."[37]

When Ne Win was displaced by a military government, India waffled. For several years it protested the eradication of democracy in Burma but was unable to apply pressure on Rangoon. Burma tolerated the movement of Indian separatists to and from Bangladesh and moved even closer to China, allowing the Chinese a facility that reportedly provides intelligence and obtaining weapons from China. China sees this as innocuous and part of a strategy to give its western provinces an alternative outlet to the Indian Ocean.[38]

After 1991, the Indian government decided to stop lecturing Burma and supported ASEAN's "constructive engagement" with it. Trade and economic links have thus been restored, political contacts expanded, and the two states work together on a common narcotics and drug trafficking problem. In 1997 India took an even greater step and established BIMSTEC, which Burma joined one year later.

India's dilemma is that its long and morally gratifying record of supporting democratic governments in Burma (now Myanmar)—even incompetent ones—poses a threat to the present Burmese military regime. The tension between idealist inclinations and realist calculations increased after the most prominent Burmese dissident, Aung San Syu Kyi, received the Nobel Peace Prize in 1991. Meanwhile, China is expanding its position in Burma, but India seems unwilling to offer itself as an alternative to China, or to attempt to balance Chinese influence. It not only lacks China's resources, but no major outside power seems likely to back it in such a venture, and there is residual anti-Indian sentiment in Burma. India's strategy is to increase its engagement with the regime, while working for a long-term transformation of Burmese politics without offending its ruling military council.

The question for India is how to promote the development of the entire region included in India's northeast, parts of Bangladesh, and parts of Burma and China. This is one of the least developed regions of Asia, yet it has enormous resources. With an industrializing China and a developing India, this subregion has become a new political and strategic frontier.

To the east of Burma lie many of the newly rich "tigers," states that were once decidedly inferior to India in economic capability. Under the Raj, the Indian Army served as a postwar occupation force, helping Britain, France, and other European states reclaim their former colonies. Nine years later an independent India returned to the region as the "neutral" member of the UN International Control Commissions in Indochina, the other two states being Poland and Canada. This was in keeping with India's self-image as a state that could interpose itself between the imperial powers and their former colonies, making peace the "third way," a philosophy embedded in India's own constitution.

India's relations with Southeast Asia have changed drastically in recent years. For many decades, Indians knew their economy was still behind Western levels but thought it was far ahead of all of the countries of Southeast Asia, plus Taiwan, and North and South Korea. The superior performance of the economic "tigers" among these states came as a rude shock, because Indians had assumed that they lacked the size, the social structure, or the centralized planning system necessary to become economic powers.

Although several of these states had large Indian ethnic communities, India remained true to its policy of not interfering in their domestic politics. In any case, New Delhi did not have the resources to do so: although Indonesia was only 90 miles from India's Andaman Islands, India did not regard itself as a Southeast Asian state. There was a brief period, at the end of the 1980s, when India was seemingly expanding its presence in Southeast Asia, but this passed quickly when it became bogged down in Sri Lanka and its economy faltered.

This policy of dismissing Southeast Asia's economic capabilities and heaping scorn on the pro-Western policies of states such as Singapore and Malaysia changed rapidly once India itself began to liberalize its own economy. Prime Minister Rao's Look East policy brought new links to the Southeast Asian tigers, and various Indian states began developing their own ties with individual ASEAN countries. This economic promise—and perhaps strategic cooperation—is replacing the old hostility caused by India's great military expansion in the 1980s, and its strong relations with Vietnam, which alienated many Southeast Asian states and Australia. India's reputation in Thailand, Singapore, Malaysia, and other tigers was very poor at that time: it was seen as a major power that could not bring itself to face economic reform, yet it still claimed for itself a preeminent role in the world.

The Look East policy is designed to repair relations with the tigers, while preserving a strategic relationship with Vietnam. In recent years India's trade and investment ties with ASEAN states have grown rapidly and now exceed India's trade with Japan.[39] The new regional economic arrangements just mentioned bring India into Southeast Asia, as does India's membership in the Asian Regional Forum. These ties to Southeast Asia offer economic benefits for both India and the ASEAN states, but they also have a strategic potential. India's BJP government has sent a number of ships to the region on goodwill missions, during which it has engaged in naval maneuvers with Japan and Vietnam. This sent a signal to China that any Chinese interference in South Asia could be countered by India in China's backyard, and also that India sits astride the vital oil routes that run from the Persian Gulf to Southeast and East Asia.[40] No longer as fearful of India because of the demise of the Soviet Union, many of these states think of India as a means of "saving for a rainy day," in that it is a potential balance to powerful China.

## China: Model, Rival, or Ally?

In the Western imagination, India and China have been coupled for more than a century. They have always been among the world's largest states (ranking number three and six, respectively), as well as among the most populous and in recent times the poorest (in the seventeenth century both were richer than any European country). Both were subjected to Western imperialist domination in the nineteenth century, and both achieved independence in the middle of the twentieth. During the cold war, however, India was seen as a responsible state, China as a giant "rogue."

While many Indians subscribe to this characterization, it is obviously not the perception of China's leaders. For them, China's civilization is older and greater than India's, China has been and remains more independent, and is strategically far more important than India. For China's leaders, the idea of Asia and the idea of China are practically synonymous. As visitors to China are often told, "You cannot ignore a billion Chinese," and China borders on more countries than any other power in the world.[41]

India-China relations are greatly affected by China's generally dismissive views of India. A second important factor is China's role as a South Asian power and its relations with regional states, particularly Pakistan, and also with the United States. A third factor is the degree of congruence between the strategic goals of these two states, including the disposition of their complex territorial/border dispute and their potential nuclear rivalry.

### Mismatched Perceptions

In 1998 a group of young Indian strategists meeting with their counterparts in Shanghai were asked what surprised them about China. One Indian responded: "Whenever we ask different Chinese participants a question, we always get the same answer." The Chinese participants laughed: "Whenever we ask different Indians a question, we always get different answers."[42] The anecdote reveals something of the difference between the political styles of the two countries: what the Chinese regard as a virtue (group harmony, a united front to outsiders) Indians see as cold, calculating behavior; and what Indians consider natural (an eagerness to develop original and different ideas, and to share these with total strangers), the Chinese see as a lack of control and coherence. In the words of an informed Indian observer, awareness in each country about the other is "abysmal," even at the level of political and cultural elites, where perceptions "are mired in stereotypes."[43] Misunderstanding comes easy to these states, since both have very strongly held (and often inaccurate) images of each other. The "Asian-ness" of India and China is a myth.

Indian stereotypes concerning the "inscrutable," arrogant, and self-centered Chinese abound. What particularly galls Indian officials is the Chinese disdain for India's position in the region, in Asia, and the world. In the words of one leading Indian strategic writer, "The Chinese [regard] India only as a semi-power which could be put down."[44] Indians also have various ideas about China's regional strategic objectives. Some think that China wants to encircle India and has therefore developed close relations with Pakistan and the other smaller South Asian states, especially Nepal. In the heyday of close India-Soviet relations, a view often expressed in Delhi was that China wanted to sabotage the India-Soviet relationship. China was also seen as a critical component of an encircling alliance that included the United States and Pakistan, each of which was jealous, envious, or fearful of India, which was considered a "growing threat."[45]

But mostly the Indian response to the question of "Why does India have conflict with China?" is puzzlement. Two years after the 1962 India-China war, Lieutenant General B. M. Kaul, the one Indian Army general of his generation with substantial experience in dealing with the Chinese in Korea and China, could still ask a visitor for a coherent theory of its origin. Even for Nehru, "the Chinese are a mystery," according to veteran diplomat T. N. Kaul, who served as ambassador to Washington and Moscow and as foreign secretary under Indira Gandhi. Nehru once told Kaul:

It is difficult to know what is in their mind. They smile while saying the most callous and ruthless things. Mao told me [Nehru] with a smile that he was not afraid of an atomic war. The Soviet leaders . . . are not isolated like the Chinese leaders. Their reactions are predictable . . . but with the Chinese, you never know and have to be prepared for unexpected reactions. This may be partly due to their isolation, but it is mainly the Chinese character, I think.[46]

Many Indians find Chinese officials to be smug and arrogant, which is ironic because many Chinese have a similar reaction to Indians. Compounding this, the Chinese victory in 1962 is still regarded as a yet-to-be cleansed stain by the Indian Army. Senior Indian strategists, especially in the Congress party, resented the casual response of China to Nehru's attempts to facilitate China's "entry" into the world at the Bandung meeting of the Afro-Asian states.[47] Indians can readily imagine the strategic and political responses of Pakistanis, Bangladesh, or other Islamic countries and can draw on their experience with the British to figure out likely U.S. policies and strategies, but until recently they have had no comparable experience in dealing with China. Only in the past ten years have Indians traveled to China in any significant numbers. Several incidents also deepened Indian suspicion of China and served to remind them of Beijing's "duplicity" in 1962: in 1979 China invaded Vietnam just as the then foreign minister, Atal Behari Vajpayee, was on a mission to China's capital to mediate between the two states, and in May 1992 China detonated several nuclear weapons just as the Indian president, R. Venkataraman, was on a state visit.

India's image of China is changing, however, as television and an occasional trip to Shanghai or Beijing by journalists, strategists, and others reveal a country of astonishing economic prosperity, compared with India today or China only fifteen years ago. The knowledge that their country has slipped behind China and that China seems to be emerging as a rival to the United States both intrigues and frightens Indians.

The Chinese view of India is also strongly conditioned by cultural assumptions. Like the Japanese and the Koreans, Chinese elites are baffled by India, especially by its caste system, widespread poverty, and mass democratic politics. The Chinese find it difficult to imagine how a country as complicated as India and lacking in discipline and coherence can make much progress at home or in international affairs.

On balance, the Chinese also view India as a country lacking significant natural resources and whose leaders have failed miserably to modernize their society. What perplexes Chinese leaders (and other East Asians, as well as many leaders of Southeast Asia) even more is that India aspires to be a major international player. States with modest accomplishments should behave in a suitably modest fashion; Indian assertiveness, the Chinese believe, does not seem to be justified, given New Delhi's feeble economic and strategic record.

Chinese strategists also dwell on what they regard as India's unremitting regional hegemony. The view in Beijing is that India inherited and still pursues British imperial policies.[48] India's insistence on observing the British-imposed McMahon line along their border, Delhi's absorption of Sikkim (not fully recognized by China), India's treaties with Nepal and Bangladesh, and its dream of Subcontinental unity are evidence that "hegemonism is the essence of Indian strategy, [that] India wants to be leader or master of the Subcontinent."[49]

India's gravest threat to China resides in Tibet. Not only have the Indians harbored the Dalai Lama and about 100,000 Tibetans, but they seek to turn Tibet into a buffer state. China fears that the day may come when Tibetans rise against China (perhaps during a moment of internal Chinese disarray), and Tibet might gravitate to the Indian sphere of influence. This contingency is the "true threat of India to China." According to one Chinese India-watcher: "Peace in the Subcontinent will always be in peril: India will never give up her ambitious goal—determined to grasp nuclear strategic power and become a superpower of the region, then a world superpower like America, at least equal to China."[50]

### Strategic Rivals?

From Beijing's perspective, India is a second-rank but sometimes threatening state. It poses little threat to China by itself, and it can be easily countered, but Beijing must be wary of any dramatic increase in Indian power or an alliance between New Delhi and some hostile major state. To counter these contingencies, China has long pursued a classic balance of power by supporting Pakistan. Pakistan is China's Israel, the largest beneficiary of Chinese aid, and a recipient of its nuclear and missile technology. For China, Pakistan is the perfect ally. Support for Islamabad balanced out Soviet *and* Indian power (and initially, U.S. power), and Pakistani criticism of China has been muted. Instead, support has been offered in various international fora. After the cutoff of American aid in 1965, China's support enabled Pakistan to offer a credible defense against Indian conventional weapons and to acquire nuclear weapons that have both a defensive and a deterrent capability.

Nepal and Sri Lanka also share the view that good ties with China can provide a useful counterweight to Indian dominance, although they are acutely aware of the risk of moving too close to China and possibly triggering an Indian military reaction. Although China is its ultimate security blanket, Pakistan understands there are limits to Chinese support, as shown during the 1965 and 1971 wars with India. While grateful for Chinese assistance in very sensitive areas (now paid for in hard currency), Pakistan has had to accept a major shift in Chinese policy on Kashmir, the issue most sensitive to Islamabad. China's position has moved from unqualified support for Pakistan to urging both sides to cease their armed provocations, "normalize" their relationship, and wait for the future, when a peaceful settlement may be possible, which is exactly the approach that China claims to have taken in its dispute with India. The shift in Chinese policies came about both because of a desire to look like a peacemaking moderate, and because China was increasingly concerned about the rise of Islamic fundamentalism in Kashmir and the possibility that Kashmiris might achieve a recognized independent status, unacceptable to China, given its position on Taiwan. India has been gratified by this change in Chinese policies but remains suspicious of China's overall regional ambitions, since Beijing retains the capacity to influence dissident groups elsewhere in India and has become a major supporter of Burma.

The United States plays a special role in India-China relations. From China's perspective, the early American support of New Delhi, culminating in outright condemnation of China during the 1962 war (and American support for the Indian position on the territorial dispute in Aksai Chin and the northeast part of India), signified that New Delhi was still under the influence of the imperial powers. This American support fit into a pattern of opposition to the Communist government but ran counter to America's early romance with China, when the two were allies during World War II in the fight against Japan.

The convoluted history of American engagement with India and China took still another turn with the recent rediscovery of democratic India and the denigration of China by American human rights activists and some labor unions and political conservatives. India has tried to take advantage of this shift in U.S. opinion, knowing that the tide of opinion might again turn against India. New Delhi has tried to persuade

U.S. officials that China represents a threat both to India and to the West through its expansionist policies in Burma, its repression in Tibet, and its promiscuous supply of weapons and missiles to Pakistan and other states. These arguments have met with only limited success, but the ground has been laid for closer strategic cooperation should China turn into a hostile state. Yet India does not want to be a surrogate for the United States, allowing Americans to fight China to the last Indian jawan. As India acquires a more far-reaching nuclear capability, this question will arise again in a more acute form: if there should be a major confrontation between the United States and China, would India want to become a target for Chinese nuclear weapons?

According to India's hawks, China will never make concessions on the border dispute until India becomes its nuclear equal. This was an objective of the 1998 tests, which some Indians thought would speed up the hitherto fruitless dialogue on the border dispute. This has not yet occurred, and the first meeting of the India-China joint working group held after the tests saw no change in the Chinese (or Indian) positions.

The basic "deal" Beijing officials have been offering India since 1960 would allow each side to keep the territory it now controls (China would keep Aksai Chin in the west; India, Arunachal Pradesh in the east), while giving up other claims (for each state's claim, see figure 4-1). So far this has been unacceptable to India for political reasons. The Congress party has long been opposed to such a swap, remembering China's humiliation of Jawaharlal Nehru, and the BJP and its allies came into power proclaiming an ever tougher strategy. The border issue remains hostage to intense feelings about the sanctity of territory on both sides. In India's case, the Himalayas hold a strong place in Hinduism as the abode of the gods and a place of pilgrimage. Inasmuch as India's other territorial disputes with its neighbors have been difficult or impossible to resolve, Delhi is unlikely to contemplate a territorial settlement with China as long as nationalist feelings on both sides remain intense.

Beyond their bilateral and border disputes, India and China have often been cast as rivals in Southeast Asia, the Middle East, and Africa, partly because they are similar in their overall economic capabilities, levels of technology, and administrative competence. Usually, India has been at a disadvantage in these rivalries; while it has a rich pool of experts to draw on and a large diaspora, New Delhi has stood back in one area where China has been very active, namely, the sale of weapons and military technology. China, like France, views arms sales as part of a strategy of developing its own arms industries and earning hard currency, while India sees them through a moral prism. It remains to be seen whether the BJP government will break with the past in this area. Military collaboration with Israel and other states has increased, and this could be the prelude to a more active military diplomacy throughout India's expanded region.[51]

## A Nuclear Rivalry?

India's 1998 tests reflected the classic assertiveness of a rising power. They were coupled with a ringing attack on the weakest of the great powers (China) and an appeal for strategic cooperation with the largest (the United States). Washington was surprised at the notion that China might pose a threat to India and subsequently issued a joint statement with Beijing condemning the Indian tests. This infuriated India all the more, as it was China that had reportedly supplied Pakistan with its nuclear technology and the United States that ignored the transfer of technology.

Since that moment, there have been recalculations in Delhi and Beijing.[52] India's earlier statements about acquiring a nuclear capability that could respond to the Chinese nuclear threat have been scaled back, and its nuclear program seems incapable of achieving such an objective until 2005–10. At the same time, New Delhi has hastened to repair the damage done to its political ties with Beijing, and the two states have resumed normal relations. Nevertheless, one wonders how their nuclear programs might interact in years to come. As noted in chapter 6, any Indian attempt to develop a nuclear capability aimed at China could easily be countered by China, leading to an arms race that India could not win.

Although India's program capitalizes on the *political* ramifications of being a nuclear weapons state, this is unlikely to cause China to alter its position on the border dispute, its support for Burma, or even its support for Pakistan. Beijing can be expected to respond to the Indian nuclear program indirectly, by marginally increasing its support for India's neighbors without giving New Delhi the pretext for a truly large-scale nuclear program. China's main concern would be that outside powers, especially the United States, might come to see India as a nuclear bulwark against China. This raises the possibility that India will develop an enhanced nuclear force, or that it will supply nuclear technology to other neighbors of China, even Taiwan, and pose serious strategic problems for Beijing.

In 2000, just as the United States was testing part of a national missile defense (NMD) system, Washington and New Delhi opened discussions on the linkage between NMD and South Asia. It was argued that if the United States deployed an NMD, then China would be forced to expand its nuclear forces, which would in turn force India to expand its capabilities, and then Pakistan to do the same. The weakness in this argument is that, first, China appears to be modernizing its forces regardless of American decisions; second, an increase in Chinese capabilities might be absorbed by the effort to defeat an American system, and third, India is so far behind China that there is little chance of New Delhi catching up with Beijing for many years to come unless India was able to invest huge amounts of money in its own offensive systems or could acquire a theater missile defense (TMD) or NMD system of its own. Given India's weak resources in this area, there may be no way to establish and stabilize an India-China nuclear balance. It looks as if Indian (and some American) fears that an American NMD could act as an accelerant are not based on analysis, but on an abstract opposition to the American program. By early 2001, some Indian commentators were taking a more realistic view of the proposed NMD, arguing that it did not have any direct implications for India.

## India's China Options

China has elevated itself to the first rank of powers without Indian assistance or even a close relationship with New Delhi. Beijing cares little for India, and though the India-China border dispute is in abeyance, China could reactivate it at any time with little risk of Indian retaliation. Indeed, some Indian hawks believe that China is using its military, economic, and strategic resources to encircle India.

In the realm of speculation, developing a strategic relationship with China has its attractions for India but risks alienating the United States. However, India has closer cultural, social, and economic ties with the United States than with its giant neighbor. Furthermore, an alliance with China directed against Washington would still leave Delhi at the mercy of Beijing, since India would only be able to fend off the pressures of the United States and the West with China's assistance. Moreover, the cost of such a relationship would be that India would have to sacrifice any claim it might have concerning its own border problem with China.

Another possible strategy for India would be to confront the Chinese directly, perhaps joining with the United States and Russia or other states that might be subjected to Chinese pressure (Taiwan, Vietnam, and Japan). However, Russia has become a neutral power in Asia and is a significant military supplier for China, while the United States is extremely unreliable, praising China one year, condemning it the next. India will not build its China policy on American Sinophobia.

India could also "pick off" vulnerable friends and allies of China, such as Burma and Pakistan. This tactic would confront China on ground close to India and possibly on Indian terms. However, this would run the risk of triggering a Chinese response. Pakistan is already an unstable state, and, as discussed earlier, a collapsed Pakistan could be a greater security threat to India than a Pakistan that merely posed its present threat. Ironically, India and China have a common interest in preventing Pakistan from evolving into an extremist, Islamist state. Rather than working against Chinese interests in Pakistan, India could conceivably find itself working with China to stabilize that state.

The optimal strategy would be to build on areas of common interest with China and avoid a confrontation for which India is not prepared. China is still an intensely nationalist country, and antiforeign attitudes can be used to drum up popular support. With a mixture of pragmatic cooperation, a strengthened economic base, and improved military capabilities, India can present itself to China as a state that is to be taken seriously but is not a threat. India is becoming more like China as it modernizes and transforms its own economy; China will become more like India as the process of social and political transformation continues. It is too early to predict "convergence," but the two countries may come to the realization that they have important common strategic interests, reminding the Americans of the limits of their power and preventing the inevitable political disruption of their smaller or less stable neighbors that would ensue if they precipitated a conflict between them. It may yet turn out that Nehru's dream of India-China cooperation and a shared vision of regional cooperation are not as far-fetched as they seemed after the catastrophe of 1962.

## India as a Great Asian Power?

In the past four centuries India's influence in Asia has reached two high tides: under the Mughals, India was one of Asia's two dominant cultural and economic powers; under the British, it became the center of a pan-Asian empire. During the cold war, its power dwindled because of competition from the United States, Britain, and France in regions where (during the Raj) it had once held considerable influence. Then China emerged as a significant Asian strategic power, expanding its presence up to India's frontiers and providing Pakistan with major military capabilities

Since the end of the cold war, the prospect of a resurgent India-in-Asia has become more realistic, although it has taken the Indian strategic community a number of years to discard the empty shell of institutions it no longer needs, such as the NAM and the dream of Asian (or Afro-Asian) solidarity, and to sort out its vital interests from those that are merely important. This is a very difficult task, particularly because of India's rivalry with Pakistan, and potential rivalry with China. To complicate matters, it has overseas Indian communities that in many cases are under grave threat, it is energy-deficient and must maintain good ties with some of the major oil producers, and above all, it has overlapping ethnic, cultural, and economic interests with its own neighbors, many of whom are weak and vulnerable. In brief, India has the interests and ambitions of a great Asian power, although it still lacks some critical resources. India's Asian diplomacy will therefore have to address a number of issues in the next decade.

First, it will have to determine its relationship with the one non-Asian power that remains a power in Asia, the United States. In the past, New Delhi considered American interventions in Asia largely detrimental to its interests. Yet as long as American power remains in the region, India must come to grips with it. Hitherto, it has done this in an ambivalent fashion, on the one hand providing facilities for refueling American aircraft during Desert Storm, for example, but on the other hand withdrawing them when the public became aware of them. However, India cannot move freely in the region without at least tacit American support and must come to some understanding of the limits and direction of that support. Although American and Indian interests in Asia do overlap, the two states have found it very difficult to work together in the region except for brief periods and within narrow limits, as was the case during the 1960s after the India-China war.

Second, India must balance its China policy in such a way that Beijing does not come to see India as a threat or a rival yet accommodates India in their long border dispute. If pressured too much, China might retaliate by increasing its assistance to Pakistan, meddling in Indian domestic affairs, or supporting a smaller South Asian neighbor. Yet a passive strategy toward China would leave the border dispute unresolved for an indefinite period. This is not necessarily a bad thing, since the present line is not unfavorable to India. Both sides clearly need to search for a political formula that will allow for minor adjustments in their respective claims so that political honor is served on both sides. Unless China's dismissive attitude toward India changes, this may not be possible.

For Asians and for Indians alike, Beijing is the measuring stick of India's "emergence" as a great power. India is certainly not China, but it clearly has qualities that will serve it well in the next decade. It has an established democratic political system, whereas China is on the verge of a vast domestic upheaval if the Communist party should falter. India's economic performance has also improved markedly; many informed businessmen and economists believe that China's lead is not so large that India could not catch up after a period of sustained economic growth. Although the great military humiliation of 1962 still rankles, even that is fading from memory.

Forty years ago the last British commander of the Indian Army, Sir Claude Auchinleck, lamented Partition, not because of any moral considerations or the loss of life during the division of the two states (although these were bad enough). Rather, it was because Partition had permanently divided the Indian Subcontinent as a strategic entity. Until then, India counted for something in every country from the Persian Gulf to Southeast Asia. It will take an act of heroic imagination to restore that strategic unity. Until then India will always be constrained by the vulnerability of its weaker neighbors as well as by its tense relationship with Pakistan.

Third, as long as India's domestic politics are tied closely to developments in Nepal, Bangladesh, and Sri Lanka, there will be pressures to intervene. Obviously, the best policy is one that encourages these states to manage their own affairs so that outside intervention is unnecessary; to this end, India has often behaved like an imperial state, and Indian officials are deeply resented in the capitals of these smaller neighbors. Experience is a great teacher, and the humiliation in Sri Lanka seems to have produced a generation of Indian officials far more cautious and restrained in their propensity to meddle in the affairs of neighbors; the operations of a coalition government in the center may also be a restraining factor even if one of the partners wants greater involvement.

Finally, two trends seem to be very encouraging as far as India's regional role is concerned. First, the revolution in economic policy that has swept over India makes it a far more attractive country for all of its neighbors and the more developed states of Southeast Asia. Indian management expertise, technology, and organizational skills are now widely exported to the rest of Asia, giving substance to the Indian claim that it is a major power. Second, India's democracy is having a great impact on many of its Asian neighbors. For the smaller states of the region, India is something of a model of how to peacefully manage a multiethnic, multireligious state. India's more distant neighbors, particularly in the Gulf and Southeast Asia, see India's democracy as less than perfect, but it provides some assurance that India is unlikely to transform itself into an aggressive, expansionist state. India is a growing power, but few of its neighbors (except Pakistan, and perhaps China) see this growth as threatening.

NINE    *India and the United States*

In late March 2000, Bill Clinton became the first president to visit India in more than twenty-two years. At the core of his five-day stay was a brilliant speech to Parliament that acknowledged India's civilizational greatness, noted its economic and scientific progress, and praised India's adherence to democratic norms. However, the speech tactfully set forth areas of American concern: Kashmir, India's relations with Pakistan, and nuclear proliferation. These led Clinton to state that South Asia was the most dangerous place in the world, a characterization that was publicly contested by India's President, K. R. Narayanan. During the trip, Clinton also signed a "vision" document with Prime Minister Atal Behari Vajpayee, committing both sides to expanded government-to-government interaction. During a five-hour stopover in Pakistan, Clinton also delivered a "tough-love" (encouraging but critical) television speech to the Pakistani people.[1]

The visit was a triumph as far as images and symbols were concerned. Departing from his prepared speech to the Asia Society in New York on April 14, 2000, India's finance minister, Yashwant Sinha, acknowledged that Clinton swept away fifty years of misperception and that the two countries appeared to be on a path of realistic engagement.[2] This may be true, but it took Clinton seven years to make a journey to South Asia. Moreover, his was only the fourth visit to India by a U.S. president and the first in two decades. This suggests that the long history of strained relations between these two democracies is based on more than misperceptions.[3] This chapter explores the suggestion that major structural changes in the India-U.S. relationship are occurring and may change perceptions and policies in both Washington and New Delhi, with a wider range of strategic choices opening up for both countries.

## India and the United States: Distanced Powers

The strategic distancing of the United States and the leadership of what was to become free India took place several years *before* the onset of the cold war, when neither side saw a close relationship as vital. Each allowed other interests to deflect any plans for strategic cooperation.

Other than early humanitarian and missionary ties and an interest in Mahatma Gandhi, the first important contacts between the United States and India began in 1942, five years before independence, when Americans first perceived a significant strategic stake in the Indian Subcontinent.[4] Support for the independence movement was especially strong among American liberals, and President Franklin D. Roosevelt needled Winston Churchill about India. The pro-nationalist media gave Mahatma Gandhi and Jawaharlal Nehru extensive publicity in *Life,* the *New York Times,* and other major American publications.[5]

The turning point in U.S. policy, which anticipated later India-U.S. disputes, was precipitated by the 1942 decision of the Indian National Congress not to support the war effort and to launch the Quit India Movement. With Allied fortunes then at their low point, this action forced the Roosevelt administration to choose between Britain, its key ally (then under military attack), and India, a potential friend. Not surprisingly, Washington chose Britain.

While disappointing, the loss of U.S. support was not critical for Indian nationalists. Their overseas lobbying efforts had focused on Great Britain, especially the British Labor Party. Many Indian leaders had been educated in Britain or in British-oriented institutions in India and had little personal or intellectual interest in the United States. If anything, they had absorbed leftist British views that the United States was the epitome of capitalism, and they shared a prejudice that Americans lacked the cultural refinements of the British. Only a few Indian leaders of these years had ever been to the United States—Nehru was not one of them—and the most prominent of these (J. P. Narayan and B. R. Ambedkar) were not members of the Congress party.

*The Cold War and Containment*

The cold war brought the United States back to South Asia in search of allies in a struggle against a comprehensive communist threat. It also led Americans to think again about the strategic defense of the region. South Asia had come under attack by Japanese ground and naval forces in World War II. What kind of threat did it face from Soviet and (after 1949) Chinese forces? The goal of America's containment policy, as implemented in South Asia, was to help India and Pakistan defend themselves against external attack, to obtain bases and facilities from which the United States might strike the Soviet Union with its own forces, and to help both states meet the threat from internal (often communist-led) insurrection and subversion. U.S. analysts saw India as the "pivotal" state of the region and Pakistan as a useful place to base long-range U.S. bombers as well as a potential ally in the tense Persian Gulf region.[6]

Eventually, Pakistan joined the Baghdad Pact (later CENTO) and SEATO. It received significant military and economic aid from 1954 to 1965.[7] Although India declined to join any of the American-sponsored alliances because it was nonaligned, it received considerably more than Pakistan in economic loans and grants (although much less on a per capita basis) and purchased about $55 million in military equipment from the United States. In addition, New Delhi received $80 million in U.S. military assistance after the India-China war of 1962.[8]

The United States also pursued cold war objectives in other parts of South Asia, often with the cooperation of regional states. As the internal vulnerabilities of Pakistan and India became more evident (especially in light of the Comintern's 1949 call for revolutionary uprisings throughout the world), Washington mounted a variety of developmental, intelligence, and information programs directed at both. Fearing that Indian communists were under the influence of the Soviet Union, the United States provided huge amounts of surplus food, economic aid, and technical and agricultural missions in an effort to help India and Pakistan counter communist influence. Many of these programs assumed a correlation between poverty and susceptibility to communism: by encouraging economic growth (and redistributive policies, such as land reform) the communists could be beaten at their own game, and democracy would have a chance, even in the poorest regions of India and Pakistan. Substantial information/propaganda campaigns were also developed to counteract the much larger Soviet operations. Although this ideological cold war peaked in the 1950s and 1960s, Washington was still vigorously countering Soviet disinformation programs in the mid-1980s.

Although Pakistan had become a useful ally in 1954, India was the main prize, and several U.S. administrations believed that the most significant contest in Asia was that between Communist China and democratic India. Echoing Leninist logic (that the vulnerability of the metropolitan country lay in its colonies), some saw India as a key battleground in the cold war.[9] The extreme form of this argument was expounded by Walt W. Rostow, who justified U.S. intervention in Vietnam on the basis of the "domino theory": if communist aggression succeeded there, then India, the most important of all of the dominoes, would eventually fall to communism.[10] (For their part, Indian diplomats were surprised to learn from Rostow that their country was the reason why America had intervened in Southeast Asia).

John Foster Dulles once remarked that Indian "neutrality" in the cold war was immoral. Yet he and other U.S. officials eventually came to see Nehru's nonalignment as less and less problematic. Indians were simply difficult to get along with. Not unlike Dulles, they were moralistic and preachy, but Delhi's influence in the nonaligned movement was an important fact of life and American critics concluded that as long as India was not an enemy, it need not be an ally. By the time of the "second" cold war of 1980–89, Washington did not try to punish India for its close relationship with the Soviet Union but sought an opening to New Delhi in the hope of luring it away from Soviet influence and protecting Pakistan's southern flank. By this time, India was no longer a strategic prize to be courted and cultivated; at best, it had nuisance value but was not in the same economic or strategic league as the other two major Asian powers, China and Japan.

## The Cold War as Seen from Delhi

Indians never saw the cold war in quite the same way as Americans did. From its beginning, Nehru opposed the cold war, although he placed India in a position where it could receive assistance from both sides. There were many reasons for this opposition, which remained a central feature of Indian foreign policy for forty years.

First, India believed the cold war was excessively militarized. This militarization included an arms race that quickly became a nuclear arms race, endangering the entire world. Nehru was appalled by the bombing of Hiroshima, and while he permitted Homi Bhabha to develop the facilities that eventually produced an Indian bomb, he remained strongly opposed to nuclear weapons, their testing, and the risk of a global holocaust created by American and Soviet nuclear stockpiles. Furthermore, the division of the world into two heavily armed blocs meant less support for the peoples of Asia, Africa, and Latin America. Nehru and other Indian leaders tirelessly criticized the cold war for its detrimental effect on the economic development of the former colonies and poorer regions of the world, including India.

Thus India had close ties to neither the United States nor the Soviet Union. At the time of independence, it saw the United States as an overdeveloped, materialistic power driven by a Manichaean view of the world. The Americans had stepped into the shoes of the British, and even noncommunist Indians suspected the United States wanted to undercut India's natural and rightful regional dominance. It saw the Soviet Union as an errant but fundamentally friendly state. Nehru had written in 1927 that it was inconceivable that Russia could ever become a threat to India in the foreseeable future.[11] To Indians, the Soviet Union "is not a colonial power, it doesn't have a colonial past." The Soviet Union, said India, was not interested in colonial expansionism and "Indo-Soviet relations [were] free of irritants, such as territorial conflict, or historical antagonisms." In the words of a leading Indian foreign policy specialist, the Soviet Union was "a harmless country."[12] It was admired for its economic accomplishments and defiance of the West, although Nehru and the Indian noncommunist left understood its essentially totalitarian structure.

The Soviet Union was a dictatorship, but Indian advice to the United States was to avoid pressuring it. As Morarji Desai told President John F. Kennedy, "There is a possibility of converting them to some extent if the method of friendly persuasion is adopted."[13] Indians were thus highly critical of the American policy of containment. Indian policymakers ridiculed American fear of the Soviet Union and regarded Soviet military preparations as essentially defensive, a response to the provocative containment strategy of the West.

Thus when the Soviet Union invaded Afghanistan on Christmas Eve of 1979, New Delhi was plunged into a state of confusion. India had become highly dependent on Moscow for military supplies and political support in several international fora, especially the United Nations. The

Soviet invasion had precipitated a "second" cold war, revived the Pakistan-U.S. military relationship, and brought the United States and China into South Asia on Islamabad's side. There had been no significant Pakistan-U.S. relationship for fifteen years, but in the decade after the Soviet invasion of Afghanistan, Pakistan was to receive more than $7 billion in loans and credits for military and economic assistance, as well as steady political support from Washington. Privately, Indian officials acknowledged the damage to their position caused by the Soviet action, but the burden of their criticism fell on the United States and Pakistan for their failure to seek a "political" solution to the Afghan crisis.

While Indians had practical and conceptual difficulties with the U.S. approach to the cold war, the most persistent and important objection to American policy stemmed from the military relationship with Pakistan. This was objectionable on every ground. It seemed to establish a strategic and moral equivalence between India and Pakistan (at least in American eyes) that was not justified by the objective military, economic, and strategic capabilities of the two states, or India's stature as a free state with a liberal outlook. Indians resented this equivalence just as many Americans resented the way that nonaligned India seemed to equate the United States and the Soviet Union.

Furthermore, by supporting Pakistan, the United States had forced India into an unnecessary and costly arms race.[14] The American arms program, agreed to in 1954, turned Pakistan into a lesser but still significant military power. It enabled Pakistan to field an armored division equipped with first-line Patton M-48 tanks, to acquire a number of modern F-85 jet aircraft, and to build a small navy. The Pakistan military also received extensive training and technical support, including NATO briefings on nuclear war. These acquisitions, essentially completed by the end of 1959, made it unlikely that India could militarily dominate Pakistan. Until 1965, aid continued at a more modest pace and new weapons systems were not introduced. In 1981 a major aid package to Pakistan provided forty F-16 aircraft, old but upgraded M-48 tanks, modern artillery, and the loan of several warships. While this did not tilt the military balance in Pakistan's favor, it neutralized India's ongoing arms buildup.

Indians had other problems with the U.S.-Pakistan relationship. First, American assistance gave Pakistan the means and the inspiration to challenge New Delhi. Air Marshal K. D. Chadha, a former Indian Air Force chief, expressed the Indian view of the relationship when he wrote that

Pakistan's affiliation with the United States aroused "ambitions and delusions of grandeur" in Pakistan's power elite. Military officers exposed to American training and doctrines "began to see themselves as invincible superior beings. They held the Indian military forces . . . in derisive contempt. Arrogant, flamboyant and impregnated with American doctrinal proclivities, they were more than convinced that militarily India was a push-over."[15] When coupled with the predominant view (in Pakistan) that one Pakistani soldier was the match of eight or ten Indians, the Americans had made it even less likely that Pakistan would come to a settlement of Kashmir, and more likely that they might pursue a military solution to the dispute, or use force to pressure India into dangerous concessions.

The American connection also distorted Pakistani politics, and the army became the country's dominant political force. After Ayub Khan's military coup in 1958, Delhi was concerned that the American-encouraged militarization of Pakistan might spread to India itself. This was an additional reason to restrict the ties between Indian officers and their Pakistani counterparts, and between the Indian and the U.S. military establishments. Not surprisingly, Delhi came to see the Pakistan-U.S. relationship as a move not against communism, but against India. Formally, the only American commitment to Pakistan was to consult, should the latter be faced with "communist" aggression.

From Delhi's perspective, U.S. pressure on India began with military aid and support for the Pakistan Army. The crowning event of this support for India's enemy occurred during the final days of the 1971 India-Pakistan war, when Richard Nixon ordered the nuclear aircraft carrier *Enterprise* to sail toward the Bay of Bengal. According to Henry Kissinger, the *Enterprise* deterred India from attacking Pakistan in the west, but it was in all likelihood intended as a gesture to China, showing American support for a mutual friend, Pakistan.[16] From that day onward, this *Enterprise* episode influenced Indian naval and strategic policy, directing Delhi's attention toward the threat from the sea for the first time since World War II. The *Enterprise* sailed on for twenty years more in the pages of Indian strategic journals and books, epitomizing American hostility in reaction to India's rise as a major power.

## The China Factor: From Ally to Betrayal

Pakistan may have been the longest-lasting irritant in U.S.-Indian relations during the cold war, but the wild oscillations in American ties to China were also distressing. After the communists seized power in 1949, Washington warned New Delhi of the danger from the "Chicoms." This did not deter Nehru from trying to be neutral in Korea and seeking to accommodate China in Tibet and on the disputed India-China border. But when the two Asian powers went to war in 1962, it appeared that the American view of China was correct, and for several years New Delhi and Washington entered into a close intelligence and strategic relationship.[17] In the early 1960s, in anticipation of an expected Chinese nuclear test, there was some talk of providing India with a nuclear capacity of its own, but the idea never went very far.[18] With the growing American involvement in Vietnam, the area in which China (and the Soviet Union) had to be contained shifted from South Asia to Southeast Asia.

In 1965 the India-Pakistan war provided a good reason to end military assistance programs to both sides. New Delhi saw this as an unfriendly act, but it was nothing compared with the sensational news that Henry Kissinger had traveled to China, via Pakistan, in July 1971 on a secret mission, further normalizing American relations with the People's Republic of China and incurring some new obligations toward Islamabad.

Again, American cold war calculations had bypassed India. After encouraging India to stand up to communist China, Washington was using Beijing to balance the Soviet Union, India's friend. Furthermore, China and Pakistan had begun a military relationship that was to supplant Washington's and that included nuclear and missile technology. Washington's flip-flop on China was devastating. Although Washington acknowledged India's regional dominance after the victory over Pakistan, this meant little.[19] In the Indian view, the United States had failed to act on its own principles and was supporting a communist dictatorship that was a direct threat to the world's largest democracy. Washington had compounded its misjudgment of India with an excessively emotional approach to Delhi's Asian rival. V. P. Dutt, a leading China expert, mixed irony and sarcasm when he wrote:

> The Americans . . . have finally come around to the policies that Jawaharlal Nehru pleaded with them for many years and which they spurned so haughtily and for which they described Jawaharlal Nehru as the "lost leader" of Asia. Suddenly they found everything Chinese unique. The Chinese food was the best in the world;

Chinese art incomparable, Chinese acupuncture the most felicitous system of treatment, and so on. The refrain in USA today was "there are no flies in Beijing."[20]

## A History of Good Intentions

The cold war also saw a number of American efforts designed to help India and Pakistan resolve their disputes, especially over Kashmir. These included a variety of incentives and disincentives to India that continued after the end of the cold war. The first such effort took place in 1948, the most recent in 1999, during the height of the Kargil war. These episodic interventions have not been part of a thought-out regional U.S. strategy, and like so many other aspects of the U.S.-Indian relationship, they are regarded quite differently by the two sides.

The Truman, Eisenhower, and Kennedy administrations each attempted to resolve the Kashmir conflict. Shortly after the first India-Pakistan war, Washington and Great Britain worked through the framework of the United Nations to support several peacekeeping missions and help establish an observer force along the cease-fire line in Kashmir. The Eisenhower administration, worried about the possibility of another India-Pakistan war, tried but failed to persuade India and Pakistan to come to a settlement on Kashmir, although it helped bring the Indus Waters dispute to a successful conclusion during its second term. The negotiations were conducted under the auspices of the World Bank, with the United States providing half of the $1 billion needed for construction projects. Washington had kept a low profile, but its financial support and diplomatic encouragement made the final settlement possible.

The last significant American effort on Kashmir was mounted by the Kennedy administration in 1962–63, during and after the China-India war. This also failed, despite high-level presidential interest and considerable pressure (and inducements) by the United States and Britain. Pakistan never took the China-India conflict seriously and believed that the Indians were exaggerating the threat in order to attract foreign support and military assistance.

All of these American efforts at resolving the conflict sprang from the calculation that a strategically divided South Asia would be vulnerable to communist pressure. India and Pakistan had to be encouraged to work out a settlement on Kashmir, lest they become targets of communist aggression. Lyndon Johnson, who was less enamored of South Asia than Kennedy, broke the pattern. When the 1965 war between India and Pakistan began, he refused to become directly involved and backed efforts by the United Nations to broker a cease-fire. Johnson later supported the postwar peace conference at Tashkent that the Soviet Union had organized, "standing cold war policy towards South Asia on its head."[21]

Six years later, Richard Nixon tried but failed to avert another India-Pakistan war, this time over East Pakistan. Nixon urged Pakistan to reach an accommodation with the dissident East Pakistanis and offered refugee aid to India. Nixon wanted to preserve Pakistan's integrity, less because of affection for Islamabad or dislike of India (although both were abundant) than because of his desire to show the Chinese, his new strategic partner, that Washington would stand by its friends. The next fifteen years saw very little American interest in India. It was assumed that the 1972 Simla Agreement had provided a regional framework for conflict resolution.

Just as the cold war was ending, Washington was again drawn into South Asia to deal with emerging regional crises. There were three such efforts, the first taking place in the waning years of the cold war. When India's 1987 Exercise Brasstacks threatened to erupt into a full-scale war, Americans assumed that the crisis had been triggered by misperceptions. Washington reassured both sides that there was no evidence of hostile behavior or intentions by either. The American analysis was wrong, because Brasstacks was part of a larger Indian strategy designed to put pressure on Pakistan, but Washington's diplomatic intervention did no harm. During a second crisis in 1990 (which occurred during a mass popular uprising in Kashmir), Washington, aware of what had almost happened during the Brasstacks crisis, was concerned that India might strike across the Line of Control or the international border, triggering a Pakistani response, and even a nuclear exchange. This led to active diplomacy by the American ambassadors in Islamabad and Delhi and a high-level mission headed by Deputy National Security Adviser Robert Gates.[22] In a third effort, in 1999, the United States urged Pakistan to withdraw its forces from across the LOC. The Indians threatened retaliation, but held off until Clinton persuaded Nawaz Sharif during a July 4 meeting to pull Pakistan's forces back. The incident inadvertently contributed to Nawaz's downfall, as the Pakistan Army regarded his turning to the United States, and subsequent pressure to stop the war, as undercutting a carefully crafted military strategy.

Although Washington did help prevent the crises of 1987, 1990, and 1999 from escalating into larger wars, these actions made no dent in the underlying India-Pakistan conflict, nor were these exercises in crisis-management intended to do so. Nevertheless, many Americans have concluded that their well-intentioned offers of mediation or conflict resolution were little appreciated and almost never accepted. No issue was more important and more frustrating in this regard than Kashmir. From the first year of independence, American officials, private citizens, foundations, and scholars pressed India and Pakistan to resolve, or at least suspend, the conflict. At first, Americans argued that this conflict made it hard for India and Pakistan to manage the joint defense of the Subcontinent from threats stemming from the Soviet Union and China. In the 1950s and 1960s, their conflict was said to be diverting attention from urgent economic and developmental needs. More recently, the specter of a nuclear war has been the spur to American intervention.

All told, fifty years of American efforts to resolve the Kashmir conflict—and other regional disputes—have yielded few positive results, even as tensions in the region rose higher in 2000 than at almost any time in modern history. After the efforts of Eisenhower, Dulles, and Kennedy, American policymakers seem to have concluded that these are unreasonable and intransigent states. After the first fifteen years of the cold war there seemed to be no compelling diplomatic reasons for the United States to enter the region, nor did it have domestic or economic interests there. In recent years a pattern of limited, sporadic engagement, usually in response to a crisis, seemed to be adequate to protect these marginal interests.

## From Carrots to Sticks

The United States grew disillusioned with South Asia as the cold war proceeded. It also moved from a diplomacy designed to encourage Indians and Pakistanis to settle their differences on Kashmir to a policy of restrictions on economic and technical assistance, or the threat of such restrictions, amounting to sanctions. This position hardened as American differences with India over non–cold war issues came to overshadow India's declining value as a player in the cold war.

The first such change occurred in the 1960s and early 1970s, in response to India's economic policies, and also its support for the Vietnam government. In July 1965 President Lyndon Johnson applied economic pressure on India's agricultural policy by ordering the suspension of long-term PL-480 food assistance, at a time when India was experiencing a severe famine. Though short-term food-aid shipments to India were allowed, the threat of a more lasting grain embargo remained until 1967, and this ultimately influenced the Indian government to adopt a changed agricultural policy. Washington (or at least Johnson) saw the "ship-to-mouth" strategy as a clever way to bring about reform. This was not a sanction as such, but severely damaged U.S.-Indian relations, which were not yet ready for an act of "tough love." The policy elicited deep anger, as Indira Gandhi and much of the Indian public felt that it constituted an attack on Indian sovereignty. Since the United States was then deeply enmeshed in Vietnam, many Indians came to see the policy not as a well-meaning act but the behavior of a bully, and one with Asian blood on its hands. American military and economic aid to India (and Pakistan) was also suspended during their 1965 and 1971 wars.[23] In the following years, military sales and assistance to both countries were steadily reduced.

Jimmy Carter reintroduced the carrot in the American diplomatic repertoire when he and the World Bank offered massive assistance for an Eastern waters regional development program. This was and remains an important economic project, though Carter's broader regional goal was to contain proliferation. India never considered the proposal seriously, partly because it thought it could work out a bilateral agreement with Bangladesh and Nepal and partly because it did not want a repeat of the Indus Waters experience, which had been managed by outsiders. In addition, some Indians saw Carter as a friend turned hypocrite: he promised aid and praised India but was really pushing a nonproliferation agenda that threatened vital Indian interests.

In response to the 1974 Indian nuclear test, the United States turned to technology export controls as a central instrument of policy. These controls, often coordinated with other countries, have been entirely nuclear or missile related. After 1974 the restrictions of the Zangger Committee and Nuclear Suppliers Group reduced and eventually halted the transfer of nuclear-related technology not just to India but to several other states of proliferation concern.[24] In March 1978 Congress passed the Nuclear Nonproliferation Act, which made approval of nuclear exports dependent on the buyer's acceptance of safeguards, with a two-year grace period. In 1980 President Carter approved a temporary waiver allowing 32 tons of uranium for India's Tarapur reactor, and in

1982 an agreement allowed France to supply Tarapur in return for India's acceptance of safeguards on the facility. Apart from nuclear sanctions, India also faced embargoes on missile-related technology from 1987 onward, after the advent of the Missile Technology Control Regime. Under them, the United States blocked the transfer of a Russian cryogenic rocket engine to India in 1992–94 but eventually allowed its sale without the related technology.

While India was denied dual-use and sensitive technologies, it did not actually lose American or international economic aid until its 1998 nuclear tests (by contrast, Pakistan lost access to American aid much earlier).[25] The Glenn Amendment required Washington to vote against international loans to non-NPT states conducting nuclear tests. As a result, India lost about $2 billion in foreign aid from international financial institutions and Japan, and another $300 million from other Western donors, including the United States. Before its 1998 tests, India had received annual aid worth approximately $2 billion from international financial institutions and $1 billion from Japan, which together accounted for three-fourths of India's total aid. After the tests, Japan banned all new foreign-aid commitments to India (as a result of which India lost about $1 billion in aid). Furthermore, with American and G-7 coordination, the World Bank halted another $1 billion in economic development and infrastructure-related loans to India, although it cleared approximately $1 billion worth of social development loans.[26]

From the U.S. perspective, these nuclear-related economic sanctions were not aimed at reducing India's status as a great power or at preventing it from emerging as a major power. They were deemed necessary to maintain a common front against the worldwide menace of proliferation. India (and Pakistan) seemed to be clear violators. While the Iraqis could be dealt with by force, the North Koreans by offers of economic aid, and the Israelis ignored, India was ripe for sanctions and other forms of denial and punishment. These were believed to be a deterrent to India, a "lesson" to other possible nuclear violators, and part of the pledge that Washington had made to its allies and to nonnuclear states that had signed up to support the constraints embedded in the NPT. Sanctions had earlier been used to cajole India into economic reform (for the most part, they had failed), and when they were applied to what many Indians regarded as a vital national interest—the maintenance of the nuclear option—they proved to be ineffective and even counterproductive.

New Delhi sees things differently. These interventions, it argues, serve American, not Indian interests. Even Indians who would have preferred a negotiated settlement with Pakistan on a wide range of issues found U.S. interventions untimely and crude. Some Indian officials also criticized the Indus Waters agreement, seemingly a satisfactory solution to a difficult problem, for having diminished India's share of the waters. When coupled with its military support for Pakistan, U.S. concerns about the security of South Asia and a possible crisis there are regarded as exaggerated at best and deceptive at worst. In India's view, Washington's recent sanctions-led policy has not only been punitive but is designed to cripple a potential great state. For the more hawkish members of the Indian strategic community, the purpose of these interventions was to prevent the dominant regional power, India, from achieving its natural dominance over Pakistan. They conveniently overlooked the fact that American sanctions on Pakistan were tougher still. No other issue has influenced Indian-U.S. relations as much as the downward trajectory in America's support for India's nuclear ambitions.

### Some Cold War Lessons

The United States and India drew very different lessons from their long and usually frustrating engagement during and immediately after the cold war. Several generations of American policymakers have concluded that with India and Pakistan unable to settle their differences, there was never much prospect for a strategically united South Asia. At times, Americans toyed with the idea of choosing between India and Pakistan to help contain the Soviet Union or China (or, at times, both). However, no administration could bring itself to make such a choice and stick with it, although Kennedy was ready to do so when he died. Time and again, a movement toward one country was partly offset by programs with the other as the United States responded to the zero sum mentality prevalent in both Islamabad and New Delhi.

By 1965 the United States had concluded that there was a danger of overcommitment, which meant being dragged into a purely regional crisis by India or Pakistan when no American interests were at stake. That year, Lyndon Johnson, frustrated by the outbreak of the second India-Pakistan war, suspended military aid to both countries and yielded the role of regional conflict manager to the Soviet Union. The United States was not so much opposed to India, but disillusioned with it. Delhi had been unable to compromise on its differences with Pakistan, and in any case the cold war had receded from South Asia. President Johnson and his secretary of state, Dean Rusk, concluded that there was little risk in letting the Soviet Union try its hand at being a regional peacemaker.

It took a crisis to build a policy, or at least to rouse America's strategic interest. Absent a crisis (either a threat to the region by an outside power or a threat to regional stability by an India-Pakistan war), American officials tended to regard South Asia as a strategic sideshow. While it may have been the site of cold war competition, it was not consistently judged to be vital territory, at least compared with the oil-rich Middle East or an industrially vital Europe and northeast Asia. For much of the cold war, the threat was posed by the Soviet Union, China, or communism; by the mid-1970s, this had been joined by the proliferation threat, which dominated American policy from 1974 on, except for the Afghan interregnum.

In the absence of significant economic, cultural, or ethnic ties, these strategic concerns—the cold war and proliferation—shaped the larger relationship with India but did not entirely crowd out two other American interests. One was support for Indian democracy and the notion that the United States and India—as democracies—had much in common. The other was the theme that ran through American policy from the 1940s, namely, that India was deserving of economic and developmental aid because of its poverty.

For the Indian strategic community, the lesson of America's cold war policies was that Washington was an untrustworthy, sometimes hostile state. While appreciative of large-scale American economic assistance in the 1950s and 1960s, India judged both superpowers primarily by their willingness to recognize its regional dominance in word and deed. In other words, were they reluctant to support India's smaller neighbors in regional disputes, or were they willing to provide those neighbors with military hardware or other supplies and thus encourage them to pursue anti-Indian policies? On these points, American policy during the cold war seemed at best ambivalent, at worst malevolent.

Comparisons between Washington and Moscow often came down on the side of the latter. India could not rely on the United States as a military supplier; Washington was erratic and prone to imposing sanctions that affected military readiness. Even American economic assistance had strings attached and was manipulated by Washington, and the humanitarian interventions that took place when the cold war ended were seen as potentially threatening to India. Well meaning or not, Washington's military assistance to Pakistan was directly threatening to India. When the Soviet Union experimented with aid to Pakistan in the late 1960s, Delhi was able to pressure it to terminate its program; the United States was not susceptible to complaints.

India's strategic expectations for their relationship fluctuated over a wider range than Washington's: from an early hope that the United States would be a staunch supporter of New Delhi to the suspicion for a number of years that the United States was India's major strategic opponent and that it had masterminded a coalition of hostile powers. In sum, the U.S.-Indian relationship was asymmetric. The United States had preponderant military and economic power; it was insensitive to Indian concerns and ambitions. The view from New Delhi for much of the cold war—and the decade that followed it—was that the United States was bent on preventing India from "emerging" as a dominant regional state and as a political and strategic factor on the global level. The United States could be held responsible for many of India's ills, a belief encouraged by Delhi's quasi ally, the Soviet Union. New Delhi's difficulties with the United States ran deeper than those associated with the cold war.

## A Changing Relationship

Over the past twenty-five years, U.S. policy toward India has focused on nonproliferation, in reaction to the expanding nuclear programs of India and Pakistan. The primary tools of U.S. policy have been not economic aid, diplomacy, or military force, sales, or assistance, but technology embargoes and economic sanctions. These put great strain on the relationship with India, a relationship that was further challenged by the 1998 nuclear tests.

### Proliferation Takes Command

The Indian nuclear test of 1974 led Americans to believe that the world was on the edge of a rapid burst of nuclear proliferation. Jimmy Carter made nonproliferation the centerpiece of his foreign policy (until the Soviet invasion of Afghanistan), and, as mentioned earlier, South Asia became a target of U.S. nonproliferation legislation that included technology denials and sanctions. This concern with proliferation was partly suspended when the Soviet Union invaded Afghanistan, and

Washington practiced a policy of "see no evil, hear no evil, and speak no evil" concerning Islamabad's weapons program.

By the time of the 1990 India-Pakistan crisis, many in Washington felt that South Asia was out of control. The conflict over Kashmir seemed to be moving toward a conventional war, which in turn could ignite a nuclear conflagration. Furthermore, there was a strong disposition for the United States, as the sole superpower, to assume the leadership role in heading off this chain of events. America was thought to have the best intelligence on these sensitive issues and the greatest leverage over India and Pakistan. Nonproliferation again became the centerpiece of U.S. regional policy. It had bipartisan support, the offspring of a liaison between strategic conservatives (who wanted to make the world safe for American nuclear weapons) and antinuclear liberals (who wanted to get rid of all nuclear weapons and who thought that other countries would be more susceptible to pressure than the Department of Defense).

India was one of the few near-nuclear states with which the United States could have a dialogue. American officials were at liberty to travel to New Delhi to lecture their counterparts on the perils of nuclear weapons. They were unable or unwilling to do so in Teheran, Pyongyang, or Tel Aviv. So India (and Pakistan) received a disproportionate amount of official and unofficial attention aimed at "capping, freezing, and rolling back" their nuclear programs, very little of it addressed to the motives and causes of these programs. In this respect, the failure of the United States to take seriously, or even respond to, the 1988 "Rajiv Gandhi initiative" on regional and global disarmament when it was initially proposed, or when it was revived in 1992, was an egregious error, reflecting the assumption that Washington knew better than India what was right in the area of nuclear disarmament. The Rajiv initiative was one of several missed opportunities to engage the Indians on one of their central objections to the NPT and to work out an alternative formulation that might have obtained their limited adherence to the NPT (and subsequently, the CTBT) even if Delhi did not formally sign them. By the mid-1990s, however, American nuclear theologians were uninterested in compromise and in any case did not take the Indian position seriously.

Overall, American sanctions slowed but did not stop the development of India's nuclear weapons. They convinced the Indian scientific and strategic communities that the United States, the world's dominant power, regarded India as a threat. If anything, this contributed to India's incentive to go nuclear. Indian strategists talked of defying the United States, joining with Russia or China in an alliance to counter American power, and developing a nuclear capability that could reach U.S. territory. In Washington, the immediate response mandated by law was to impose additional sanctions. Washington and New Delhi seemed on a collision course and reconciliation unlikely. The five nuclear tests of May 1998 appeared to have erected an insuperable barrier to a more normal relationship between these two powers. Indeed, some Americans came to see New Delhi as a potential military opponent, taking seriously the claims of the BJP and its supporters that Delhi could join with others in challenging American hegemony.

None of these predictions have materialized or are likely to materialize in the near future. While the nuclear tests were traumatic, both India and the United States have backed away from a costly confrontation. Second and more important, the deeper links between the United States and India are being transformed as the two states find their economies and their populations coming into closer alignment. Despite the nuclear tests, the strategic choices for both have become much wider than at any other time in the past fifty years, and the well-known points of disagreement are fading, while several important areas of agreement are emerging.

## Recalibrating the Relationship

Washington and New Delhi entered into an unexpected, prolonged, high-level dialogue after India's nuclear tests. On one side was the deputy secretary of state, Strobe Talbott, who had assumed control over America's South Asia policy. His counterpart, Jaswant Singh, was to become India's foreign minister in December 1998. In all, Washington held eight rounds of talks with New Delhi and nine with Islamabad between June 1998 and February 1999, and then resumed talks in November following India's elections. These became the longest extended strategic dialogue between senior American and Indian officials, and they broadened out from questions of proliferation and nuclear policy to larger issues such as the shape of the international system, terrorism, and strategic cooperation between the two states. The talks proved to be surprisingly valuable in the summer of 1999, when India was confronted by the Pakistani move across the LOC at Kargil. Talbott and Singh had established a more positive relationship that persuaded India to respond cautiously to the Pakistani attack while giving Washington the chance to pressure Pakistan to withdraw.

On nuclear issues, Washington gradually accepted New Delhi's and Islamabad's nuclear programs but tried to ensure that they remained within mutually acceptable limits and refused to grant India or Pakistan official nuclear status. New Delhi and Islamabad did agree to maintain a moratorium on nuclear testing (but did not sign the CTBT) and to strengthen their export controls. However, they did not agree to other arms control measures, such as a fissile material freeze or missile restraints, let alone nondeployment and nonweaponization.

Changes in the U.S.-China relationship also affected Washington's perception of India. While the Clinton administration had sought a "normal" relationship with Beijing, this proved hard to define and difficult to maintain in the face of increased Chinese domestic repression and pressure on Taiwan during the 2000 elections. When added to the usual tensions over trade and security issues, these concerns suddenly made India more attractive. Although nuclear issues remain at the center of U.S. policy toward New Delhi, Americans now realize that direct pressure might be counterproductive and that a more subtle, long-term strategy was called for in dealing with the Indian nuclear program.

Such a strategy had been outlined in a number of nongovernmental and think-tank reports produced during the 1990s.[27] These studies—sponsored by the Asia Society, the Brookings Institution, the Carnegie Endowment for International Peace, and the Council on Foreign Relations—were inspired in part by concern about the Clinton administration's single-issue approach to the region. Among their conclusions was that U.S. policy had not given India's economic and strategic potential enough weight and that its sanctions were crude instruments ill-suited to the region's problems. The reports called for a more nuanced approach, with incentives as well as punishment. Finally, they urged higher-level attention to India, including a presidential visit, on the grounds that only then would the U.S. government be informed fully enough to deal with India and the rest of South Asia. Some studies urged a more accommodating attitude toward Indian proliferation. Others felt that the U.S.-India relationship should form the core of America's South Asia policy. And still others called for a more balanced approach to India and Pakistan. Perhaps the most significant aspect of these studies was what they did not advocate: none felt that the United States should play a major role in settling the Kashmir problem or invest substantial economic or military assistance in the region. Although such studies may have influenced U.S. policy on the margins (there was a shift, in the second Clinton administration, toward a broader approach to the region), nonproliferation was still its primary emphasis.

Although these studies had grasped the major changes then under way in Indian-U.S. relations and had concentrated not on strategy or security, but on deeper social and economic questions, some officials found them too pro-Indian. After the nuclear tests of 1998, however, the administration began to consult regularly with many members of these study groups, and while they played no official role, they helped improve American understanding of Indian political and strategic compulsions and thus helped accelerate the move to replace what Hans Morgenthau used to call a "policy of making faces" with a policy of engagement.

### New Social and Economic Ties

For many decades, the image of Indians in the United States has been bimodal. At one extreme, there were pictures of hungry children, wandering cows, naked sadhus, and teeming cities. At the other extreme, there were saints and sadhus, ranging from the revered Mahatma Gandhi (whose writings influenced a whole generation of Americans through Martin Luther King Jr.) to Mother Teresa, and an assortment of transient Indian gurus.[28] American policymakers and elected officials shared these images, which made it difficult to come to a balanced assessment of Indian strengths and weaknesses. In the past twenty years, however, India has acquired a new "face." No longer an abstraction, India has a visible and tangible presence in the United States through the 1.5 million Indian-Americans who have created a positive image and are likely to have an enduring impact on the bilateral relationship.

This transformation originated in the changes in U.S. immigration law in 1965, which eliminated the Europe-weighted immigration system and permitted a greater flow of Indian immigrants, including extended families. By the late 1970s, Americans of Indian origin had begun to establish themselves. They fell into three broad groups. The first consisted of doctors, academics, and other professionals, especially engineers, who were evenly distributed through the United States. This brought many Americans into very close and positive contact with professionals of South Asian origin. Indeed, American hospitals and emergency rooms would have collapsed without their contribution. Another group was the Indian business community, which pursued more or less traditional business interests, often in imports-exports, jewelry, or gems. These were concentrated in the eastern metropolitan areas of the United States. The third group comprised Indians who came to the United States to study and work in high-technology fields. Many found employment in the aerospace industry, telecommunications, and in software and computer development. Concentrated in Silicon Valley and its Washington, Boston, and Austin counterparts, they have achieved fabulous personal and professional success. ꞏ

Indian-Americans have been high achievers in some important fields. There are approximately 300 Indian-American entrepreneurs with a personal net worth of at least $5 million, many in the high-technology sector.[29] Nearly 40 percent of start-up companies in the Silicon Valley and Washington, D.C., areas are owned by Indians or Indian-Americans, and there are at least 774 Indian-American companies in Silicon Valley alone. These high-technology entrepreneurs have their own networks, one of which, TiE (The IndUS Entrepreneurs), has 1,000 members in nine chapters in the United States, India, Pakistan, and Singapore.[30] In other fields as well, Indian-Americans have moved quickly into important managerial and administrative positions. Overall, the community is extremely prosperous, and its per capita income of over $50,000 places it at the top of levels earned by "hyphenated" Americans.

The Indian-American community has also begun to organize itself along political lines and has become an important source of funding in several House and Senate races. It influenced the relaxation of sanctions legislation following the 1998 nuclear tests.[31] Leaders of the community regularly visited the Clinton White House. The 2000 election was the first presidential election in which they played a visible and influential role. This new activism complemented the growth of corporate American interest in India.

With the transformation of Indian economic policy since 1991, corporate America has begun to take India seriously. U.S. two-way trade to India rose from $5.3 billion in 1990 to $8.5 billion in 1995 and $12 billion in 1999, with $9.1 billion in imports and $3.7 billion in exports.[32] Even so, India was still only America's twenty-fifth largest trading partner (the volume of American trade with its four largest partners (Canada, Mexico, Japan, and China) is in excess of $100 billion each.

American corporations have grown more and more interested in India in the wake of these and other changes. Its fleet of civilian jet aircraft (just over 200) is about the same size as China's was when the Chinese had been liberalizing for about the same period of time. India has pushed open the energy sector to foreign investment, and a number of American firms, notably Enron and Cogentrix, have entered the market, albeit with mixed results. Estimates are that India will require more than $100 billion investments in power, roads, and transportation and will have to make major investments to bring its antiquated ports, airports, and air traffic control systems up to modern standards. And of course the recent great success in high technology, especially software, has attracted many major American firms to India and also increases India's exports to the United States: its software exports are growing at a rate of 50 percent annually and could reach $40 billion by 2008, two-thirds of which would go to the United States and Canada.[33]

While the size of the Indian middle-class market, estimated to be anywhere between 100 million and 300 million, may be exaggerated, American firms understand the advantages of South Asia as a production site as well as a place to sell goods. This new perception of India has rippled through the bureaucracy and Congress. American corporations now actively lobby Congress for legislation favorable to the region, although they are reluctant to side with India or Pakistan on contentious issues if it might mean criticizing another country in which they have important economic interests.

These developments open possibilities that were unimaginable just ten or twenty years ago. There is for the first time the prospect of a substantial economic relationship between the United States and India. The economic benefits of this interdependence are obvious, but the political ones are no less important: strong economic ties between the United States and India will provide an incentive to manage other issues more carefully. It is premature for Indians to envision the kind of reverse dependency relationship that China has achieved with the United States, but even a limited expansion of economic ties has changed the context in which contentious political, economic, and strategic issues are discussed.

These new economic links mean, first, that differences on economic issues can be managed more cordially. The balance of trade favors India, but some Indians remain concerned that American capital and finance will come to dominate their economy. Indian economic policies of the past twenty years have been based upon this "East India Company syndrome." New ways of regulating and transforming these disparities have been developed, including the membership of both states in the World Trade Organization, enhanced bilateral contacts between commercial and economic officials on both sides, and the role of the Indian court system in ensuring compliance on both sides.

Better economic ties can also create important political dependencies, especially through "lobbies" in both countries. These provide continuity and a balanced perspective when conflict develops in other areas, as demonstrated in interactions between the United States and Japan, and between the United States and most of the "tigers" of Southeast Asia. In these cases labor unions, distributors, and others join American corporations in their quest for a balanced and positive relationship with the respective country. They all have direct and powerful access to the American political system. India lacks this access, but as it grows, it will change the overall relationship.

If the image of India is undergoing rapid change in the United States, that of America in India is also being transformed, at least for the moment. The hostility of India's leaders toward the United States—more persistent than in any other democracy—has declined.[34] Earlier, in the absence of much in the way of a positive connection between the two states, negative images (American racism, the cold war mentality, aid to Pakistan, and a patronizing view toward India) tended to dominate Indian perceptions. These were not offset (indeed, perhaps they were exacerbated) by the ritual of all Indian-U.S. meetings nor by the cliché that Washington and New Delhi represented the world's oldest and largest democracies (or, latterly, the world's most powerful and largest democracies). These terms meant little to either side: Washington was closely engaged with dictatorships that were India's rivals, and India itself had close relations with a number of autocracies. Furthermore, its post-1970 policies definitely were "tilted" in the direction of Moscow.

In the 1980s Indian governments pursued various strategies to change Washington's policies. Culture displays played a role, and a festival of India was held in the mid-1980s in the hope of broadening American understanding of Indian culture. Yet, U.S.-Indian academic ties were still restricted, and such subjects as caste, security policy, or relations with Pakistan and China discouraged. As the Indian-American community grew in numbers, the Indian government tried to use it to influence Congress and the executive branch, and in 1998 the Indian embassy in

Washington even hired a public relations firm to assist it in shaping American policy.[35]

The gradual increase in the influence of the Indian-American community proved particularly important. While not necessarily in tune with "official" Indian positions and in some cases actually critical of Indian government policies, the community gained a foothold in American society and lobbied for India, especially in matters involving Pakistan.

Although this community has no exact counterpart in India, many Indians have studied or worked in the United States, and they also bring a more realistic assessment of the United States to the Indian strategic and political community. A number of the reform-minded Indian economists have been trained in the United States, and publicist/journalists such as Arun Shourie (once editor of the *Indian Express* and now a BJP minister), had extensive contact with Americans in the 1960s. This generation represents a major shift from the British-educated elites of the period from the 1930s to the 1950s. The trend to seek higher education in the United States was sharply accelerated in the 1980s when the Thatcher government made it more expensive for Indians (and other former colonials) to study in Britain. Now that the United States is the place of choice for higher education, there is a new generation of Americans of Indian origin and of Indians with American experience.

Bill Clinton's visit to India in 2000 was a dramatic success because it reconciled (in the Indian mind) the great gap between the popular understanding of Americans as a friendly people and the belief that the United States was hostile to India. The major goal of the Clinton trip planners was to demonstrate that this dichotomy no longer existed. Both governments wanted to use the trip to present a more balanced image of India's economy and society to America. The sites Clinton visited—especially the high-tech and commercial centers—were carefully chosen to reflect a "new" India and the close personal ties between the United States and India.

For the United States, the strategic goal of the trip was to stress that its policy in South Asia was no longer steered by cold war concerns, that such problems as terrorism, the expansion of democracy, and developing an equitable global economic order could be addressed in a cooperative spirit. Equally important was the message Clinton delivered in Pakistan, warning Islamabad that the Line of Control could not be transgressed by force, thus echoing Indian policy that the LOC's sanctity should be upheld. The fact that Clinton spent only five hours in Pakistan, as opposed to five days in India, was also meant to convey the importance Washington accorded to India (although Indian officials had foolishly tried to prevent the stopover entirely).

Although the two states reached no substantive agreements during the visit, the trip was correctly hailed as a breakthrough in Indian-U.S. relations. For the first time in thirty-five years, it became acceptable to view the United States in a generally positive way. The trip was largely symbolic with few clues as to direction the relationship may take in years to come. This will depend largely on whether the United States and India can manage their political and strategic disputes, as well as build on their growing mutual interests.

## Points of Difference

Ironically, India's nuclear tests shattered U.S. policy, with its single-minded focus on proliferation, and forced a reconsideration of relations with New Delhi. While the Clinton administration was reluctant to formally abandon its nonproliferation goals (a year after the 1998 tests, officials were still calling for the capping, roll-back, and elimination of India's nuclear capabilities), there was widespread agreement that relations with India had to be more carefully managed and that the treaty-dominated, sanction-enforced strategy had not worked. On the Indian side, too, there is a new eagerness for a close relationship with the United States. Both countries seem to see eye to eye on one thing: that India might become a more significant power, and that they should explore the limits of cooperation, and conceivably restructure their relationship. While there are also important differences between them on such issues as humanitarian intervention and the shape of a desirable world order, the Talbott-Singh dialogue led to a closer working relationship on international trade, terrorism, health and environmental problems and other subjects. There also remains the common commitment to democracy, given some substance in Indian-U.S. cooperation on the community of democracies hosted by Poland in June 2000 and co-convened by India, the United States, and several other states. However, India demonstrated its independent streak—and angered officials in the Clinton administration—when it declined to assume the leadership of an informal caucus of democracies, representing some 100 countries in the United Nations.[36] Indian officials were supportive in the abstract but did not want to be put in a position where they would be required to speak out against undemocratic states with which they have good strategic, economic, or political relations. Like the reversal of policy on the CTBT, where India had been one of the original advocates of a comprehensive test ban, India had pragmatic reasons for going its own way on the democratization initiative. Still, this baffled American officials who had assumed that India would be a "partner" in the one area (democracy) where the two countries had a long-standing, shared commitment. As in the case of the CTBT, agreement on a lofty principle is not enough for either state when more pressing strategic calculations suggest a different policy.

## Economic Risks and Gains

While trade between India and the United States is increasing, several issues remain in dispute. These include the American practice of linking human rights issues with economic policies, the question of child labor, the disappearance of Indian brands, and the danger of a political backlash from uneven economic growth within India. These seem to be balanced by the benefits to India's new high-technology sector and the growing competitiveness of many Indian firms. Nevertheless, the possibility remains that intense Indian nationalism (or American protectionism) might lead to an economic backlash. While this relationship will require nurturing, powerful economic forces on both sides are now interested in maintaining it.

Looking over the horizon, some economists have floated the idea of an Indian-U.S. free trade agreement, arguing that this would be of benefit to both countries.[37] For India, such an agreement would help reduce tariff barriers on textiles and improve access to American high technology. Although it is unlikely to transpire in the short run, the growing ties between the two economies may make it easier to reach such an agreement in a few years, and the idea should be developed further. Although the deepening economic relationship will also create new problems, on balance these will be outweighed by the new ties and alliances, which will be a stabilizing factor, providing the "ballast" for a closer relationship between the two states.

## Containing Nuclear Differences

The subject of sharpest disagreement between the two states in the past fifteen or twenty years has been India's nuclear program. This is likely to become less important in the next few years providing India keeps its nuclear and missile program within certain limits. Limiting the range of its own nuclear forces and cooperating with the United States in preventing the further spread of nuclear weapons will shape the way in which Washington views India—as a "responsible" nuclear power or as a potential rogue—and will affect the degree to which the United States would engage in strategic cooperation with India and even sell it advanced military equipment or dual-use technology.

## Pakistan and Kashmir

Unless India can foster a more normal relationship with Pakistan, its perceptions of Washington's relationship with Islamabad will color its own relationship with Washington. If the Americans continue to play a constructive role in ameliorating the India-Pakistan conflict, that is one thing; but if Pakistan should deteriorate, India might escalate its goals dramatically by attempting to dominate Pakistan and asking for American assistance in the process, perhaps by locating Pakistani nuclear weapons or neutralizing a possible Chinese involvement. The challenge for the United States will be to maintain a close relationship with Pakistan without suggesting a threat to New Delhi while encouraging India to normalize its relations with Islamabad, working albeit slowly, toward a resolution of the Kashmir problem.

In the 1950s and 1960s the United States tried to be a regional peacemaker and offered a range of inducements designed to promote the peaceful resolution of the Kashmir problem, the river waters dispute, and other issues. If it were to return to such a strategy of conflict resolution or peacebuilding, it would have to take a more active role in South Asia, not to promote or oppose India, but to shape the regional environment in such a way that conflict between India and Pakistan could be averted. There have been no American efforts along these lines for many years, although the interventions during the three recent crises demonstrated that a U.S. role of this nature might be accepted by both sides if the conditions were right. The most obvious model for such a sustained engagement is the Middle East peace process, although it would have to be constructed quite differently in South Asia. For such an effort to succeed, the United States would have to assume a low profile, there might have to be a careful restoration of military sales to one or both sides, and other technical assistance could be offered (such as technologies to verify agreements reached by the two countries).

## A New Global Order?

Americans and Indians have very different conceptions of a just international order. The United States is comfortable with what it regards as a benign hegemony, whereas India has long preferred a world of six or seven major powers, each responsible for peace and stability in its own region, each refraining from meddling in the affairs of other major powers, but working cooperatively in the United Nations Security Council. These differences have led the two states to disagree on three important issues: the limits of humanitarian peacekeeping, the makeup of the UN Security Council, and the emergence of China.

Most Indians have trouble accepting the principle of humanitarian intervention, although they are willing to concede the need for it in many recent conflicts. Such intervention by the United States, especially in Kosovo, left India wondering whether Kashmir too might become the subject of international inquiry and whether the United States might sponsor such a move in South Asia against India's wishes. Despite American denials, Indians think the United States would support the principle of "self-determination" within sovereign states and press for a plebiscite in Kashmir. For the West, humanitarian intervention is a charitable, discretionary activity; for India, it represents a direct threat to its control over Kashmir. The Kosovo and earlier Desert Storm operations led New Delhi to question the motives behind American behavior since it was no longer necessary to balance Soviet power. Indians concluded that the major second-tier states (such as India, Iraq, and others) could become the object of American aggression, whether under the pretext of economic need or humanitarianism. Given the overpowering military superiority of the United States and the demonstrable inability of Soviet-era equipment to deter or defend against an American force, Indian strategists had to treat the United States as a potential enemy. With the new difficulties in Kashmir, there was widespread concern that the United States might seize upon that conflict and focus its diplomatic—and perhaps its military—resources on the dispute.

The two states also disagree strongly on whether the Security Council should be expanded and a permanent seat be given to India. Symbolically, such a move would amount to the full recognition of India as a great power, something that the Indian elite still craves. Indians also attach great practical and political value to a Security Council seat, especially since the veto power it would confer on India could quash any unwelcome Kashmir policy. The very early UN resolutions on Kashmir still stand, though India has argued for many years that these have been overtaken by events and by the Simla Agreement. With the distancing that has occurred between Russia and India, such a veto is more important than ever.

From the American perspective, the Indian demand for a council seat is problematic, and many Americans are wary of admitting India into this particular club. There is no history of U.S.-Indian strategic collaboration, and some Americans would regard a UN seat as a "reward" for India's nuclear program and fear that this would further accelerate the trend toward nuclear weapons, even among allies such as Japan, which also seeks a council seat. Furthermore, if India were made a member of the council, would it become less sensitive to American interests? Many Americans find New Delhi's diplomacy to be like that of France: contrary, oppositional, and sometimes destructive. But France is embedded in a European and NATO framework. Would a veto-wielding India be a threat to UN and American policies, especially in the area of peacekeeping and humanitarian intervention?

American and Indian intentions aside, India's quest for a Security Council seat is not likely to be acceptable to other members of the council. Russia, for example, has adopted the same "wait-and-see" attitude as the United States; the two European seatholders would be opposed, especially if it weakened their position on the Council; and China, while publicly noncommittal, would certainly find reasons to oppose an Indian seat. For India, however, the effort to obtain a seat has a strong positive payoff at home and among nonresident Indians abroad, but unless India can propose an arrangement for the reorganization of the council that did not lessen the influence of present members and that allowed for several new members—probably an impossible combination—India's efforts are likely to go unrewarded.

India and the United States are each groping for a strategy to cope with the emergence of China as a major world power. In the early 1960s the United States viewed India as a major free, democratic Asian power that could balance a threatening, expansionist China. Initially, India was reluctant to assume this role, and Nehru sought an accommodation with Beijing. After 1962 there was a de facto U.S.-India alliance directed against China, but that faded as the United States drifted away from India and engaged China in a strategic relationship aimed at the former Soviet Union. Now the wheel has turned once more, and both the

United States and India find themselves again regarding China with a mixture of concern and uncertainty, and China could again draw the two together. The United States is especially concerned about China's threatening posture toward Taiwan, India about China's support for Pakistan. Can these two threads be tied together? Probably not, if Chinese diplomacy does not press too hard on either front and force a response. However, it does seem that both sides are seeking strategic "reinsurance" through a good working relationship that could allow for much closer ties if necessary.

## Learning to Engage

One of the few substantive agreements to come out of the Clinton trip to India was a commitment by both sides to explore the content of this relationship more systematically and regularly. From the perspective of both states, this was probably the wisest decision, rather than trying to reach some major agreement in areas of significant dispute. The "vision" document pledged regular summit meetings, ministerial-level meetings, and working groups in a variety of subjects. For this reason, the subsequent visit of Prime Minister Atal Behari Vajpayee in October 2000 was welcomed both in India and in the United States. No new agreements were reached, but the two countries consulted further on a number of issues, and plans went forward for additional meetings. For example, shortly afterward a joint official working group on antiterrorism met in New Delhi to explore steps that both states might take to ensure smoother cooperation in any joint international operations.

If the measures set forth in the document are implemented, there will still be no guarantee that the two states would engage in close cooperation or form anything resembling an alliance. But they will have a more "normal" relationship, with certain disparities between them either better understood, or not as painful as they were in the past. India will continue to pursue a complex and many-sided diplomacy. Shortly after the Clinton visit, India had high-level summit meetings with the leaders of both China and Russia, indicating that by the end of 2000, it had repaired much of the damage to its international position and was again being courted as a lucrative market for arms and technology.

The United States and India have clearly grown distant over the years, not only because of abundant misperceptions on both sides but also because of fundamental differences on the best way to peacefully organize the international system, the nature of the Soviet Union, the virtue (or sins) of alliances, and above all, the degree to which in Indian eyes the United States resisted India's emergence as a major power. In the absence of many positive economic or human ties, it is surprising that the two states got along as well as they did over the years, although even some of the positive dimensions of the relationship—such as the large economic aid programs to India—were considered patronizing and condescending. It has been difficult to manage a relationship with such military and economic asymmetries when both sides view themselves as unique, major powers. The relationship will remain more important to India than to the United States for the foreseeable future, but in the past few years the latter has come to recognize that Indian power is balanced internally and that New Delhi's many weaknesses are increasingly offset by new strengths. The degree to which the two states can act upon this better understanding of the possibilities inherent in a relationship between the "sole superpower" and a rising India will be a major determinant of India's role in the world in the next two decades.

TEN       *India*
          *Rising*

AS THIS BOOK POINTS OUT, India has begun to
overcome its many deficiencies and has discovered new strengths. Ten
years ago India was struggling to find a role in the post–cold war world,
its economy was in disarray, and its social and political systems were
undergoing rapid and unsettling change. India seemed to be plunging
into chaos. Despite frequent changes in leadership, it systematically
addressed most of these problems:

—A new approach to economics and development has turned India
into one of the world's fastest-growing economies. Although this growth
is stronger in some parts of the country than in others, its policymakers
are committed to further reform, and some are predicting the annual
growth rate will rise to 7–9 percent. If such growth continues for the
next four or five years, India would have the resources to rebuild its
weak physical infrastructure and thus make more rapid (and equitable)
growth possible. It would also provide additional resources that could
be devoted to defense and security.

—India's democratic political system, valuable in its own right, is no
longer seen as a liability. Some Indians and others used to argue that
India needed a dose of authoritarianism to bring about rapid economic
and social change. Now both the economy and Indian society are wit-
nessing rapid reform within the context of a democratic framework.
Rather than being a handicap, India's metastable democracy provides
governments the legitimacy to make tough decisions. Indian governments at the center and in the states can strike out on their own, confi-

dent that they do so with a popular mandate. India's elites have also demonstrated a flexibility that has been absent in other complex, multi-ethnic, multinational states such as Pakistan, Yugoslavia, and the former Soviet Union. Like a ship with many watertight compartments, India is relatively immune to the kinds of large-scale, extremist, or totalitarian movements that have afflicted other states.

—India's cultural influence, once a marginal factor in its relations with the rest of the world, is growing. At one level this takes the form of popular culture, including films, music, and food. At another level it is transmitted through the example and writings of leading Indian spiritual and political figures. Gandhi's influence may have leveled off in India, but it has had a profound impact on democratic struggles in places ranging from South Africa to the American South and remains a powerful influence in Latin America, Africa, and even Europe. The "new" rich Indian diaspora has exposed Indian values and ideas to many important countries, including the United States. These are all aspects of India's civilizational power.

—Once again, India has a central geostrategic position. Interaction with the major energy producers of the Persian Gulf and Central Asia, as well as with the economic "tigers" of Southeast Asia, is no longer constrained by a cold war framework, and Indian strategists are learning how to function successfully in this reconceived Asia, developing new bilateral ties and exploring multilateral arrangements that will link South Asia to adjacent regions, especially to its east.

—India is part of a chain of actual or potential nuclear weapons states that stretches from Israel to North Korea and includes Iraq, China, Pakistan, Iran, Taiwan, and South Korea. Any global nonproliferation policy will have to take India into account.

—India's reputation is also undergoing an important change. Past stereotypes of poverty and backwardness are being displaced by new images. Some of these, including the belief that Indians are inherently computer-savvy, are also stereotypes, but on the whole a more balanced and accurate picture of India's assets and liabilities is emerging, and India is being courted by the major powers of the world.

On the whole, the rate of change seen in recent years seems likely to continue for at least another half-decade. On most "hard" and "soft" measures of influence and power, India will advance slowly but steadily. By the end of this decade, India and China will again be routinely compared, as they were forty years ago. Then, they were seen as classic

Asian rivals: India was the great democratic state of Asia, China was the world's largest state. India claimed leadership of the nonaligned movement, China leadership of the communist world. Today, each still sees itself as the embodiment of a great civilization, but since 1980 China's economic performance has been strikingly better than India's, although five or six years of high Indian growth rates will narrow the gap. India has yet to decide whether it will emulate China as a military power building a small strategic arsenal and engaging in extensive sales of military equipment abroad, which made China a factor to be reckoned with in Africa and the Middle East. India is unlikely to move in this direction, but it will increasingly exert its influence in its own region—South Asia—as well as in Southeast Asia, Africa, and even Central Asia, and in selected world fora. Both India and China have domestic vulnerabilities, but here India may have the advantage. China's ideologically defunct communist system will sooner or later have to be supplanted by a form of government more suitable to Chinese culture and the modern era. It is not inconceivable that over the next decade China will become more open, just as India will begin to resemble China in its growing self-assurance in foreign policy. Whether or not India follows closely behind China in its emergence as a major Asian state will depend largely on Indian decisions in a few critical areas.

## Revolutionary Indians, Cautious India

Perhaps the most difficult challenge for the Indian leadership is to conduct an essentially conservative foreign policy while managing the domestic revolutions discussed in chapter 4. This turmoil is the consequence of vast new revolutionary forces. If India used to be easy to rule but hard to change, now it is quick to change and difficult to govern. The old bureaucratic systems have weakened, and political parties have mushroomed in number and strength and are voicing the demands of newly empowered castes and ethnic groups.

India's leaders have tried to balance the demands of an active foreign policy with these domestic political pressures. Nehru was able to persuade the world that India "counted for something" and used foreign policy to bolster national pride and self-confidence. Indira Gandhi more firmly established the link between foreign policy and domestic politics when she intervened in the domestic politics of several neighbors (and achieved the dismemberment of the original Pakistan). In the present era of coalition governments, domestic and foreign policies remain tightly intertwined. This is especially the case concerning India's ties to Bangladesh, Nepal, and Sri Lanka.

As its economic and military power grows, New Delhi will be tempted to exploit foreign policy for narrow domestic political advantage. There will be occasions when intervention in the affairs of India's neighbors will seem to be justified, as when ethnic Indians are being persecuted, strategic interests seem to be threatened, or intervention might yield some economic advantage. However, an unwise unilateral intervention abroad will alarm some of India's important neighbors and could prove to be counterproductive if other powers determine that India threatens their interests. Recent Indian governments have wisely sought to use regional fora as a way of developing closer economic and political ties with states that lie just beyond South Asia. Such arrangements are a way of exercising power without appearing to do so; India could use these cooperative mechanisms in its own region as well, by increasing its support for the South Asian Association for Regional Cooperation.

There is some speculation, however, that India will again fall under the spell of authoritarianism, this time inspired by the Hindu right. This could do enormous damage to India's reputation as a tolerant and secular state and could lead to significant social unrest. India ventured down the authoritarian path under Mrs. Gandhi, but its leaders have by and large rejected zealotry, authoritarianism, and totalitarianism. Even the RSS-influenced BJP has found itself defending the liberal nationalism once propounded by Nehru. The balance between the secular, democratic, pluralist, and nationalist elements of the basic framework established by India's first generation of leaders is deeply rooted in the social and political fabric of the country, and no government is likely to tip it sharply in another direction. This is not a country that can be ordered to march to a single beat.

## Rethinking the Policy Process

Indian leaders will have to rebuild the archaic and inefficient process by which policy is made at the center if the country is to sustain an innovative and balanced foreign policy. The foreign policy machinery derives from the Raj and still bears the imprint of the Nehru-Gandhi dynasty. Decisions are excessively centralized, parliamentary consultation is weak, the talents of outsiders are rarely utilized, and coordination among differing ministries and bureaucracies is poor. During the cold war, India could conduct a coherent foreign policy by relying on a handful of individuals without much input from the public or the armed forces. This is impossible now, and reform is long overdue. Some attempts have been made to use parliamentary standing committees to this end, but Parliament's overall contribution to the policy process remains weak and uninformed. Ad hoc arrangements such as the National Security Advisory Board have also been introduced, but this is no substitute for a government that openly and regularly consults with experts from all sectors of society and all regions of the country and that treats intraministry cooperation and decisionmaking as the norm, rather than the exception. Also, the virtual exclusion of the armed forces from the policy process is dysfunctional. The services are still viewed through the prism of civilian control, not professional competence. As India emerges as a great power, it will have to find better ways of ensuring that the armed forces offer the best available professional advice on weapons purchases, threat assessment, and tactical and strategic military decisions.

## India's Pakistan Options

In international affairs, states are known by the enemies they keep. India is destined to be compared with Pakistan until it can accommodate Islamabad, or Pakistan "withers away" to the point where it is no longer a major factor in Indian strategy. While much of the world has urged India and Pakistan to work together to settle their differences, cooperation remains an abstract idea. This is seen most clearly in Kashmir. For the next few years this problem may become more, not less difficult. For a region that is about to be swamped by the conflicts of the twenty-first century, everyone seems obsessed with the problems of the past. Failing any bold diplomacy from Delhi or Islamabad, or a cataclysmic failure of Pakistan, the present crisis-ridden relationship could continue indefinitely.

As the larger power with larger ambitions, India will have to figure out a way to initiate and sustain a credible dialogue with Pakistan, either directly or through intermediaries. The difficulty of doing this is evident in the failure of the formal negotiations and secret diplomacy of recent years. Indians feel themselves besieged by Pakistan and have retreated to the moral high ground. While this position may be gratifying, New Delhi now needs to attempt a fresh start. Until a few years ago, many Indians would have welcomed Pakistan's decline and disappearance, but with the rise of Islamic extremism and Islamabad's acquisition of nuclear weapons, a weak and failing Pakistan could be a greater threat to India than a coherent Pakistan. Such a Pakistan could serve as a base for radical Islamic movements that target Indian Muslims, it could accelerate the spread of nuclear weapons to states hostile to India, and it could spew out millions of refugees in India's direction.

Dealing with the Kashmir problem means ultimately grappling with larger questions of a contested people, a contested territory, and two contested national identities. There will also have to be a great deal of "stage management" because India and Pakistan have invested so much in their position over the years. While Pakistan must move some distance from its entrenched view of how Kashmir could be resolved, prospects for agreement would be enhanced if India came to the realization that conflict with Islamabad is an important barrier to India's full emergence as a major power. A more tranquil domestic political order, expanded regional economic cooperation, a greater role in the Middle East and other adjacent regions, and perhaps a Security Council seat would all follow if India removes this millstone from around its neck. If it does not, then it may have to learn to live with a Pakistan that can threaten and undercut it in many ways, but as long as this state of affairs continues, Indian influence will suffer.

## Nuclear Decisions

The 1998 tests increased India's prestige and status, thus indirectly improving its net security. India will always be seen as a "nuclear weapons state," an accomplishment more politically significant than technically impressive. How long the reputational spinoff from the nuclear tests will last is hard to tell, but if the Indian government can avoid any crisis that demonstrates how weak and superficial its nuclear capabilities really are, and if it can use its nuclear status as a way of leveraging a seat on various arms control fora, then the decision will prove to have been a correct one from the perspective of helping to elevate India to the rank of major power.

India must now confront a number of issues that had been smoothed over by the option strategy. After thirty years of oversimple and uninformed debate on these issues, Indians cannot be expected to reach a consensus on them soon. Looking ahead to the next several years, India has a number of critical nuclear-related decisions ahead of it.

The first is whether India will be satisfied with the political payoff of the 1998 tests, or whether it will feel compelled to renew testing or otherwise expand the nuclear and missile programs to again attract global attention and jack up its reputation as a "hard" state. If India's international environment remains benign, then its policymakers are unlikely to deviate from the present modest path of nuclearization and India will continue to follow a policy of nuclear ambiguity. At the same time, it would no doubt have difficulty agreeing to any arms control initiative that would limit future choices. This would allow India to develop a nuclear doctrine and move slowly but steadily on missile deployment while reaping the benefit of being a nuclear-armed state. Pakistan would likely follow, and South Asia will experience an "arms crawl" rather than an "arms race."

On the other hand, if India should feel pressured by the United States or other countries, it could resume an active nuclear testing program, increase the rate of deployment, and attempt to again draw attention to itself via the nuclear program. The program could move in directions advocated by the nuclear maximalists, with India obtaining a first strike capability against Pakistan, developing an ICBM capability, and seeking parity with China. Should this happen, then Beijing is likely to balance India by supporting Pakistan; China could also increase its pressure on the border with India, thus providing another reason for Indian maximalists to press for an all-out nuclear capability.

Economic developments over the next several years will also influence Delhi's nuclear choices. As India becomes richer, it is possible that both the armed forces and the scientific/military/industrial complex will have adequate funds for a full-scale nuclear program, complete with seaborne delivery systems, satellite reconnaissance capabilities, and an elaborate command and control system with modern permissive-action links. With assistance from abroad, India might be able to develop and deploy a theater missile defense against another nuclear power.

Furthermore, as its capacities grow, India will have the option of selectively selling or transferring nuclear and missile technology to other states. So far, New Delhi has shied away from the role of arms exporter, partly because its weapons were unattractive to potential consumers and partly because of Nehruvian qualms about the morality of the arms industry. But India's new realpolitik and its comparative advantage in some areas of high technology may lead to India joining the major industrial powers, China, and North Korea as a supplier of advanced military or nuclear technology.

One wild card in India's nuclear hand would be the occurrence of a nuclear accident or a misjudgment. Near-war scares and nuclear accidents elsewhere in the world have influenced attitudes toward nuclear weapons. Given India's overcrowded cities, its long tradition of being critical of nuclear weapons in the hands of other powers, and a growing environmental movement, such an event might sweep aside all of the theorizing and lead to radical changes in Indian opinion and policy. The tremendous earthquake that devastated the state of Gujarat on January 26, 2001 (coincidentally, India's Republic Day) reminded many Indians of the devastation that a nuclear strike would cause and made it evident that the country's disaster relief capabilities were limited: the best performers being the armed forces, which would be presumably otherwise occupied should India have a nuclear exchange with another state.

## Relations with the United States

As long as the world remains unipolar, New Delhi has a much greater stake than Washington in a closer relationship. This asymmetry is likely to continue indefinitely and puts India at some risk. The economic dimensions of the relationship also favor Washington, and it will be a long time before New Delhi acquires significant leverage in this regard. For this reason, recent Indian policymakers have all but abandoned the view that the United States is a strategic threat and that India should join with other countries in balancing the "sole superpower." The underlying strategic logic of this position was pure Krishna Menon–think: namely, that emerging powers like India will inevitably be opposed by dominant world powers. The problem with this position was that two likely partners in the containment or counterbalancing of America (Pakistan and China) are themselves allies and potential rivals of New Delhi. The attempt by Inder Gujral to reinvigorate the non-aligned movement as a force of the "have nots" against the "haves" also had inherent limits: compared with most of those states, India is a major power, and in any case most of them need a close relationship with the United States for economic or strategic purposes.

For the next several years India is likely to pursue a policy that combines accommodation of some American interests with an attempt to influence Washington to better appreciate Indian concerns. It would be premature to imagine India accepting recent American positions concerning nuclear proliferation, or moving more quickly toward a settlement on Kashmir. Rather, New Delhi will attempt to persuade Washington that Indian nuclear weapons and India's policies on Kashmir are compatible with American interests. Both of these issues touch vital Indian interests, and it is unlikely that any Indian government can make significant concessions to the United States without a severe domestic backlash. However, movement toward American positions on such issues as combating terrorism and expanding trade has already occurred.

In pursuing a new relationship with the United States, strategists may begin talking of a "natural alliance" between the two, but New Delhi still retains close ties to Russia and has cultivated France and Israel in recent years. All three countries are far more likely to provide India with advanced military technology than the United States, which has bound itself tightly with its sanctions policies. Even if Washington were to eliminate these sanctions, the Indian strategic community would not soon trust it.

In dealing with United States, India now has another and more enduring asset than cultural shows. The million-strong American-Indian community represents a bridge between the two countries. The 2000 presidential election was the first major opportunity this community had to play a role in the American political system. Although this community cannot be expected to support all Indian policies (many Indian-Americans have been highly critical of India's sluggish pace of economic reform, for example), it is generally supportive of Indian ambitions and can perform the invaluable function of educating influential Americans about India and helping to shape a more realistic assessment of Indian society in the minds of other Americans.

## Between Kautilya and Moralism

The enduring national debate in any major democracy revolves around the balance between considerations of realpolitik and its idealist inclinations. The former are necessary because the world is imperfect, since even other democracies may pursue policies that threaten it—just as alliances with distasteful or dissimilar states may be necessary. Yet democracies have an urge to proselytize, and many, including India, assume that foreign policy should be an extension of cherished domestic values.

India has for many years projected an image of indecision as it has oscillated between grand proclamations of idealism and actions that appear to be motivated by the narrowest of realpolitik considerations. It has treated some of its neighbors as vassals, while declaring its support for the equality of all states; it has bowed low before totalitarian regimes, while professing an eternal commitment to democracy.

To some outsiders, these oscillations suggest that India lacks a strategic culture. Indians themselves are engaged in an endless debate as to which parts of its periphery are most important and why. While indecision and ambiguity might have had certain advantages in the bipolar cold war, they are liabilities today. In recent years, there seems to be a new effort to resolve the realism-idealism conundrum and to determine priorities in Indian foreign policy. Perhaps the breakthrough came during the CTBT debate, when India's representative, Ambassador Arundati Ghosh, stated that India had to oppose the treaty (as then written) because security issues were involved. This may have been the first time that India invoked this argument; hitherto, Indian positions on such treaties were stated in terms of high principle, although they may have been guided by considerations of realpolitik. It is essential that India learn to bridge the gap between idealistic inclinations and realist compulsions. This will make India a more credible country, improve the quality of debate within the Indian foreign policy community, and make India a more predictable state, hence one that other major powers will find it easier to work with.

In the past, India has been a less-than-great power attempting to act like a great one, which sometimes made it look foolish. A new generation of Indian strategists, politicians, and officials is increasingly aware that a hectoring style is counterproductive and is letting a new realism creep into India's Foreign Ministry, still famed as one of the world's bureaucracies most skilled at "getting to no." If Indian diplomacy of the past five years is any indication, the gaps between Indian ambitions and capabilities, and between Indian rhetoric and Indian intentions, are slowly closing.

## Rising India

I have argued that India has "emerged" as a major—even great—power, but in different ways than expected. The hopes that India would become a wealthy state have been belied, although there is enough wealth in

India to ensure that the state can bring substantial resources to bear on any problem when it wants to, and future growth is expected to be equitably distributed. The revolutions under way in India have produced strains and stresses, but as long as these stem from the aspirations and achievements of hitherto ignored and depressed social groups, they are to be welcomed, not condemned. India has been threatened and hurt by outside powers, and in turn it has inflicted suffering on others. A new realism in the Indian strategic community suggests that Indians will fantasize less about various plots to encircle or weaken it, without losing the expectation that India has a special role to play in the world. That role is primarily to "be India," and to address the human security issues that stem from its own imbalances and injustices. By doing that India will make one-quarter of the world more secure, not a trivial accomplishment. As India moves ahead into the future its central identity is likely to remain pretty much the same: there is a recognizably Indian world view and a recognizably Indian way of dealing with that world. But the rate of change both within India and in that larger world seems to be accelerating, as are notions of what constitutes a "great" power. Given the problems of many of its neighbors and its success in managing its own experiment in democracy, the greatest in human history, it would seem that the future favors India, which does not mean that this future will inevitably be pleasant or peaceful.

## The United States and India

As India becomes more than a regional power, how should the United States respond? Traditionally, the great states of the world resist the entry of new members into the great power club. America's failure to address India's aspirations has been costly. An India that did not seem to count for very much over the past ten years (in Washington, at least) became embroiled in two major crises, exploding five nuclear devices, spurring Pakistan to do the same, and challenging the U.S. nonproliferation strategy. These events at least got America's attention.

There are many incentives for the United States to learn how to deal with a rising India. India could make an important contribution to international peacekeeping, it is a critical country as far as nonproliferation policies are concerned, it could be a balancer to China, its newly liberated economy has growing ties with that of the United States, there are about one and a half million Americans of Indian origin, and above all, the success of the Indian democratic and social revolutions is an indirect but still important interest of the United States.

There are also negative reasons for the United States to reexamine its policies. India is capable of behaving irresponsibly. Preemptive diplomacy is in order, to ensure that India does not conclude that widely exporting sensitive technologies to earn hard currency or to tweak the nose of the West (and China) is in its best interest. In addition, while India is unlikely ever to become an ally of China, it could side with Beijing (and Russia) to challenge the American-dominated alliance system in East and Southeast Asia. India could also pursue a riskier strategy for dealing with Pakistan.

### Stability in American Policy

It is premature for the United States to pursue a strategic alliance with India. India rejects dependency, whether economic, strategic, moral, or cultural. For its part, the United States works well with countries whose dependencies match its strengths. India should be acknowledged as South Asia's regional dominant power and as a major Asian power, and reasonable Indian ambition can be supported. But the United States should not let Indian hawks shape the relationship. Some of them would define India's sphere of influence as including part of Pakistan, parts of China, and much of the Indian Ocean. It is inappropriate to write a blank check and let the Indians fill in the figure. Washington has strategic interests in these countries and in the Indian Ocean. These do not threaten India, and right now there appears to be no good reason to break with such states, pull out of Diego Garcia and the Indian Ocean, or subcontract to India a regional peacekeeping role. A strategic alliance must rest on strong, enduring, and shared interests and friendships: there must be a degree of trust and coming together of goals between the strategic elites of both states. The United States does have a shared interest with Indian leaders in working toward orderly change and a peaceful region, but the two sides disagree on how to bring this about. Slowly, however, the perceptions of India and the United States are moving closer, and further dialogue, such as the strategic discussions held in the last two years of the Clinton administration, might lead to a greater convergence of policy.

If there is to be a new relationship, both sides would have to find a model that fits their idiosyncratic styles, can withstand the scrutiny of

Congressional and parliamentary democracy, and meets their respective strategic interests. Even then, in a world of regions—a world that lacks a core strategic rivalry—there might not be common permanent interests between members of different strategic regional groupings so much as permanent friendships based on ideological, personal, and economic ties.

Strategically, the United States should regard India not as another Asian state comparable to Pakistan or Indonesia, but as a player in the larger Asian sphere, one of the five most important states in the world, whether from a strategic, political, or ideological perspective. India may not be China, but neither is it an insignificant "third world" state. An India that continues to reform its economy and comes to terms with Pakistan could be a force for stability in Asia, a partner in humanitarian intervention in Africa and other war-torn regions. Should the contingency arise, it could be a partner in the containment of a threatening or expansionist China. Even an India that grows slowly and cannot solve its Pakistan problem will continue to have great influence in the non-Western world.

Treating India as a rising power would mean the expansion of American engagement with Delhi, including discussion of shared policy concerns (terrorism, narcotics, humanitarian intervention, political stability in fragmented, ethnically complex countries, and China). Treating India as a rising power also means Delhi should be one of the capitals—along with London, Berlin, Beijing, Moscow, and Tokyo—that senior American officials contact concerning important global developments. Like the French, Indians have a different and not necessarily hostile view of how the world should be organized, and regular consultation will temper their sometimes abrasive style.

Washington should also offer qualified support for India's candidacy for a seat on the UN Security Council. A country of India's size and importance should take its place on the council, but only after the Kashmir problem appears to be on the road to resolution. This would provide an incentive to India to work with Pakistan and other countries on this dispute and would ensure that it was not acquiring a seat merely to gain a veto over international initiatives on Kashmir. Furthermore, a decision to expand the council to include India would force a debate on the future political role of the United Nations, and its place in American diplomacy. Recent American administrations have gone back and forth on this issue.

Holding India in higher regard does not mean abandoning important American interests in Pakistan. The United States can also do more than merely point out the virtues of regional accommodation. It should encourage a greater sense of realism in Pakistan about possible solutions to the Kashmir conflict, while also urging India to accommodate Pakistan's concerns about the treatment of Muslim Kashmiris. A more active yet low-key diplomacy is in order. It will not lead to an easy or rapid resolution of the Kashmir dispute, but it will enable the United States to retain influence in both countries should its services again be required to avert a war or even a future nuclear crisis.

This prescription for the U.S.-India relationship calls for neither opposition nor alliance, but for something in between. There is no need to contain or oppose an India that is still struggling to reshape its economic and political order, especially since it is in U.S. interests that those domestic reforms proceed apace. However, the United States cannot expect a strategic alliance that Delhi would view as part of an anti-Pakistan or anti-China campaign. An "in-between" relationship would require developing new understandings in several areas: the conditions under which India and the United States might jointly engage in humanitarian intervention in various parts of the world, deploying new defensive military technologies (such as theater missile defense) without triggering regional arms races in Taiwan and South Asia, and joint steps that the two might take to strengthen fragile democratic regimes in Asia and elsewhere. A relationship with India provides an opportunity to directly influence the Indian world view on issues that are of importance to the United States. It would also provide early warning of potentially harmful policies.

India is not a great power in the classic sense; it cannot challenge American military or economic power outside of South Asia, although it is increasingly able to resist American intrusion in its own region. However, in a transformed international order, its assets and resources become more relevant to a wide range of American interests than they have been for the past fifty years. They cannot be safely ignored in the future, as they have been in the past.

## India's Nuclear Program

The nonproliferation policies at the core of U.S. policy strategy toward South Asia throughout the 1990s failed to prevent India from testing nuclear weapons and declaring itself a nuclear weapons state. While the Indian tests angered many officials in the Clinton administration, future American administrations must understand that India is essentially a status quo power when it comes to the proliferation of nuclear weapons. New Delhi wanted to be the last country to "go nuclear," and it has an interest in working with the United States and other responsible countries to ensure that proliferation proceeds at a very slow pace. The United States must put nuclear proliferation in its proper perspective. South Asia has proliferated. The major task for American diplomacy lies in the realm of management, not abolition. India and Pakistan need to be brought into as many international containment regimes as possible, while their own uncertain nuclear standoff is stabilized and secured.

As far as the United States is concerned, the development of Indian and Pakistani nuclear programs raises three immediate and one long-term concern: how to discourage the two nations from using nuclear weapons in a crisis, how to ensure that nuclear weapons do not add to regional instability or cause an inadvertent detonation, and how to prevent the transfer of the technology to produce these weapons to other nations or nonsovereign separatist or terrorist organizations. This list suggests that a "cap, roll-back, and eliminate" approach is not a realistic option in South Asia. Actually, it never was. That was the goal of U.S. policy for more than a decade, and it was both ineffective and counterproductive.

There are a number of ways to reduce the risk of accidental or inadvertent use of nuclear weapons. Some are technical: better command and control arrangements would enhance Indian and Pakistani confidence that nuclear weapons would be used only when intended. The best arrangement (from the perspective of crisis stability) would be if neither side deployed its nuclear arsenal, perhaps by leaving warheads unassembled and separated from their delivery systems. The United States should be prepared to share its experience in developing command and control arrangements and nuclear doctrine to help the two states maintain a credible nuclear deterrent with the fewest possible number of weapons and the highest level of stability.

Stabilizing the India-Pakistan nuclear relationship is all the more important since in a few years both states may have medium-range ballistic missiles capable of reaching other countries. The United States also has an interest in making sure that these new nuclear systems do not interact with those of other Middle Eastern or Asian powers: Israel and Pakistan, for example, or India and China. The United States must also remain concerned about the transfer of nuclear weapons expertise, fissile material, and whole devices from South Asia to other states, legitimate or rogue. While both India and Pakistan have pledged to enforce legislation prohibiting such transfers, the fact is that four of the world's five declared nuclear weapons states (Britain being the exception) have assisted one or more other countries with their nuclear programs. This situation calls for a strategy that moves beyond one of mere prevention to one that enlists India and Pakistan in limiting the further spread of weapons of mass destruction and the problems raised by the introduction of ballistic missile systems. This strategy will have to combine incentives with sanctions.

One incentive is status. India wants the legitimacy of its nuclear programs to be recognized. However, it cannot be a member of the Nuclear Nonproliferation Treaty, which defines a "nuclear weapon state" as a country that tested nuclear devices before 1967. That said, India should be associated with the various international nuclear and missile control regimes and the larger effort to contain weapons proliferation. For its part, the United States should be prepared to discuss various ideas for promoting nuclear stability, including a greater role for defensive systems with India and its stated preference for the eventual elimination of nuclear weapons. India should also participate in the global dialogue on the reduction of strategic nuclear weapons.

Another incentive would be to provide civilian nuclear technology to India. This would not violate the NPT once India's civilian programs were separated from military nuclear programs. Affording India such assistance could also be part of a trade-off that brought it into the various international nuclear and missile control regimes and encompassed the larger effort to contain weapons proliferation. The prospect of a continuing positive relationship with the United States provides another incentive for Delhi to restrain its military nuclear programs and join in global nonproliferation efforts.

In exchange, Washington should be prepared to provide early warning devices and technologies to help prevent accidental war; it should bring both states into nuclear and control regimes such as the Missile Technology Control Regime and the London Suppliers Group, and it should be willing to assist civilian nuclear energy programs that are under adequate international safeguards. Washington should also explore the possibility of selling defensive antimissile technologies to India (or Pakistan) in exchange for limiting their deployment of offensive systems.

The development of theater missile defense systems also provides a new opportunity for creative and useful American initiatives in South Asia. These technologies could be shared with any state that helped in other ways to constrain a nuclear arms race, or that avoided provocative and destabilizing actions.[1] TMD systems serve, to some extent, as substitutes for offensive nuclear weapons, and it is in the overall interest of the United States to see the world move away from nuclear and military doctrines based on the assumption that security rests on the threat of the destruction of millions of innocent people.

Second, military exchange programs with India need to be restored and the practical aspects of military cooperation with India explored. India, along with other South Asian states, has been a major contributor to UN peacekeeping operations but lacks air and sealift capabilities. The Indian and American military establishments need to work closely to prepare for contingencies in which they can help stabilize war-torn or fragmenting states around the world.

These security ties cannot be expanded as long as the United States has military sanctions in place. A sanction-led policy must be supplanted by a grand bargain that would emphasize political incentives and mutual security rather than punishment. As part of such a bargain, India and Pakistan might agree to limit their nuclear systems, develop better command and control systems, institute serious confidence-building measures, and work closely with international agencies to ensure that their nuclear and missile technologies do not leak to other states. These steps would bring the two states in alignment with many of the core provisions of the Non-Proliferation Treaty.

## Democracy Matters

Many years ago, Western observers saw that a great experiment had been launched in India. Its society was widely recognized as the most unequal in the world in terms of social hierarchy, regional disparity, and economic distribution. Could India reduce these inequalities and achieve development by democratic means? Other former colonial states had become military dictatorships, some nationalist movements had slipped into autocracy, and the People's Republic of China was born totalitarian. Could India forge integrative institutions while simultaneously promoting economic growth under conditions of political democracy? This is a feat that no other large state except the United States has attempted (and then, under far more favorable geopolitical and economic circumstances). It is a task of awe-inspiring magnitude. It remains the strongest basis for an Indian claim for the support, sympathy, and assistance of the United States and other developed states.

The success of the Indian democratic approach to state- and nation-building should be the core of regional policies of the United States and its democratic allies. In this regard, India resembles contemporary Russia. If either was to lapse into militarism or dictatorship, or break apart, the strategic consequences for U.S. and Western interests would all be negative. It is hard to imagine what would be worse: a region dominated by an extremist Indian government, thrashing about, crushing its neighbors, or an India broken up into five, ten, or twenty states in conflict with each other, and some within reach of a nuclear capability. Some Indians think the West is unsympathetic to this American interest in India's great experiment in state-and nation-building. To an Indian policymaker, beset by problems of staggering magnitude, the motives of outsiders are sometimes sinister. Comments on India's human rights record, its actions in Kashmir, its restrictive economic policies, and even intellectual property rights are dismissed as "anti-Indian." Outsiders should continue to provide these comments and criticisms, but should not be surprised by hostile Indian reactions.

This is why regular, high-level, symbol-rich state visits are important to convey the depth and stability of American interests in India. These visits, such as President Clinton's March 2000 trip, can be used to convey America's interest in the broad range of human, social, and economic developments under way in India. They serve strategic purposes, of course, but in India's case (as in that of Russia and China), the long-term American interest lies in the orderly development of the societies of these countries and their increasing openness. One by-product of the Clinton visit, the ambitious vision statement, provided a blueprint, calling for regular summit meetings and high-level consultations. Given India's past reluctance to engage the United States—except as a critic—these dialogues can help reduce anti-American suspicions in Delhi, acquaint American officials with Delhi's unique world view and provide an opportunity to influence that view.

An adjunct to a policy of supporting and strengthening India's democracy, but now a valuable goal in its own right, is a closer economic engagement with a newly liberalizing India. Economic ties will eventually provide the ballast for a more stable U.S.-Indian relationship. However, because the economic relationship was for so many years fraught with distrust and irritation, both countries should fully use the conflict resolution procedures available in the World Trade Organization (WTO) to resolve differences between the two states over allegations of discriminatory tariffs, unfair trade practices, and violations of intellectual property rights.

Washington should also look for new ways to expand economic contacts between the two countries. India is not a member of any of the major free-trade agreements. The new Bush administration should consider the possibility of negotiating the introduction of a phased free-trade zone between the two countries. Along with India's active membership in the WTO, this would accelerate the liberalization of the Indian economy and could have a major impact on the rate of Indian economic development. It would also give American firms greater access to the Indian market.

## A More Active Regional Role

With the nuclearization of the India-Pakistan relationship, Washington must find a role for itself in the Kashmir dispute somewhere between doing nothing and being an unwelcome intruder. South Asia has a number of conflicts, but three are interconnected and threaten the stability of India and Pakistan, and the wider world. The Afghanistan and Kashmir conflicts are linked, as are Kashmir and the threat of regional nuclear war. Together, these three disputes make the region one of the most dangerous places in the world.

In the case of Kashmir, India officially rejects the idea of a mediator, but many Indians would welcome a sympathetic outsider. Similarly, Pakistan's military leadership (and many of its civilians) believe that Islamabad should have a controlling role in Afghanistan. Both Afghanistan and Kashmir could benefit from a peace process, and success in resolving or ameliorating these disputes would also make a nuclear conflict less likely. A regional peace process would have to be tailor-made for South Asia. Any American role would have to be low-profile but persistent; it would also have to involve America's key allies and friends, some of which are interested in untying the Afghan, Kashmir, and nuclear knots. In the case of nuclear issues, the United States must work closely with Japan, a state that has a special interest in proliferation and is a strong economic force in both India and Pakistan. In the case of Afghanistan, it would be wise for the Untied States to let selected European countries take the lead. And in the case of Kashmir, where there is now considerable American expertise, it would be appropriate for Washington to increase its engagement with India, Pakistan, and Kashmiris of various political hues, encouraging a return to the negotiating table and offering technical and other assistance to the parties.[2] South Asia needs a process that will encompass, ameliorate, stabilize, and eventually resolve the core disputes between its major states. To some Indians, such U.S. efforts will seem to be an intrusion, but this indirect route may be the most effective way of enhancing Indian power and influence over the long term.

# Notes

## Introduction

1. Stephen P. Cohen and Richard L. Park, *India: Emergent Power?* (New York: Crane, Russak, 1979), p. xiv. We argued that India was already a regional "hegemon" but would emerge as an Asian power.

2. The best summary of this relationship, routinely characterized as a "roller-coaster" or as a series of "ups and downs" by various authors is in Dennis Kux, *Estranged Democracies: India and the United States 1941–1991* (New Delhi: Sage, 1993).

3. For an early collection, see Selig S. Harrison, ed., *India and the United States* (Macmillan, 1961), with contributions by a wide range of eminent Americans including Senators John F Kennedy and Hubert Humphrey, Hans Morgenthau, Richard L. Park, Averell Harriman, and others. See also John W. Mellor, ed., *India: A Rising Middle Power* (Boulder, Colo.: Westview Press, 1979), with contributions largely by academics.

4. India's stagnation, internal conflict, and disorder have been themes of many books, including those by a number of American correspondents based in New Delhi. See Bernard D. Nossiter, *Soft State: A Newspaperman's Chronicle of India* (Harper and Row, 1970); Selig S. Harrison, *India: The Most Dangerous Decades* (Princeton University Press, 1960); and Barbara Crossette, *India Facing the Twenty-First Century* (Indiana University Press, 1993).

5. Katherine Mayo eventually produced three books on India. For the first and most influential, originally published in 1927, see Katherine Mayo, *Mother India* (New York: Greenwood Press, 1969).

6. An early and still valuable analysis of American stereotypes of India is in Harold R. Isaacs, *Images of Asia: American Views of China and India* (Harper,

319

1972; originally published under the title *Scratches on Our Minds,* 1958). A more recent survey is Sulochana Raghavan Glazer and Nathan Glazer, eds., *Conflicting Images: India and the United States* (Glenn Dale, Md.: Riverdale Company, 1990).

7. Carla Hills and Arthur Hartman, co-chairs, *South Asia and the United States* (New York: Asia Society, 1994); and Devin T. Hagerty, rapporteur, *Preventing Nuclear Proliferation in South Asia* (New York: Asia Society, 1995).

8. See George Perkovich, *India's Nuclear Bomb: The Impact on Global Proliferation* (University of California Press, 1999).

9. Sandy Gordon, *India's Rise to Power in the Twentieth Century and Beyond* (London: St. Martin's, 1995).

10. Two important studies of India by eminent Indian expatriates either ignore or devote little attention to Indian foreign policy and its regional or global role. See Shashi Tharoor, *India: From Midnight to the Millennium* (New York: Arcade, 1997); and Sunil Khilnani, *The Idea of India* (Farrar, Straus and Giroux, 1998). However, a comprehensive overview of Indian strategy by a retired Indian navy admiral does present a careful examination of the linkage between internal politics and economic development and security and foreign policy matters. See Verghese Koithara, *Society, State and Security, The Indian Experience* (New Delhi: Sage, 1999)

11. Richard N. Haass and Gideon Rose, *A New U.S. Policy toward India and Pakistan* (New York: Council on Foreign Relations Press, 1997). See also the balanced council-sponsored study by Shirin Tahir-Kheli, *India, Pakistan, and the United States: Breaking with the Past* (New York: Council on Foreign Relations Press, 1997). Of the twenty-eight signatories to the report, thirteen signed a "dissent" or an additional opinion; some signed both. A subsequent letter to the president by the same group achieved a greater degree of consensus and was signed by fifteen members of the original task force. See Richard N. Haass, "Open Letter to the President," March 13, 2000 (www.brook.edu/views/articles/haass/20000313.htm [January 24, 2001]).

12. See Khilnani, *The Idea of India*; Tharoor, *India;* and also two collections, one Indian, one American: P. R. Chari, ed., *India towards Millennium* (New Delhi: Manohar, 1998); and Selig S. Harrison, Paul Kreisberg, and Dennis Kux, eds., *India and Pakistan: The First Fifty Years* (Washington: Woodrow Wilson Center Press, 1999).

## Chapter 1

1. For a recent overview see Paul Kennedy, *The Rise and Fall of the Great Powers: Economic Change and Military Conflict from 1500 to 2000* (Random House, 1987).

2. For a classic overview of historical imperial systems see S. N. Eisenstadt, *The Political Systems of Empires: The Rise and Fall of the Historical Bureaucratic*

*Systems* (London: The Free Press of Glencoe, 1963); and Adda B. Bozeman, *Politics and Culture in International History: From the Ancient Near East to the Opening of the Modern Age,* 2d ed. (New Brunswick, N.J.: Transaction, 1994).

3. For a discussion, see Janet Abu-Lughod, "Discontinuities and Persistence: One World System or a Succession of Systems?" in Andre Gunder Frank and Barry K. Gills, eds., *The World System: Five Hundred Years or Five Thousand?* (New York: Routledge, 1993), p. 279.

4. Jonathan Pollack, "China and the Global Strategic Balance," in Harry Harding, ed., *China's Foreign Relations in the 1980s* (Yale University Press, 1984), pp. 173–74.

5. For two informed discussions of the proposition that China could be a superpower, see Andrew J. Nathan and Robert S. Ross, *The Great Wall and the Empty Fortress: China's Search for Security* (W. W. Norton, 1997); and Michael D. Swaine and Ashley J. Tellis, *Interpreting China's Grand Strategy* (Santa Monica, Calif.: Rand, 2000).

6. A recent Indian statement of the way in which culture is a component of state power, arguing that this is an area where India has a special advantage, is found in B. P. Singh, *India's Culture: The State, the Arts and Beyond* (Oxford University Press, 1999), pp. 47–58.

7. Joseph E. Schwartzberg, ed., *A Historical Atlas of South Asia,* 2d impr. (Oxford University Press, 1992), pp. 254–61.

8. Ibid., p. 16.

9. Charles Drekmeier, *Kingship and Community in Early India* (Stanford University Press, 1962), p. 282.

10. Romila Thapar, *A History of India,* vol. 1 (London: Penguin Books, 1966), p. 91.

11. The Cholas were based in Southern India. For an overview of their expansion from 850 to 1200 A.D., see Schwartzberg, *A Historical Atlas of South Asia,* pp. 32, 189–90.

12. The *Arthashastra* was probably a compilation made over many years. For a modern translation by an Indian diplomat, see Kautilya, *The Arthashastra,* L. N. Rangarajan, ed. (New Delhi: Penguin Books, 1987). The American political scientist George Modelski provided an excellent survey of the realist principles embedded in the mandala. See Modelski, "Kautilya: Foreign Policy and the International System in the Ancient Hindu World," *American Political Science Review,* vol. 53 (September 1964), pp. 549–60.

13. Here is an important difference between India and China; in China, only the Manchus were absorbed and Sinicized in this way.

14. See Joel Larus, *Culture and Political-Military Behavior: The Hindus in Pre-Modern India* (Columbia, Mo.: South Asia Books, 1979), p. 191.

15. It began to decay when Aurangzeb tried to extend Mughal rule to the South, well beyond the capability of the empire to impose its authority. See John Richards, *The Mughal Empire* (Cambridge University Press, 1993), pp. 242–46.

16. See the survey by Nehru's contemporary, the scholar-statesman K. M. Panikkar, *Problems of Indian Defence* (London: Asia Publishing House, 1960), p. 14. For more recent scholarship on the spread of Western military technology, see the survey by Geoffrey Parker, *The Military Revolution* (Cambridge University Press, 1988).

17. Ronald Inden, "Ritual, Authority and Cyclic Time in Hindu Kingship," in John F. Richards, *Kingship and Authority in South Asia,* 2d ed. (University of Wisconsin South Asia Program, 1981), p. 34.

18. Percival Spear, *A History of India,* vol. 2 (London: Penguin, 1965), p. 37.

19. For an official discussion of British India's grand strategy, see the excellent survey by the Historical Section (India and Pakistan), *Official History of the Indian Armed Forces in the Second World War, 1939–45, Defense of India: Policy and Plans* (New Delhi: Orient Longmans, 1963).

20. Kanti P. Bajpai and Amitabh Mattoo, eds., *Securing India: Strategic Thought and Practice, Essays by George K. Tanham with Commentaries* (New Delhi: Manohar, 1996). Paraphrase of Tanham by the editors, p. 17.

21. British skepticism concerning Indian self-rule can still be seen emblazoned above the main portal of the North Block of the Central Secretariat Building in New Delhi: "Liberty will not descend to a people. A people must raise themselves to liberty. It is a blessing that must be earned before it can be enjoyed."

22. There had been a limited franchise before this date, but in 1935 one-sixth of the Indian people voted for a government that lasted until World War II began in 1939. Robert L. Hardgrave and Stanley A. Kochanek, *India: Government and Politics in a Developing Nation,* 6th ed. (Harcourt, 2000), p. 49.

23. Sri Aurobindo (Aurobindo Ghose, 1872–1950) was one of the "extremist" highly Westernized intellectuals drawn into politics after the British partitioned Bengal. He spent only four years in active politics, but strongly influenced Gandhi and other nationalists. Aurobindo lived the remainder of his life in Pondicherry, a French possession in India, as an accomplished yoga and spiritual guide. For a summary of his views, see the various excerpts presented in Stephen Hay, ed., *Sources of Indian Tradition, vol. 2: Modern India and Pakistan,* 2d ed. (Columbia University Press, 1988).

24. Jawaharlal Nehru, *The Discovery of India* (London: Meridian Books, 1960), p. 545.

25. S. Gopal, *Jawaharlal Nehru, A Biography, vol. 1: 1889–1947* (Harvard University Press, 1976), p. 356. Jaswant Singh, foreign minister in the 1999 BJP-led government, cited a personal communication from Nehru's cousin, B. K. Nehru, indicating that Jawaharlal Nehru never accepted the creation of Pakistan. See Singh, *Defending India* (St. Martin's Press, 1999), pp. 23ff.

26. For a survey of impressions of India by foreign visitors, see Raj Thapar, *Traveler's Tales* (New Delhi: Vikas, 1977).

27. Drekmeier, *Kingship and Community*, pp. 69–88.

28. A. L. Basham, *The Wonder That Was India*, 3d ed. (New York: Taplinger, 1967), p. 149.

29. For an excellent overview, see the recent book by noted Indian anthropologist Dipankar Gupta, *Interrogating Caste: Understanding Hierarchy and Difference in Indian Society* (New Delhi: Penguin, 2000).

30. Ibid., pp. 202–03.

31. The "untouchables" have borne many names over the millennia: Achhut, Harijan, scheduled caste, and most recently, Dalit. Their resurgence is reviewed in chapter 4.

32. For a history, see Philip Mason, *A Matter of Honour* (Holt, Reinhart and Winston, 1974). See also Stephen P. Cohen, *The Indian Army: Its Contribution to the Development of a Nation*, 2d ed. (Oxford University Press, 1990).

33. The idea of "Asia" is a fiction, invented by Greek navigators as they sailed through the Dardanelles, the Bosphorus, and the Straits of Kerch. This navigational convenience sparked a mythic feud between Europe and Asia and was put into broader circulation by Herodotus: "For Asia, with all the various tribes of barbarians that inhabit it, is regarded by the Persians as their own; but Europe and the Greek race they look on as distinct and separate." See Arnold Toynbee, *A Study in History*, abr. ed., vol. 2 (1957), "Note: 'Asia' and 'Europe': Facts and Fantasies," pp. 238–40. See also John M. Steadman, *The Myth of Asia: A Refutation of Western Stereotypes of Asian Religion, Philosophy, Art and Politics* (Simon and Schuster, 1969). For Herodotus, see *The Persian Wars*, trans. George Rawlinson (Modern Library, 1942), bk. I, chap. 5, p. 5. "West Asia" is supplanting the Middle East, although all of the major states of the world, including India, have a somewhat different definition of it.

34. See K. M. Panikkar, *Asia and Western Dominance* (Macmillan, 1969).

35. Jawaharlal Nehru, *India's Foreign Policy* (New Delhi: Publications Division, 1961), p. 22, speech in Constituent Assembly, March 8, 1949, Reflecting this Indian influence, the British used to call present-day Southeast Asia "Farther India."

36. Jawaharlal Nehru, *Glimpses of World History* (Oxford University Press, 1989), pp. 428–35, 449–52.

37. Joseph S. Nye, "The Changing Nature of World Power," *Political Science Quarterly*, vol. 105 (Summer 1990), pp. 177–92.

38. Ainslie Embree, *Imagining India: Essays on Indian History* (Oxford University Press, 1989), especially the chapter "Anti-Americanism in South Asia: A Symbolic Artifact," pp. 182–92.

39. World Bank, *World Bank World Development Report 1999/2000* (Oxford University Press, 2000), pp. 230–31.

40. Ibid.

41. Ibid.

42. United Nations Development Program (UNDP), *Human Development Report 2000* (Oxford University Press, 2000), p. 149.

43. Ibid., p. 154.

44. Ibid., pp. 158–59. For the 1947 estimate, see Bipan Chandra, "The Colonial Legacy," in Bimal Jalan ed., *The Indian Economy* (New Delhi: Penguin, 1992), pp. 12–13.

45. UNDP, *Human Development Report 2000,* pp. 158–59; and Chandra, "The Colonial Legacy," p. 12.

46. India has an estimated 237,687 local and state jurisdictions, far exceeding the United States (with over 70,000) and the rest of the world combined. World Bank, *World Development Report, 1999/2000,* p. 216.

47. These and other figures in the following paragraphs are drawn from the various national entries in International Institute for Strategic Studies, *The Military Balance, 1999–2000* (Oxford University Press, 1999), pp. 20, 112, 161–63, 166–67, 186, 300–05.

48. Ibid., pp. 300–05.

49. See the scathing pre-Kargil critique by a BJP sympathizer, Mohan Guruswamy, "Modernise or Perish," *Indian Express,* January 26, 1998. After Kargil, he and others pointed out the considerable qualitative disadvantages held by India's larger forces when confronted by the Pakistani forces.

50. International Institute for Strategic Studies, "India's Military Spending: Prospect for Modernization," *Strategic Comments,* vol. 6 (July 2000).

51. For an analysis, confirmed in part by recently retired U.S. officials, see Robert Windrem and Tammy Kupperman, "Pakistan Nukes Outstrip India's, Officials Say," MSNBC News, at (www.msnbc.com/news/417106.asp?cpl=1 [January 24, 2001]).

52. This included a $3 billion agreement to produce aircraft under license and acquire modern tanks and an aircraft carrier. "India, Russia Sign $3 Billion Arms Deal," *Times of India,* December 29, 2000; "India, Russia Ready Military Arms Dealer," CNN.com, October 4, 2000.

53. For a comprehensive discussion of middle powers, see Carsten Holbraad, *Middle Powers in International Politics* (St. Martin's Press, 1984), pp. 4, 10ff.

54. Ibid, p. 76.

55. Mohammed Ayoob, "India in South Asia: The Quest for Regional Predominance," *World Policy Journal,* vol. 7 (Winter 1989–90), p. 108.

56. See William T. R. Fox, *The Super-Powers: The United States, Britain, and the Soviet Union—Their Responsibility for Peace* (Harcourt, Brace, 1944).

## Chapter 2

1. Stephen P. Cohen, *The Pakistan Army,* rev. ed. (Oxford University Press, 1998).

2. Extract from *Modern Review,* reprinted in Jawaharlal Nehru, *Toward Freedom* (Boston: Beacon, 1958; first published 1941), pp. 436–37.

3. Nehru, reply to debate on foreign affairs in the Lok Sabha, December 9, 1958, in *India's Foreign Policy, Selected Speeches* (New Delhi: Publications Division, 1961), p. 80.

4. The most complete presentation of Menon's views and influence is in Michael Brecher, *India and World Politics: Krishna Menon's View of the World* (Oxford University Press, 1968). One of India's leading foreign policy experts, Jagat Mehta, has made a strong case that Nehru's errors are due to too rich and sophisticated a vision of the problem and warns against the emergence of an Indian "national security state." See "Nehru's Failure with China: Intellectual Naivete or the Wages of a Prophetic Vision?" paper prepared for a conference on Nehru and the Twentieth Century, University of Toronto, October 1989.

5. Kanti Bajpai, "War, Peace and International Order: India's View of World Politics," in Harvard Academy for International and Area Studies, *Project on Conflict or Convergence: Global Perspectives on War, Peace and International Order* (Cambridge, Mass.: Weatherhead Center, 1998), p. 2.

6. This and the following quotations are from an essay written just before Gujral became foreign minister: I. K. Gujral, "The Post Cold-War Era: An Indian Perspective, *World Affairs,* vol. 1 (January–March 1997), pp. 44–55.

7. K. Subrahmanyam, "Hedging against Hegemony: Gandhi's Logic in the Nuclear Age," *Times of India,* July 16, 1998.

8. Edward C. Sachau, ed., trans., *Alberuni's India* (New Delhi: Low Price, 1991), p. 23. Alberuni was born in 973 A.D. in Khiva, taken prisoner by Mahmud of Ghazni, and served as court historian during the invasion of India. His full name was Abu-Raihan Muhammed ibn Ahmad Alberuni.

9. Sometimes called revivalist or fundamentalist. For a discussion of these terms, see R. Scott Appleby, *The Ambivalence of the Sacred : Religion, Violence, and Reconciliation,* Carnegie Commission on Preventing Deadly Conflict (www.ccpdc.org/pubs/apple/frame.htm [January 24, 2000]).

10. I am indebted to Kanti Bajpai for discussions on the following points. His own book will provide the definitive discussion of India'a different approaches to grand strategy.

11. Before entering politics, Singh was in the Indian army. He comes from a distinguished Rajput princely family.

12. Jaswant Singh, *Defending India* (St. Martin's Press, 1999), pp. 326–37.

13. Ibid., p. 33.

14. Some of the leading neoconservative thinkers include Bharat Karnad, a journalist/academic specializing in strategic and nuclear matters, and Mohan Guruswamy, a management consultant and specialist on foreign and domestic policy. Both have consulted frequently with government officials and senior political leaders. For Karnad's views, see Bharat Karnad, ed., *Future Imperiled:*

*India's Security in the 1990s and Beyond* (New Delhi: Viking, 1994); for Guruswamy's, see a critique of the lack of preparedness of the Indian defense forces, "Modernise or Perish," *Indian Express,* January 26, 1998.

15. "Revitalism" is a term used to describe groups that wish to infuse "traditional" social values, often defined in religious terms, with modern technologies, whereas "fundamentalist" carries pejorative overtones. The revitalist RSS, like the Christian Right in the United States or various Islamic groups such as the Jamaat-i-Islam in Pakistan, sees itself as thoroughly "modern," yet guided by values and standards embedded in civilizational tradition.

16. The role of the RSS in the founding of the Jana Sangh and the BJP is discussed in Christophe Jaffrelot, *The Hindu Nationalist Movement in India* (Columbia University Press, 1996); see also Walter Andersen and Shridhar Damle, *The Brotherhood of Saffron* (Boulder, Colo.: Westview Press, 1987); and Partha S. Ghosh, *The BJP and the Evolution of Hindu Nationalism: From Periphery to Centre* (New Delhi: Manohar, 1999).

17. This theme was an important component of the earliest Indian response to the British and is central to the thinking of the nineteenth-century Indian reformers Swami Dyananda and Sri Aurobindo, and subsequently Mahatma Gandhi.

18. M. S. Golwalker, *Bunch of Thoughts* (Bangalore: Vikrama Prakashan, 1966), p. 83. See also Golwalker, *WE, or Our Nationhood Defined* (Nagpur: P. N. Indurkar/Bharat Publications, 1939). The text is available at the RSS website, www.rss.org.

19. Golwalker, *Bunch of Thoughts,* p. 280.

20. For an explication, see Balraj Madhok, *Indianization* (Delhi: S. Chand, 1969). For an early objective study, see Mohammed Ali Kishore, *Jana Sangh and India's Foreign Policy* (Delhi: Associated Publishing House, 1969).

21. For contemporary discussions, see Sunil Khilnani, *The Idea of India* (Farrar, Straus Giroux, 1997); and Shashi Tharoor, *India: From Midnight to Millennium* (New York: Arcade, 1997).

22. For a testimonial to Vajpayee's "Churchillian" qualities by a distinguished former foreign secretary, Jagat S. Mehta, see "Man with Churchillian Blend," on the BJP website (www.BJP.org/leader/dream3.html#chur [January 25, 2001]).

23. See Atal Behari Vajpayee, "India's Experience Has Taught That Peace Lies in Strength," *International Herald Tribune,* September 21, 2000, p. 10.

24. Ibid.

25. Bajpai, "War, Peace and International Order," pp. 4–5.

26. Quoted in Romila Thapar, *A History of India,* vol. 1 (London: Penguin Books, 1966), p. 239.

27. Jawaharlal Nehru, *Glimpses of World History* (New Delhi: University Press, 1989; reprint of 1934–35 edition).

28. A major struggle is currently under way for control of the Indian Council for Historical Research and other academic institutions. The issue is which aspects of the Indian past are to be emphasized: liberal-secular or nationalist-Hindu? Each approach seeks to define "India" in a particular way. For an extended discussion of the identity question, see Khilnani, *The Idea of India.*

29. A. L. Basham summarizes the contribution of Indian civilization to the world, especially to Europe and Southeast Asia, in *The Wonder That Was India,* 3d ed. (London: Sidgwick and Jackson, 1993), pp. 486ff. See also Donald F. Lach and Edwin J. Van Kley, *Asia in the Making of Europe: A Century of Advance,* bk. 2, vol. 3: *South Asia* (University of Chicago Press, 1993).

30. Constitution of India, "Directive Principles of State Policy," Part IV, Article 51.

31. For example, a speech by Rajiv Gandhi to the United Nations on June 9, 1988, entitled "A World Free of Nuclear Weapons," proposing a three-stage timetable for global disarmament was dismissed by most Western governments as "unrealistic." They failed to recognize not only a good faith effort by Delhi to reassert its leadership on the issue of disarmament but also a subtle retreat from India's earlier self-serving position on global disarmament.

32. Minister of Defense K. C. Pant, "Philosophy of Indian Defense," address to the Massachusetts Institute of Technology, July 1, 1989. Reprinted in Institute of Defense Studies and Analyses, *Strategic Analysis,* vol. 12 (August 6, 1989), p. 486.

33. For example, Henry Kissinger, *White House Years* (Boston: Little, Brown, 1979), p. 843.

34. India is treated as one of the nine "pivotal" states in Robert Chase, Emily Hill, and Paul Kennedy, eds., *The Pivotal States: A New Framework for U.S. Policy in the Developing World* (New York: Norton, 1999).

35. For a discussion of the concept of pivotal state and a critique, see Stephen P. Cohen and Sumit Ganguly, "India," in Chase, Hill, and Kennedy, *The Pivotal States,* pp. 40–63.

36. Constitution of India, Article 51.

37. For a critique of the Indian position opposing "mediation" on Kashmir, see P. R. Chari, "Advantages of Third Party Mediation Are Cited," *India Abroad,* July 30, 1999.

38. U. S. Bajpai, *India's Security: The Politico-Strategic Environment* (New Delhi: Lancers, 1983), pp. 65–66.

39. Ibid., pp. 118–19.

40. Abdul Kalam, then director of the Defense Research and Development Organisation, quoted in "Boom for Boom," *India Today,* April 26, 1999.

41. Manoj Joshi, "Commitment in Sri Lanka," *The Hindu* (International Edition), May 19, 1990.

42. For a fuller study of regional proliferation, regional attitudes, and suggestions for averting a nuclear arms race, see Stephen P. Cohen, ed., *Nuclear Prolif-*

*eration in South Asia: The Prospects for Arm Control* (Boulder, Colo.: Westview Press, 1990).

43. Major General E. D'Souza (retired), "Generals for Peace and Disarmament," *Indian Defense Review,* July 1989, pp. 116–21.

44. For an insightful critique of India's problems as a military power, see Verghese Koithara, *Society, State and Security: The Indian Experience* (New Delhi: Sage, 1999).

45. See L. Chibber, "India-Pakistan Reconciliation: The Impact on International Security," in Kanti P. Bajpai and Stephen P. Cohen, eds., *South Asia after the Cold War: International Perspectives* (Boulder, Colo.: Westview Press, 1993).

46. Ibid., p. 153.

47. The view of the Indian diplomatic corps on such exaggerated expectations is nicely laid out in a novel by Kiran Doshi, a retired Indian Foreign Service officer, set largely in the Indian embassy in Washington, D.C. See Doshi, *Birds of Passage* (Mumbai: Strand Book Stall, 1999).

48. For a brief discussion, see Bajpai, *India's Security,* p. 124. There is considerable evidence of a large-scale governmental effort to use the American-resident Indian community to advance Indian interests. The process was begun in 1970, when the lobbying efforts of both Indians and sympathetic Americans were coordinated from the Embassy of India in Washington. More recently the Indian government has created a ministry for "persons of Indian origin" (PIOs) and "nonresident Indians" (NRIs).

49. See Tanham's core essay, "Indian Strategic Thought: An Interpretive Essay," originally a RAND study, reprinted in Kanti P. Bajpai and Amitabh Mattoo, eds., *Securing India: Strategic Thought and Practice, Essays by George K. Tanham with Commentaries* (New Delhi: Manohar, 1996), pp. 28–111.

## Chapter 3

1. The Chinese influence took the form of a professional bureaucracy recruited on the basis of ability and promoted on the basis of performance and competence. The British developed a professional bureaucracy for India (in their recruitment of civil servants for the East India Company) before it was widespread in Europe.

2. See Dennis Kux, *Estranged Democracies: India and the United States, 1941–91* (New Delhi: Sage, 1993), pp. 47–48. No Congress nationalists were included in the Indian delegation to the San Francisco conference that established the United Nations, although President Harry Truman met with Nehru's sister, Vijaya Lakshmi Pandit, who led an alternative delegation to the meeting.

3. For a survey of Congress's pre-independence international activities devoted not only to acquiring independence but also to actively supporting

other nationalist movements, see Bimla Prasad, *The Origins of Indian Foreign Policy* (Calcutta: Bookland Private, 1960).

4. For a discussion of Indianization, see Stephen P. Cohen, *The Indian Army: Its Contribution to the Development of a Nation,* 2d ed. (Oxford University Press, 1990).

5. For the authoritative history of this remarkable institution, see Terence Creagh Coen, *The Indian Political Service: A Study in Indirect Rule* (London: Chatto and Windus, 1971). Jagat Mehta, who was to become foreign secretary in Indira's second administration, had been selected for the Indian Political Service, but when it was terminated he became the first person selected to join the new Indian Foreign Service.

6. See David C. Potter, *India's Political Administrators, 1919–1983* (Oxford University Press, 1986), p. 117.

7. Perhaps the most influential member of the ICS was Sir Girja Shankar Bajpai, who served as a key adviser on foreign policy matters to the Raj. (He opened up and directed an office representing India in Washington, purchasing the buildings that became the present Indian embassy residence and chancery.)

8. There is no provision in the constitution for a declaration of war. For an excellent survey, see Granville Austin, *The Indian Constitution: Cornerstone of a Nation* (Oxford University Press, 1966).

9. Nehru had earlier been prodded into invading Goa by Menon.

10. J. N. Dixit, "Foreign Policy Decision Making Process in India," in Foreign Service Institute, *Indian Foreign Policy: Agenda for the 21st Century,* vol. 1 (New Delhi: Konarak, 1997), p. 450.

11. A similar, but less extreme change took place in the British parliamentary system

12. See www.tehelka.com.

13. Dixit, "Foreign Policy Decision Making Process in India," p. 453.

14. For Appleby's comments on India and the response, see Paul H. Appleby, *Report of a Survey: Public Administration in India* (Delhi: Manager of Publications, 1953); and *Report on India's Administrative System: Comments and Reactions* (New Delhi: Lok Sabha Secretariat, 1956).

15. When an opportunity for service in Kosovo arose (to rebuild that province-state's civil service), more than 1,000 IAS officers volunteered for duty, largely because of the pay, which would have meant the equivalent of $100,000, or Rs. 42 lakhs, a lifetime's salary. See "Stampede in IAS to Rebuild Kosovo," *Indian Express,* August 12, 1999.

16. Personal communication from Shivaji Sondhi.

17. For a history of the ICS and IAS, see Potter, *India's Political Administrators.*

18. For a comprehensive contemporary overview of the Indian Foreign Service and India's diplomacy, see Kishan S. Rana, *Inside Diplomacy* (New Delhi:

Manas, 2000). RAW has both internal and external responsibilities. It is located in the Prime Minister's Office, and thus is subject to neither parliamentary nor cabinet scrutiny. See Asoka Raina, *Inside RAW: The Story of India's Secret Service* (New Delhi: Vikas Publishing House, 1981).

19. A separate bureaucracy, based in the Ministry of Finance, has officers in the Ministry of Defense, where they exercise tight control over defense spending; this practice, which is detached from the policy process per se, is an antiquated remnant of the Raj.

20. For an overview of the organizational infirmities of the MEA, see Kishan S. Rana, "Restructuring the MEA," in Foreign Service Institute, *Indian Foreign Policy: Agenda for the 21st Century,* vol. 1 (New Delhi: Konarak, 1998), pp. 431–45.

21. For an extended presentation of this perspective, see Jagat S. Mehta, *Rescuing the Future: Coming to Terms with Bequeathed Misperceptions* (New Delhi: Manohar, forthcoming).

22. Two IAS officials who have served in high positions in the defense community are K. Subrahmanyam and P. R. Chari. Both are world-class strategic writers and thinkers, and each served as director (Subrahmanyam twice) of the government-funded think tank the Institute for Defense Studies and Analyses.

23. P. R. Chari, "The Interface between Defence and Diplomacy: Institutional Arrangements and Domestic Structures in India," in Foreign Service Institute, *Indian Foreign Policy: Agenda for the 21st Century,* vol. 1 (New Delhi: Konarak, 1998), pp. 170–71.

24. Ibid.

25. For a criticism of the Kargil report from the perspective of a former RAW official, see B. Raman, *The Kargil Review Committee Report* (Institute of Topical Studies) (www.saag.org/papers/paper108.html [January 29, 2001]).

26. One of the regular duties of the Indian intelligence agencies is to detect and inform on alleged plots by the military to seize power. Conversations with senior intelligence officers indicate that they have "detected" at least three major coup attempts by Indian generals (the most recent being that of General K. Sundarji in 1987). There is no credible evidence of such plots, but insecure politicians and bureaucrats, many of whom have a stereotyped image of the military, listen to these warnings.

27. For details, see Cohen, *The Indian Army,* pp. 201–33.

28. For a discussion of the expansion of the army's role in domestic politics, see Stephen P. Cohen, "The Military and Indian Democracy," in Atul Kohli, ed., *India's Democracy: An Analysis of Changing State-Society Relations* (Princeton University Press, 1988).

29. Arun Singh, *The Military Balance: 1985–1994* (Program in Arms Control, Disarmament, and International Security, University of Illinois, March, 1997), p. 21.

30. For an inside account of the tests, based on interviews with the scientists and military personnel that organized and conducted them, see Raj Chengappa, *Weapons of Peace: The Secret Story of India's Quest to Be a Nuclear Power* (New Delhi: HarperCollins, 2000), esp. chap. 2.

31. For some of Kalam's extraordinarily optimistic and ambitious views on the transformation of India, see A. P. J. Abdul Kalam with Y. S. Rajan, *India 2020: A Vision for the New Millennium* (New Delhi: Viking, 1998).

32. J. N. Dixit, *My South Block Years: Memoirs of a Foreign Secretary* (New Delhi: UBS, 1996).

33. Utpal K. Banerjee, "Role of Cultural Diplomacy," in Foreign Service Institute, *Indian Foreign Policy: Agenda for the 21st Century,* vol. 1 (New Delhi: Konarak, 1998), p. 408.

34. The Indian government never released the major study of the 1962 war, the Henderson-Brookes report, nor has it released the military histories of this and other wars commissioned by the Ministry of Defense Historical Section. The recent "Kargil Report" represents a significant break with the past, and while the report has its flaws, it is comprehensive, compared with past efforts.

35. The MEA had traditionally been aloof from India's think tanks, but this has changed in recent years. See Rana, "Restructuring the MEA," pp. 442–43.

36. These include the Delhi Policy Group, the Institute of Peace and Conflict Studies, the Centre for Policy Research, and the government-funded Institute for Defence Studies and Analyses.

37. For an excellent survey of the nuclear issue, see the anthology edited by A. Subramanyam Raju, *Nuclear India: Problems and Perspectives* (New Delhi: South Asia Publishers, 2000), with contributions from scholars based in Hyderabad, Pondicherry, Mumbai, Chennai, and Bangalore. The meeting was sponsored by a non-Indian organization, the Regional Centre for Strategic Studies based in Colombo, which has encouraged research and dialogue by the non-Delhi academic and strategic communities.

38. A full-scale study of Indian and Pakistani negotiating styles is in order, perhaps along the lines of the examples in Hans Binnendijk, ed., *National Negotiating Styles* (Washington: Foreign Service Institute, 1987).

39. My observation, based on discussions with Indian audiences beginning in 1964.

## Chapter 4

1. The numbers pertaining to baby girls come from UNICEF and are cited in Barbara Crossette, *India: Facing the Twenty-First Century* (Indiana University Press, 1993), p. 50. A number of major scandals have dominated the headlines for years; the most sensational was the conviction of former prime minister P. V. Narasimha Rao for attempting to bribe other members of Parliament to keep his shaky (1993) government from falling.

2. For an influential and devastating critique of Indian planning and economic and social policy, see Gunnar Myrdal, *Asian Drama: An Inquiry into the Poverty of Nations* (New York: Pantheon, 1968).

3. See Verghese Koithara, *Society, State and Security: the Indian Experience* (New Delhi: Sage, 1999), p. 218.

4. An excellent survey of the influence of domestic political and ideological forces on Indian foreign policy in the early 1980s is A. Appadorai, *Domestic Roots of India's Foreign Policy 1947–1972* (Oxford University Press, 1981).

5. These sensitivities proved to be imaginary, more the product of the Indian elite's tilt to the Arab states than any deep concern among Indian Muslims, who did not raise any loud protests at the normalization of India-Israel relations in the mid-1990s.

6. "Happy Anniversary?" *Economist*, August 16, 1997, p. 17.

7. For a survey of the issue and an excellent guide to constitutional changes, see Granville Austin, "Turbulence in Federal Relations," in *Working a Democratic Constitution: The Indian Experience* (Oxford University Press, 1999), pp. 534–51.

8. One perceptive examination of the linkage between external security and India's democracy is Raju G. C. Thomas, *Democracy, Security and Development in India* (St. Martin's Press, 1996).

9. V. S. Naipaul, *India: A Million Mutinies Now* (New York: Penguin Books, 1992).

10. M. N. Srinivas, "On Living in a Revolution," in James P. Roach, ed., *India 2000: The Next Fifteen Years* (Riverdale, Md.: Riverdale, 1986), p. 4.

11. For a lucid summary written as the reform process was beginning, see Jagdish Bhagwati, *India in Transition: Freeing the Economy* (Oxford: Clarendon Press, 1993); and for an inside account of the process, see Ashok V. Desai, *My Economic Affair*, 2d ed. (New Delhi: Wiley Eastern, 1994), p. 7.

12. The latest chapter in the saga of the LCA has the plane making a maiden test flight, but the Indian government seeking outside technical assistance for the program, reportedly from the Russians. See "LCA Production Requires Tie-ups," *The Hindu,* February 8, 2001.

13. Angus Donald, "Foreigners Eye Air India," *Financial Times*, November 6, 2000.

14. Swaminathan S. Aiyar, *India's Economic Prospects: The Promise of Service,* Center for Advanced Study of India Occasional Paper 9 (Philadelphia, April 1999), p. 5 (www/sas.upenn.edu/casi/reports/aiyerpaper042299.html). For a British survey of Indian reforms, see David Gardner, "Survey-India, Part One, Part Two," *Financial Times,* November 6, 2000.

15. "Happy Anniversary?" *Economist*, p. 17.

16. Montek Singh Ahluwalia, "Economic Performance of States in Post-Reforms Period," *Economic and Political Weekly,* May 6, 2000, p. 1638.

17. Ibid., p. 1648.

18. Aiyar, *India's Economic Prospects,* p. 10.

19. According to the New York credit rating agency, Standard and Poor's, India's software exports were about $6 billion in 2000. Industry advocates think this figure will likely grow to $20 billion (about 4 percent of GDP, half of all nonservices exports) by 2003. They expect the number of people employed by the industry to grow tenfold by 2008. According to various other estimates, the growth in software exports should range from $40 billion to $100 billion by 2010. Even by the more conservative estimates, Indian software exports can be expected to become an increasingly significant portion of India's economy and export revenue. Seventy percent of the software sales are exports, two-thirds of which go to the United States and Canada. See "Information Technology in India: Yet Another Missed Opportunity?" *Standard & Poor's Credit Week,* July 12, 2000. Also, "Fixing India's Karma," *Far Eastern Economic Review,* August 13, 2000.

20. The International Institute of Strategic Studies thought the subject so important that it devoted an entire conference in India in September 1997 to the linkage between strategic developments and economic policy.

21. www.worldbank.org/data/wdi2000/pdfs/tab4-1pdf (January 25, 2001).

22. I am grateful to Devesh Kapur of Harvard University for sharing his analysis of this issue.

23. Koithara, *Society, State and Security,* p. 380.

24. Ibid., pp. 379–80.

25. "India to Design ABM on U.S. Lines," *Times of India,* January 5, 2000.

26. DRDO's travails and India's problems with defense acquisition are reviewed in Amit Gupta, "Building an Arsenal: The Indian Experience," in Amit Gupta, ed., *Building an Arsenal: The Evolution of Regional Power Force Structures* (Westport, Conn.: Praeger, 1997).

27. See "Information Technology: Yet Another Missed Opportunity?" *Standard and Poor's Credit Week,* July 12, 2000, pp. 18–25.

28. Ibid., p. 19.

29. Ibid., pp. 20–21.

30. "Emerging-Market Indicators: Risky Economies," *Economist,* September 30, 2000.

31. Standard and Poor's, *Sovereign Rating Service, India,* May 2000.

32. Rajni Kothari, "Cultural Context of Communalism in India," *Economic and Political Weekly,* January 14, 1989.

33. Congress was further weakened by its inability to keep up with the social changes that were taking place in many districts, and it was unable to keep intact its old coalition of high castes, low castes, and Muslims.

34. Of course, this creates great strains in the state units of the BJP when the party enters an electoral arrangement with a powerful state party. Congress

faces the same dilemma, as would any "third" force alliance of leftist and centrist parties that might emerge.

35. Joseph Schwartzberg and associates provide several tables and maps that illustrate the continuity of regional political forces in different parts of India. Joseph E. Schwartzberg, ed., *A Historical Atlas of South Asia,* 2d ed. (Oxford University Press, 1992).

36. Congress never received 50 percent of the popular vote, but because of the "first-past-the-post" system and lack of unity among opposition parties, it was able to form stable majorities in the center and most of the states for decades. Typically, it would win 50–70 percent of the seats with 40–45 percent of the votes. See Robert L. Hardgrave Jr. and Stanley A. Kochanek, *India: Government and Politics in a Developing Nation,* 6th ed. (New York: Harcourt College Publishers, 2000), pp. 351ff.

37. For figures and an analysis, see ibid., pp. 333, 352–62. See also the website of the Indian Parliament (www.parliamentofindia.nic.in [January 25, 2001]).

38. For a view of the process, see the critical comments by the distinguished journalist Harish Khare, "For Whom Are These States?" *The Hindu,* November 5, 2000.

39. Hardgrave and Kochanek, *India,* p. 316.

40. For a discussion and description of coalition politics, see Philip Oldenburg, *The Thirteenth Election of India's Lok Sabha* (New York: Asia Society, 1999), pp. 8–9.

41. Ibid, p. 7.

42. Even so it was deceptive, as party leaders assured coalition partners and foreigners alike that they would not act rashly and test nuclear weapons right away.

43. See "BJP Will Adhere to Coalition Politics," *Times of India,* December 28, 1999; "BJP Will Stick to NDA Agenda," *Hindustan Times,* December 28, 1999.

44. Arati R. Jerath, "Naidu Leads Revolt on Revenue Sharing," *Indian Express,* August 19, 2000.

45. For an overview of Andhra's political economy, see Rajen Harshe and C. Srinivas, "Andhra Pradesh: Dilemmas of Development," *Economic and Political Weekly,* vol. 35 (June 3, 2000).

46. The noted economist Jairam Ramesh has praised Naidu and his Congress counterpart in Madhya Pradesh in "Tale of Two CMs," *India Today International,* September 20, 1999, p. 34.

47. For a brief survey of Naidu's relationship with the leading Indian software company, Satyam Computer Services, based in Hyderabad, see Khozem Merchant, "Agri-business Sprouts Indian Software Success," *Financial Times,* September 6, 2000. Satyam began by servicing overseas computer and software needs and pioneered "offshore" technology services. It is now listed on

NASDAQ. Many of the leading software and computer experts in the world are Telugus, including the chair of President Bill Clinton's Information Technology Advisory Group, Raj Reddy. Telugus constitute the second largest group of Indian-Americans.

48. For the strategies available for dealing with separatist or insurrectionary movements or state-level violence in India, see Ved Marwah, *Uncivil Wars: Pathologies of Terrorism in India* (New Delhi: Indus, 1995).

49. The Nagas (many of whom were Christians and had strong foreign links to both China and Christian missionaries) were eventually beaten down after a ten-year insurrection. More recently, separatist Mizos and Bodos, Assamese, Manipuris, and tribal guerrillas in Tripura have taken up arms and bombed trains in protest against New Delhi. Since these movements were in a distant corner of India, public and international access could be tightly controlled, and since the numbers involved were relatively small, they never received much publicity in the human rights community.

50. One look at a map shows how improbable Khalistan would have been as a state, without access to the sea, and with two hostile and far more powerful neighbors.

51. As a rule, Indian Muslims are not "militant" and most are content to live within a more or less secular India. The one place where "Islamic" extremism has taken root is in Kashmir. For an extended discussion of the origins of the Kashmir insurgency, see Sumit Ganguly, *The Crisis in Kashmir: Portents of War, Hopes of Peace* (Cambridge University Press, 1997).

52. Naipaul, *India: A Million Mutinies Now.*

53. If the reader can imagine an America where, simultaneously, the Civil Rights movement was at its height in the south and the urban north had to accommodate a massive inflow of immigrants, one would have some idea of the second, or "cultural," revolution under way in India right now.

54. The name derives from the schedules, or lists, that enumerated these groups, their particular social disadvantage, their numbers, and their location. The British government in India regularly issued these.

55. For a comprehensive overview of the Dalit community, see Oliver Mendelsohn and Marika Vicziany, *The Untouchables: Subordination, Poverty and the State in Modern India* (Cambridge University Press, 1998). For a penetrating study of an untouchable family over the years, see Siddharth Dube, *Words Like Freedom: The Memoirs of an Impoverished Indian Family, 1947–97* (New Delhi: HarperCollins, 1998).

56. India's Dalit population in the 1990s was about 140 million, or 16.48 percent of the population; the population of scheduled tribes was just under 70 million, or about 8 percent of the total. See *Statistical Outline of India, 1997–98* (Bombay: Tata Services, 1997), p. 49. According to their publicists, the term "Dalit" means split or torn asunder and was first used in the nineteenth century

as a name for untouchables/scheduled castes. It was revived in the 1960s as part of a mass movement of Dalit Christians, Hindus, Muslims, and Sikhs (http://dalitchristians.com/Word%20dalit.html [January 31, 2001]).

57. The name BIMARU is also a pun, since in Hindi the term means "sickly." For an overview of Bihar, see Arvind N. Das, *The Republic of Bihar* (New Delhi: Penguin Books, 1992); and Human Rights Watch, *World Report 1999* (www.hrw.org/wr2k/Asia-04.htm [January 21, 2001]).

58. C. Rammanohar Reddy, "Another Divide," *The Hindu,* August 19, 2000.

59. Figures are from B. P. Singh, then secretary in the Ministry of Home Affairs, as reported by United News of India; Rediff on the Net, July 31, 1998.

60. Freedom House, "Annual Survey of Freedom Country Scores, 1972–73 to 1998–99" (http://freedomhouse.org/ratings/index.htm [February 3, 2001]).

61. For an overview of the IIT-U.S. link, see Chidanand Rajghatta, "Brain Curry: American Campuses Crave for IIT of Glory," reprinted by the IIT Delhi chapter (www.stockpulse.com/iitdaa/newslet/v5/braincurry.htm [January 24, 2001]). Other sources indicate that over a quarter million Indians work in the United States as software developers. Joydeep Mukherji, "Information Technology in India: Yet Another Missed Opportunity?" Standard and Poor's *Credit Week,* July 12, 2000, pp. 18–25. An excellent overview of the Indian-American community has been developed by the India Abroad Center for Political Awareness on its website, at www.iacfpa.org/iapop.html.

62. There were three basic causes for this migration: the 1965 changes in American immigration law, the stagnation of the Indian economy in the 1970s, and the obstacles to immigration imposed by the Thatcher government in Great Britain in the 1980s.

63. For a discussion of this term, see R. Scott Appleby, *The Ambivalence of the Sacred: Religion, Violence, and Reconciliation* (Carnegie Commission on Preventing Deadly Conflict) (www.ccpdc.org/pubs/apple/frame.htm [February 14, 2000]).

64. Some important Congress party members were not Indians. An Englishman founded Congress, and the English social and political activist Annie Besant was a prominent member.

65. BJP and supportive organizations no longer publicly call for a "Hindu" India so much as for the extension of the ideal of "Hindutva," which they point out is untranslatable but which might be read as "Hindu-like," or "Hindu-derived," or compatible with Hindu values.

66. A Rath Yatra is, literally, a "chariot procession" and is part of Hindu religious festivals in many regions of India, with some becoming tourist attractions.

67. For a brief history of communalism in India, see Asghar Ali Engineer, "Communal Violence in India," *The Hindu,* January 12, 2000; for a summary

of major communal riots in the 1980s and 1990s, see Praveen Swami, "A Catalog of Crimes," *Frontline*, vol. 16 (January 30–February 12), 1999.

68. Ishan Joshi, "Gujarat: Sangh's Los Alamos," *Outlook Online*, January 16, 2000.

69. Editorial, "The BJP's Reverses in Gujarat," *The Hindu*, October 6, 2000.

70. Mookerjee was not an RSS member but rather an academic who was vice-chancellor of Calcutta University at the age of thirty-three and subsequently a member of the Union cabinet under Nehru.

71. India's Muslim population is approximately 12 percent of the total and amounted to just under 102 million in 1991. Allowing for the increase in population, Muslims total at least 120 million in India proper and another 2 million or 3 million in Jammu and Kashmir. A new census is being undertaken in 2001. See 1991 Census of India, "India at a Glance: Religions" (www.censusindia.net/religion.html).

72. For an account by a former Indian intelligence analyst, who notes that in this area Pakistan seems to be doing better than India, see B. Raman, "Proxy War in Cyber Space," Paper 150, South Asia Analysis Group (www.saag.org/papers2/paper150.html [January 31, 2001]).

73. For an account by a leading reporter who covered both states, see Shekhar Gupta, "The Punjab Parable," *Indian Express*, August 19, 2000.

## Chapter 5

1. Jawaharlal Nehru, *Toward Freedom* (Boston: Beacon, 1958, reprint of 1941 publication), p. 284.

2. Ibid., pp. 3–4.

3. Around this time the only Indian interested in developing strategic doctrine was the diplomat-scholar K. M. Panikkar, who emphasized the importance of seaward defense. Panikkar's works were ignored for years, but he is now frequently cited. See K. M. Panikkar, *Problems of Indian Defence* (London: Asia Publishing House, 1960).

4. For a discussion of Indian defense budgets by an economist who served as a Ministry of Defense official, see Amiya Kumar Ghosh, *India's Defence Budget and Expenditure Management in a Wider Context* (New Delhi: Lancers, 1996).

5. For the authoritative survey of these issues, see A. Martin Wainwright, *Inheritance of Empire: Britain, India, and the Balance of Power in Asia, 1938–55* (Westport, Conn.: Praeger, 1994).

6. Ibid., p. 29.

7. A complete presentation of Menon's views and discussion of his influence is Michael Brecher, *India and World Politics: Krishna Menon's View of the World* (Oxford University Press, 1968).

8. Some of the Indian government's international treaties and agreements are on the Internet (www.indiagov.org/economy/ibta/mainpg.htm [January 31, 2001]).

9. There is a vast literature on the diplomacy leading up to the war, and on the war itself. The best Indian account of the fighting is by a retired Indian officer, D. K. Palit, who was director of Military Operations at the time. See Major General D. K. Palit (retired), *War in High Himalaya: The Indian Army in Crisis, 1962* (New Delhi: Lancer International, 1991). A balanced scholarly account is Steven A. Hoffman, *India and the China Crisis* (University of California Press, 1990).

10. One of Pakistan's early grievances against India was that it did not share this equipment as agreed upon; Gandhi's final fast was, ironically, in protest of this policy.

11. For a discussion of the defense-versus-development issue in the Indian context by two influential retired Ministry of Defense officials, see H. C. Sarin, *Defense and Development* (New Delhi: USI of India, 1979); and K. Subrahmanyam, *Defense and Development* (Calcutta: Minerva, 1973).

12. A useful history of the 1965 war is contained in the three volumes by Major General Sukhwant Singh (retired) under the general title *India's Wars since Liberation,* vols. 1, 2, and 3 (New Delhi: Vikas, 1980, 1981, and 1982). The official history has recently been leaked and contains a blunt assessment of India's mediocre performance. See B. C. Chakravorty, *History of the Indo-Pak War, 1965* (New Delhi: History Division, Ministry of Defense, 1992). The official histories of the 1962 and 1971 wars have not been released.

13. Dieter Braun, *The Indian Ocean: Region of Conflict or Peace,* trans. Carol Geldart and Kathleen Llanwame (London: C. Hurst, 1983), p. 130. Braun notes that the Soviet Union came to view India as the regional dominant power as early as 1955, whereas most Western states did not do so until 1971 or later.

14. See Shashi Tharoor, *Reasons of State* (New Delhi: Vikas, 1982), pp. 64–74, a critical study of Indira Gandhi's foreign policy; a more sympathetic account is in Surjit Mansingh, *India's Search for Power* (New Delhi: Sage, 1984).

15. For a discussion of civilian militarism and Indira Gandhi's governance, see Stephen P. Cohen, "The Military," in Henry C. Hart, ed., *Indira Gandhi's India: A Political System Reappraised* (Boulder, Colo.: Westview Press, 1976).

16. The best overview of the diplomacy leading to the war, the war itself, and its implications is Leo Rose and Richard Sisson, *War and Secession: Pakistan, India, and the Creation of Bangladesh* (University of California Press, 1990).

17. For a lengthy account by the general involved, see Lieutenant General Jack Jacobs, *Surrender at Dacca: Birth of a Nation* (New Delhi: Manohar, 1997), p. 130.

18. The *Enterprise*'s mission was one reason India acquired a large number of submarines from the Soviet Union. These provide the backbone of the Indian Navy's strategy of defending against intrusions by a major naval power.

19. Major General D. K. Palit (retired), a former director of military Intelligence during the 1962 war, became a military correspondent in the late 1960s and kept up a drumbeat of warning about Pakistan. When the war was over he was among the first to predict the revival of Pakistani power. See *The Lightning Campaign* (New Delhi: Thomson Press, 1972). Palit worked closely with K. Subrahmanyam, then director of the Institute of Defense Studies and Analyses.

20. Commander V. Koithara, "India and the Indian Ocean," USI of India *Journal,* July–September, 1975, pp. 227–37. Koithara's later book is *Society, State and Security: The Indian Experience* (New Delhi: Sage, 1999).

21. Baldev Raj Nayar, "Regional Power in a Multipolar World," in John W. Mellor, ed., *India: A Rising Middle Power* (Boulder, Colo.: Westview Press, 1979), p. 147.

22. Mansingh, *India's Search for Power.* For a penetrating study of personality in Indian foreign policy, especially the Indira Doctrine, see Bharat Wariavwalla, "Personality, Domestic Political Institution, and Foreign Policy," in Ram Joshi and R. K. Hebsur, eds., *Congress in Indian Politics: A Centenary Perspective* (Bombay: Popular Prakashan, 1987).

23. See the 1991 Census of India (www.censusindia.net/religion.html [March 8, 2001]).

24. The Janata's view of security policy during this period is presented in a remarkable forty-three page speech, "India's Defense Strategy in the Next Decade," delivered by the then defense minister, C. Subramaniam (who earlier had chaired an important Aeronautics Committee), to the officer students of the National Defense College in New Delhi. The address bears the imprint of K. Subrahmanyam. Though it was delivered by a Janata minister, its arguments and assumptions were widely shared.

25. For the authoritative summary of this debate, including its many nuances, see U. S. Bajpai, *India's Security: The Politico-Strategic Environment* (New Delhi: Lancers, 1983).

26. The International Institute of Strategic Studies (IISS) notes that India's arms exports were valued at $50 million to $100 (or 1–2 percent of the world market) for the period 1992–98, placing it in the same category as Australia, Iran, and Poland. IISS, *The Military Balance 1999–2000* (Oxford: 1999), p. 281.

27. For basic figures on Indian defense spending, see Air Commodore Jasjit Singh, *India's Defence Spending* (New Delhi: Knowledge World, 2000), pp. 22–66.

28. For a careful study of Siachin, see Robert G. Wirsing, *India, Pakistan and the Kashmir Dispute: On Regional Conflict and Its Resolution* (St. Martin's Press, 1994), pp. 195–216.

29. For a discussion of Chibber's role, see ibid., p. 208.

30. For a comprehensive overview, see Kanti Bajpai, P. R. Chari, Pervaiz Cheema, Stephen P. Cohen, and Sumit Ganguly, *Brasstacks and Beyond: Crisis Perception and Management in South Asia* (New Delhi: Manohar).

31. There is widespread confusion between "exercise" and "operation." When asked about the difference, Sundarji told a group studying the crisis that "an exercise is an EXERCISE, and an operation is an OPERATION!" The difference became immediately clear; Brasstacks as an exercise continued for several months, even though parts of the Indian army had mounted a military operation that wound down when the crisis dissipated, allowing Brasstacks to conclude quietly.

32. For studies of this operation, see S. D. Muni, *Pangs of Proximity: India and Sri Lanka's Ethnic Crisis* (New Delhi: Sage, 1994); P. R. Chari, "The IPKF in Sri Lanka," ACDIS Occasional Paper (University of Illinois at Champaign-Urbana, 1993); Rohan Gunaratna, *Indian Intervention in Sri Lanka: The Role of India's Intelligence Agencies* (Colombo: South Asian Network on Conflict Research, 1993).

33. For a study of this crisis, see P. R. Chari, Pervaiz Iqbal Cheema, and Stephen P. Cohen, *1990: A Compound Crisis* (Champaign, Ill.: ACDIS, 2000). A widely read but inaccurate history of the crisis appeared in 1993. Seymour Hersh, "On the Nuclear Edge," *New Yorker,* March 29, 1993, pp. 67–68.

34. This had been discussed within the Pakistan army as early as 1983. Stephen P. Cohen, *The Pakistan Army,* 2d ed. (Oxford University Press, 1997).

35. The Maldivians had first asked the Sri Lankans and then the United States for assistance; India was their third choice. When the Indian forces arrived by air from New Delhi, the coup leaders had already gone; the Indian Navy was vectored onto the fleeing ship by a nearby American frigate, and the plotters were rounded up and turned over to Maldivian authorities.

36. *Time Magazine* (Asian edition), April 3, 1989. The cover story by Ross H. Munro was titled "The Awakening of Asian Power: Armed and Assertive, The World's Most Populous Democracy Takes Its Place as a Military Heavyweight."

37. Sandy Gordon, *India's Rise to Power in the Twentieth Century and Beyond* (St. Martin's Press, 1995), p. 224.

38. Shekhar Gupta, "India Redefines Its Role," Aldelphi Paper 293, International Institute for Strategic Studies (Oxford University Press, 1995), p. 38.

39. Ibid., p. 38.

40. These and other observations on Kargil reflect conversations with senior Pakistani military leaders in Islamabad, February 2000.

41. The phrase was freely used by Prime Minister Vajpayee after the 1998 tests and was picked up in 2000 by Vice President Al Gore during Vajpayee's visit to Washington.

## Chapter 6

1. Three books offer a comprehensive history of the Indian nuclear weapons program. George Perkovich, *India's Nuclear Bomb: The Impact on Global Pro-*

*liferation* (University of California Press, 1999), is a careful account that draws on extensive interviews with the Indian participants; Itty Abraham, *The Making of the Indian Atomic Bomb* (London: Zed Books, 1998), places the program in the context of India's search for a national identity; and Raj Chengappa, *Weapons of Peace: The Secret Story of India's Quest to Be a Nuclear Power* (New Delhi: HarperCollins, 2000), contains rich anecdotal information about the personalities involved in both the nuclear and missile programs.

2. Abraham, *The Making of the Indian Atomic Bomb,* p. 126.

3. This debate was contemporaneously recorded by G. G. Mirchandani, a former director of information of the Ministry of Defense. See Mirchandani, *India's Nuclear Dilemma* (New Delhi: Popular Book Service, 1968).

4. For a discussion of the BJP's foreign and nuclear policy, see Partha S. Ghosh, *BJP and the Evolution of Hindu Nationalism* (New Delhi: Manohar, 1999), pp. 313–65.

5. Bhabha also provided an early public analysis of the importance of nuclear weapons to "smaller" neighbors of China, with its "huge population." He suggested that "with the help of nuclear weapons," a state can acquire a "position of absolute deterrence even against another having many times greater destructive power under its control." Homi J. Bhabha, "The Implications of a Wider Dispersal of Military Power for World Security and the Problems of Safeguards," in *Proceedings of the Twelfth Pugwash Conference on Science and World Affairs,* January 27–February 1, 1964, Udaipur, India, p. 75, cited in Kargil Review Committee, *Report, March 2000* (New Delhi: Government of India, 2000), n. 71, p. 174.

6. Personal conversations with Menon, 1965.

7. D. S. Kothari, *Nuclear Explosions* (Delhi: Publications Division, 1958), contains the foreword to the first and to the second editions.

8. The NPT commits the nuclear weapons states to pursue "effective measures relating to the cessation of the nuclear arms race at an early date and to nuclear disarmament." (Article VI)

9. V. C. Trivedi, speech, in B. M. Jain, *Nuclear India,* vol. 2 (New Delhi: Radiant, 1974), pp. 192–93.

10. Stephen P. Cohen and Richard L. Park, *India: Emergent Power?* (New York: Cranc, Russak, 1979), pp. 52–53.

11. For his version of the development of Indian strategic thought, plus his own role in the process, see K. Subrahmanyam, "Indian Nuclear Policy—1964–98 (A Personal Recollection)," in Air Commodore Jasjit Singh (retired), ed., *Nuclear India* (New Delhi: Knowledge World, 1998), pp. 26–53. For a concise statement of his views about the future Indian nuclear program, see K. Subrahmanyam, "India's Security Perspective," in P. R. Chari, ed., *India towards Millennium* (New Delhi: Manohar, 1998).

12. The locus classicus for Sundarji's writings is the unpublished monograph "Strategy in the Age of Nuclear Deterrence and Its Application to Developing

Countries," written in 1984 when he was a lieutenant general. This drew upon a number of unpublished, classified documents that Sundarji had prepared over the years. Later, he was to widen his audience with two important publications: one was a "mail seminar" that he ran while commandant of the College of Combat, Mhow; the other was a novel, *Blind Men of Hindoostan, Indo-Pak Nuclear War* (New Delhi: UBSPD, 1993), published after retirement. Sundarji frequently cited Kenneth Waltz's aphorism, "More is not better if less is enough," which has become the banner of the "pragmatists" in Pakistan as well as India. For a systematic presentation of Sundarji's views about a year before he became army chief, see Lieutenant General K. Sundarji, "Strategy in the Age of Nuclear Deterrence and Its Application to Developing Countries," unpublished manuscript, Simla, June 21, 1984.

13. K. Subrahmanyam, "Effects of Nuclear Asymmetry on Conventional Deterrence," Combat Papers 1 (Mhow: College of Combat, May 1981).

14. Though not public, some of its findings appear to guide the work of one of its staff members, Brigadier Vijay K. Nair (retired), *Nuclear India* (New Delhi: Lancer International, 1992). Nair served on both the Army Expert's Committee in 1989 and then under Arun Singh on the latter's Committee on Defense Expenditure. Arun Singh was later to produce one of the few internal studies examining the implications of becoming a nuclear weapons state. For his views see, Arun Singh, *The Military Balance: 1985–1994* (University of Illinois, 1997).

15. Sundarji agreed with Subrahmanyam that the NPT treaty was flawed because it legitimized the possession (and by implication, the use) of nuclear weapons by the great powers. As he indicated in "Strategy in the Age of Deterrence," he favored the use of tactical nuclear weapons against China in the Himalayas, arguing that they would do little damage (p. 5), that India "only" needed 10–60 megaton equivalents to cope with China, Pakistan, and any possible threat from Washington, agreeing with Waltz that the logic of international relations led to deterrence stability (p. 39) while reducing the influence of the superpowers (pp. 39–40).

16. K. Subrahmanyam, "Hedging against Hegemony: Gandhi's Logic in the Nuclear Age," *Times of India*, June 16, 1998.

17. This is my own conclusion after conversations with several of the principals on both sides. For an overview, see Kanti P. Bajpai, P. R. Chari, Pervaiz Iqbal Cheema, Stephen P. Cohen, and Sumit Ganguly, *Brasstacks and Beyond: Perception and Management of Crisis in South Asia* (New Delhi: Manohar, 1995).

18. Subrahmanyam, "Indian Nuclear Policy—1964–98, A Recollection," in Singh, *Nuclear India*, pp. 43–44. India's missile program, which formally began in 1983, also gained momentum from 1988 onward. The first Prithvi missile test took place in 1988 (with fifteen more Prithvi tests through 1997), and the first Agni missile test in 1989 (with subsequent tests in 1992 and 1994). These tests

were sometimes coordinated with India's diplomatic efforts to resist American pressure.

19. Statement by India on March 21, 1996, at the Conference on Disarmament cited in George Perkovich, *India's Nuclear Bomb* (University of California Press, 1999), p. 371.

20. There is a vigorous but somewhat abstract academic debate on the question of how much "security" or "domestic" considerations influenced the decision to "go nuclear." The role of scientists is stressed in Abraham, *The Making of the Indian Atomic Bomb*. Security threats are given preeminence in Sumit Ganguly, "India's Pathway to Pokhran II," *International Security*, vol. 23 (Spring 1999), pp. 148–77; and T. V. Paul, "The Systemic Basis of India's Challenge to the Global Nuclear Order," *Nonproliferation Review*, vol. 6 (Fall 1998), pp. 1–11. For a comprehensive overview of both domestic and international politics as well as issues of principle, see Perkovich, *India's Nuclear Bomb*. See also Amitabh Mattoo, ed., *India's Nuclear Deterrent: Pokhran II and Beyond* (New Delhi: Har Anand, 1999).

21. For an authoritative statement of the proliferation problem from the perspective of a leading member of the American nonproliferation "community," see Randy J. Rydell, "Giving Nonproliferation Norms Teeth: Sanctions and the NNPA," *Nonproliferation Review*, vol. 6 (Winter 1999), pp. 1–19.

22. See Amitav Ghosh's interview with Fernandes in Ghosh, "Countdown: Why Can't Every Country Have the Bomb?" *New Yorker*, October 26–November 2, 1998, pp 186–91. For an authoritative overview of the South Asian nuclear balance, see Neil Joeck, "Nuclear Developments in India and Pakistan," *Access Asia Review*, vol. 2 (July 1999), pp. 5–45.

23. Personal interview, 1999.

24. A. P. J. Kalam has become the chief icon of the program not only because of his scientific skills but because these were largely acquired within India and because, although a Muslim, he has a strong interest in Hindu philosophy and culture. Subrahmanyam and other staunch nationalists jokingly referred to the bomb as purely "indigenous" because of Kalam's background.

25. Inder Kumar Gujral, *A Foreign Policy for India* (New Delhi: Ministry of External Affairs, 1998), p. 50.

26. For documentation of these changes in public opinion, see David Cortright and Amitabh Mattoo, *India and the Bomb: Public Opinion and Nuclear Options* (University of Notre Dame Press, 1996).

27. For a survey of the party's foreign policy planks, including its interest in nuclear weapons, see Partha S. Ghosh, *The BJP and the Evolution of Hindu Nationalism: From Periphery to Centre* (New Delhi: Manohar, 1999), chap. 7, "Foreign Policy," pp. 313–65.

28. They had yielded to coalition partners on the revocation of Article 370 of the Constitution (which provided Kashmir with a special constitutional status),

on the further destruction of mosques built upon temple sites, and on "Swadeshi" economics.

29. A statement of the national security adviser Brajesh Misra in a television interview, November 10, 2000 (www.rediff.com/news/2000/ nov/10nuke.htm [February 2, 2001]).

30. "Draft Report of the NSAB on Indian Nuclear Doctrine," August 17, 1999 (www.indianembassy.org/policy/CTBT/nuclear_doctrine_aug_171999.html [February 14, 2001]).

31. Jaswant Singh, interview with C. Raja Mohan, "India Not to Engage in a N-Arms Race," *The Hindu,* November 29, 1999. Jaswant Singh clarified that the NSC asked the NSAB "to prepare a number of papers, including one on a possible Indian Nuclear Doctrine. This it prepared and submitted to the National Security Adviser, also releasing it publicly for a larger debate. That debate is now under way. It is thus not a policy document of the Government of India."

32. See Kanti P. Bajpai, "India's Nuclear Posture after Pokhran II," *International Studies,* vol. 37 (March 2000), pp. 267–301.

33. Among these converts are Jasjit Singh, the head of India's government-sponsored Institute of Defense Studies and Analysis, who developed the idea of a recessed deterrent.

34. The proposed numbers of such a system vary considerably, but most are in the range of 100–300 nuclear weapons. Some favor a thermonuclear capability; others believe that a first-generation fission bomb is adequate for deterrence.

35. Jaswant Singh, *Defending India* (St. Martin's Press, 1999), p. 270.

36. Lieutenant General V. R. Raghavan (retired), *India's Need for Strategic Balance: Security in the Post–Cold War World* (New Delhi: Delhi Policy Group, 1996), p. 26.

37. He may more accurately reflect the views of serving officers than the "moderates," who would only build a small nuclear force. For a concise statement of his views, see Bharat Karnad, "A Thermonuclear Deterrent," in Mattoo, *India's Nuclear Deterrent,* pp. 108–49.

38. Bharat Karnad, "A Sucker's Payoff," *Seminar 485,* January 2000, p. 45.

39. See Mohan Guruswamy, "Now Work on Real Deterrence," *Indian Express,* June 5, 1998.

40. Rear-Admiral Raja Menon (retired), *A Nuclear Strategy for India* (New Delhi: Sage, 2000). Menon's study was funded in part by the Defense Research and Development Organization and written while he was associated with the nongovernmental United Services Institution of India in New Delhi.

41. The most outspoken members of this group include novelist Amitav Ghosh and social activists Praful Bidwai and Achin Vanaik. See Bidwai and Vanaik, *South Asia on a Short Fuse: Nuclear Politics and the Future of Global Disarmament* (Oxford University Press, 1999).

42. For a recent analytical overview, see Sumit Ganguly and Ted Greenwood,

eds., *Mending Fences: Confidence- and Security-Building Measures in South Asia* (Boulder, Colo.: Westview Press, 1996).

43. This literature, almost unknown to Indians, is not classified. Some of it is discussed and cited in Stephen P. Cohen, *The Pakistan Army,* 2d ed. (Oxford University Press, 1998).

44. Kargil Review Committee, *Report, March 2000* (New Delhi: Government of India, 2000). The three-member committee included a journalist (George Verghese), a former government official (K. Subrahmanyam, as chair), and a retired general (Lieutenant General K. K. Hazari).

45. Ibid., chap. 10, "Nuclear Backdrop," pp. 151–79.

46. Raghavan, *India's Need for Strategic Balance.*

47. Karnad, "A Thermonuclear Deterrent," pp. 108–49.

48. For an overview of Chinese nuclear strategy in the context of the South Asia tests, see Ming Zhang, *China's Changing Nuclear Posture: Reactions to the South Asian Nuclear Tests* (Washington: Carnegie Endowment for International Peace, 1999).

49. Guruswamy, "Now Work on Real Deterrence." Yet he also argues that "nuclear weapons are not war-fighting weapons," only weapons of coercive diplomacy.

50. Karnad, "A Thermonuclear Deterrent," pp. 108–49.

51. See Paul Bracken, *Fire in the East: The Rise of Asian Military Power and the Second Nuclear Age* (New York: HarperCollins, 1999).

52. For an overview written in the midst of the period of American grand theorizing on nuclear weapons, see Herman Kahn, *On Thermonuclear War* (Princeton University Press, 1960), pp. 231–32.

53. D. K. Palit, *War in the Deterrent Age* (London: Macdonald's, 1966).

54. USI of India, *Journal,* vol. 124 (January–March 1999), p. 21.

55. Ibid., p. 22.

56. For a survey of the doctrinal problems associated with India's delivery of a nuclear weapon, see Rahul Bedi, "India's Nuclear Doctrine Unclear," *Jane's Defence Weekly,* vol. 34 (October 18, 2000).

57. Ibid.

58. One exception to this would be the present president of India, K. R. Narayanan, a distinguished retired diplomat.

59. So does the fact that for many years India maintained a chemical weapons capability, which was kept secret from senior politicians and even the armed services. The truth came out only when India had to prepare to sign the Chemical Weapons Treaty.

60. This baseline study is by S. Rashid Naim, "Asia's Day After," in Stephen P. Cohen, ed., *The Security of South Asia: Asian and American Perspectives* (University of Illinois Press, 1987). A revised version appears in Stephen P. Cohen, ed., *Nuclear Proliferation in South Asia* (Boulder, Colo.: Westview Press, 1990); figures cited above are from the latter version, pp. 46–56. For a graphic depiction

of a nuclear attack on a major Indian city, see M. V. Ramana, *Bombing Bombay* (Cambridge: International Physicians for the Prevention of Nuclear War, 1999).

61. Lieutenant General (retired) Eric Vas and others, "Nuclear Menace: The Satyagraha Approach," Indian Initiative for Peace, Arms Control, & Disarmament (INPAD) Monograph (Pune, India: INPAD, 1999) (www.inpad.com/publication.html [February 2, 2000]).

## Chapter 7

1. This term is my own. For an insightful discussion of how hostile groups or crowds are generated, see Elias Canetti, *Crowds and Power* (New York: Seabury Press, 1978). For the perspective of a clinical psychologist who has studied the origins of ethnic conflict and war, see Vamik D. Volkan, *The Need to Have Enemies and Allies: From Clinical Practice to International Relationships* (New York: Jason Aronson, 1988).

2. The former believe they are under a comprehensive threat from the more numerous Sinhalese, and the latter believe *themselves* to be the threatened minority, given the fact that there are 60 million Tamils across the Palk Straits. The Tigers argue that Tamils can never be secure unless there is a Tamil homeland on the island.

3. For a sympathetic biography of Jinnah, see Stanley Wolpert, *Jinnah of Pakistan* (Oxford University Press, 1984).

4. For a discussion, see Volkan, *The Need to Have Enemies and Allies,* pp. 155–79.

5. Canetti, *Crowds and Power,* pp. 138–40.

6. An influential and authoritative interpretation of India from the perspective of the Pakistan Army can be found in Lieutenant Colonel (now Major General) Javed Hassan, *India: A Study in Profile* (Rawalpindi: Army Press, 1990).

7. This is also the view of such Pakistani scholars as Ayesha Jalal and the late Eqbal Ahmed.

8. U. S. Bajpai, *India's Security: The Politico-Strategic Environment* (New Delhi: Lancers Publishers, 1983), pp. 70–71.

9. For a selection of contemporary Indian writing on Pakistan, much of it by present and former police and intelligence officials, see Rajeev Sharma, ed., *The Pakistan Trap* (New Delhi: UBSPD, 2001).

10. Ibid., p. 70–71.

11. Ibid., p. 73.

12. For a fuller discussion of Pakistan's approach to India, see Stephen P. Cohen, *The Pakistan Army,* 2d ed. (Oxford University Press, 1998).

13. Ibid., pp. 141–68.

14. There are two Punjabs, one in Pakistan and one in India. Pakistan's constitutes 48 percent of the population and includes much of Pakistan's most fertile and prosperous land.

15. For Jinnah's views, see his speech to the Constituent Assembly, discussed in Wolpert, *Jinnah of Pakistan,* pp. 333–40. For a contemporary Pakistani discussion of Jinnah's secularism, see Akbar S. Ahmed, *Jinnah and Islamic Identity: The Search for Saladin* (Oxford University Press, 1997).

16. Sisir Gupta, *Kashmir: A Study in India-Pakistan Relations* (Bombay: Asia Publishing House, 1966).

17. This image is vividly conveyed to a second and third generation of Indians (and others) by the portrayal of Jinnah in the Attenborough film *Gandhi.* This inspired a second film, produced by a distinguished Pakistani academic-administrator, Akbar Ahmed, dealing with the life of Jinnah.

18. Girilal Jain, *The Hindu Phenomenon* (New Delhi: UBSPD, 1994). Jain was one of India's most brilliant journalists, and in the last ten years of his life (he died in 1988) he wrote feelingly about Hindu-Muslim affairs and the phenomenon of Pakistan; he was, in many ways, the most successful popularizer of BJP views well before the party came to power.

19. Lieutenant General P. N. Kathpalia (retired), "Indo-Pak Relations: The Concept of National Security," *Indian Defense Review,* January 1989, pp. 116, 124.

20. For a definitive statement of army perceptions of India by an able Pakistani officer, see Hassan, *India.*

21. A summary of some of these can be found in Sundeep Waslekar, *Track-Two Diplomacy in South Asia,* ACDIS Occasional Paper (University of Illinois, October 1995); and Navnita Chadha Behera, Paul M. Evans, and Gowher Rizvi, *Beyond Boundaries: A Report on the State of Non-Official Dialogues on Peace, Security and Cooperation in South Asia* (University of Toronto Press, 1997).

22. Some of these dialogues are more thoroughgoing and reach a younger generation of scholars, strategists, journalists, and diplomats, such as the many workshops organized by the Colombo-based Regional Centre for Strategic Studies (www.rcss.org. [February 6, 2001]).

23. The SAARC home page can be found at (www.saarc.com/spotential.html [February 6, 2001]).

24. For an account of the diplomacy of the war, see Leo Rose and Richard Sisson, *War and Secession: Pakistan, India, and the Creation of Bangladesh* (University of California Press, 1990).

25. For a comprehensive overview, see Kanti Bajpai, P. R. Chari, Pervaiz Cheema, Stephen P. Cohen, and Sumit Ganguly, *Brasstacks and Beyond: Crisis Perception and Management in South Asia* (University of Illinois Press, 1995).

26. For an excellent survey of the Kashmir problem, see Jonah Blank, "Kashmir: Fundamentalism Takes Root," *Foreign Affairs,* vol. 78 (November–December 1999), pp. 36–53; and Sumit Ganguly, *The Crisis in Kashmir: Portents of War and Hopes of Peace* (Cambridge University Press, 1997).

27. For the text of the agreement, see Dorothy Woodman, *Himalayan Frontiers: A Political Review of British, Chinese, Indian, and Russian Rivalries* (New York: Praeger 1969).

28. Population figures are from the Kashmir Study Group, *Kashmir: A Way Forward* (Larchmont, N.Y.: February 2000), p. 12.

29. See Sumit Ganguly, *Origins of War in South Asia: The Indo-Pakistani Conflict Since 1947,* 2d ed. (Boulder, Colo.: Westview Press, 1994); and Ganguly, "Wars without End? The Indo-Pakistani Conflict," *Annals of the American Academy of Political and Social Science,* vol. 541 (September 1995), pp. 167–78.

30. For a discussion of the Pakistani view on the strategic importance of Kashmir, see Cohen, *The Pakistan Army,* pp. 141ff.

31. For an excellent survey of these issues, see Navnita Chadha Behera, "J&K (& L & D & G . . . ): Making and Unmaking Identities," *Himal South Asia,* November–December, 1996, pp. 26–33.

32. For the Pakistani perspective, see Pervaiz Iqbal Cheema, "Pakistan, India, and Kashmir: A Historical Review," in Raju G. C. Thomas, ed., *Perspectives on Kashmir: The Roots of Conflict in South Asia* (Boulder, Colo.: Westview Press, 1992).

33. For an extensive review of the Indian position, see Ashutosh Varshney, "Three Compromised Nationalisms: Why Kashmir Has Been a Problem," in Thomas, *Perspectives on Kashmir.*

34. For a vivid press account see W. P. S. Sidhu, "Siachin: The Forgotten War," *India Today,* May 31, 1992.

35. For a discussion of the impact of the cold war on Kashmir and South Asia by one of the chief architects of American policy during the Kissinger era, see Peter W. Rodman, *More Precious Than Peace: The Cold War and the Struggle for the Third World* (Charles Scribner's Sons, 1994). For an academic study covering the U.S.-Pakistan relationship, see Robert McMahon, *The Cold War on the Periphery: The United States, India, and Pakistan* (Columbia University Press, 1994).

36. This point is made by several Indian and Pakistani authors in Kanti P. Bajpai and Stephen P. Cohen, eds., *South Asia after the Cold War* (Boulder, Colo.: Westview, 1993). See especially the chapters by Pervaiz I. Cheema and Lieutenant General M. L. Chibber, pp. 139–72.

37. Ganguly, *The Crisis in Kashmir,* p. 27.

38. The distinguished Kashmiri Indian scholar T. N. Madan has been a close observer of developments in his home state. See T. N. Madan, *Modern Myths, Locked Minds* (Oxford University Press, 1997), pp. 257–60. For a thorough, if sometimes erratic, survey of Kashmir, see the voluminous memoir-history by a former governor of Kashmir, Jagmohan, *My Frozen Turbulence in Kashmir* (New Delhi: Allied, 1991).

39. For a brief UN history of the conflicts in Kashmir plus information about the UN peacekeeping operations in the state, see the website of the United Nations Department of Public Information, United Nations Peacekeeping Operations: UNMOGIP (United Nations Military Observer Group in India and Pakistan) (www.un.org/Depts/DPKO/Missions/unmogip.htm [February 6, 2001]).

40. Robert G. Wirsing, *India, Pakistan and the Kashmir Dispute: On Regional Conflict and Its Resolution* (St. Martin's Press, 1994), p. 190.

41. See Stephen P. Cohen, "U.S.-Soviet Cooperation in South Asia," in Roger Kanet and Edward Kolodziej, eds., *The Cold War as Cooperation* (London: Macmillan, 1990).

42. According to Abdul Sattar, a senior Pakistani foreign office official who was with Bhutto at Simla.

43. See Pervaiz Iqbal Cheema, "The Kashmir Dispute and Peace of South Asia," *Regional Studies,* vol. 15 (Winter 1996–97), pp. 170–88.

44. Some elements of the Bharatiya Janata party have recommended that Kashmir be repopulated with Hindus, once its special constitutional status (Article 370) is eliminated. The Andorra precedent of the thirteenth century—a treaty between Spain and France guaranteeing Andorra's internal autonomy—has been discussed by Jean Alphonse Bernard of Paris; Jagmohan, one of the key principals in the most recent crises in Kashmir, has written that the long-term solution rests in a revival of the Indian spirit. See his own record of Kashmir's crises in *My Frozen Turbulence.*

45. A survey of centrist thinking, which might well evolve into official policy (if the circumstances were right), can be found in Kanti P. Bajpai and others, *Jammu and Kashmir: An Agenda for the Future* (Delhi: Delhi Policy Group, 1999).

46. Nehru suggested this arrangement in conversations in 1953 with John Foster Dulles. See Dennis Kux, *Estranged Democracies: India and the United States, 1941–91* (New Delhi: Sage, 1993), p. 115–16.

47. I have discussed a peace process for South Asia in several places. See Stephen P. Cohen, "A New Beginning in South Asia," Brookings Policy Brief 55 (January, 2000) (www.brookings.edu/comm/policybriefs/pb6055/pb55.htm [February 6, 2001]).

48. The Regional Centre for Strategic Studies has issued a number of studies on confidence-building measures. See Major-General Dipankar Banerjee (retired), ed., *Confidence Building Measures in South Asia* (Colombo: RCSS, 1999); and Banerjee, ed., *CBMs in South Asia: Potential and Possibilities* (Colombo: RCSS, 2000).

49. The communal riot is a set piece in South Asia. Conflicts erupt between two ethnic, religious, or linguistic groups for both proximate and long-term reasons. In almost every case, the leaders of both sides tell their followers that they are vulnerable and threatened and must strike first, since waiting would put their side at a disadvantage.

## Chapter 8

1. See T. A. Keenleyside, "Nationalist Indian Attitudes towards Asia: A Troublesome Legacy for Post-Independence Indian Foreign Policy," *Pacific Affairs,* vol. 55 (Summer 1982), pp. 210–30.

2. Jawaharlal Nehru, speech on Asia to the Constituent Assembly, March 8, 1949, reprinted in Jawaharlal Nehru, *India's Foreign Policy* (New Delhi: Publications Division, 1961), p. 23.

3. When asked why Bhutan was one of only two countries to support India in the UN vote on the CTBT, a Bhutanese official winked and said: "You remember what happened to Grenada!" Interview, Thimpu, 1997.

4. For a brief survey of India-Nepal relations, see S. D. Muni, "India and Nepal: Towards the Next Century," in Lalit Mansingh and others, eds., *Indian Foreign Policy: Agenda for the 21st Century,* vol. 2 (New Delhi: Konarak, 1998), p. 143.

5. Ibid., p. 144.

6. For the classic study, see Leo Rose, *Nepal: Strategy for Survival* (Oxford University Press, 1973).

7. Muni, "India and Nepal," p. 155.

8. The water issue has been studied by a number of regional experts. For an overview, see B. G. Verghese and Ramaswamy R. Iyer, *Harnessing the Eastern Himalayan Rivers: Regional Cooperation in South Asia* (New Delhi: Konarak, 1993); and Q. K. Ahmad and others, *Converting Water into Wealth: Regional Cooperation in Harnessing the Eastern Himalayan Rivers* (Dhaka: Academic Publishers, 1994).

9. In 1977 India and Bangladesh signed a five-year agreement on the division of water flows; this was extended to 1988, when the agreement lapsed.

10. Sri Lanka's Human Development Index was 0.716 (on a scale of 0–1), one of the highest in the world. UNDP, *Human Development Report, 1998,* cited in Regional Centre for Strategic Studies, *Newsletter,* Colombo, January 1999. Figures for other South Asian states are India, 0.451; Pakistan, 0.453; Bangladesh, 0.371; and Nepal, 0.351.

11. The 1999 Indian Tamil film *The Terrorist* offers a chilling and realistic depiction of these operations.

12. "K. P. S. Gill to Advise Lanka on Security," *Indian Express,* May 17, 2000.

13. For an overview of regionalism in South Asia, see Kant Kishore Bhargava, Heinz Bongartz, and Farooq Sobhan, eds., *Shaping South Asia's Future: Role of Regional Cooperation* (New Delhi: Vikas, 1995). This includes several comparative studies of SAARC and other regional organizations, including ASEAN.

14. U. S. Bajpai, ed., *India's Security: The Politico-Strategic Environment* (New Delhi: Lancer International, 1983), p. 121.

15. Anirudha Gupta, "A Brahmanic Framework of Power in South Asia?" *Economic and Political Weekly,* April 7, 1990.

16. Hedley Bull, *The Anarchical Society: A Study of Order in World Politics* (London: Macmillan, 1977), pp. 213–19. For a case study of the United States in Latin America, see Carsten Holbraad, *Middle Powers in International Politics* (St. Martin's Press, 1984), pp. 98–116.

17. For a survey of the diaspora, see Raj Chengappa, "World Wide Worry," *India Today International,* North American Special, September 18, 2000.

18. For a discussion of this point, see K. Mathews, "Understanding India's Africa Policy," in *Indian Foreign Policy,* vol. 2, pp. 14–24.

19. Interview, Islamabad, Pakistan, 1998.

20. India's total trade with developing countries comes to less than 15 percent of its total. *Statistical Outline of India, 1997–98* (Bombay: Tata Services, 1997), p. 106.

21. Many Ugandan Indians fled to Britain and the United States. The movie *Mississippi Masala* traces their journey from continent to continent.

22. Asian Development Bank, "Key Indicators of Developing Asian and Pacific Countries" (www.adb.org/documents/books/key-indicators/2000/ind.pdf [February 6, 2001]).

23. One Indian passenger had been stabbed earlier by the hijackers. The Taliban had warned the hijackers that they would not tolerate further killing or the holding of innocent hostages.

24. V. P. Dutt, *India and the World* (New Delhi: Sanchar Publishing House, 1990), p. 78. This summed up the view of the pro-Soviet lobby in India.

25. See, for example, C. Raja Mohan, "Indo-Soviet Relations—the Return of Common Sense," *The Hindu,* International Edition, August 18, 1990; and Bhabani Sen Gupta, "USSR and the Changing World," *India Abroad,* July 27, 1990. Both of these pieces celebrate the visit of V. P. Singh to Moscow, though it had no palpable results and non-Indian observers (including several Soviet scholars) viewed it as a fiasco.

26. U. S. Bajpai, *India's Security,* p. 5.

27. A. K. Damodaran, in U. S. Bajpai, ed., *India and Its Neighborhood* (New Delhi: Lancer International, 1986), p. 381.

28. For a discussion of India's pipeline diplomacy, see Swapan Dasgupta, "The Great Game Revisited," *India Today International,* June 5, 2000.

29. J. N. Dixit, "India and Central Asia," in *Indian Foreign Policy,* vol. 2, p. 119.

30. India and Uzbekistan signed a "Joint Declaration on Principles" in May 2000 and several agreements on extradition, customs, and assistance. Atul Anejal, "India, Uzbekistan Sign Key Security Pacts," *The Hindu,* May 3, 2000.

31. For a current survey with different Indian perspectives, see *Seminar* (New Delhi), no. 487 (March 2000), special issue, *Looking East,* esp. Sanjaya Baru,

"The Problem," pp. 12–17. See also Mohammed Ayoob, *India and Southeast Asia: Indian Perceptions and Policies* (London: Routledge, 1990).

32. A. N. Ram, "Historical Perspectives," in *Seminar,* special issue, *Looking East,* p. 31.

33. Baru, "The Problem," p. 17.

34. V. Jayanth, "The Mekong-Ganga Initiative," *The Hindu,* November 28, 2000.

35. P. M. S. Malik, "Indo-Myanmar Relations," in *Indian Foreign Policy,* vol. 2, p. 283.

36. Ibid., pp. 283–84.

37. Ibid., pp. 283–84.

38. For a concise discussion, see "China's Ambitions in Myanmar: India Steps up Countermoves," *International Institute for Strategic Studies Strategic Comments* (London), vol. 6 (July 2000) (www.iiss.org/pub/Myanmar.asp [February 8, 2001]).

39. "India Looks East," *South Asia Monitor,* July 6, 2000.

40. For an excellent overview of India's emerging thinking on the use of its naval power to gain influence, see Rahul Roy-Chaudhury, *India's Maritime Security* (New Delhi: Knowledge World and the Institute for Defense Studies and Analyses, 2000).

41. For an authoritative statement of Chinese military perceptions of India's geostrategic setting, see Chen Ping Sheng, ed., *Studies on Indian Military Thoughts* (Beijing: Military Publishing House, 1992). China touches thirteen to eighteen states (the latter figure includes seaward neighbors), India seven.

42. Personal observation, Shanghai, China, September 1998.

43. C. Raja Mohan, "Stage Set for Productive Engagement with China," *The Hindu,* June 4, 2000.

44. Bajpai, *India and Its Neighborhood,* p. 101.

45. Lieutenant General P. N. Kathpalia (retired), "Indo-Pak Relations: The Concept of National Security," *Indian Defense Review,* January 1989, pp. 113–24.

46. T. N. Kaul, *Diplomacy in Peace and War* (New Delhi: Vikas, 1979), pp. 70–72. Kaul claims to have reproduced Nehru's thoughts "from memory."

47. This is less the case of BJP experts, who have strongly criticized Nehru for his naivete. See Jaswant Singh, *Defending India* (St. Martin's Press, 1999), chap. 1, pp. 1–60. The Chinese themselves regard such an inference as presumptuous.

48. For a realist's analysis of China's policies toward South Asia, see Yaacov Y. I. Vertzberger, *China's Southwestern Strategy* (Westport, Conn.: Praeger, 1985).

49. Interview with Chinese strategists, Beijing, 1993.

50. Ibid.

51. Defense cooperation between India and Israel is extensive but not well documented. For an authoritative examination of the prospects for India-Israel military relations, see the work of an Indian scholar long resident in Israel: P. R. Kumaraswamy, "The Limitations of Indo-Israeli Military Cooperation," *Contemporary South Asia*, vol. 5, no. 1 (1996), pp. 75–84.

52. China's response to the Indian tests is discussed in Ming Zhang, *China's Changing Nuclear Posture: Reactions to the South Asian Nuclear Tests* (Washington: Carnegie Endowment for International Peace, 1999). A perceptive, albeit unofficial, Chinese view on possible regional restraint measures is in Cheng Ruisheng, "Sino-Indian Relations after India's Nuclear Tests," unpublished memo, May 1999.

## Chapter 9

1. The vision document is "India-U.S. Relations: A Vision for the 21st Century," March 21, 2000, archived at (www.indianembassy.org/indusrel/clinton_india/joint_india_us_statement_mar_21_2000.htm [January 31, 2001]). The Pakistan speech is "Address by the President to the People of Pakistan, Islamabad, Pakistan," *Weekly Compilation of Presidential Documents*, vol. 36 (Government Printing Office, April 3, 2000), pp. 635–38.

2. His asides were not recorded in the official version of the text.

3. There are several excellent histories of India-U.S. relations. For an American perspective, see Dennis Kux, *Estranged Democracies: India and the United States 1941–1991* (National Defense University Press, 1993). For an excellent recent Indian compilation, published just before the Clinton visit, see Kanti P. Bajpai and Amitabh Mattoo, eds., *Engaged Democracies: India-U.S. Relations in the 21st Century* (New Delhi: Har-Anand, 2000).

4. The Grady Mission, discussed in chapter 5, led to heavy U.S. investment in India's military capabilities, in part setting the stage for the future India-Pakistan conflict. See Martin Wainwright, *Inheritance of Empire: Britain, India, and the Balance of Power in Asia, 1938–55* (Westport, Conn.: Praeger, 1994), pp. 36–40.

5. There were also critics, the most persistent being the feminist and iconoclast Katherine Mayo, whose views toward Gandhi and other Congress leaders grew more hostile and influential in the 1930s and 1940s. Mayo decried not only the poverty of India but also the hypocrisy and arrogance of the Indian political elite. Katherine Mayo, *Mother India* (New York: Greenwood Press, 1969).

6. Robert McMahon, *Cold War on the Periphery: The United States, India, and Pakistan* (Columbia University Press, 1994).

7. For Pakistan, this included a grant of $630 million for weapons, $619 for defense support (construction of facilities and salaries for designated units), and

$55 million worth of equipment purchased on a cash or concessional basis. See Stephen P. Cohen, *The Pakistan Army* (University of California Press, 1984), pp. 138–39. Economic aid to India was also considerable: during Eisenhower's second term, U.S. economic assistance grew from about $400 million in 1957 to $822 million in 1960; and in May 1960 Washington signed a four-year, $1.27 billion PL-480 food agreement with India. See Kux, *Estranged Democracies*, p. 150.

8. Shivaji Ganguly, *U.S. Policy toward South Asia* (Boulder, Colo.: Westview Press, 1990), p. 97. The amount might have been much greater had John F. Kennedy lived, as he was sympathetic to India. Many of the Indian (and Pakistani) loans, especially those that enabled these countries to buy American grain, were to be paid back in rupees, and large amounts were subsequently written off.

9. The view was developed fully by Chester Bowles, who twice served as U.S. ambassador to New Delhi. For an authoritative account of Bowles's views and his impact on U.S. policy, see Howard B. Schaffer, *Chester Bowles: New Dealer in the Cold War* (Harvard University Press, 1993).

10. Walt W. Rostow, *The Diffusion of Power: An Essay in Recent History* (Macmillan, 1972).

11. Nehru visited Russia in 1927. His views on the Soviet Union are found in Jawaharlal Nehru, *Toward Freedom: An Autobiography of Jawaharlal Nehru* (Boston: Beacon Press, 1941; reprinted 1958), pp. 229–31; and J. F. Horrabin, ed., *Jawaharlal Nehru: Glimpses of World History* (Oxford University Press, 1985), pp. 844–64.

12. Interview with a prominent academic scholar of geopolitics, New Delhi, 1988.

13. Morarji Desai, *The Story of My Life*, vol. 2 (New Delhi: S. Chand, 1974), pp. 171–72.

14. The facts do not quite bear out this concern. India had begun significant arms purchases before the Soviet invasion and was in the process of negotiating a number of major arms deals with France, the Soviet Union, and other states at least a year before the Reagan administration agreed to an aid package for Pakistan.

15. Air Marshal K. D. Chadha (retired), "Indo-Pak Antagonisms: Why the Impasse?" *Indian Defense Review*, January 1990, pp. 112–13. For another assessment, see Stephen P. Cohen, *The Pakistan Army*, 2d ed. (Oxford University Press, 1998).

16. For the perspective of the official most knowledgeable about the affair, see Christopher Van Hollen, "The Tilt Revisited: Nixon-Kissinger Geopolitics and South Asia," *Asian Survey*, vol. 20 (April 1980), pp. 339–61.

17. During this period, the U.S. Air Force flew training missions into India and exercised with the Indian and Commonwealth air forces.

18. George Perkovich, *India's Nuclear Bomb* (University of California Press, 1999), pp. 93–95.

19. Kux, *Estranged Democracies,* p. 318.

20. V. P. Dutt, *India and the World* (New Delhi: Sanchar Publishing House, 1990), p. 59.

21. Dennis Kux, "U.S. Foreign Policy in South Asia: Some Lessons from History," archived at the Brookings website (www.brookings.edu/fp/projects/south_asia/events/19991204.htm [February 8, 2001]).

22. For a comprehensive study of the crisis, see Kanti Bajpai, P. R. Chari, Pervaiz I. Cheema, Stephen P. Cohen, and Sumit Ganguly, *Brasstacks and Beyond: Perception and Management of Crisis in South Asia* (New Delhi: Manohar, 1995).

23. Gary Hufbauer, Jeffrey Schott, and Kimberly Ann Elliott, *Economic Sanctions Reconsidered: Supplemental Case Histories,* 2d ed. (Washington: Institute for International Economics, 1990), p. 324.

24. In 1974, after India's nuclear tests, the Zangger committee drew up a list of nuclear technology that would trigger strict safeguards against states of proliferation concern, and Washington suspended uranium supplies to South Africa. Subsequently, in January 1976, a subgroup of the Zangger committee, the Nuclear Suppliers Group, or London Club, adopted the stricter "Guidelines for Nuclear Transfers."

25. Pakistan first lost aid briefly in 1979 under the Symington amendment, and then again for almost a decade beginning in 1990, as a result of the Pressler amendment of 1985. The 1976 Symington and Glenn amendments required the suspension of economic and military assistance to countries buying and selling enrichment and reprocessing facilities that are not NPT signatories or do not have full safeguards. Aid to Pakistan was cut off in 1979 but resumed upon the Soviet invasion of Afghanistan. The Pressler amendment was implemented in 1990 and resulted in the termination of almost all American economic and military aid to Pakistan.

26. Dinshaw Mistry, "Diplomacy, Sanctions, and the U.S. Nonproliferation Dialogue with India and Pakistan," *Asian Survey,* vol. 31 (September/October 1999), pp. 753–71. U.S. sanctions curbed economic projects worth $20 million and an $8 million greenhouse gas program (that went ahead after a November 1998 sanctions waiver); however, sanctions did not hold up U.S. humanitarian and food aid and PL-480 disbursements worth $100 million to India. Sanctions also halted financing by U.S. government entities (the Ex-Im bank and OPIC) for projects estimated at $500 million, although this primarily hurt American investors rather than India. Small amounts of aid to India were held back by Australia, Canada, Denmark, Germany, the Netherlands, and Sweden. France and Britain did not cancel their aid programs.

27. See, for example, Brookings and Council on Foreign Relations, *After the Tests: U.S. Policy toward India and Pakistan,* Report of an Independent Task Force, September 1998.

28. A few notable Indian-American successes in academia (the physicist S. Chandrasekhar) and business (Amar Bose) made a small impact in comparison with these dominant images.

29. Don Clark, "South Asian 'Angels' Reap Riches, Spread Wealth in Silicon Valley," *Wall Street Journal*, May 2, 2000, p. 81.

30. TiE's website is www.tie.org.

31. Robert M. Hathaway, "Confrontation and Retreat: The U.S. Congress and the South Asian Nuclear Tests," *Arms Control Today*, vol. 30 (January/February 2000).

32. Figures from the U.S. Trade Representative, "Foreign Trade Barriers" (ustr.gov/reports/nte/2000/pdf [January 31, 2001]).

33. "Information Technology in India: Yet Another Missed Opportunity," *Standard & Poor's Credit Week*, July 12, 2000.

34. Until a few years ago, India's American studies community was quite anti-American. For a discussion of the roots of anti-Americanism, see Ainslie Embree, "Anti-Americanism in South Asia: A Symbolic Artifact," in *Imagining India: Essays on Indian History* (Oxford University Press, 1989).

35. It eventually hired four firms, along with a former member of Congress, Stephen Solarz.

36. See Malini Parthasarathy, "India Declines U.S. Proposal to Head Caucus of Democracies," *The Hindu*, September 21, 2000.

37. Aaditya Mattoo and Arvind Subramaniam, "Intensifying U.S.-India Economic Relations: The Role of a Free Trade Agreement," unpublished manuscript, 2000.

## Chapter 10

1. For example, a seaborne theater missile defense system could protect Mumbai, Karachi, and other vulnerable cities from missiles launched from some land bases. However, such a system would be unable to protect Delhi or Islamabad and might be vulnerable to close-in attacks.

2. For a discussion of a peace process for the region, see Stephen P. Cohen, "A New Beginning in South Asia," Brookings Brief 55 (January 2000) (www.brookings.edu/comm/policybriefs/pb055/pb55.htm [February 8, 2001]); and Cohen, "India Rising," *Wilson Quarterly*, vol. 24 (Summer 2000), pp. 32–52.

# *Index*